Pergamon General Psychology Series

APPROACHES TO CHILD TREATMENT

INTRODUCTION TO THEORY, RESEARCH, AND PRACTICE

James H. Johnson

Wiley C. Rasbury

Lawrence J. Siegel

PERGAMON INTERNATIONAL LIBRARY
of Science, Technology, Engineering and Social Studies

*The 1000-volume original paperback library in aid of education,
industrial training and the enjoyment of leisure*

Publisher: Robert Maxwell, M.C.

APPROACHES TO CHILD TREATMENT
(PGPS-138)

THE PERGAMON TEXTBOOK
INSPECTION COPY SERVICE

An inspection copy of any book published in the Pergamon International Library
will gladly be sent to academic staff without obligation for their consideration for
course adoption or recommendation. Copies may be retained for a period of 60 days
from receipt and returned if not suitable. When a particular title is adopted or
recommended for adoption for class use and the recommendation results in a sale
of 12 or more copies the inspection copy may be retained with our compliments.
The Publishers will be pleased to receive suggestions for revised editions and new
titles to be published in this important international Library.

Pergamon Titles of Related Interest

Dangel/Polster TEACHING CHILD MANAGEMENT SKILLS
Gelfand/Hartmann CHILD BEHAVIOR ANALYSIS AND THERAPY,
Second Edition
Morris/Kratochwill THE PRACTICE OF CHILD THERAPY
Morris/Kratochwill TREATING CHILDREN'S FEARS AND PHOBIAS:
A Behavioral Approach
Ollendick/Hersen CHILD BEHAVIORAL ASSESSMENT:
Principles and Procedures
Santostefano COGNITIVE CONTROL THERAPY WITH CHILDREN
AND ADOLESCENTS

Related Journals
(Free sample copies available upon request)

ANALYSIS AND INTERVENTION IN DEVELOPMENTAL DISABILITIES
APPLIED RESEARCH IN MENTAL RETARDATION
JOURNAL OF CHILD PSYCHOLOGY AND PSYCHIATRY
JOURNAL OF SCHOOL PSYCHOLOGY

PERGAMON GENERAL PSYCHOLOGY SERIES
EDITORS
Arnold P. Goldstein, *Syracuse University*
Leonard Krasner, *SUNY at Stony Brook*

APPROACHES TO CHILD TREATMENT
Introduction to Theory, Research, and Practice

James H. Johnson
University of Florida

Wiley C. Rasbury
Henry Ford Hospital, Detroit

Lawrence J. Siegel
University of Texas Medical Branch—Galveston

PERGAMON PRESS
New York   Oxford   Beijing   Frankfurt
São Paulo   Sydney   Tokyo   Toronto

Pergamon Press Offices:

U.S.A.	Pergamon Press, Maxwell House, Fairview Park, Elmsford, New York 10523, U.S.A.
U.K.	Pergamon Press, Headington Hill Hall, Oxford OX3 0BW, England
PEOPLE'S REPUBLIC OF CHINA	Pergamon Press, Qianmen Hotel, Beijing, People's Republic of China
FEDERAL REPUBLIC OF GERMANY	Pergamon Press, Hammerweg 6, D-6242 Kronberg, Federal Republic of Germany
BRAZIL	Pergamon Editora, Rua Eça de Queiros, 346, CEP 04011, São Paulo, Brazil
AUSTRALIA	Pergamon Press (Aust.) Pty., P.O. Box 544, Potts Point, NSW 2011, Australia
JAPAN	Pergamon Press, 8th Floor, Matsuoka Central Building, 1-7-1 Nishishinjuku, Shinjuku-ku, Tokyo 160, Japan
CANADA	Pergamon Press Canada, Suite 104, 150 Consumers Road, Willowdale, Ontario M2J 1P9, Canada

---

First printing 1986

Library of Congress Cataloging in Publication Data

Johnson, James H. (James Harmon), 1943-
    Approaches to child treatment.

    (Pergamon general psychology series ; 138)
    Includes indexes.
    1. Child psychotherapy. I. Rasbury, Wiley C.
II. Siegel, Lawrence J. III. Title. IV. Series.
[DNLM: 1. Child Behavior Disorders--therapy.
WS 350.6 J67a]
RJ504.J63 1986   618.92'8914   86-2418
ISBN 0-08-033630-2
ISBN 0-08-033629-9 (pbk.)

Printed in the United States of America

To

Jamie, Trey, and Theda (J.H.J)

Sean, Jamie, and Mary Ann (W.C.R)

Marcia and Daniel Siegel,
and Scott and Nancy—two special people (L.J.S)

CONTENTS

Preface and Acknowledgements   xi

1. Conceptual Models and Their Relevance to
    Assessment and Intervention   1
       Conceptualizing Deviant Behavior   4
       Models, Assessment, and Treatment: A Comment   17
       Prevailing Orientations and Patterns of Clinical
          Utilization   20
       Summary   21

2. Problems That Require Treatment: The Nature
    of Child Psychopathology   25
       Normal and Abnormal Behavior: A Developmental
          View   25
       Classification of Childhood Psychopathology   28
       Problems of Activity and Attention   38
       Childhood Anxiety Disorders   42
       Affective Disorders of Childhood: Childhood
          Depression   49
       Pervasive Developmental Disorders and
          Schizophrenia   52
       Eating Disorders: Anorexia Nervosa   62
       Eliminative Disorders: Enuresis and Encopresis   65
       Conduct Disorders   69
       Summary   73

3. General Issues in Individual Treatment   81
       Children Versus Adults in Psychotherapy   82
       Elements of Change in Child Psychotherapy   84

The Intervention Process: From Referral to
    Psychotherapy   86
Ethical Issues in Child Treatment   94
The Issue of Effectiveness   98
Summary   106

4.   Psychoanalytic and Client-Centered Therapy   109
The Psychoanalytic Model of Personality
    Development   109
The Client-Centered Model   124
Outcome Research: Psychoanalytic and
    Client-Centered Approaches   134
Summary   135

5.   Behavioral Approaches   138
Definition and Scope of Behavior Therapy   139
Behavioral Assessment   139
Theoretical Foundations   144
Clinical Applications of Child Behavior Therapy   149
Outcome Research   180
Issues and Trends in Child Behavior Therapy   182
Summary   185

6.   Biological Approaches to the Treatment of
Behavior Problems   195
Psychopharmacological Treatment   197
Dietary Treatment   217
Final Comments   230

7.   Group Therapy   243
Historical Development of Group Psychotherapy
    with Children   243
Three Group Models   246
Outcome Research: Group Therapy   264
Summary   266

8.   Family Therapy   270
The Origins of Family Therapy   271
Assessment of Families   273
Models of Family Therapy   279
Variation in Family Treatment   296

	Family Therapy Outcome Research	297
	Summary	301
9.	**Treatment in Residential Settings**	306
	The Case of Billy Revisited: One Example of Residential Treatment	306
	The Nature of Residential Treatment Programs	308
	Guidelines for Residential Treatment	313
	The Effectiveness of Residential Treatment	314
	Summary	316

Epilogue	319
Permissions	323
Author Index	325
Subject Index	336
About the Authors	340

PREFACE AND ACKNOWLEDGEMENTS

Mental health professionals of various theoretical orientations employ a variety of approaches in the treatment of child psychopathology. Some rely heavily on play therapy, approaching treatment from either a psychoanalytic or client-centered point of view. Some, viewing the child's difficulties as resulting from family conflict and faulty interaction patterns, prefer to treat the child within the context of the family. Others take a behavioral approach and rely heavily on the application of learning principles in the modification of child behavior problems. Still others rely on the use of pharmacological or other biological methods. Although these approaches are often conducted on an outpatient basis, the nature of some childhood problems makes intervention within a residential setting a necessity.

Given this diversity of treatment approaches, there is a need for those preparing for careers in working with children to become familiar with the available child treatment methods, their effectiveness, and their applicability to various types of childhood problems. Although it is possible to find texts dealing specifically with drug therapies, play therapies, family therapies, child behavior therapies, and general principles of child psychotherapy—and while they may be quite valuable for those interested in a particular treatment approach—there is at present no one book that provides an overview of these various approaches. The present text was written to fill this need.

By taking a treatment method approach, as opposed to one emphasizing the treatment of specific forms of child psychopathology, we have attempted to introduce the reader to a range of approaches commonly used in clinical practice. Coverage of treatment methods is accomplished by discussing the theoretical assumptions underlying specific approaches, the techniques involved in treatment, and what is presently known regarding the effectiveness of these methods as indicated by research findings. The text is written for upper-level undergraduate and beginning graduate courses dealing with child treatment methods and child psychopathology, and more general courses concerned with the emotionally disturbed child. The material we have presented is appropriate for students in clinical psychology, social work, and special education who are pursuing training for working with children, as well as for mental health professionals who have not been trained in child treatment but desire a general introduction to the area.

It is our hope that the clinical material provided here will stimulate interest in the area of childhood intervention and that the questions of treatment effectiveness, which in some instances are left unanswered, will stimulate some readers to seek answers.

We would be remiss if we did not acknowledge the help and support of those who contributed, either directly or indirectly, to the present text. First, we would like to express a special note of thanks to Jerry Frank and the very capable staff at Pergamon Press. Their expertise has added much to the quality of the book and their support throughout this project has been appreciated. The support of our respective institutions: the University of Florida, the Henry Ford Hospital, and the University of Texas Medical Branch at Galveston, should also be noted. We would also like to express our gratitude to Cheryl Bodiford, Steve Boggs, Mary Ann Clark, and Thomas Wood for assistance in proofing and indexing the final manuscript. Finally, we would like to thank our families and significant others for the support they provided while this manuscript was being completed.

1

CONCEPTUAL MODELS AND THEIR RELEVANCE TO ASSESSMENT AND INTERVENTION

Mental health professionals come into contact with children displaying a broad range of behavioral, emotional, cognitive, and intellectual adjustment problems. The child's difficulties may be concentrated in any one of these areas, or encompass several or all of them. For example, some children show deficits in intellectual functioning to the degree that they are considered mentally retarded. Some display stereotypic or ritualistic behaviors and such severe impairments in language and in relating to others that they are diagnosed as autistic. It is not uncommon to see children who are unable to function effectively due to phobias, heightened levels of anxiety, feelings of depression, or problems in socialization, all of which may result in considerable distress. Still other children have difficulties that bring them into continued conflict with their environment. Included here are conduct disorders such as excessive aggressiveness, antisocial behavior, and hyperactivity. Additionally, there are other less serious difficulties that frequently are experienced by children during the process of development. These include problems in toilet training, noncompliance, temper tantrums, and sibling rivalry, to name but a few. Although common, and time limited if handled adaptively, these developmental difficulties can create significant child management problems for parents and require professional assistance.

Although the nature and causes of adult psychopathology have been studied extensively and with fruitful results, our knowledge of childhood disorders has lagged far behind. For example, it is only recently that comprehensive systems for the classification of childhood disorders have appeared (American Psychiatric Association, 1980; Group for the Advancement of Psychiatry, 1966; Rutter, Shaffer, & Shepherd, 1975), and it is only in the past 20 years or so that research into most forms of child psychopathology even began. Likewise, child treatment research has not compared, either in quantity or quality, with that for adult treatment (Barrett, Hampe, & Miller, 1978). It is not entirely clear why research in child psychopathology and treatment has lagged so far behind research on adults, but a number of complex factors have been suggested. These include the inferior status typically accorded children in our society, funding patterns that have favored the training of mental health professionals for working with adults rather than children, and federal funding for mental health research that has tended to favor adult studies. Thus, views of childhood problems have been shaped historically by prevailing models of adult psychopathology, and child assessment and treatment methods have represented little more than downward extensions of procedures used in working with adults. This emphasis on adults also has resulted in clinicians frequently ignoring important developmental factors that must be taken into account in order to adequately understand the nature of childhood problems and plan effective intervention strategies (Gelfand & Peterson, 1985). Despite the low priority given to developmental psychopathology research in the past, in the last decade there has been an increased interest and greater awareness of the psychological problems of childhood and how they differ from those of adults, and more research is being devoted to the causes and correlates of childhood disorders. These advances are well documented in numerous recent child psychopathology texts (Ollendick & Hersen, 1983; Wenar, 1982; Achenbach, 1982; Schwartz & Johnson, 1985). Since 1980 more than 10 major child psychopathology books have been published, in contrast to a single text available in the early 1960s (Bakwin & Bakwin, 1960). Thus, although our understanding of child problems is still less than adequate, clinicians today have a greater fund of knowledge available to them than in the past, and research on child disorders continues to be vigorously pursued.

With this increased interest in child psychopathology, there has been a corresponding increase in attention given to child treatment. Traditional models of child therapy, such as psychoanalytic and nondirective approaches, have received renewed interest in recent years (Tuma & Sobotka, 1983), and family (Levant, 1984; Zimmerman & Sims, 1983) and behavioral (Bornstein & Kazdin, 1985; Ollendick & Cerny, 1981; Ross, 1981) approaches to child treatment have achieved considerable popularity in clinical practice. There also has been an expanded use of pharmacological (Campbell, Green, & Deutsch, 1985; Werry, 1982) and dietary (Conners, 1980; Rapp, 1980) treatments of childhood problems. It is the nature of these treatments, their theoretical and empirical underpinnings, and their application and effectiveness that are the primary focus of this text.

The following clinical example illustrates the type of major childhood problem that might confront a clinician. This illustration will serve as a point of reference for discussion of various issues related to psychopathology and treatment.

The Case of Billy

Billy is a 12-year-old resident of a children's inpatient unit. Prior to his placement he lived with his parents and siblings, two sisters aged 16 and 14 and a 7-year-old brother. The family's socioeconomic status is lower middle class. Billy's father, though presently unemployed, has worked at several unskilled jobs over the years, most recently as a delivery man for a local bakery. Billy's mother is a housewife.

It is noteworthy that Billy's uncle was diagnosed as schizophrenic, and Billy's father on two occasions had "nervous breakdowns" that required psychiatric hospitalization. The father's diagnosis is not known; however, he presently is being treated with psychotropic medication by a psychiatrist at the local community mental health center. Although neither the mother nor any of the siblings have had serious psychiatric problems, the mother reported that she and the children are under considerable strain as a result of Billy's problems and those of the father. She stated that she and her husband argue a great deal and that the home environment is not pleasant for any of them.

A review of Billy's developmental history indicates that his mother's pregnancy and delivery were complicated. The mother experienced periodic bleeding during her pregnancy, the delivery had to be induced, and Billy was born with the umbilical cord wrapped around his neck. Despite possible oxygen deprivation, Billy reportedly appeared relatively normal at birth. During the neonatal and early infancy periods he displayed feeding problems and irritability. Motor and language development were mildly delayed.

Billy showed no serious behavior problems until the age of 10. However, his parents reported that he never related well to other children and at times displayed behaviors that they thought were unusual, such as biting and hitting himself. Around age 10 Billy became emotionally labile, physically and verbally aggressive toward other children, and increasingly "clingy" and dependent on his mother. He often became enraged over minor events that normally would not bother other children. These behaviors occurred at school as well and resulted in Billy's placement in a special class. At the time of his placement, testing revealed an IQ of 85 and below-average academic achievement. The test results also suggested possible neurological impairment and "peculiarities in thinking." Billy's behavior continued to deteriorate, and he finally was hospitalized.

During his first week on the unit Billy continued to exhibit serious behavior problems, frequently became extremely anxious without any apparent reason, and on a number of occasions showed almost uncontrollable emotional outbursts when mildly reprimanded by child care workers. In addition he frequently hit, bit, and scratched other residents without apparent provocation, on several occasions severely enough to cause bleeding and bruises. This behavior resulted in other patients avoiding him whenever possible. Physical restraint often was needed to control him. Given the nature of his problem, the unit staff was in agreement that a treatment plan needed to be developed quickly to cope with Billy's behavior.

CONCEPTUALIZING DEVIANT BEHAVIOR

When confronted with a case such as the one presented here, the clinician must judge the importance of various factors as possible contributors to the child's problems and make decisions regarding approaches to assessment and treatment. The approach taken typically is based on the model of psychopathology adopted by the clinician. The phrase "model of psychopathology" can loosely be defined as a collection of working assumptions regarding the role of biological, psychological, social and environmental, and other factors thought to contribute to the development of psychopathology. It represents the conceptual and theoretical framework used by the clinician in attempting to organize information about the patient and make sense of "abnormal" behavior. This conceptual framework, usually developed as a function of the therapist's training and clinical experience, determines the factors that are seen as causally related to the child's problems, the nature of assessment, and subsequent treatment recommendations. What follows is a presentation of several of the more formalized models of psychopathology and their application to the case of Billy.

THE MEDICAL MODEL

The medical or disease model, which represents the biological perspective in psychopathology, developed largely as a result of the medical profession's early attempts to account for disordered behavior. Deviant behaviors, like the symptoms of physical illness, were thought to be the result of underlying physiological aberrations or disease processes. This view heavily influenced early approaches to psychiatric classification (Kraeplein, 1883) and has continued in varying degrees to influence current classification systems (Blashfield, 1984). This model's roots in the medical profession are clearly reflected in its terminology. Psychological problems reflect "mental illness" characterized by a particular set of "symptoms." Persons displaying mental illness are referred to as "patients," treatment is termed "therapy," and the alleviation of symptoms is described as a "cure" (Achenbach, 1982). The tie to medicine, however, is most apparent in the basic assumption that deviant behavior is the manifestation of underlying biological problems. Although early views postulated the existence of actual physical disease, contemporary versions state simply that biological factors play a major role in the development of psychopathology. Because the specific nature of the biological contributors is most often unknown, emphasis is placed on the development of a taxonomy of "mental disorders." It is assumed that an accurate description of symptom clusters will result in the delineation of underlying biological causes and the development of appropriate treatment methods (Achenbach, 1983).

From this perspective various biological factors might be hypothesized as contributing to Billy's problems. For example, given the psychiatric history of Billy's father and paternal uncle, genetic predisposition would be considered. Likewise, the complications associated with the pregnancy and delivery might be seen as significantly influencing Billy's central nervous system development and contributing to his difficulties. The etiological role of other biological factors such as metabolic abnormalities might also be considered, along with less probable ones such as a tumor or seizure disorder. Finally, the interaction of these biological factors, as well as their interaction with specific interpersonal, social, and environmental factors, would be considered. Although this list of factors that might contribute to Billy's problems is not exhaustive, it does emphasize the major importance placed on the role of biological factors when psychopathology is viewed from this vantage point.

Assessment

Assessment procedures determine the extent to which the child displays features consistent with a diagnosis of psychopathology, as well as the nature of any biological factors that relate to the child's problems. In the case of Billy, assessment would most likely involve obtaining a detailed history with an emphasis on factors suggestive of biological causes. Specific areas covered in the interview with the parents might include the mother's pregnancy, labor, and delivery; a detailed developmental history beginning with the neonatal period; and a thorough medical history. Billy's evaluation would include a complete medical examination and perhaps an evaluation by a neurologist. An EEG and possibly a CAT scan (a computerized x-ray technique that assesses structural abnormalities of the central nervous system) might be suggested by the neurological examination. In some instances, laboratory tests for metabolic abnormalities or toxic substances (e.g., drugs or heavy metals such as lead or mercury) might also be obtained. The decision to use any of these procedures or to conduct laboratory studies would depend on the nature of the patient's specific symptoms. Billy's behavioral symptoms would concomitantly be delineated through the use of interviews, observation, and psychological tests to assess cognition, feelings, emotions, and thought processes, so as to arrive at a formal diagnosis.

Treatment

Assuming that psychopathology is biologically determined, it stands to reason that biological treatment approaches will be favored. Thus, clinicians adhering to a medical model are likely to rely on pharmacological and other biological approaches to treatment more than clinicians favoring some alternative model. Examples include the use of antipsychotic medications for the treatment of serious psychopathology such as schizophrenia or aggressive and destructive behaviors, stimulant medications such as Ritalin® and Cylert® for the treatment of attention deficit disorders and hyperactivity, or antidepressants for the treatment of enuresis and childhood depression. Elimination diets and megavitamin therapy are also consistent with the medical model of psychopathology. The specific treatment depends on the nature of the assessment findings; in Billy's case, the nature of his symptoms might result in drug treatments to deal with his aggressivity and other behaviors suggestive of serious psychopathology.

THE PSYCHODYNAMIC MODEL

The psychodynamic model represents a blend of the medical model and the basic tenets of psychoanalytic theory as initially postulated by Sigmund Freud (1933). At the risk of oversimplification, the Freudian position can be seen as developmental, structural, and dynamic in nature (see chapter 4 for a more detailed discussion).

The theory is developmentally oriented in that it assumes the child must successfully negotiate successive phases of development that are critical for ultimate social and emotional well-being. These phases are referred to as psychosexual stages and consist of the oral, anal, phallic, and genital periods of development during which pleasurable sensations are focused on different body areas or erogenous zones and the child must cope with specific tasks at each stage (e.g., toilet training during the anal stage).

The theory is structural in assuming the existence of several personality constructs, the expression and interactions of which are shaped by the child's experiences as the child negotiates the successive phases of psychosexual development. Freud postulated three personality constructs: the id, ego, and superego. The id is basic biological energy and the source of instinctual strivings. Its sole function is gratification of biological needs and impulses. The ego is a rational structure that attempts to mediate between the demands of the id and those of society. Whereas the id is biological in nature, the ego evolves from the interaction of the individual with the surrounding environment. A third structure, the superego, also evolves from experience. It is the representative of morality or "conscience" and reflects the internalization of the individual's moral code. The ego, in addition to mediating between the id and the external world, also mediates between the demands of the id, which are without morality or conscience, and those of the superego. At times demands of the id, directed toward immediate gratification, come into conflict with the censorship of the superego. This situation gives rise to guilt and anxiety, which are threatening to the child. It is the ego's task to protect the individual from being overwhelmed by anxiety and other threatening feelings in the face of intrapsychic conflicts. The model also postulates that conflicts are expressed at conscious and unconscious levels, and that conflict at the unconscious level is more problematic to the individual's emotional well-being. Movement of conflictual thoughts and feelings between conscious and unconscious levels is a complex process that is mediated by the ego's numerous defense mechanisms, that is, psychic operations used by the ego to reduce the anxiety associated with anxiety-provoking stimuli. If the ego is unable to cope with intrapsychic conflict at a conscious level, it seeks to banish it to an unconscious level where, ironically, it creates more problems for the individual, in that the conflict may be expressed in the form of abnormal behavior. The individual must be made consciously aware of conflicts if they are to be satisfactorily resolved.

Optimal personality functioning occurs when there is a dynamic balance between the id, ego, and superego structures. The development of this balance is largely a function of adequate development of the ego, because it is the principle mediator between the id and superego and the demands of the external world.

The psychoanalytic model is basically a medical model; however, no assumptions are made about underlying physical causes. Instead, it is assumed that the disease processes are psychological in nature. Just as symptoms of physical illness result from physical pathology, symptoms of mental illness are seen as resulting from underlying psychological problems such as repressed conflicts, traumatic experiences, or fixation at a particular psychosexual stage of development. Except for the assumption of underlying psychological rather than physical aberrations, the psychoanalytic perspective is quite consistent with the medical model and has been considered a variant of it.

When viewed from this perspective, Billy's behavior would be seen as the result of unresolved intrapsychic conflicts, inadequate ego development resulting in a poor balance between psychic structures, or possible fixation at a specific level of psychosexual development giving rise to poor social and emotional adaptation.

Assessment

The nature of Billy's difficulties would be determined through parent and child interviews and psychological tests designed to elicit evidence of unconscious conflicts and personality dynamics that might be contributing to his problems.

Although the specific nature of the interview can vary, that with the parents would be directed toward gaining information regarding Billy's physical and developmental history (pregnancy and birth complications, childhood illnesses or injuries, and age of meeting developmental milestones such as walking, talking, and toilet training) as well as toward obtaining specific information regarding his relationships with other family members and with peers, and the general nature of his social environment. Detailed information would also be obtained regarding Billy's past and current behavior, with particular attention given to events occurring during phases of psychosexual development, because these problems often are thought to result in specific types of psychopathology. For example, problems at the oral stage of development can greatly influence the subsequent development of the child's ego, and problems at the anal stage can significantly influence superego development. Development of all three structures is not limited to a specific stage, however; specific stages should be thought of as focal points, with development seen as an ongoing process.

Generally, interviews with older children and adolescents take the form of an oral interchange directed toward obtaining information about the presenting problems and possible contributing factors, and interviews with younger children involve observing the child's play, with verbal interaction centered around this play behavior. It is assumed that through play the child will reveal meaningful information regarding his or her emotional problems. Given Billy's age, the use of play as opposed to a more talk-oriented interview would be largely dependent on the clinician's judgment as to which of these approaches is more likely to yield useful information. As a result of information obtained from the interview, the clinician formulates hypotheses about the child's problems that are tested through obtaining other types of information. For an overview of interview methods consistent with this general model, see the work of Greenspan and Greenspan (1981).

The psychological tests given to Billy would be directed toward uncovering the nature of his underlying psychopathology. Although child clinicians use a variety of test instruments, ranging from quite structured, such as personality inventories, to those that are very unstructured, the ones most consistent with the psychodynamic model are the projective techniques. Excellent overviews of these techniques as used with children are provided by French, Graves, and Levitt (1983) and by Krahn (1985).

Representative of these projective techniques are the Rorschach Test, a series of 10 inkblots to which the child responds by describing what the inkblot looks like as well as the features that influenced his or her responses, and the Thematic Apperception and Children's Apperception Tests, in which children are presented with a series of cards depicting either humans or animals engaging in some activity and asked to make up stories about what is going on in the cards. Other projective tests commonly used with children include sentence completion and figure drawing tests. In sentence completion tests, children are presented with a series of sentence stems assumed to relate to important areas such as ''I love . . . ''; ''My mother . . . ''; ''School is . . . ''; ''Boys should . . . '' and asked to complete these sentences with the first thing that comes to mind. In the Draw-a-Person Test, the child is asked simply to draw a picture of a person, and then a person of the opposite sex, on the assumption that these drawings may reflect personality variables such as body image and the child's view of others. In addition to these projective techniques, French et al. (1983) describe others that have received less attention in clinical practice.

All of these techniques are based on what has been referred to as the ''projective hypothesis'' that when a child is presented with some unstructured test stimulus, he or she will attempt to impose structure, and in doing so will reveal important information about personality dynamics and areas of conflict.

Treatment

Within this model therapy would focus on helping Billy develop an awareness of the unconscious factors that relate to his problems, either through direct verbal interactions with the therapist or somewhat less directly through play. As his difficulties were brought to light, attempts would be made to help him resolve them and develop more adaptive coping skills through increased insight into the nature of his problems and the use of various therapeutic techniques (see chapter 4).

Because this model focuses on underlying processes, the therapist is not primarily concerned about overt symptoms, which are seen as manifestions of the underlying psychological disorder. It is assumed that overt symptoms will dissipate when the underlying conflicts and problems are resolved. Psychoanalytic therapy with children can take a variety of forms, such as individual talk therapy with older children, play therapy with younger children, and verbal- or play-oriented group therapy approaches. Any one of these therapeutic approaches may involve the parents, depending on the age of the child and the specific philosophy of the therapist. Given Billy's level of social and emotional immaturity, the psychoanalytically oriented clinician might prefer play therapy to a more verbal interactive form of analytic treatment.

THE BEHAVIORAL MODEL

Several features characterize the behavioral perspective. First, an emphasis is placed on environmental determinants of behavior instead of the underlying biological or intrapsychic factors suggested by the medical and psychodynamic models. The focus is usually on overt behavior, and psychopathology is usually thought of in terms of behavioral excesses or deficits, or as behavior occurring within an inappropriate context. The problematic behaviors displayed by the child are seen as the primary problem rather than as surface manifestations of some more basic underlying difficulty. There is increasingly a greater tendency to view cognitions (self-statements, self-instructions, and other thoughts) as relevant behaviors in addition to the more overt behaviors emphasized by early proponents of the behavioral view (Kendall & Braswell, 1985).

Whether behavior is viewed in terms of overt responses, cognitions, or basic physiological responses, it is assumed that much of this abnormal behavior is learned according to the same principles that govern the acquisition of other more adaptive behaviors: classical conditioning, operant conditioning, and observational learning. These learning paradigms and their relevance for behavioral views are presented in chapter 5.

From a behavioral point of view, Billy's psychopathology is a learned pattern of behavior that has given rise to emotional stress, frustration, and maladaptive interactions with those around him. Given the degree of apparent stress and instability in the family, one might assume that Billy's difficulties might have emerged partly because of having poor role models for the development of social skills and emotional control, or because of his inappropriate behaviors being reinforced by other persons in the environment, for example, adults paying a lot of attention to him when he shows these behaviors or other children giving in to him when he becomes aggressive. Although it seems likely that these variables contribute to Billy's problems, their adequacy as explanations can only be determined through proper assessment.

Assessment
The focus is on determining the specific behaviors that have resulted in the child being considered maladaptive and the environmental (or other) factors that elicit and maintain these behaviors or contribute to the child's behavioral deficits.

As with other approaches, an interview typically is the starting point in assessment. Behavioral interviews, like other interviews, are directed toward obtaining a developmental history, social history, information concerning peer and family relationships, and information concerning the nature of the child's problem behavior. Despite these similarities, much more detailed information usually is obtained regarding the specific details of problem behaviors and environmental variables that may contribute to the child's difficulties.

A variety of authors have suggested that the basic information necessary for an adequate behavioral assessment is reflected in the acronym SORKC (see Feldman, 1985; Goldfried & Sprafkin, 1974; Kanfer & Saslow, 1969). "S" refers to the stimuli in the child's environment that elicit maladaptive behaviors or control their occurrence, 'for example, stimuli that are typically present when the problem behavior occurs. "O" stands for the organismic variables, such as physical factors or cognitions, that influence behavior. "R," for response, refers to the problematic behaviors of primary concern and their parameters of frequency, duration, and intensity. The term "K" has to do with specific contingency factors, such as the schedule of reinforcement for a particular behavior. Finally, "C" relates to the consequences of the child's behaviors or, in simple terms, what the payoff (C) is for the child as a result of his or her behavior (R). After obtaining preliminary information of this type from the interview, an attempt usually is made to supplement it with other procedures.

Parents or teachers may be asked to complete checklists to indicate the range of problematic behaviors displayed. Parents may be asked to observe specific problem behaviors and record their frequency of occurrence along with any antecedents and consequences. Independent observers may be used to make naturalistic observations of the child's behavior in the home, school, clinic, or hospital setting. In some cases, rather than observing behavior in the natural environment, analogue assessment methods are used in which the child is presented with specific stimuli thought to elicit a particular behavior, so that the child's response to the stimulus can be observed in a controlled setting. These are but a few of the behavioral assessment methods that might be used in making an assessment of Billy's problem behaviors and the factors that contribute to their occurrence. For an excellent detailed presentation of behavioral assessment methods for children, the reader is referred to Ollendick and Hersen's work (1984).

Treatment

Treatment approaches derived from the behavioral model have taken various forms. Each, however, is based on the assumption that most "abnormal" behavior is learned and can be modified through the systematic application of learning principles or other empirically derived methods of behavior change. Child behavior therapy methods include systematic desensitization, modeling, operant conditioning, and cognitive behavior therapy, among others. Procedures such as systematic desensitization, which involves gradually presenting the person with anxiety-arousing stimuli while deeply relaxed, have been used to treat childhood fears and phobias, as has modeling (observational learning). Modeling procedures also have been used with other procedures in social skills training with children who are deficient in this area and in teaching language and self-help skills to mentally retarded and autistic children. Operant conditioning procedures such as positive reinforcement, extinction, and punishment have been used widely in increasing desirable behaviors, for example, toileting, compliance, social skills, and improved academic performance, and in decreasing undesirable behaviors such as aggressiveness, self-injury, temper tantrums, and disruptiveness. Cognitive behavioral approaches—which seek to modify behaviors through changing self-statements, or what children say to themselves— recently have become popular in treating hyperactive and impulsive children and others with self-control difficulties.

Returning to our example, it would seem that the use of learning principles might be particularly relevant in Billy's case. For example, if assessment data supported the hypothesis, suggested earlier, that Billy's aggressive behavior was being maintained by the attention it elicited from those around him, an operant approach might be quite useful. Billy's aggression might be dealt with by manipulating environmental contingencies so that aggressive behaviors were no longer followed by attention, such as holding him, telling him to stop, or reasoning with him about his behavior. Removal of the reinforcement that usually followed his aggressive behavior would be expected to bring about a reduction in its occurrence.

The use of a time-out procedure might also be made contingent on Billy's aggressive behaviors. This procedure is based on the notion that if a child is removed from a potentially reinforcing situation as soon as maladaptive behavior occurs and before it can be reinforced, the probability of the behavior will be weakened through extinction. For Billy, time out might involve immediately removing him from the unit each time he behaved aggressively and placing him in an empty room devoid of any reinforcers. The brief time-out period of 5 to 10 minutes serves only to insure that the child's behavior is not reinforced. In Billy's case time-out procedure would not only eliminate reinforcement for aggressive behavior, but by removing him from the unit would also decrease the likelihood that he might endanger other children.

As a treatment program should involve increasing a child's appropriate behaviors, rather than simply teaching him or her what not to do, it would be useful to include as part of Billy's treatment program opportunities to receive positive reinforcement for adaptive and socially appropriate behaviors, especially those incompatible with aggression. The specific rewards or incentives would be based on Billy's desires and interests. For example, the staff may note that Billy enjoys playing video games and watching certain TV programs, and that his inappropriate behavior seems to be reinforced by attention. Access to these activities or free time with staff members might be made contingent on the occurrence of adaptive behavior. Because Billy's problems not only involve aggressive behavior but also a lack of adequate social skills, other procedures designed to increase these skills, perhaps involving a combination of modeling and positive reinforcement, would also be of value. In essence, a broad range of learning principles could be implemented to deal with Billy's complex and varied behavior problems. For a more detailed coverage of various child behavior therapy techniques, see chapter 5.

THE CLIENT-CENTERED MODEL

The client-centered model is the outgrowth of the work of Carl Rogers with adults and Virginia Axline with children. Basic to this view is the belief that individuals have within themselves the capacity for personal growth and adaptive functioning. Psychopathology occurs as a result of social or environmental conditions imposed on the individual that somehow interfere with personal growth. As a result of this interference, the individual begins to behave in ways that are not self-enhancing. Self-esteem and a sense of emotional well-being are lost or significantly impaired, and behavior becomes even more dysfunctional. From the client-centered perspective, the conflict and apparent instability in Billy's family would be viewed as a major factor in inhibiting his emotional growth and development. His inappropriate behavior would be viewed as symptomatic, as well as contributing to the maintenance of his pathology.

Assessment

Because it is designed to provide information regarding what is "wrong" with the client, assessment is frequently seen as judgmental in nature and not consistent with a client-centered orientation. Given the belief that the direction of therapy should largely be controlled by the patient rather than influenced by assessment information, a formal assessment of Billy's problems would probably not be undertaken.

Treatment

Therapy most often is conducted within the context of play activities, but like analytic child therapies, it may emphasize verbal interaction with older children. The therapist relates to the child in such a way as to communicate an empathic understanding of the child's situation and an unconditional and genuine acceptance of the child as a person. Instead of interpreting the meaning of the child's play or verbal behavior, as within a psychoanalytic framework, primary attention is given to the therapeutic relationship and to a clarification of the child's feelings through the process of reflection. More specifically, reflection refers to the therapist's attempts to comment on the child's communications in such a way as to help the child understand his or her feelings and to increase the congruence between feelings and behavior. As suggested by the term "client-centered," the client rather than the therapist determines the direction therapy takes, except perhaps when the therapist needs to set limits on in-therapy behavior (see chapter 3).

In client-centered therapy, Billy would probably be seen in a playroom where the therapist could allow him to act out his emotional conflicts and aggressions through the medium of play. The therapist would provide reflective comments on Billy's behavior to help clarify and focus his feelings and emotions. Equally important, the therapist would not judge or restrict Billy's aggressive play, unless it became potentially injurious to Billy or the therapist. Thus, the therapist conveys to Billy that he is accepted as a person of worth and, except under specific circumstances, has full freedom of expression. Such an accepting and noncontrolling environment would enable Billy to shed his emotional conflicts, and develop his inherent capacity for positive emotional growth. Client-centered approaches to child treatment are considered in chapter 4.

THE FAMILY MODEL

This model differs from the others presented here in that the emphasis is placed not on the patient, but on the larger family system of which the patient is a part. This perspective is well presented by Achenbach (1974, p. 610):

The family model is based on the assumption that the family is a social system and that each member's behavior is a function of pressures existing within the system. The symptoms of a child brought to treatment are thus not regarded as manifestations of the child's pathology, but as manifestations of the family's pathology. Moreover, the child's symptoms are regarded as having a definite function in the family so that their disappearance without other changes in the family may produce new symptoms in other family members or a dissolution of the family system. Consequently, the child is referred to as the identified patient, i.e., the one identified as a patient by other family members.

From the perspective of the family model, Billy has emerged as the identified patient. His problems would be seen as resulting from deviant patterns of interaction and communication within the family, and his behaviors would be viewed as symptomatically reflective of a basic family disturbance.

Assessment

There are various methods of assessment that have been developed for use with families rather than individuals, for example, a range of observational measures for assessing dysfunctional family systems. Included here are a number of behavioral coding systems for assessing dyadic interactions between family members (Eyberg, Robinson, Kniskern, & O'Brian, 1978; Robinson & Eyberg, 1981; Patterson, Ray, Shaw, & Cobb, 1969; Wahler, House, & Stambaugh, 1976). These have been designed to provide ratings of problem behaviors displayed by family members and, in some instances, the degree to which specific problem behaviors are elicited by the behaviors of other family members. In addition to these coding systems, which have been designed for use in the home, school, or clinic, other assessment methods such as the Revealed Differences Test (Farina, 1960) also have been used. Here each family member is individually asked how he or she would deal with a series of situations (e.g., which TV programs to watch). After responding to these situations, usually in a different manner, the family is asked to reach a mutually acceptable solution. Ratings of simultaneous speech, number of interruptions, and disagreements provide measures of family conflict. Additionally, several self-report measures such as the Family Adaptability and Cohesion Evaluation Scales (Olson, Bell, & Portner, 1978) and the Family Environment Scale (Moos, 1974) have been developed for use in working with families.

Despite their usefulness in research, most observational measures are not well suited for actual clinical practice, due to the complexity of the measures and the difficulty in obtaining trained raters to code behaviors. One notable exception is the Dyadic Parent–Child Interaction Coding System (DPICS), which was specifically developed by Eyberg et al.,

1978, for use in the clinic setting. Most of the other measures noted above have not been used widely in clinical practice. Whether or not such procedures would be effective with a family such as Billy's would be determined by the particular training of the clinician and practical considerations specific to the case.

Clinical assessment of Billy's family would begin within the context of an initial family interview, with the focus on the delineation of pathological processes operative within the family. Based on the assumption that problematic behavior results from a dysfunctional family unit, emphasis would be placed on the patterns of communication and interaction that contribute to the inappropriate behavior of, or distress experienced by, various family members. Attention might be given to assessing degree of rigidity of family members, the extent to which family members could be differentiated in terms of their roles in the family, the lines of authority, and the capacity of family members for conflict resolution. An attempt would be made to determine the function of Billy's behavior within the family system and the extent to which the communications of family members, especially parents, were confusing and inconsistent. Also of relevance to some family therapists would be the degree to which Billy's problematic behaviors were inadvertently reinforced by others within the family.

Treatment

Family therapy approaches typically involve a therapist and possibly a co-therapist interacting with an entire family unit or subset of family members. Although therapy usually deals with family issues thought to underlie the problem behaviors of family members, the actual approach may vary. Some therapists deal with basic family pathology by taking a systems approach that focuses largely on communication and interaction patterns. Other more psychodynamic approaches focus on the pathology of individuals in the family as well as the family as a whole. Behavioral approaches deal mainly with family-based contingencies that contribute to the dysfunctional behavior of family members. Any of these approaches might be taken in working with Billy's family, depending on the particular orientation of the therapist. The specific family members included in these approaches vary as a function of the specific problems and family dynamics displayed. Less conventional methods have involved extended families and even entire kinship systems and social networks.

Some approaches have been developed to deal with acute family crises rather than ongoing family issues. For example, in multiple-impact family therapy an entire team of therapists works intensively with a family over a period of 1 to 2 days to deal with the acute problems of the family. This approach to family therapy is considered in chapter 8.

MODELS, ASSESSMENT, AND TREATMENT:
A COMMENT

Diverse models of psychopathology have led to the development of many assessment and treatment approaches. As we have seen, these models range from those that emphasize the individual to those that focus on the entire family, and from those that emphasize biological factors to those that focus on social and environmental causes of pathology. Models also vary in terms of viewing the patient's maladaptive behavior as a symptom of some underlying pathological process, as opposed to seeing symptoms as pathology. As has been noted, both assessment and treatment vary as a function of the specific model used to conceptualize the clinical problem under consideration.

Is the clinical world divided into proponents of various models with no intermingling of approaches in the management of clinical cases? Basically the answer to this question is a qualified "no." It is true that many clinicians align themselves with the major psychoanalytic, client-centered, behavioral, and family models. However, each of these models and the therapeutic approaches derived from them have limitations. The models presented in this chapter should be viewed simply as collections of working assumptions or ways of attempting to organize and make sense of clinical phenomena. Because our present state of knowledge does not provide clear information regarding the causes of most forms of child psychopathology, we cannot assume that any of these models represent well-validated systems of thought. Although some models may be more consistent with research findings, none should be viewed as presenting an adequate explanation of the range of childhood psychopathology seen in clinical practice. Neither should we assume that assessment and treatment methods derived from these models will be applicable to all childhood problems. Given our rudimentary understanding of child psychopathology, it is premature to assume that any one of these views provides an adequate way of understanding and treating all of the childhood disorders that are seen clinically. Although it is important for the clinician to have some theoretical and conceptual framework to guide his or her thinking and clinical activities, it is desirable that those working with children (and adults) keep an open mind and be willing to view clinical problems from several perspectives. Indeed, we advocate an eclectic approach to clinical work in which treatment techniques are determined by a careful consideration of the complexities of the individual case and by what is known regarding the efficacy of each technique in dealing with specific clinical problems. An eclectic approach can take many forms, depending on the specifics of each clinical case, as illustrated in the following case presentation.

The Case of Terri

Terri is a 5-year-old girl who has been in seven foster homes in the past 3 years. She became a ward of the state at 2 years of age, when her mother abandoned the family and the father was unable to care for her. Her longest foster care placement was for 9 months and the shortest for 2½ months. Terri adjusted well to her early placements and reportedly developed positive emotional attachments to most of her foster parents. During her sixth placement, however, she was sexually molested by her foster father, with a pattern of repeated instances of abuse occurring over a 4- to 6-month period.

Shortly after placement in her seventh foster home with a family who cared for her a great deal and wished to adopt her, Terri began to display many problem behaviors. She frequently made sexually suggestive remarks to the foster father and talked very explicitly about sexual behaviors. On several occasions she was found engaging in sexual play with her younger foster brother. The foster parents were aware of Terri's history of sexual abuse, but were frankly surprised at her sexually inappropriate behavior and unsure of how to handle it. Terri also became unusually aggressive toward the younger boy when he was given any degree of attention by the foster parents. On several occasions Terri became aggressive toward her foster mother, hitting her when scolded, and on other occasions threw temper tantrums when she could not have her own way. Self-abusive behaviors occurred on numerous occasions when Terri was reprimanded or felt rejected by the foster parents. She would bang her head on the wall or floor and on occasion scratch her face seriously enough to cause bleeding. Although sometimes affectionate, Terri seemed to be generally apprehensive of developing a close emotional relationship with her new foster family.

Although it is possible to view Terri's behavior from the perspective of several of the models we have discussed, her background and the diverse nature of her difficulties make it inappropriate to restrict attempts to understand and treat her problems from a single perspective.

To illustrate, it might be argued that Terri's sexually provocative behaviors reflect learned and obviously inappropriate ways of relating, and that the application of behavioral procedures would be the most effective way to decrease these behaviors and replace them with more socially appropriate ways of behaving toward her foster father and brother. The causes and treatment of her tantrums and self-destructive and aggressive behaviors might be viewed in a similar manner. Despite the likelihood that prior learning has played some role in the development and maintenance of Terri's problems, one could argue that other factors also are involved and need to be addressed in any treatment plan that is developed.

It would not be unreasonable to assume that Terri's sexually provocative behaviors result from unresolved conflicts centering around her prior sexual abuse and that her tantrums, aggressive behaviors, and self-destructiveness reflect feelings of jealousy and fear of rejection because of having to share parental attention with another child, whom she perceives as being more secure in the family due to the fact that he is the natural child of her foster parents. From a relationship perspective it might also be hypothesized that Terri's hesitancy to quickly develop a close relationship with the foster parents is due to a fear of being hurt again; of being rejected and having to leave this home as she has had to leave all the others. Given her history, this hesitancy to become involved in a close emotional relationship may be seen as an adaptive self-protective defensive maneuver that, although understandable, is potentially maladaptive.

Assuming that prior learning experiences, current environmental contingencies, ongoing relationships, and unresolved conflicts associated with her history of molestation all contribute to Terri's difficulties, it is appropriate that each of these variables be considered in treatment planning. Thus, the therapist might help the parents to develop behavior management skills to deal with Terri's temper tantrums and her aggressive and self-destructive behaviors. They might also be given specific help in learning how to discourage Terri's sexually provocative behavior, yet neither make her feel that she has been emotionally rejected nor cause her to develop more negative attitudes toward sexuality. It would also be useful to help the parents understand the dynamics of Terri's behavior and how her past experiences, both sexual and nonsexual, have contributed to her present problems. Additionally, the parents would need emotional support in the face of what appears to be a partial rejection of them by a child they love and want to adopt.

Involving Terri in individual therapy would also be of value. Given her age, therapy is likely to take place within the context of play activities, but in an atmosphere in which there would also be opportunities for Terri and the therapist to discuss important issues. This sort of therapeutic involvement would be seen as especially useful in helping Terri clarify and work through any feelings and conflicts that might be related to the sexual abuse she experienced. Terri's problems in the area of relationship development suggest that therapy focusing on relationships but that also is designed to facilitate the development of insight into the nature of significant problem areas would be most appropriate. Indeed, simply learning in therapy that it is possible to develop a long-term relationship with a caring adult that will not be terminated unexpectedly is of therapeutic value. It would be especially important to have Terri seen by a therapist who has developed particular expertise in helping sexually molested children.

This multimodal approach suggested for Terri represents only one combination of treatment methods that might be pursued in clinical practice. In the case of Billy, for example, treatment might include a combination of behavioral, family, and psychopharmacological treatments. Other cases require other combinations of treatment methods. As a general rule, the child's problems should always be treated in the most efficacious and least invasive manner possible. In some cases successful treatment might consist of a single consultation with a child's parents; other cases require more time and the use of multiple approaches. In general, serious problems involve longer single or multimodal therapeutic interventions. Finally, we should reiterate that present knowledge regarding the causes and effective treatments for most forms of child psychopathology is limited. Therefore, it is important to keep an open mind and not be restricted to a single conceptual model and treatment paradigm that may be inappropriate or ineffective in dealing with certain forms of childhood psychopathology.

PREVAILING ORIENTATIONS AND PATTERNS OF CLINICAL UTILIZATION

Some comment is in order regarding the relative popularity of theoretical orientations among child clinicians and the degree to which treatments derived from various models are actually used in clinical practice. Some information regarding these issues can be found in the results of a recent survey by Tuma and Pratt (1982). These investigators surveyed a diverse group of clinical psychologists who were all members of the clinical child psychology section of the American Psychological Association. Information regarding theoretical orientation and the major types of therapeutic techniques used with children was obtained along with other data. The frequency of endorsement of various theoretical orientations by the 342 clinicians who provided such information is presented in Table 1.1. As can be seen, approximately one-fourth of the clinicians reported a primary theoretical orientation that was either psychodynamic or behavioral in nature. Consistent with the view that it is often necessary to consider clinical phenomena from diverse perspectives, approximately half reported an eclectic orientation.

Tuma and Pratt also obtained data on the types of therapeutic approaches these clinicians used with children. Information was provided regarding the degree to which respondents employed different treatment methods generally, and the extent to which the type of treatment used varied with the age of the child. These results are presented in Table 1.2.

Table 1.1. Theoretical Orientations of
Clinical Child Psychologists

ORIENTATION	%
Psychodynamic	28
Behavioral	25
Humanistic-existential	4
Psychodynamic and behavioral	12
Psychodynamic and humanistic-existential	4
Behavioral and humanistic-existential	7
All three orientations	5
Eclectic only (none of the above)	15

Note. Tables 1.1 and 1.2 are from "Clinical Child Psychology Prac-
tice and Training: A Survey" by J. M. Tuma and J. M. Pratt, 1982,
Journal of Clinical Child Psychology, 11, pp. 27–34. Copyright 1982 by
Section on Clinical Child Psychology. Reprinted by permission.

Although the results in Table 1.2 suggest that child therapists use a variety of therapeutic approaches, perhaps of greater significance is the fact that the specific techniques employed in treatment vary widely with the age of the child. Although it is unclear what types of specific play, individual, family, or behavior therapies were employed by the respondents, the results do indicate that many therapeutic approaches are employed by practicing clinicians. It also seems clear that a combination of approaches frequently is used in the treatment of childhood problems, as in the combined use of parental counseling and either play or behavior therapy with younger children. Finally, there are many variations in the specific ways each of these approaches are employed in the clinical setting (Koocher & Pedulla, 1977; Schaefer & O'Conner, 1983).

SUMMARY

Many childhood problems come to the attention of the child clinician. When seen clinically, these problems may be conceptualized in a variety of ways depending on the experience of the clinician and the nature of

Table 1.2. Intervention Techniques Used by Clinical Child Psychologists

INTERVENTION	PRESCHOOL (%)	SCHOOL AGE (%)	ADOLESCENTS (%)	ALL AGES (%)
Individual psychotherapy	5	35	74	54
Play therapy	44	53	—	28
Behavior therapy	36	29	24	35
Family therapy	18	37	46	38
Parent counseling	63	29	32	25

the model of psychopathology to which he or she subscribes. These models of psychopathology are simply ways of organizing our thoughts about complex clinical phenomena. Several of these models of psychopathology were discussed, including the medical or disease, psychodynamic, behavioral, client-centered, and family models. In brief, the medical model assumes that psychopathology is the result of underlying biological factors. The outward manifestations of the child's problems are viewed as symptoms of an underlying disease or physiologically dysfunctional state. The psychodynamic model, like the medical model, assumes "abnormal behavior" to be the result of some underlying cause, psychological rather than biological in nature. From the perspective of the behavioral model, the child's problematic behaviors result from learning experiences and are elicited and maintained by the environment. The nondirective perspective views deviant behavior as emerging from aspects of the child's social and psychological environment that impede emotional growth. Finally, according to the family model, the child's problem behaviors are symptomatic of a dysfunctional family system, and the family rather than the individual child is the focus of intervention efforts. In considering these models it was suggested that assumptions basic to these differing views of abnormal behavior have led to the development of diverse treatment approaches, many of which are widely used in child treatment.

In the absence of adequate knowledge concerning the etiology of and optimal treatment for many childhood problems, conceptual models like those described here may serve as useful guides for clinical work. However, it is important not to become rigidly aligned with one perspective to the exclusion of other potentially useful views of abnormal child behavior.

REFERENCES

Achenbach, T. M. (1974). *Developmental psychopathology*. New York: Ronald Press.
Achenbach, T. M. (1982). *Developmental psychopathology* (2nd ed.). New York: Wiley.
Achenbach, T. M. (1983). Taxonomic issues in child psychopathology. In T. Ollendick & M. Hersen (Eds.), *Handbook of child psychopathology*. New York: Plenum.
American Psychiatric Association (1980). *Diagnostic and statistical manual of mental disorders* (3rd ed.). Washington, DC: American Psychiatric Press.
Bakwin, H., & Bakwin, R. M. (1960). *Behavior disorders in children*. Philadelphia: Saunders.
Barrett, C. L., Hampe, E., & Miller, L. C. (1978). Research on psychotherapy with children. In S. L. Garfield & A. E. Bergin (Eds.), *Handbook of psychotherapy and behavior change* (2nd ed.). New York: Wiley.
Blashfield, R. (1984). *The classification of psychopathology*. New York: Plenum.
Bornstein, P. H., & Kazdin, A. E. (1985). *Handbook of clinical behavior therapy with children*. Homewood, IL: Dorsey.

Campbell, M., Green, W. H., & Deutch, S. I. (1985). *Child and adolescent psychopharmacology*. Beverly Hills, CA: Sage.

Conners, C. K. (1980). *Food additives and hyperactive children*. New York: Plenum.

Eyberg, S. M., Robinson, E. A., Kniskern, J. R., & O'Brian, P. (1978). *Dyadic parent–child interaction coding system: Manual* (rev. ed.). Unpublished manuscript. University of Oregon, Health Sciences Center, Portland.

Farina, A. (1960). Patterns of role dominance and conflict in parents of schizophrenic patients. *Journal of Abnormal and Social Psychology, 61*, 31–38.

Feldman, R. S. (1985). Functional analysis of children's behavior. In D. Shaffer, A. A. Ehrhardt, & L. L. Greenhill (Eds.), *The clinical guide to child psychiatry*. New York: Free Press.

French, J., Graves, P. A., & Levitt, E. E. (1983). Objective and projective testing of children. In E. Walker & M. Roberts (Eds.), *Handbook of clinical child psychology*. New York: Wiley.

Freud, S. (1933). *Collected papers*. London: Hogarth.

Gelfand, D. M., & Peterson, L. (1985). *Child development and psychopathology*. Beverly Hills, CA: Sage.

Goldfried, M., & Sprafkin, J. N. (1974). *Behavioral personality assessment*. Morristown, NJ: General Learning Press.

Greenspan, S. I., & Greenspan, N. I. (1981). *The clinical interview with children*. New York: McGraw-Hill.

Group for the Advancement of Psychiatry (1966). *Psychopathological disorders of childhood: Theoretical considerations and a proposed classification*. Washington, DC: Group for the Advancement of Psychiatry.

Kanfer, F. H., & Saslow, G. (1969). Behavioral diagnosis. In G. Franks (Ed.), *Behavior therapy: Appraisal and status*. New York: McGraw-Hill.

Kendall, P. C., & Braswell, L. (1985). *Cognitive behavior therapy with impulsive children*. New York: Plenum.

Koocher, G. P., & Pedulla, B. M. (1977). Current practices in child psychotherapy. *Professional Psychology, 8*, 275–286.

Kraepelin, E. (1883). *Psychiatrie*. Leipzig: Barth.

Krahn, G. L. (1985). The use of projective assessment techniques in pediatric settings. *Journal of Pediatric Psychology, 10*, 179–194.

Levant, R. F. (1984). *Family therapy: A comprehensive overview*. Englewood Cliffs, NJ: Prentice-Hall.

Moos, R. (1974). *Preliminary manual: Family, work and group environment scales*. Palo Alto, CA: Consulting Psychologists Press.

Ollendick, T. H., & Cerny, J. (1981). *Clinical behavior therapy with children*. New York: Plenum.

Ollendick, T. H., & Hersen, M. (1983). *Handbook of child psychopathology*. New York: Plenum.

Ollendick, T. H., & Hersen, M. (1984). *Child behavioral assessment*. New York: Pergamon.

Olsen, D. H., Bell, R., & Portner, J. (1978). *Faces-11*. St. Paul, MN: University of Minnesota.

Patterson, G. R., Ray, R. S., Shaw, D. A., & Cobb, J. A. (1969). *Manual for coding family interactions*. New York: ASIS/National Auxiliary Publications Service.

Rapp, D. (1980). *Allergies and the hyperactive child* (2nd ed.). New York: Cornerstone.

Robinson, E. A., & Eyberg, S. M. (1981). The dyadic parent–child interaction coding system: Standardization and validation. *Journal of Consulting and Clinical Psychology, 49*, 245–250.

Ross, A. O. (1981). *Child behavior therapy.* New York: Wiley.

Rutter, M., Shaffer, D., & Shepherd, M. (1975). *A multi-axial classification of child psychiatric disorders.* Geneva: World Health Organization.

Schaefer, C. E., & O'Connor, K. (1983). *Handbook of play therapy.* New York: Wiley.

Schwartz, S., & Johnson, J. H. (1985). *Psychopathology of childhood: A clinical-experimental approach* (2nd ed.). New York: Pergamon.

Tuma, J. M., & Pratt, J. M. (1982). Clinical child psychology practice and training: A survey. *Journal of Clinical Child Psychology, 11,* 27–34.

Tuma, J. M., & Sobotka, K. R. (1983). Traditional therapies with children. In T. Ollendick & M. Hersen (Eds.), *Handbook of child psychopathology.* New York: Plenum.

Wahler, R. G., House, A. E., & Stambaugh, E. E. (1976). *Ecological assessment of child problem behavior.* New York: Pergamon.

Wenar, C. (1982). *Psychopathology from infancy through adolescence.* New York: Random House.

Werry, J. S. (1982). Pharmacotherapy. In B. Lahey & A. Kazdin (Eds.), *Advances in clinical child psychology* (Vol. 5). New York: Plenum.

Zimmerman, J., & Sims, D. (1983). Family therapy. In E. Walker & M. Roberts (Eds.), *Handbook of clinical child psychology.* New York: Wiley.

2

PROBLEMS THAT REQUIRE TREATMENT: THE NATURE OF CHILD PSYCHOPATHOLOGY

Any discussion of child therapy methods requires some familiarity with the problems that result in children being referred for treatment. This chapter considers a range of childhood disorders, with an emphasis on how these conditions are manifested clinically and on the types of treatments most often employed in dealing with them. Before discussing specific forms of child psychopathology, however, it is important to consider those criteria used in distinguishing between normal and abnormal child behavior, and contemporary approaches to classifying child psychopathology.

NORMAL AND ABNORMAL BEHAVIOR: A DEVELOPMENTAL VIEW

The clinician must often make judgments as to whether child behaviors are normal or abnormal. The distinction between normal and abnormal can be difficult at any age, but is especially challenging in the case of children, as their behavior problems may be more reflective of developmental processes than actual psychopathology.

It is noteworthy that several large-scale studies have found normal children to display rather high frequencies of problem behaviors. Consider, for example, the findings of the classic Berkeley Growth Study (MacFarlane, Allen, & Honzik, 1954) presented in Table 2.1. These results, obtained on children followed from the age of 21 months to 14 years, clearly suggest that normal children show a range of behaviors that are a significant source of concern for parents. Lapouse and Monk (1958) also have provided cross-sectional data concerning behavior problems in normal

Table 2.1. Incidence of Selected Problem Behaviors at 4 Age Levels

PROBLEM	SEX	PROBLEM INCIDENCE (%)			
		AGE 3	AGE 5	AGE 10	AGE 14
Disturbing dreams	B	29	20	33	6
	G	29	29	47	4
Nocturnal enuresis	B	18	8	11	11
	G	31	10	6	0
Soiling	B	4	3	0	0
	G	0	0	0	0
Tics and mannerisms	B	0	5	0	0
	G	4	5	0	0
Nailbiting	B	8	8	18	33
	G	10	17	32	22
Thumbsucking	B	18	5	0	0
	G	35	19	6	0
Excessive activity	B	37	46	26	11
	G	33	35	15	0
Speech problems	B	24	18	11	0
	G	18	8	3	4
Lying	B	14	49	15	6
	G	12	42	12	0
Stealing	B	12	10	4	0
	G	18	4	0	0

Note. From *A Developmental Study of the Behavior Problems of Normal Children Between 21 Months and 14 Years* by J. W. MacFarlane, L. Allen, and M. P. Honzik (1954). Berkeley: University of California Press. Copyright 1954 by the University of California Press. Reprinted by permission.

children. Data presented in Table 2.2 indicate the proportion of children between the ages of 6 and 12 years who displayed behavioral difficulties significant enough to be reported as problems by their parents.

These findings, along with those of others (see Achenbach, 1978; Crowther, Bond, & Rolf, 1981; Werry & Quay, 1971), suggest that it is common for normal children to exhibit aggressiveness, hyperactivity, noncompliance, fearfulness, temper tantrums, nightmares, and other behaviors considered to be problematic without being labeled pathological. Because of their frequency in the normal child population and the fact that they often decline with age, one could argue convincingly that these behaviors be characterized as developmental difficulties rather than as symptoms of psychopathology. A relevant question, however, concerns the criteria to be used in distinguishing between common developmental problems and childhood disorders.

In a particularly cogent discussion, Wenar (1982) has advocated defining all child psychopathology in terms of a deviation from normal development and has presented several developmentally related criteria for distinguishing between normal and deviant behavior. Two of these criteria are fixations and regressions in behavior. Fixations refer to behaviors that persist beyond the age when they are considered developmentally appropriate. The behavior of a 7-year-old who wets the bed would be considered abnormal according to this criterion, as most children develop nighttime control over urination by the age of 4 or 5. The term regression refers to a child who, having initially achieved a normal level of development in some area, reverts back to behaviors characteristic of an earlier age. An example would be a 6-year-old child who has been toilet trained and then begins to wet the bed again.

Psychopathology can also be indicated by a failure to show behaviors expected at a certain age. For example, an 18-month-old child may be considered normal despite the fact that he or she does not have well developed speech. A 3-year-old would not be considered normal. Likewise, deviant development may be indicated by an exaggeration of behaviors that would be considered normal if displayed in a milder form. Some aggressive behavior is considered normal in young children, but violent behav-

Table 2.2. Frequency of Selected Behaviors as Reported by Mothers in a Sample of Children Aged 6–12 Years

BEHAVIOR	CHILDREN (%)
Fears and worries, 7 or more present	43
Wetting bed within the past year	
All frequencies	17
Once a month or more	8
Nightmares	28
Temper loss	
Once a month or more	80
Twice a week or more	48
Once a day or more	11
Overactivity	49
Restlessness	30
Stuttering	4
Unusual movements, twitching or jerking (tics)	12
Biting nails	
All intensities	27
Nails bitten down (more severe)	27
Grinding teeth	14
Sucking thumb or fingers	
All frequencies	10
"Almost all the time"	2
Biting, sucking, or chewing clothing or other objects	16
Picking nose	26
Picking sores	16
Chewing or sucking lips or tongue or biting inside of mouth	11

Note. "Fears and Worries in a Representative Sample of Children" by R. Lapouse and M. Monk, 1959, *American Journal of Orthopsychiatry, 29,* pp. 803–818. Copyright 1959 by American Orthopsychiatric Association. Reprinted by permission.

iors are not. Some nightmares are to be expected. Frequent and extremely upsetting nightmares are not normal. High activity levels, even at a level that might be problematic for some parents, may be seen as normal at a young age. If, however, the activity level is such that it seriously interferes with the child's ability to function, then it might be considered pathological.

Finally, Wenar has noted that some behaviors are considered abnormal because they are qualitatively different from those seen in children at any age. The idiosyncratic and sometimes bizzare behavior and language patterns of autistic children and the delusional behaviors noted in some psychotic children fall into this category of qualitatively different behaviors.

With a background in normal child development and a knowledge of behaviors expected at various age levels, it should be possible to employ developmentally based criteria, like those suggested here, to make appropriate judgments concerning the normality–abnormality of child behaviors. These judgments can then serve as guides in determining whether intervention may be necessary.

CLASSIFICATION OF CHILDHOOD PSYCHOPATHOLOGY

Formal methods for classifying abnormal behavior can be traced to 1883, when the German psychiatrist Emil Kraepelin proposed the first scheme for classifying adult mental disorders. Kraepelin's system was essentially descriptive in providing a listing of characteristics thought to be reflective of various types of psychopathology that existed at that time. Its development was based on two general assumptions: (a) specific mental disorders with specific etiologies can be defined by constellations of symptoms that differentiate one disorder from another, and (b) proper diagnosis is necessary for proper treatment. Although contemporary classification systems differ in various ways from this scheme, many significant features are retained.

Although several child classification systems have been developed, the most widely accepted one is embodied in the third edition of the *Diagnostic and Statistical Manual of Mental Disorders* (DSM-III) (American Psychiatric Association, 1980).

ESSENTIAL FEATURES OF DSM-III

DSM-III represents a significant revision and expansion of earlier versions of this system (DSM-I, DSM-II). It is similar to earlier versions in its emphasis on the descriptive features of psychopathology. However, it differs in a number of important respects. For example, DSM-III contains approximately four times as many categories appropriate for use with younger age groups than did either DSM-I or DSM-II. The range of diagnostic categories are presented in Table 2.3.

DSM-III also provides more objective diagnostic criteria. For example, the DSM-II criteria for making a diagnosis of "Hyperkinetic Reaction of Childhood" were as follows (American Psychiatric Association, 1968; p. 48): "This disorder is characterized by overactivity, restlessness, distractibility, and short attention span, especially in young children. The behavior usually diminishes in adolescence." In contrast, the description in Table 2.4 for "Attention Deficit Disorder with Hyperactivity" in DSM-III replaced Hyperkinetic Reaction. It can be seen that the DSM-III criteria are more objective and behaviorally oriented, and that specific rules are given for diagnosis. This greater degree of objectivity also is found in other child and adolescent categories.

Finally, DSM-III differs from earlier versions in its multiaxial approach to classification. Rather than simply providing for a psychiatric diagnosis (Axis I), it is possible to classify the individual along several dimensions. Children are assessed in terms of any developmental disorder they may display, in addition to their primary psychiatric disorder (Axis II), any physical condition that may be relevant to their condition (Axis III), the severity of psychosocial stressors experienced during the previous year (Axis IV), and the highest level of adaptive functioning displayed during the past year (Axis V). The inclusion of Axes II through V encourages the assessment of dimensions in addition to the psychiatric disorder and takes into account the fact that individuals may show more than one type of difficulty. For a more detailed discussion of DSM-III as it is used with children, see Cantwell (1985).

DSM-III represents a significant improvement over its predecessors in terms of the expanded number of child and adolescent categories, its more objective nature, and its multiaxial format. However, questions can be raised regarding its adequacy. Many of these questions have to do with issues of reliability and validity.

Reliability

For a classification system to be useful, it must be reliable. Two clinicians using the system with the same patient should arrive at a similar diagnosis on most occasions. As reliability has been a serious problem with earlier versions of the DSM system (Schmidt & Fonda, 1956; Sandifer, Pettus, & Quade, 1964), there has been considerable interest in the reliability of DSM-III, especially in view of its greater objectivity. Findings from two of the more adequate child studies (Mattison, Cantwell, Russell, & Will, 1979; Werry, Methven, Fitzpatrick, & Dixon, 1983) provide useful data regarding the reliability of the child and adolescent categories.

Table 2.3. Outline of DSM-III Classification System with Emphasis on
Disorders of Childhood and Adolescence

I. *Disorders of Childhood or Adolescence*
   A. Mental Retardation: mild, moderate, severe, profound.
   B. Attention Deficit Disorder: with hyperactivity, without hyperactivity,
      residual type.
   C. Conduct Disorder: undersocialized aggressive, undersocialized
      nonaggressive, socialized aggressive, socialized nonaggressive, atypical.
   D. Anxiety Disorders of Childhood and Adolescence: separation anxiety
      disorder, avoidant disorder, overanxious disorder.
   E. Other Disorders of Childhood and Adolescence: reactive attachment
      disorder of infancy, schizoid disorder, elective mutism, oppositional
      disorder, identity disorder.
   F. Eating Disorder: anorexia nervosa, bulimia, pica, rumination disorder of
      infancy, atypical eating disorder.
   G. Stereotyped Movement Disorders: transient tic, chronic motor tic, Tourette's
      syndrome, atypical tic, atypical stereotyped movement.
   H. Other Disorders With Physical Manifestations: stuttering, functional
      enuresis, functional encopresis, sleepwalking, sleep terror.
   I. Pervasive Developmental Disorders: infantile autism, childhood-onset
      pervasive developmental disorder, atypical pervasive developmental
      disorder.
   J. Specific Developmental Disorders (Axis II): reading, arithmetic, language,
      articulation, mixed specific developmental disorder, atypical specific
      developmental disorder.
II. *Organic Mental Disorders*: e.g., senile and presenile dementias, substance-induced
    organic disorder, other organic brain syndrome.
III. *Substance Abuse Disorders*: e.g., alcohol abuse, barbiturate abuse, other substance
     abuse.
IV. *Schizophrenic Disorders*: e.g., disorganized, catatonic, paranoid, undifferentiated,
    residual.
V. *Paranoid Disorders*: e.g., paranoia, paranoid state.
VI. *Psychotic Disorders* (not elsewhere classified): e.g., schizophreniform disorder,
    brief reactive psychosis.
VII. *Affective Disorders*: e.g., manic disorder, depressive disorder, mixed cyclothymia.
VIII. *Anxiety Disorders*: e.g., phobic disorders, obsessive compulsive disorder,
      generalized anxiety.
IX. *Somatoform Disorders*: e.g., conversion reaction, psychogenic pain.
X. *Dissociative Disorders*: e.g., psychogenic amnesia, multiple personality.
XI. *Psychosexual Disorders*: e.g., transsexualism, gender identity disorder of childhood,
    sexual sadism, psychosexual dysfunction.
XII. *Factitious Disorders*: e.g., factitious illness with physical or psychological
     symptoms.
XIII. *Disorders of Impulse Control* (not elsewhere classified): e.g., pathological gambling,
      kleptomania.
XIV. *Adjustment Disorder*: e.g., with depressed mood, anxious mood, mixed emotional
     features.
XV. *Psychological Factors Affecting Physical Condition*
XVI. *Personality Disorders* (Axis II): e.g., dependent, passive-aggressive.
XVII. *Conditions Not Attributable to Mental Disorders*

Note. The section on childhood disorders lists conditions usually manifest in childhood or adolescence.
According to this scheme any appropriate adult diagnosis can also be used with children. Adapted from
Diagnostic and Statistical Manual of Mental Disorders (3rd ed.) by the American Psychiatric Association (1980).
Washington, DC: American Psychiatric Press. Copyright 1980 by the American Psychiatric Association.

Table 2.4. DSM-III Diagnostic Criteria for Attention Deficit Disorder with Hyperactivity

The child displays, for his or her mental and chronological age, signs of developmentally inappropriate inattention, impulsivity, and hyperactivity. The signs must be reported by adults in the child's environment, such as parents and teachers. Because the symptoms are typically variable, they may not be observed directly by the clinician. When the reports of teachers and parents conflict, primary consideration should be given to the teacher reports because of greater familiarity with age-appropriate norms. Symptoms typically worsen in situations that require self-application, as in the classroom. Signs of the disorder may be absent when the child is in a new or one-to-one situation.

The number of symptoms specified is for children between the ages of 8 and 10, the peak age range for referral. In younger children, more severe forms of the symptoms and a greater number of symptoms are usually present. The opposite is true of older children.

A. *Inattention.* At least three of the following:
   1. Often fails to finish things he or she starts.
   2. Often doesn't seem to listen.
   3. Easily distracted.
   4. Has difficulty concentrating on schoolwork or other tasks requiring sustained attention.
   5. Has difficulty sticking to a play activity.
B. *Impulsivity.* At least three of the following:
   1. Often acts before thinking.
   2. Shifts excessively from one activity to another.
   3. Has difficulty organizing work (this not being due to cognitive impairment).
   4. Needs a lot of supervision.
   5. Frequently calls out in class.
   6. Has difficulty awaiting turn in games or group situations.
C. *Hyperactivity.* At least two of the following:
   1. Excessively runs about or climbs on things.
   2. Has difficulty sitting still or fidgets excessively.
   3. Has difficulty staying seated.
   4. Moves about excessively during sleep.
   5. Is always "on the go" or acts as if "driven by a motor."
D. Onset before the age of 7.
E. Duration of at least 6 months.
F. Not due to schizophrenia, affective disorder, or severe or profound mental retardation.

Note. DSM-III also provides for a diagnosis of attention deficit disorder without hyperactivity (same criteria except child is judged never to have displayed signs of hyperactivity—Criterion C) and for the diagnosis of attention deficit disorder, residual type (child once met criteria for attention deficit disorder with hyperactivity but hyperactivity is no longer present). From *Diagnostic and Statistical Manual of Mental Disorders* (3rd ed.) by the American Psychiatric Association (1980). Washington, DC: American Psychiatric Press. Copyright 1980 by the American Psychiatric Association. Reprinted by permission.

Mattison et al. (1979) had clinicians review a number of child clinic cases and make diagnostic judgments using both DSM-II and a preliminary version of DSM-III. Using the DSM-II system, the clinicians showed an average agreement level of 57%. When agreements on Axis I (major psychiatric diagnosis) of DSM-III were considered, the average level of agreement was only 54%. Although level of agreement was considerably higher for Axes II through V (Axis II = 78%, Axis III = 90%, Axis IV = 63%, Axis V = 64%), the lack of agreement regarding the primary psychiatric disorder

Table 2.5. Reliability of DSM-III Diagnostic Categories with Children and Adolescents

DIAGNOSTIC CATEGORY	DEGREE OF AGREEMENT (KAPPA)
I. Child and Adolescent Categories	
Mental Retardation	.62
Mild	.62
Attention Deficit Disorder (ADD)	.76
ADD with hyperactivity	.73
ADD without hyperactivity	.05
Conduct Disorder	.53
Undersocialized aggressive	.57
Undersocialized nonaggressive	.18
Socialized aggressive	−.04
Socialized nonaggressive	.32
Unspecified subtype	.40
Anxiety Disorders of Childhood and Adolescence	.67
Separation anxiety disorder	.72
Avoidant disorder	.05
Overanxious disorder	.65
Other Disorders of Childhood and Adolescence	.39
Schizoid disorder	.37
Oppositional disorder	.39
Identity disorder	.28
Eating Disorder	.91
Anorexia nervosa	1.00
Other Disorders with Physical Manifestations	.91
Enuresis	.96
Encopresis	.91
II. Adult Categories	
Organic Mental Disorders	.89
Delirium	1.00
Substance Abuse Disorders	1.00
Other, mixed and unspecified	.62
Other specified	.02
Schizophrenic Disorders	.70
Paranoid type	.16
Undifferentiated	.35
Psychotic Disorders (not elsewhere classified)	.47
Schizophreniform	.19
Atypical psychosis	.05
Anxiety Disorders (Adult)	.91
Simple phobia	.27
Obsessive compulsive	.94
Atypical	.27
Factitious Disorders	.05
With psychological symptoms	.05
Somatoform Disorders	.49
Somatization	.11
Conversion reaction	.37
Psychogenic pain	.50
Adjustment Disorders	.23
Depressed mood	.67
Anxious mood	−.04
Mixed emotional features	.06
Disturbances of conduct	.05
Mixed disturbance of emotions and conduct	.20

Table 2.5. (*Continued*)

DIAGNOSTIC CATEGORY	DEGREE OF AGREEMENT (KAPPA)
III. Other Codes	
Malingering	−.10
Parent–child problem	.22
Unspecified disorder	.28
No Axis-I diagnosis	.41

Note. Several DSM-III diagnostic categories are not listed, as the frequency of occurrence of these diagnoses was too low to compute reliability. Adapted from "The Inter-Rater Reliability of DSM-III in Children" by J. S. Werry, R. J. Methven, J. Fitzpatrick, and H. Dixon, 1983, *Journal of Abnormal Child Psychiatry*, *11*, pp. 341–354. Copyright 1983 by Plenum Publishing Co. Adapted by permission.

is disappointing. These findings are generally consistent with results obtained from earlier uncontrolled field trials with the child and adolescent system (American Psychiatric Association, 1980).

More recently, Werry et al. (1983) assessed reliability in a more naturalistic setting. Experienced clinicians made diagnostic judgments on a total of 195 children admitted to a large child psychiatry inpatient unit. Independent diagnoses were made after hearing a detailed presentation of each case at a conference held within a week after the child's admission to the hospital. Kappa coefficients, which index percentage of agreement among judges when corrected for chance, were used to indicate agreement for major diagnostic categories (e.g., attention deficit disorder) and subcategories (e.g., attention deficit disorder without hyperactivity). Reliability findings for the various DSM-III child and adolescent categories, as well as "adult" categories used with children, are presented in Table 2.5.

Considering that a Kappa coefficient of .70 is considered an acceptable level of agreement (Spitzer, Forman, & Nee, 1979), these results suggest adequate reliability for some major categories. However, level of agreement for many specific categories (e.g., attention deficit disorder without hyperactivity, avoidant disorder, schizoid disorder, oppositional disorder, identity disorder, and various subcategories of conduct disorder) is unacceptably low. The findings of this study are somewhat more positive than those of earlier investigations, but even these results indicate that the system may be inadequate for diagnosing many specific childhood disorders. Werry et al. (1983, p. 353) conclude: "While the major categories appear robust and could well be tidied up with a little effort, our results suggested that the subcategories have serious problems. . . . If other studies can confirm our results, a great deal of work will need to be done in the area of diagnostic criteria themselves and/or in the data-collection process in child psychiatry to justify the continued existence of subcategories." Despite the apparent improvements in the DSM system, additional work may be necessary to enhance the reliability of this classification scheme for children and adolescents.

Validity

The validity of DSM-III categories has also been questioned. For a classification system to be considered valid, diagnostic categories (and the criteria associated with them) should be reflective of disorders actually displayed by children. To illustrate, with the DSM-III category "oppositional disorder," for example, it should be possible to find youngsters in the general child and adolescent population who show the constellation of features defined by the criteria for this disorder in Table 2.6. In addition, it should be demonstrable that these characteristics not only occur together, as suggested by the criteria, but in a way unrelated to any other disorder, such as conduct disorder, or attention deficit disorder with hyperactivity. Whether this is the case with DSM-III categories remains to be seen.

It is important to note that the many new DSM-III categories were not based on empirically defined patterns of deviant behavior, but on the judgments of clinicians regarding disorders that they assumed to exist. Although certain of these categories may possess a degree of "face validity," one might question whether all of the syndromes are actually displayed by children.

The question of validity is especially pertinent when one considers the results of multivariate studies of childhood behavior problems. These studies usually have involved collecting data on various behavioral characteristics of clinic cases and subjecting these data to factor analysis. Simply put, factor analysis is a statistical method that involves assessing the intercorrelations among behaviors to determine empirically defined classes of behavior. With this method it is possible to define clusters or dimensions of behaviors that are highly intercorrelated with one another and independent from other dimensions—the empirical counterpart to a clinical syndrome. To the extent that DSM-III categories are valid, one would expect dimensions of psychopathology derived from multivariate studies at least to approximate diagnostic categories included within the DSM-III system.

In reviewing some 55 studies of child behavior problems, Quay (1986) has identified a number of empirically derived dimensions that have been well replicated in multivariate investigations. These dimensions and the characteristics associated with each of them are presented in Table 2.7. Quay notes that although there is some correspondence between these empirically derived dimensions and certain DSM-III categories, this is not the case for most child and adolescent categories. The degree of agreement between specific, empirically defined factors and DSM-III child and adolescent categories is reflected in Table 2.8.

Findings such as these fail to support the validity of many child and adolescent categories in DSM-III. It is important to note, however, that no study has assessed the entire range of criteria included within the DSM-

Table 2.6. DSM-III Criteria for Oppositional Disorder

A. Onset after 3 years of age and before age 18.
B. A pattern, for at least 6 months, of disobedient, negativistic, and provocative opposition to authority figures, as manifested by at least two of the following:
  1. Violations of minor rules.
  2. Temper tantrums.
  3. Argumentativeness.
  4. Provocative behavior.
  5. Stubborness.
C. No violation of the basic rights of others or of major age-appropriate societal norms or rules (as in conduct disorder); and the disturbance is not due to another mental disorder, such as schizophrenia or a pervasive developmental disorder.
D. If age 18 or older, does not meet the criteria for passive-aggressive personality disorder.

Note. From *Diagnostic and Statistical Manual of Mental Disorders* (3rd ed.) by the American Psychiatric Association (1980). Washington, DC: American Psychiatric Press. Copyright 1980 by the American Psychiatric Association. Reprinted by permission.

III system. Also, many studies have not included children who could reasonably be expected to show certain types of psychopathology. One cannot define dimensions of behavior through multivariate studies if relevant behaviors are not assessed, or if children with particular types of psychopathology are not sampled. Adequate tests of validity will come from studies that assess the full range of behaviors reflected in the various

Table 2.7. Behavior Dimensions Replicated in Multivariate Investigations

BEHAVIOR DIMENSION	CHARACTERISTICS
Conduct Disorder	Disobediant, defiant, fights, hits, destructive, uncooperative, resistant.
Socialized Aggression	Has "bad" companions, truant from school, loyal to delinquent friends, steals in the company of others.
Motor Overactivity	Restless, overactive, overtalkative, excitable, impulsive, squirmy, jittery.
Attention Problems	Poor concentration, short attention span, daydreams, preoccupied, stares into space, impulsive.
Anxious-Depressed Withdrawal	Anxious, fearful, tense, timid, depressed, sad, disturbed, feels inferior, worthless.
Somatic Complaints	Stomachaches, vomiting, nausea, headaches, elimination problems.
Psychotic Disorder	Bizzare, odd, peculiar behavior, incoherent speech, visual hallucinations, strange ideas.

Note. Adapted from A critical analysis of DSM-III taxonomy of psychopathology in childhood and adolescence by H. C. Quay (1986). In T. Millon & G. Klerman (Eds.), *Contemporary Directions in Psychopathology.* New York: Guilford. Copyright 1986 by Guilford Publishing Co. Adapted by permission.

Table 2.8. Behavior Dimensions Corresponding to
DSM-III Child and Adolescent Categories

DSM-III CATEGORY	BEHAVIOR DIMENSION
Attention Deficit Disorder	
With hyperactivity	Attention Problems with Motor Excess
Without hyperactivity	Attention Problems without Motor Excess
Conduct Disorder	
Undersocialized aggressive	Conduct Disorder
Undersocialized nonaggressive	
Socialized aggressive	Socialized Aggression
Socialized nonaggressive	
Anxiety Disorders	
Separation anxiety disorder	
Avoidant disorder	
Overanxious disorder	Anxious-Depressed Withdrawal
Other Disorders	
Reactive attachment disorder of infancy	
Schizoid disorder	
Elective mutism	
Oppositional disorder	
Identity disorder	
Pervasive Developmental Disorder	
Infantile autism	Psychotic Disorder
Childhood-onset pervasive	
developmental disorder	Psychotic Disorder

Note. Only dimensions that have been replicated in at least 10 studies are listed. Quay notes two additional "weakly replicated" dimensions, "social ineptness" and "schizoid unresponsiveness," which relate to the DSM-III categories of avoidant disorder and schizoid disorder, respectively. Adapted from *A critical analysis of DSM-III taxonomy of psychopathology in childhood and adolescence* by H. C. Quay (1986). In T. Millon & G. Klerman (Eds.), *Contemporary Directions in Psychopathology.* New York: Guilford. Copyright 1986 by Guilford Publishing Co. Adapted by permission.

DSM-III criteria and employ a diverse sample of clinic cases displaying various forms of psychopathology.

GENERAL CONCERNS REGARDING CLASSIFICATION

Many clinicians have reservations regarding the general issue of classification. As Schwartz and Johnson (1985) have noted, these concerns are of several types. Some clinicians argue that the use of any classification system is problematic, as classification results in a loss of information about the person. It is undeniable that only selected aspects of behavior are used in making diagnostic judgments, but the real issue is whether important information is lost; that is, whether classification results in a loss of information necessary for making important judgments regarding prognosis and appropriate treatment approaches. It is likely that the potential loss of information will vary with the type of classification system employed. A multiaxial system such as DSM-III should result in fewer problems of this type than one that only provides for a primary diagnosis. Future research is needed to address this issue adequately.

In addition to the loss of information that may occur with classification efforts, the assignment of a diagnostic label may create problems because of excess meaning attributed to the label. To illustrate, a child may be diagnosed as displaying a socialized/nonaggressive conduct disorder on the basis of a limited number of characteristics, such as persistently lying to the parents. Although this child may not display any of the other features often associated with conduct disorder (e.g., stealing, seriously aggressive behavior, running away from home, alcohol use, or truancy), persons aware of the diagnosis and unaware of the specific reasons for it may attribute such characteristics to this person, when they in reality do not apply. The point is that labels sometimes carry excess meaning that may lead to an inappropriate view of the person.

A diagnosis may also have an effect on the way others behave toward the child. Parents, for example, may behave very differently toward a child who has been labeled as having a particular disorder than toward a child who shows the same behaviors but has not been diagnosed. There is also evidence from a number of studies to suggest that professionals respond differently to individuals depending on the labels they carry, even when these individuals display the same behaviors (Langer & Abelson, 1974; Temerlin, 1968). It is also likely that a child's awareness of the diagnosis that he or she has been given may have important implications for that child's view of himself or herself. It is possible that a diagnosis may become a self-fulfilling prophecy.

Despite these problems, it is difficult to do away with classification entirely. We not only classify individuals in the formal sense when we make DSM-III diagnostic judgments, but we classify when we make decisions as to whether a child is a candidate for therapy, has a good or poor prognosis, or would respond to one type of therapy better than another. Thus, classification is inevitable and in fact quite useful for purposes of communication among professionals. It must be emphasized, however, that diagnosis and labeling are not inconsequential acts. Professionals involved in making such judgments have the responsibility of being aware of the impact of labeling and striving to minimize any possible negative consequences.

With this general discussion of developmental issues and classification as background, the following sections describe a range of childhood problems often seen by mental health professionals. Although research findings are presented, the emphasis is on how these disorders are manifested clinically and the treatment methods that have been used in dealing with them. The relatively greater emphasis on clinical features relates to the fact that there are a number of recent sources (e.g., Schwartz & Johnson, 1985; Shaffer, Erhhardt, & Greenhill, 1985) that deal with both theory and research related to these disorders, and a consideration of clinical features is most relevant to discussions of treatment.

PROBLEMS OF ACTIVITY AND ATTENTION

Tommy, a 6-year-old first grader, was referred to the child development clinic of a large medical center by his teacher, who reported that Tommy seldom sat in his seat for more than a few minutes, was easily distracted, and had trouble concentrating on school-related tasks. She noted that his behavior had become increasingly problematic, and he constantly disrupted other children while out of his seat and moving about the room. On several occasions Tommy left the room during class and was found wandering through the halls, doing nothing in particular.

Tommy's parents reported that they had had difficulty with him from the age of 2. He was said to be "always on the go," into everything, and never content to sit still. In addition to his heightened activity level, Tommy was quite impulsive and engaged in many behaviors that troubled his parents, such as running into the street without looking and wandering off while shopping. According to his parents, Tommy's behavior made it impossible for them to have any sort of social life. They reported being unable to go to church, to have friends over, or even to leave Tommy with a babysitter because of his behavior.

Clinicians frequently see youngsters like Tommy who are hyperactive, impulsive, and generally difficult to manage both at home and in school. These children may also display perceptual-motor problems, problems in learning, and emotional lability, as well as various conduct problems such as aggressiveness, destructiveness, noncompliance, and temper tantrums (Whalen, 1983). Over the years this syndrome has been referred to as the hyperactive child syndrome, the hyperkinetic syndrome, minimal brain dysfunction, and most recently in DSM-III as attention deficit disorder with or without hyperactivity. The DSM-III criteria for this disorder were presented in Table 2.4. A diagnosis of this disorder typically is based on observations of the child's behavior during a formal assessment, which may include an interview, psychological testing, and observing the child's behavior in the classroom or home, and on reports of the child's behavior provided by parents or teachers. These parent or teacher reports may be obtained by using checklists such as the one in Table 2.9

Table 2.9. Conners' Teacher-Rating Scale

	Not at All	Just a Little	Quite a Bit	Very Much
1. Sits fiddling with small objects.	___	___	___	___
2. Hums and makes other odd noises.	___	___	___	___
3. Falls apart under stress of examination.	___	___	___	___
4. Coordination poor.	___	___	___	___
5. Restless or overactive.	___	___	___	___
6. Excitable.	___	___	___	___
7. Inattentive.	___	___	___	___
8. Difficulty in concentration.	___	___	___	___
9. Oversensitive.	___	___	___	___
10. Overly serious or sad.	___	___	___	___
11. Daydreams.	___	___	___	___
12. Sullen or sulky.	___	___	___	___
13. Selfish.	___	___	___	___
14. Disturbs other children.	___	___	___	___
15. Quarrelsome.	___	___	___	___
16. "Tattles."	___	___	___	___
17. Acts "smart"	___	___	___	___
18. Destructive.	___	___	___	___
19. Steals.	___	___	___	___
20. Lies.	___	___	___	___
21. Temper outbursts.	___	___	___	___
22. Isolates himself or herself from other children.	___	___	___	___
23. Appears to be unaccepted by group.	___	___	___	___
24. Appears to be easily led.	___	___	___	___
25. No sense of fair play.	___	___	___	___
26. Appears to lack leadership.	___	___	___	___
27. Does not get along with opposite sex.	___	___	___	___
28. Does not get along with same sex.	___	___	___	___
29. Teases other children or interferes with their activities.	___	___	___	___
30. Submissive.	___	___	___	___
31. Defiant.	___	___	___	___
32. Impudent.	___	___	___	___
33. Shy.	___	___	___	___
34. Fearful.	___	___	___	___
35. Makes excessive demands for teacher's attention.	___	___	___	___
36. Stubborn.	___	___	___	___
37. Overly anxious to please.	___	___	___	___
38. Uncooperative.	___	___	___	___
39. Attendance problem.	___	___	___	___

Note. Adapted from A teacher's rating scale for use in drug studies with children by C. K. Conners, 1969, *American Journal of Psychiatry, 126*, 152–156. Adapted by permission of the author.

Prevalence

This disorder is more common in males than females, with sex ratios as high as 5 : 1 or 10 : 1 reported (Greenhill, 1985; Whalen, 1983). Kerasotes and Walker (1983) have reported prevalence estimates of 4 to 5% in the general population.

Etiological Factors

Given that professionals often have assumed this syndrome to be reflective of minimal brain dysfunction, it is not surprising that research has focused on biological variables. In reviewing studies on pregnancy and birth complications, neurological soft signs, and neurological abnormalities as reflected in EEG recordings, Dubey (1976) found little support for the view that most children with this disorder are brain damaged, minimally or otherwise. Indeed, it has been suggested that perhaps 95% of such children show no evidence of neurological impairment (Safer & Allen, 1976).

Although research clearly has questioned the notion of minimal brain dysfunction, there is evidence that other biological factors may play some role in this disorder. For example, some studies have documented a relationship between hyperactivity and increased lead levels (David, Hoffman, Sverd, & Clark, 1977). Others have found hyperactivity to be associated with minor physical anomalies, such as deviant head size, misshapen ears, curved fifth finger, high palate, and very fine hair, which are associated with deviant fetal development (Waldrop & Goering, 1971; Firestone & Prabhu, 1983). Psychophysiological studies have found these children to show attenuated responses to stimulation (Hastings & Barkley, 1978), suggesting that a decreased responsiveness to stimulation may account for the apparent stimulation-seeking behavior of such children. Finally, there is some evidence that genetic factors may play a role (Cantwell, 1975). Taken together, these studies suggest that there are a number of variables that have some relationship to this disorder. The range of variables identified strongly suggests that problems of activity and inattention may result from multiple causes rather than from a single etiological factor.

Prognosis

What is the long-term outlook for these children? At one time it was believed that the disorder resolved itself as children entered adolescence. Follow-up studies, however, have suggested that although activity level may decrease in adolescence, distractibility and problems in concentration and restlessness continue. Antisocial behavior is found in a substantial minority (Borland & Heckman, 1976; Weiss, Minde, Werry, Douglas, & Nemeth, 1971). Although the manifestations of the disorder may change with age, the long-term outlook suggests that certain problems displayed by these children may continue into adulthood (Ross & Ross, 1982; Wallander & Hubert, 1985).

Treatment of Attention Deficit Disorders

A variety of treatment approaches have been tried with this disorder, but only a limited number have been found to be useful. Kerasotes and

Walker (1983) note that play therapies and relationship-oriented treatments have met with relatively little success. Psychopharmacological and behaviorally-oriented treatment methods have been more successful, but no one treatment has been found to be uniformly effective. The pharmacological agents most often used are stimulants, such as Dexedrine®, Ritalin®, and Cylert®, with a favorable response in as many as 75% of the cases. Although these drugs may make the child's behavior more manageable, this improvement is not necessarily accompanied by other changes, such as better academic performance (Kerasotes & Walker, 1983). The use of stimulant drugs also has been associated with a significant number of side effects (e.g., loss of appetite, weight loss, sleep disturbance, and flu-like symptoms). The long-term effects of stimulant drug usage are unknown.

Behavioral treatments have been of several types. Operant approaches involve reinforcing children for not engaging in hyperactive, impulsive, and distractible behaviors or, alternatively, rewarding behavior that is incompatible with heightened activity and inattention. Another behavioral approach in treating hyperactive and impulsive children which is receiving increased attention is cognitive behavior modification (Kendall, 1981, 1984; Kendall & Braswell, 1985; Meichenbaum, 1979). This method focuses on cognitive in addition to observable behavior, and involves the use of procedures such as modeling and guided participation to teach the child adaptive self-instructions that facilitate less impulsive ways of responding. An illustration of the application of these procedures is presented in Table 2.10. Although cognitive behavioral procedures are relatively new, there is accumulating evidence that these methods are of value (Kendall & Braswell, 1985).

Considering that no single treatment approach has been found to be totally adequate, Kerasotes and Walker (1983, p. 519) suggest a multimodal approach may be most appropriate:

In terms of the present state of the art, it would appear that a multifaceted treatment package is most likely to result in the greatest amount of success for these youngsters. It would appear that medication might profitably be employed in the early stages of treatment in order to bring the activity under control and make the child more manageable for other programs. The medication might then be reduced as the child progresses in the treatment program. Along with the medication, behavioral treatments involving training in cognitive self-control as well as relaxation and biofeedback training, along with reinforcement for on-task behavior, would be important components of the treatment regime. Likewise, coaching and training of teachers and parents in appropriate child management techniques that would be consistent with the behavioral program would be advisable. It appears that this type of treatment package, along with some discussion and modeling for the young person that would lead to improvements in self-concept and re-

Table 2.10. Content and Sequence of Self-Instructional Procedures
with Impulsive Children

Content of Self-Instructions

Problem definition	"Let's see, what am I supposed to do?"
Problem approach	"I have to look at all the possibilities."
Focusing of attention	"I better concentrate and *focus in*, and think only of what I'm doing right now."
Choosing an answer	"I think it's this one . . ."
Self reinforcement	"Hey, not bad. I really did a good job."
or coping statement	"Oh, I made a mistake. Next time I'll try and go slower and concentrate more, and maybe I'll get the right answer."

Sequence of Self-Instructions

- The therapist models task performance and talks out loud while the child observes;
- The child performs the task, instructing himself or herself out loud;
- The therapist models task performance while whispering the self-instructions; followed by
- The child performing the task, whispering to himself or herself;
- The therapist performs the task using covert self-instructions with pauses and behavioral signs of thinking (e.g., stroking beard or chin);
- The child performs the task using covert self-instruction.

Note. From Cognitive behavioral interventions with children by P. C. Kendall (1981). In B. Lahey & A. Kazdin (Eds.), *Advances in Clinical Child Psychology* (Vol. 4). New York: Plenum. Copyright 1981 by Plenum Publishing Co. Reprinted by permission.

duction in hostile and aggressive behavior, would provide the highest probability of overall success.

This sort of treatment strategy is quite consistent with the eclectic approach to intervention that was advocated in the preceding chapter. Along with these treatment components, there may be cases where the use of other more traditional relationship or insight-oriented approaches is called for. Although we have no good evidence that these therapies are useful in decreasing activity level, for example, such approaches may in some instances help children deal with certain of the emotional difficulties and problematic interactions with the social environment that may have developed as secondary symptoms of their hyperactivity.

CHILDHOOD ANXIETY DISORDERS

DSM-III lists several childhood disorders in which anxiety is the most obvious symptom. In some cases anxiety is associated with some specific object or situation, and in other cases it is of a more generalized nature. Included within this category are separation anxiety disorder, avoidant disorder of childhood and adolescence, and overanxious disorder. Although phobias are not listed among the child and adolescence disorders because they can develop at any age, childhood phobias may also be considered under this heading.

SEPARATION ANXIETY DISORDER

The DSM-III criteria for separation anxiety disorder are presented in Table 2.11. Children with this disorder show obvious distress upon separating from the parents. They are often overly demanding of parents, constantly cling to them, and refuse to let them out of their sight. Distress associated with separation may be exaggerated to the point of a panic reaction (Gittelman, 1985). These children may refuse to go to school, to stay overnight with friends, or to go anywhere without their parents. Because of their anxiety, such children may show physical symptoms such as nausea, vomiting, headaches, or stomachaches. They frequently have accompanying fears of accidents, illness, monsters, getting lost, being kidnapped, or any number of other things that could be seen as a threat to their closeness to their parents. Except for separation anxiety, the child may show little evidence of other difficulties.

Although there has been little research on this disorder, clinical experience suggests it is a relatively common problem. It occurs with ap-

Table 2.11. DSM-III Criteria for Separation Anxiety Disorder

A. Excessive anxiety concerning separation from those to whom the child is attached, as manifested by at least three of the following:
   1. Unrealistic worry about possible harm befalling major attachment figures or fear that they will leave and not return.
   2. Unrealistic worry that an untoward calamitous event will separate the child from major attachment figures; e.g., the child will be lost, kidnapped, killed, or the victim of an accident.
   3. Persistent reluctance or refusal to go to school in order to stay with major attachment figures or at home.
   4. Persistent reluctance or refusal (a) to go to sleep without being next to a major attachment figure, or (b) to go to sleep away from home.
   5. Persistent avoidance of being alone in the home and emotional upset if unable to follow the major attachment figure around the home.
   6. Repeated nightmares involving a theme of separation.
   7. Complaints of physical symptoms on school days; e.g., stomachaches, headaches, nausea, vomiting.
   8. Signs of excessive distress upon separation, or when anticipating separation, from major attachment figures; e.g., temper tantrums or crying, pleading with parents not to leave (for children below the age of 6, the distress must be of panic proportions).
   9. Social withdrawal, apathy, sadness, or difficulty concentrating on work or play when not with a major attachment figure.
B. Duration of disturbance of at least 2 weeks.
C. Not due to a pervasive developmental disorder, schizophrenia, or any other psychotic disorder.
D. If age 18 or older, does not meet the criteria for agoraphobia.

Note. From *Diagnostic and Statistical Manual of Mental Disorders* (3rd ed.) by the American Psychiatric Association (1980). Washington, DC: American Psychiatric Press. Copyright 1980 by the American Psychiatric Association. Reprinted by permission.

proximately equal frequency in boys and girls and shows some tendency to run in families. It may occur as early as preschool age, often in response to some major life event, and it seems to develop most frequently in children from close-knit and caring families. The typical course of the disorder is marked by exacerbation and remission over a period of years (American Psychiatric Association, 1980). For a general overview of separation anxiety disorder, particularly as it relates to refusal to go to school, see Gardner (1985).

AVOIDANT DISORDER OF CHILDHOOD AND ADOLESCENCE

Like separation anxiety, this condition involves anxiety associated with a particular area of functioning, in this case contact with strangers. DSM-III criteria for diagnosis are presented in Table 2.12. Although most young children are somewhat fearful of strangers, the symptoms of avoidant disorder develop after the age when these fears are to be expected, and they clearly interfere with adaptive functioning. The child typically appears excessively shy, may have difficulty even speaking to strangers, and tends to cling to the parents in order to alleviate his or her fear and anxiety. These children tend to lack self-confidence, are unassertive, and are frequently bothered by feelings of isolation that result from their restricted social interactions.

These descriptions, like those for separation anxiety disorder, are based on case reports and clinical experience rather than on empirical research. There is no available information concerning prevalence or sex ratio, but the disorder is thought to be relatively uncommon. Thus, it is not surprising that there is little information regarding treatment and prognosis. In fact, there is some question as to whether a meaningful distinction can be made between separation anxiety and avoidant disorder, as in both

Table 2.12. DSM-III Criteria for Avoidant Disorder

A. Persistent and excessive shrinking from contact with strangers.
B. Desire for affection and acceptance, and generally warm and satisfying relations with family members and other familiar figures.
C. Avoidant behavior sufficiently severe to interfere with social functioning in peer relationships.
D. Age at least 2½. If age 18 or older, does not meet the criteria for avoidant personality disorder.
E. Duration of the disturbance of at least 6 months.

Note. From *Diagnostic and Statistical Manual of Mental Disorders* (3rd ed.) by the American Psychiatric Association (1980). Washington DC: American Psychiatric Press. Copyright 1980 by the American Psychiatric Association. Reprinted by permission.

cases the child avoids separation from the parents and may exhibit similar behavioral and emotional characteristics.

OVERANXIOUS DISORDER

In "Overanxious Disorder of Childhood" the child displays an exaggerated level of generalized anxiety. This excessive worry and fearfulness is not focused on any specific person, place, or event. Specific criteria are presented in Table 2.13. The excessive worries noted in these children include injuries, their ability to live up to expectations, being accepted by others, or any number of other things. They tend to be perfectionistic, often spending a great deal of time wondering what others think of them. Their heightened anxiety often contributes to physical symptoms such as headaches, dizziness, shortness of breath, and upset stomach.

As with the two conditions just discussed, there is relatively little empirical research on overanxious disorder. Case studies and clinical experience suggest that it is somewhat more common in boys than girls and is a relatively common problem. The disorder may have either a sudden or gradual onset. The condition typically is exacerbated with increased stress (American Psychiatric Association, 1980). There also has been little research regarding effective treatments. Behaviorally-oriented anxiety reduction techniques, however, perhaps combined with social skills training (in the case of separation anxiety and avoidant disorder), may be of value in treating children with such problems.

CHILDHOOD FEARS AND PHOBIAS

Childhood fears are quite common. Indeed, Lapouse and Monk (1958), in their survey of behavior problems displayed by 6- to 12-year-old children, found that some 43% had seven or more fears. Childhood fears range from those related to very specific and concrete objects (e.g., animals and strangers) to those that are more abstract (e.g., monsters, war, death). Some fears seem to be age or developmental-stage specific, such as fear of strangers at age 6 to 9 months, fear of separation at age 1 to 2 years, and fear of the dark around age 4. Many fears resolve themselves with time and do not require treatment, but others are more problematic. In these instances the term phobia is appropriate. Miller, Barrett, and Hampe (1974, p. 90) have defined phobia as a specific type of fear that "(1) is out of proportion to the demands of the situation, (2) cannot be explained or reasoned away, (3) is beyond voluntary control, (4) leads to avoidance of the feared situation, (5) persists over an extended period of time, (6) is unadaptive, and (7) is not age or stage specific." This list reflects the essential nature of the DSM-III criteria for phobic disorders.

Table **2.13.** DSM-III Criteria for Overanxious Disorder

A. The predominant disturbance is generalized and persistent anxiety or worry (not related to concerns about separation), as manifested by at least four of the following:
  1. Unrealistic worry about future events.
  2. Preoccupation with the appropriateness of the individual's behavior in the past.
  3. Overconcern about competence in a variety of areas; e.g., academic, athletic, social.
  4. Excessive need for reassurance about a variety of worries.
  5. Somatic complaints, such as headaches or stomachaches, for which no physical basis can be established.
  6. Marked self-consciousness or susceptibility to embarrassment or humiliation.
  7. Marked feelings of tension or inability to relax.
B. The symptoms in A have persisted for at least 6 months.
C. If age 18 or older, does not meet the criteria for generalized anxiety disorder.
D. The disturbance is not due to another mental disorder, such as separation anxiety; avoidant, phobic, obsessive compulsive, or depressive disorder; schizophrenia; or pervasive developmental disorder.

Note. From *Diagnostic and Statistical Manual of Mental Disorders* (3rd ed.) by the American Psychiatric Association (1980). Washington, DC: American Psychiatric Press. Copyright 1980 by the American Psychiatric Association. Reprinted by permission.

Jenny: A Case of Balloon Phobia

Jenny, a 6-year-old girl, was brought to the clinic by her mother, who had become increasingly concerned over her fearfulness. The major problem was that Jenny had recently become increasingly afraid of balloons, and this fear was causing her serious difficulties in a number of situations. In discussing the problem with her mother, it was determined that Jenny had a long history of being afraid of inflatable toys. The mother recalled that as early as age 2 Jenny frequently became upset when confronted with any toy that could be blown up. In trying to determine whether Jenny had experienced some specific negative experience with inflatables that might account for the fear, the mother was unable to relate any such incident. She stated that these fears, which the parents dealt with by not having such toys in the house, had gradually become more restricted to balloons, although the intensity of the fear seemed to have increased.

In describing Jenny's fear of balloons the mother appeared almost apologetic, indicating that in many ways a fear of such objects might seem quite insignificant. She noted, however, that there had been a number of instances in which this fear had created significant difficulties for her daughter. In one instance Jenny, along with other children in her class, was asked to make paper-mache animals by covering inflated balloons. Jenny became quite frightened, left the room, and refused to come back until the other children were through. On another occasion, Jenny and her mother attended a wedding where well-meaning friends of the groom filled the couple's car with balloons during the service. Upon walking with the bride and groom to the car, Jenny became so upset she had to leave the area. The mother indicated that recently she and Jenny had to leave a parade Jenny was enjoying because she became so afraid of the balloons that were present, and there was one toy store in the local mall that Jenny refused to enter or even walk past because there was a balloon display at the entrance.

Jenny, in speaking with the interviewer, indicated that she was "just afraid of them" (balloons). She was unable to identify exactly what about balloons she was afraid of, except that she became more afraid if they were full enough to pop. In assessing Jenny's reaction to balloons shown to her in the clinic, she showed no signs of anxiety toward those that were not inflated, and only a small degree of anxiety when asked to blow up a balloon halfway. When presented with a fully inflated balloon blown up by the interviewer, however, she became upset and started to cry, asked for her mother, and indicated that she wanted to leave the room. (Schwartz & Johnson, 1985, p. 190)

Prevalence

Although there is a fair amount of information pertaining to childhood fears, there is less information on the prevalence of childhood phobias. Figures derived from various sources, however, suggest that a reasonable estimate can be placed at .5 to 1% of the general child population (Kennedy, 1983).

Prognosis

With the literature dominated by case studies, it is difficult to make clearcut statements regarding prognosis. Based on the results of case reports, it would appear that the prognosis is relatively good in most instances. Agras, Chapin, and Oliveau (1972) have suggested that childhood phobias often show spontaneous remission. They found at a 5-year follow-up of phobic individuals that all of those under the age of 20 were symptom-free. Although the results of such studies suggest that childhood phobias may often be self-limiting, Miller (1983) has cautioned that phobias can become chronic and in some cases are symptomatic of more pervasive psychopathology.

Etiological Factors

There are many theoretical views regarding the origins of phobic behavior. Psychoanalytic theory asserts that phobias result from anxiety associated with threatening impulses that are repressed and then displaced onto some symbolic object in the environment. Behaviorists believe that phobias result from learning experiences. From a classical conditioning perspective, it has been suggested that phobias are learned because the phobic object or situation has been paired with some noxious stimulus. The classic example of this model was described by Watson and Raynor (1920), who demonstrated that a young child (Little Albert) could be conditioned to display fear in response to a previously neutral stimulus (a rat) by pairing the rat with an aversive noise. Other behaviorally-oriented clinicians have suggested that phobic responses may develop vicariously when children observe other persons (e.g., parents, siblings) who show exaggerated fear in response to specific stimuli. It also has been suggested that operant factors may be related to the maintenance of phobic responses. Here the avoidance behavior displayed by the phobic individual is likely to be negatively reinforced as avoidance responses typically result in anxiety reduction; that is, the person avoids feeling anxious by avoiding the phobic stimulus. Finally, some theorists have postulated that phobias may be related to genetic or other biological factors (see Delprato, 1980). In general, although there are some data to support several of the explanations presented here, none appear adequate to account for all cases of phobic behavior. Reviews of the literature related to etiology are provided by Emmelkamp (1982) and by Morris and Kratochwill (1983).

Treatment of Childhood Phobias

Childhood phobias have been treated from a variety of perspectives. One classic approach was taken by Freud (1909), who described the first psychoanalysis (see chapter 4) of a young child who displayed a phobia of horses. The analysis actually was carried out by the child's father, who treated the child under Freud's direction. Although there are numerous other case studies that describe this approach, little research designed to assess the effectiveness of this treatment with phobic children has been done.

Behavioral approaches typically have involved either desensitization or modeling. As noted in chapter 1, desensitization involves gradually exposing the child to a feared stimulus while the child is relaxed or engaging in some other response incompatible with anxiety (e.g., eating). In modeling, which has been used widely in dealing with childhood fears, the child observes a model (usually another child) who initially seems fearful but gradually approaches and interacts with the phobic stimulus. A particularly useful approach is "contact desensitization," which represents a blend of desensitization and modeling. In this method the child gradually is exposed to the phobic object, with each step toward the object being modeled first. The model helps the child engage in the modeled behavior and provides encouragement and verbal praise for approach behaviors. As the child becomes more proficient in approaching the feared stimulus, the model gradually withdraws and allows the child to proceed alone. In addition to these approaches, several published reports provide some support for the usefulness of cognitive behavioral interventions (of the type described above for hyperactivity) in the treatment of childhood fears. Whereas much of the research is based on case studies and/or has involved the use of subjects with less severe (e.g., nonphobic) fears, there does seem to be sufficient evidence that behavioral procedures are of value in the treatment of childhood phobias (Johnson, 1985; Morris and Kratochwill, 1983).

AFFECTIVE DISORDERS OF CHILDHOOD: CHILDHOOD DEPRESSION

For many years it was assumed that only adults displayed depressive disorders. Now, although there is still controversy regarding the issue of childhood depression (Cantwell, 1982; Lefkowitz & Burton, 1978), the idea that children can become depressed is increasingly accepted by mental health professionals. Consider the case of Jimmy.

Jimmy: A Case of Childhood Depression

Jimmy's parents consulted a psychiatrist because of their concern that he might be emotionally disturbed. Their concerns stemmed from the fact that over the past year or so Jimmy had changed from being a fairly "happy-go-lucky boy, who liked most everything," to one who seemed to be constantly "down." The parents first became concerned when Jimmy's third-grade teacher reported that he was unable to concentrate at school and seemed to have become poorly motivated. Shortly afterward they began to note that he was more irritable, seemed to be eating less, and appeared to lose interest in many of the toys and activities he had always enjoyed. The parents indicated that now he always looked sad, cried more frequently than he ever had before, and just wanted to sit around the house rather than engage in any activities. Jimmy's mother was especially concerned over his behavior, as she had previously had a serious problem with depression and did not want her son to have to go through what she had experienced.

In comparing Jimmy's behavior to the DSM-III criteria for depressive disorder (see Table 2.14) it is obvious that many of his characteristics are consistent with this diagnosis.

Prevalence

Prevalence estimates vary depending on the criteria employed in making the diagnosis. This relationship is nicely illustrated by the results of a study by Carlson and Cantwell (1980). In a random sample of 210 child cases seen at the UCLA Neuropsychiatric Institute, these researchers found that 60% displayed "depressive symptoms" at intake; 49% were judged depressed, based on scores on a depression inventory; but only 28% met DSM-III criteria for depressive disorder. If one assumes that childhood depression is defined adequately in terms of DSM-III criteria, a prevalence estimate of 28% of the clinical population seems reasonable. There are relatively little data regarding prevalence in the general population, although Kashani and Simonds (1979) have suggested a rate of approximately 2% using DSM-III criteria.

Table 2.14. DSM-III Criteria for Depressive Disorder

A. Dysphoric mood or loss of interest or pleasure in all or almost all usual activities and pastimes. The dysphoric mood is characterized by symptoms such as the following: depressed, sad, blue, hopeless, low, down in the dumps, irritable. The mood disturbance must be prominent and relatively persistent, but not necessarily the most dominant symptom, and does not include momentary shifts from one dysphoric mood to another, e.g., anxiety to depression to anger, such as are seen in states of acute psychotic turmoil. (For children under 6, dysphoric mood may have to be inferred from a persistently sad facial expression.)

B. At least four of the following symptoms have been present nearly every day for a period of at least 2 weeks (in children under 6, at least three of the first four).
1. Poor appetite or significant weight loss when not dieting, or increased appetite or significant weight gain (in children under 6, failure to make expected weight gains).
2. Insomnia or hypersomnia.
3. Psychomotor agitation or retardation, but not merely subjective feelings of restlessness or being slowed down (in children under 6, hypoactivity).
4. Loss of interest or pleasure in usual activities, or decrease in sexual drive (in children under 6, signs of apathy).
5. Loss of energy; fatigue.
6. Feelings of worthlessness, self-reproach, or excessive or inappropriate guilt which may be delusional.
7. Complaints or evidence of diminished ability to think or concentrate, such as slowed thinking, or indecisiveness not associated with marked loosening of associations or incoherence.
8. Recurrent thoughts of death, suicidal ideation, wishes to be dead, or a suicide attempt.

C. Neither of the following dominate the clinical picture when an affective syndrome is not present, i.e., symptoms in criteria A and B above, that is, before it developed or after it has remitted.
1. Preoccupation with a mood-incongruent delusion or hallucination.
2. Bizzare behavior.

D. Not superimposed on either schizophrenia, schizophreniform disorder, or paranoid disorder.

E. Not due to organic mental disorder or uncomplicated bereavement.

Note. From *Diagnostic and Statistical Manual of Mental Disorders* (3rd ed.) by the American Psychiatric Association (1980). Washington, DC: American Psychiatric Press. Copyright 1980 by the American Psychiatric Association. Reprinted by permission.

Prognosis

Because it is only recently that childhood depression has been taken seriously, there is little longitudinal research available on the subject. In a rare follow-up study of depressed children, Poznanski, Krahenbuhl, and Zrull (1976) followed 10 children for 10 years after they initially were diagnosed as depressed. Over half of these children were judged to be depressed at the time of follow-up. Although these data are limited, they do suggest that in a substantial number of cases depression may persist and become chronic.

Etiological Factors
Little is known regarding the factors that contribute to childhood depression. Nevertheless, some data are beginning to provide leads regarding potentially important variables. For example, descriptive studies frequently suggest that a high proportion of depressed children have one or more parents who also are depressed. There is also some suggestion that depressed children have parents who are hostile and rejecting, and families characterized by high levels of discord (Cantwell, 1982). These findings, although tentative, suggest that depression in children may be related to family variables, and genetic factors may contribute to the development of this disorder. Other studies have documented relationships between negative life changes and child or adolescent depression (Johnson & McCutcheon, 1980; Mullins, Siegel, & Hodges, 1985). Some research has suggested biological (biochemical) correlates of childhood depression (see McKnew and Cytryn, 1979). Despite the importance of this area of study, inconsistent findings obtained thus far make it difficult to draw meaningful conclusions regarding the role of such variables. Although biological factors may prove important in the development of childhood depression, as in the case of adult affective disorders (Carson & Carson, 1984), descriptions of the family environments of depressed children suggest that research on the role of family variables also is warranted.

Treatment of Childhood Depression
There is little consensus regarding the most effective treatment for childhood depression. Individual, group, and family treatments have all been used with reported success, but there has been virtually no systematic assessment of the effectiveness of these methods. Antidepressants such as Tofranil® and Elavil® also have been reported to be effective, especially with children meeting DSM-III criteria for depressive disorder (Ambrosini & Puig-Antich, 1985; Puig-Antich et al., 1979; Puig-Antich, 1982). In reviewing the findings of available drug studies, Cantwell (1982) suggested an overall improvement rate in the 75% range. Given the uncontrolled nature of these investigations, however, these findings must be viewed with caution.

In light of the documented role of antidepressants in the treatment of depressed adults (Carson & Carson, 1984) and the likelihood that antidepressants may also be of value in treating depressed children, one might ask whether it is necessary to pursue other approaches. No clear answer to this question is available. However, given the problems in social and family relationships that seem to characterize depressed children, intervention approaches designed to deal with these issues also may be productive.

PERVASIVE DEVELOPMENTAL DISORDERS AND SCHIZOPHRENIA

The DSM-III category of "Pervasive Developmental Disorders" includes several severe forms of child psychopathology that historically have been referred to by a variety of labels, such as atypical psychosis, child psychosis, symbiotic psychosis, and infantile autism. As these disorders have been found to bear little relation to the psychotic conditions of adulthood, they are considered within DSM-III to be "developmental" rather than "psychotic" disorders. These "pervasive" developmental disorders, however, are to be distinguished from "Specific Developmental Disorders" (i.e., reading, articulation, arithmetic, and language disorders), as being characterized by severe disturbances in many basic areas of development that may be reflected in behaviors having no counterpart in normal development. Thus, children with these conditions may display distorted rather than simply delayed development (American Psychiatric Association, 1980).

INFANTILE AUTISM

Connie: An Autistic Child

Connie was 3½ years old when her pediatrician recommended her for a developmental evaluation. The referral was prompted by the fact that Connie had not yet begun to speak normally, and she showed an extreme lack of responsiveness. Connie's parents reported that she always had been much less responsive than other children, seldom showed any signs of affection, and usually seemed unaware that others were even present. She spent most of the time playing by herself, actively avoided interacting with others, and generally appeared to be "in a world of her own."

Connie was almost 2 before she said even single words. The parents reported that although her vocabulary had increased considerably since that time, she showed no spontaneous speech, seemed unable to communicate verbally, and did not seem to comprehend what others said to her. Much of her speech was characterized by simply parroting back what others said, sometimes long after she had heard it. Her father found it peculiar that despite her deficient language, Connie was able to sing almost perfectly a number of songs she had heard on the radio, and to recite numerous television commercials word for word.

The mother had observed Connie display a number of "strange" behaviors, including the tendency to become extremely distraught if furniture or other things in the house were changed in some way. She indicated that Connie often spent long periods of time staring at her hands while making unusual movements with her fingers. Connie also was reported to sometimes hit her head on the wall or bite on her arm when upset over a trivial incident.

In summarizing their concerns, the father stated that both he and his wife knew that something was "very wrong," but they did not know what the problem could be. Both were very concerned about what would happen to Connie in the future and expressed guilt over possibly having contributed to their daughter's problem in some way.

Infantile autism is characterized by a number of features that were first described by Kanner (1943) in his classic paper "Autistic Disturbances of Affective Contact." This early description, which continues to heavily influence present-day views of the disorder, emphasized a number of features.

Early Onset. Unlike other severe disorders of childhood, Kanner considered autism to be present from birth, or at least to become manifest during the first year or so. Indeed, he has referred to autism as an "inborn disturbance." According to Kanner, early onset differentiated the disorder from other problems which at that time were categorized as manifestations of childhood psychosis.

Inability to Relate. Autistic children have a primary disturbance in social relationships. They seem aloof, often oblivious to the presence of others, and are described as being in a world of their own. This characteristic may be reflected in early life by a failure to show anticipatory posturing when the parent attempts to pick up the infant, and by the failure of the infant to mold itself to the body of the parent. An inability to relate may be displayed at later ages by the failure of the child to respond to parents and others. Sometimes these children are thought to be deaf because of their lack of responsiveness. In some instances children may treat parents as if they were strangers and show almost no response when a parent returns home even after being gone for some time. This lack of emotional responsivity prompted Kanner to describe the disorder as primarily a disturbance of affective contact (Kanner, 1943).

Severe Language Disorder. All autistic children have serious problems with language. Many remain mute. Those that develop speech typically show unusual features such as (a) echolalia, the repetition of what someone else has said, in exactly the same way, or (b) pronominal reversal, the failure to use pronouns correctly (e.g., referring to oneself as "you" and to others as "I"). Even though some autistic children develop fairly large vocabularies, they usually cannot use speech to communicate with others. In describing 11 cases of autism in his 1943 paper, Kanner noted that although some of the children had developed language, they were no better able to communicate than those who remained mute. "Speaking" autistic children often have no difficulty in naming a large number of objects and sometimes have a facility for memorizing complex verbal constructions such as poems, songs, and lists. Such learning, however, seems to be devoid of any appreciation of content. There is usually minimal evidence of spontaneous speech serving a communicative function. For an excellent selection of papers on communication problems in autism, see Schopler and Mesibov (1985).

Desire for Sameness. Kanner and others have noted that autistic children seem to display an anxious desire for the maintenance of sameness. Such children often become upset when various aspects of their environment are changed; when furniture is moved, when routines are changed, or when toys the child has left in a particular position are moved. These minor changes may result in a catastrophic reaction that continues until things are returned to their former state. The desire for sameness may lead some autistic children to display a wide range of ritualistic behaviors.

In addition to the characteristics suggested by Kanner, there are other features that are found in some autistic children. For example, many autistic children show stereotyped behaviors. They may mouth objects, spend long periods of time flapping their arms and hands, rock back and forth, or display other self-stimulating behaviors. They may appear either under- or over-responsive to environmental stimuli, at different times. Under-responsiveness occasionally is reflected in an apparent insensitivity to pain and associated self-injurious behaviors. As can be seen in Table 2.15, a number of the features described here are represented in current DSM-III criteria.

Table 2.15. DSM-III Criteria for Infantile Autism

A. Onset before 30 months of age.
B. Pervasive lack of responsiveness to other people (autism).
C. Gross deficits in language development.
D. If speech is present, peculiar speech patterns prevail, such as immediate and delayed echolalia, metaphorical language, and pronominal reversal.
E. Bizzare responses to various aspects of the environment, e.g., resistance to change or peculiar interest in or attachments to animate or inanimate objects.
F. Absence of delusions, hallucinations, loosening of associations, and incoherence, as in schizophrenia.

Note. From *Diagnostic and Statistical Manual of Mental Disorders* (3rd ed.) by the American Psychiatric Association (1980). Washington, DC: American Psychiatric Press. Copyright 1980 by the American Psychiatric Association. Reprinted by permission.

Prevalence

Although autism has always been seen as a rare disorder, it is difficult to determine its exact frequency of occurrence. This is because investigators have often used different criteria for diagnosis, the disorder has frequently been confused with other severe disorders of childhood, and not all children with autism come to the attention of researchers. Despite these difficulties, data from a number of studies suggest a frequency of occurrence of 4 or 5 cases per 10,000 children (Wing, Yeates, Brierly, & Gould, 1976). The disorder is more frequent in boys than in girls, with sex ratios ranging from 3 : 1 to 5 : 1 (Ando & Tsuda, 1975; Rutter, 1985).

Prognosis

Autism is indeed a severe disorder. In reviewing follow-up studies of autistic children, DeMyer, Hingtgen, and Jackson (1981) noted that 60 to 70% live a life of complete or semi-dependence, either at home or in an institution. Only about 1 to 2% achieve "normal" levels of independence, and anywhere from 5 to 19% show a borderline level of functioning. A better prognosis seems to be associated with an IQ greater than 60. In a particularly interesting paper entitled "How Far can Autistic Children Go in Matters of Social Adaptation?" Kanner (1973) followed up on 96 autistic children that he had seen prior to 1953. Although the majority did not fare as well, 11 of the 96 achieved what he described as a favorable outcome. Of the 11, 3 obtained college degrees, 3 went to junior college, and 1 was reported to be doing well in college. The other 4 did not go beyond high school or special education. The occupations of these grown-up autistics included accountant, duplicating machine operator, lab technician, and bank teller, along with several types of unskilled work. Kanner noted that although these 11 children showed a favorable outcome, none in adulthood seemed to have any interest in the opposite sex or in marriage, suggesting continued problems in the development of close relationships. Kanner found outcome to be unrelated to prior psychiatric treatment. The single best predictor seemed to be useful speech by the age of 5, which probably was correlated with higher IQ.

Etiological Factors

Views regarding the causes of autism can generally be classified as being psychogenic or biogenic. Psychogenic theorists, citing early reports that characterized the parents of autistic children as cold, aloof, obsessional, "refrigerator" personalities (see Kanner, 1943), have emphasized the role of parental variables in the development of autism. Some clinicians such as Bettelheim (1967) have suggested that negative maternal attitudes are of major importance in the development of this disorder. For the most part, however, research attempting to link family variables to autism has provided little support for such views. In reviewing the literature DeMyer et al. (1981, p. 432) noted:

> In sharp contrast to early portrayals of parents of autistic children as "refrigerator" personalities, the last decade of investigation has characterized these parents as similar to those with children exhibiting other severe childhood disturbances. . . . Parents of autistic children have been found to display no more signs of mental or emotional illness than parents of children with organic disorders (with or without psychosis). In addition, they do not manifest extreme personality traits such as coldness, obsessiveness, social anxiety, or rage, nor do they possess specific deficits in infant and child care.

There is a growing conviction on the part of most researchers and clinicians that autism is a biologically based disorder. This point of view is supported by studies that in one way or another have implicated the role of biological factors. Thus, autism has been shown to be related to other biological problems such as rubella, pregnancy and birth complications, abnormal levels of certain neurotransmitters, minor physical anomalies, and abnormal EEGs (brain waves), as well as structural abnormalities of the left hemisphere (DeMyer et al., 1981). Although methodological problems inherent in most studies make it difficult to draw firm conclusions, taken together these findings provide strong support for a biogenic perspective. The specific biological factors most relevant to understanding the etiology of autism remain to be uncovered.

Treatment of Autistic Children

Probably due to the severe cognitive impairment that they display, autistic children do not benefit from insight-oriented "talk therapies" (NIMH, 1975). Although there is presently no available treatment to make autistic children normal (or even approach normality), behavioral approaches have achieved some measure of success. Operant procedures combined with modeling have been found useful in teaching language and other socially adaptive skills and in decreasing many inappropriate behaviors (Lovaas, 1977; Stevens-Long & Lovaas, 1974). Despite these accomplishments, it must be noted that bringing about such behavioral changes requires not only skills that very few clinicians possess, but an enormous amount of time. There is also the problem of maintaining the treatment gains that are made.

Although many medications have been used with autistic children without much success, there is evidence that some drugs may be beneficial. For example, haloperidol, which has been used with adult schizophrenics and some other clinical groups, has been shown to improve the learning ability of autistic children (Campbell et al., 1982). The most recent drug used is fenfluramine, a diet drug that appears to reduce levels of serotonin in the blood and which is in the process of being studied intensively in a large nationwide study. Serotonin is one of the neurotransmitters that biochemical studies have found to be elevated in some autistic children. Two preliminary studies published to date (Geller, Ritvo, Freeman, & Yuwiler, 1982; Ritvo, Freeman, Geller, & Yuwiler, 1983) provide evidence that fenfluramine does in fact reduce serotonin levels and bring about improvements in functioning, as indexed by social and intellectual indices. When the treatment was interrupted, behavior deteriorated. Future research will clarify the degree to which this drug can significantly modify the core problems in infantile autism.

CHILDHOOD-ONSET PERVASIVE DEVELOPMENTAL DISORDER

This category, along with the category "Atypical Pervasive Developmental Disorder," was included in DSM-III for use with children between the ages of 2 years and adolescence showing severe psychopathology. Children with these conditions may exhibit some features suggestive of infantile autism, but the later age of onset is thought to be a major characteristic differentiating them from autistic youngsters. DSM-III criteria for childhood-onset pervasive developmental disorder are presented in Table 2.16. The diagnosis of atypical pervasive developmental disorder is used for children who show somewhat similar features that represent "distortions in the development of multiple basic psychological functions" (American Psychiatric Association, 1980, p. 92), but who do not meet the criteria for either infantile autism or childhood-onset pervasive developmental disorder.

Any discussion of these disorders is hampered by the fact that there is almost no information available on them. Whereas childhood-onset pervasive developmental disorder is purported to represent a specific syndrome defined by a number of features such as severe difficulties in social relationships, exaggerated anxieties, bizarre ideas, unusual preoccupations, inappropriate emotional responses, and strange behaviors, we know little else about it clinically. Likewise, there is little information regarding prevalence, except that it is said to be less frequent than autism. Virtually nothing is known with regard to etiological factors and efficacy of various treatment methods. The same is true for atypical pervasive developmental disorders.

Despite being included in DSM-III, it is presently unclear whether

Table 2.16. DSM-III Criteria for Childhood-Onset Pervasive Developmental Disorder

---

A. Gross and sustained impairment in social relationships, e.g., lack of appropriate affective responsivity, inappropriate clinging, asociality, and lack of empathy.
B. At least three of the following:
  1. Sudden excessive anxiety manifested by such symptoms as free-floating anxiety, catastrophic reactions to every-day occurrences, inability to be consoled when upset, and unexplained panic attacks.
  2. Constricted or inappropriate affect, including lack of appropriate fear reactions, unexplained rage reactions, and extreme mood lability.
  3. Resistance to change in the environment (e.g., becoming upset if dinner time is changed), or insistence on doing things in the same manner every time (e.g., always putting on clothes in the same order).
  4. Oddities of motor movement, such as peculiar posturing, peculiar hand or finger movements, or walking on tiptoe.
  5. Abnormalities of speech, such as a questionlike singsong or monotonous tone.
  6. Hypersensitivity or hyposensitivity to sensory stimuli, e.g., hyperacusis.
  7. Self-mutilation, e.g., biting or hitting self, head banging.
C. Onset of the full syndrome after 30 months of age and before 12 years of age.
D. Absence of delusions, hallucinations, incoherence, or marked loosening of associations.

Note. From *Diagnostic and Statistical Manual of Mental Disorders* (3rd ed.) by the American Psychiatric Association (1980). Washington, DC: American Psychiatric Press. Copyright 1980 by the American Psychiatric Association. Adapted by permission.

there is in fact a specific syndrome characterized by the constellation of symptoms said to define this disorder (Rutter, 1985). Rather, it seems likely that this category, and to an even greater extent the category of atypical pervasive developmental disorder, may classify a heterogeneous group of children who display severe pathologies with differing etiologies. As these diagnostic categories seem to represent little more than convenient ways of referring to a range of severe pathologies that elude more precise classification, their actual value is unclear (Schwartz & Johnson, 1985).

SCHIZOPHRENIA IN CHILDHOOD

Some children and adolescents manifest symptoms similar to those seen in adults who are diagnosed as schizophrenic. When these symptoms are observed in children, a diagnosis of schizophrenia is considered appropriate. The symptoms of schizophrenia in children include disordered thinking, disturbed perceptions of the environment, interpersonal inadequacies, and a lack of control over ideas, affect, and behavior (Weiner, 1982). These symptoms are reflected in the DSM-III criteria for ''Schizophrenic Disorder'' presented in Table 2.17 and in the following case illustration.

Jason: A Schizophrenic Child

Jason, age 13, was referred to a child psychiatrist by his family physician at the request of his parents, who had become increasingly concerned over the changed nature of his behavior. Jason, described by his parents as always somewhat shy and sensitive, had developed relatively normally intellectually and physically, although he was reported to have been somewhat more sickly and awkward than his two siblings. Despite this reasonably normal development, the parents reported that Jason's behavior had shown a dramatic, although gradual change during the past 8 to 10 months. His grades had dropped from mostly B's and C's to D's and failures, and he no longer seemed to take care of his basic grooming needs, such as brushing his teeth and bathing, unless forced. His parents also noted that Jason had become progressively withdrawn and no longer chose to spend any time with his former friends.

Of special concern was the fact that Jason's behavior had become more and more inappropriate. The parents noted, for example, his tendency to giggle uncontrollably for no apparent reason. Other examples included his tendency to talk "without making sense." The parents indicated that Jason's answers to questions frequently had little or nothing to do

Table 2.17. DSM-III Diagnostic Criteria for Schizophrenic Disorder

A. At least one of the following during a phase of the illness:
   1. Bizarre delusions (content is patently absurd and has no possible basis in fact), such as delusions of being controlled or of thought broadcasting, thought insertion, or thought withdrawal.
   2. Somatic, grandiose, religious, nihilistic, or other delusions without persecutory or jealous content.
   3. Delusions with persecutory or jealous content if accompanied by hallucinations of any type.
   4. Auditory hallucinations: Either a voice keeps up a running commentary on the individual's behavior or thoughts, or two or more voices converse with each other.
   5. Auditory hallucinations on several occasions, with content of more than one or two words, and with no apparent relation to depression or elation.
   6. Incoherence, marked loosening of associations, markedly illogical thinking, or marked poverty of content of speech if associated with at least one of the following: (a) blunted, flat, or inappropriate affect; (b) delusions or hallucinations; or (c) catatonic or other grossly disorganized behavior.
B. Deterioration from a previous level of functioning in such areas as work, social relations, and self-care.
C. Continuous signs of the illness for at least 6 months at some time during the person's life, with some signs of the illness at present. The 6-month period must include an active phase, during which there were symptoms from A.

Note. From *Diagnostic and Statistical Manual of Mental Disorders* (3rd ed.) by the American Psychiatric Association (1980). Washington, DC: American Psychiatric Press. Copyright 1980 by the American Psychiatric Association. Reprinted by permission.

with what he was asked and that they often could not understand what he was saying because his thinking seemed so disorganized. The parents also found it unusual that Jason had recently begun to avoid touching the television set. In response to his parents' request for an explanation, Jason stated that his body was so charged with electricity that he might cause the TV to explode if he came into contact with it. On occasion he made other comments concerning his belief that "others" would like to hurt him with "electrical impulses." Jason's parents also reported that he frequently made "strange faces" and assumed unusual postures for no obvious reason, while talking to himself. Jason's father was especially concerned that Jason's behavior had deteriorated from being simply withdrawn and self-absorbed to being more and more bizarre and out of touch with reality.

Prevalence

Childhood schizophrenia frequently is not distinguished from other severe psychopathologies of childhood, and deriving accurate estimates of its prevalence is difficult. From information currently available, the disorder would seem to be quite rare, with 3 to 4 cases per 10,000 children representing an approximate rate (Lotter, 1966). The disorder appears to be more common in boys than girls by a ratio of 2 : 1 to 3 : 1 (Kolvin, 1971). The disorder occurs most frequently in early adolescence, although the age of onset can be earlier (Dawson & Mesibov, 1983).

Prognosis

Even though the prognosis for schizophrenia in childhood seems more favorable than that for autism, the long-term outlook is generally poor. In a follow-up of 57 schizophrenic children, Eggers (1978) found only 20% to show complete remission, with 50% displaying a moderate to poor outcome. Lower IQ and onset before age 10 were predictive of a less favorable outcome. Similar results were obtained by Howells and Guirguis (1984) in a 20-year follow-up study of adults who had been diagnosed as childhood schizophrenics. Even those adults who were able to function independently still remained relatively aloof and emotionally detached from others.

Etiological Factors

Unfortunately, as with autism and childhood-onset pervasive developmental disorders, the etiology of schizophrenia has not been determined. Implicated as causal have been disturbed mother–child relationships and faulty parenting by "schizophrenogenic" mothers, deviant family communication patterns, genetic factors, biochemical abnormalities, and environmental stressors (Carson, 1984).

Of these possible causes, genetic factors have received the most consistent support. Although the available research suggests a significant genetic component to schizophrenia (Buchsbaum & Haier, 1982), it is clear that genetics are not sufficient to account for the development of schizophrenia in either adults or children.

Currently, the most widely accepted view is that genetic (and perhaps other biological) factors may predispose one to schizophrenia, but the development of the disorder is dependent upon an interaction between genetic predisposition and environmental factors (Dawson & Mesibov, 1983). This position is consistent with what is popularly referred to as the diathesis-stress model of schizophrenia. Basic to this model is the assumption that both biological and psychosocial factors are necessary in the development of schizophrenia. As Weiner (1982, p. 202) has suggested, ''the stronger the biogenetic predisposition (diathesis) to the disturbance, the more likely it is to arise in response to minimal psychosocial stress. Conversely, persons with little or no predisposition to schizophrenia either cope adequately with severe family disorganization and environmental pressures or develop other forms of psychopathology.'' A clearer delineation of the psychosocial variables that interact with genetic predisposition awaits further research.

Treatment of Childhood Schizophrenia

None of the approaches that have been employed in the treatment of schizophrenia have been very successful in resolving the fundamental psychopathology of the schizophrenic child. Specific approaches have included psychodynamic therapies, behavior therapy, and antipsychotic drugs similar to those used with adult schizophrenics. Residential and day-treatment programs are commonly needed, due to the severe nature of the problems these children display. In reviewing treatments, Weiner (1982) has noted that although much anecdotal evidence supports the psychodynamic approach, which emphasizes the development of a permissive and trusting therapeutic atmosphere within which the child may feel free to give up psychotic symptoms, there is little empirical research to support its effectiveness. Behavior therapy has been found to be effective in dealing with both the behavioral deficits and specific maladaptive behaviors of such children. Both of these approaches, however, fall short of bringing about a ''normal'' level of functioning. Drug treatments have met with some limited success. Among those drugs found most useful are the phenothiazines, psychotropic medications that are used in the treatment of adult psychoses. These drugs are useful in controlling the symptoms of schizophrenia, but they are problematic in that they also have a sedating effect at effective treatment doses. Such side effects may make it difficult for the child to benefit from adjunct forms of treatment necessary to improve his or her ability to function. More work related to the treatment of schizophrenic children and adolescents is needed.

EATING DISORDERS: ANOREXIA NERVOSA

She looked like a walking skeleton, with her legs sticking out like broom-sticks, every rib showing, and her shoulder blades standing up like little wings. Her mother mentioned, "When I put my arms around her I feel nothing but bones, like a frightened little bird." Alma's arms and legs were covered with soft hair, her complexion had a yellowish tint, and her dry hair hung down in strings. Most striking was the face—hollow like that of a shriveled-up old woman with a wasting disease. . . . Alma insisted that she was fine and that there was nothing wrong with her being so skinny. (Bruch, 1978, pp. 2–3)

Anorexia nervosa is a potentially life-threatening disorder characterized by an active refusal to eat, often in the context of a good appetite, which results in severe weight loss and a variety of physical symptoms second-ary to starvation (e.g., changes in skin, hair, nails, teeth, and complex-ion; swelling of the extremities; and hypotension). Amenorrhea, that is, cessation of menstruation, may occur. Starvation can result in amenor-rhea, but the fact that it usually precedes or coincides with the beginning of weight loss suggests that it may be a symptom of the disorder rather than a consequence of malnutrition.

Individuals with anorexia nervosa frequently engage in behaviors to facilitate weight loss. They may go on calorie-burning exercise binges, con-sume large quantities of laxatives, or force themselves to vomit in order to avoid weight gain. Sometimes individuals with this disorder also show evidence of bulimia, which can also occur apart from anorexia nervosa, in which they engage in binge eating episodes only to purge themselves later through the use of laxatives and self-induced vomiting.

Persons with this disorder usually also display accompanying psycho-logical features that help to define the syndrome. They may be preoccu-pied with food while refusing to eat, actively deny their illness, seem un-concerned with the dangerous level of their weight loss, and in fact "feel fat" despite their emaciated appearance. Indeed, distorted body image is a central feature of the disorder. The specific criteria for diagnosis ac-cording to DSM-III are presented in Table 2.18.

Prevalence

Anorexia nervosa occurs primarily among females, with only about 5 to 15% of the cases being found among males (Andersen, 1984). Onset is usually in adolescence or young adulthood and frequently coincides with puberty. Halmi (1985) has noted that in 85% of the cases anorexia nervosa develops between the ages of 13 and 20. Prevalence estimates vary widely, depending on the diagnostic criteria used, but studies employ-ing fairly stringent weight-loss criteria (30% of normal body weight) sug-gest a frequency of one case among every 100 adolescent females (Crisp,

Table 2.18. DSM-III Diagnostic Criteria for Anorexia Nervosa

A. Intense fear of becoming obese, which does not diminish as weight loss progresses.
B. Disturbance of body image, e.g., claiming to "feel fat" even when emaciated.
C. Weight loss of at least 25% of original body weight. If under 18 years of age, weight loss from original body weight plus projected weight gain from growth charts may be combined to make the 25% weight loss assessment.
D. Refusal to maintain body weight over a minimal normal weight for age and height.
E. No known physical illness that would account for the weight loss.

Note. From *Diagnostic and Statistical Manual of Mental Disorders* (3rd ed.) by the American Psychiatric Association (1980). Washington, DC: American Psychiatric Press. Copyright 1980 by the American Psychiatric Association. Reprinted by permission.

Palmer, & Kalucy, 1976). There appears to be evidence that the frequency of the disorder is increasing and that this increase cannot be explained solely on the basis of more careful diagnostic procedures (Leon & Phelan, 1985).

Prognosis

The seriousness of anorexia nervosa is suggested by the fact that a significant proportion of those affected either die of the disorder or from complications associated with it. Death rates ranging from 3 to 21% have been reported in the literature (Leon & Dinklage, 1983). For many persons it is a chronic condition, characterized by periodic remissions and relapses, with the long-term outlook being less than positive. Crisp, Kalucy, Lacey, and Harding (1977) have suggested an overall recovery rate of 40 to 60%.

Relationship to Bulimia

Bulimia is characterized by uncontrolled binge-eating episodes in which the individual consumes large volumes of high-calorie foods within a brief period of time. The person usually realizes that the binge eating is abnormal but feels unable to control it, and may even fear being unable to stop eating. Behavior may alternate between binge eating and fasting, self-induced vomiting, and laxative use to get rid of the large amount of food eaten. This syndrome has been given a number of labels: "bulimarexia," "purge vomiters," "bulimia nervosa," "dysorexia," and "abnormal weight-control syndrome." Although bulimic eating can occur as a separate disorder (American Psychiatric Association, 1980) it often is seen as a feature of anorexia nervosa.

In a study investigating the relationship between anorexia nervosa and bulimia, Casper, Eckert, Halmi, Goldberg, and Davis (1980) assessed the eating habits of 105 patients hospitalized for anorexia nervosa. Weight loss was achieved in 53% by fasting, and 47% were found also to engage in bulimia. In studying the differences between these two groups, Casper et al. found that those relying on fasting for weight loss showed more introversion and little overt distress in relation to the bulimic patients, who had higher levels of anxiety, depression, and guilt and also more bodily complaints. These findings led the authors to conclude that bulimic patients should be viewed as a distinct subgroup among individuals with anorexia nervosa. Particularly important is the fact that binge vomiters may show high levels of depression, because suicide is the most common cause of death in this disorder (Crisp, 1982; Maloney & Klykylo, 1983).

Etiological Factors

As with most other disorders discussed to this point, the factors that contribute to anorexia nervosa are unclear, although a number have been implicated. Some insight-oriented writers, noting that the disorder frequently coincides with puberty, have focused on the reluctance of these individuals to grow up. Their point of view is that the refusal to eat, and the subsequent weight loss and failure to develop, are ways of avoiding adult responsibilities and sexual issues (Dally, 1969). High concordance rates for monozygotic twins have suggested that genetic factors may play some role (Garfinkle & Garner, 1982). Other biologically-oriented hypotheses have focused on possible hypothalamic dysfunction and abnormalities in neurotransmitter regulation (Gold, Pottash, Sweeny, Martin, & Davies, 1980; Lupton, Simon, Barry, & Klawans, 1976). Behavioral therapists do not usually address the etiology of the disorder, but focus instead on the role of attention and other reinforcers in maintaining the disorder (Ullmann & Krasner, 1975). Of interest is the fact that anorexia nervosa often is said to be preceded by the experiencing of stressful life events (Dally, 1969), thus suggesting that stress plays a role. Determining the importance of these variables in the development of anorexia nervosa will require much additional research.

Treatment of Anorexia Nervosa

Psychoanalytic psychotherapy; family therapy; various behavioral approaches, for example, reinforcement for eating and desensitization for the fear of gaining weight; and medical interventions, such as high-calorie diets, tube feeding, hospitalization, and drug treatment, have all been employed in the treatment of anorexia nervosa (Andersen, 1984; Leon & Phelan, 1985; Maloney & Klykylo, 1983). Van Buskirk (1977) has stated the need for a dual perspective that focuses both on treatments that are most effective in bringing about rapid weight gain and those that maintain adequate food intake over time. Among the approaches seen as most useful in helping patients gain weight and perhaps getting them out of danger due to starvation, are operant conditioning (rewarding food intake), high-calorie diets, and drug treatments (e.g., chlorpromazine). To maintain the weight gain, Van Buskirk suggests supplementing these approaches with supportive therapies that involve the family in the treatment process. This point of view would suggest that family therapies, such as those considered in chapter 8, may prove to be of significant value in the treatment of this disorder.

ELIMINATIVE DISORDERS: ENURESIS AND ENCOPRESIS

ENURESIS

Children are diagnosed as enuretic if they do not have control over their urination by an age at which it is usually acquired. Daytime control typically is accomplished by the age of 3 or 4, and nighttime control is present by the age of 4 or 5. According to DSM-III criteria (see Table 2.19), a diagnosis of enuresis is only to be used with children older than 5 years. It should be noted that even when a diagnosis of enuresis is made, the condition often resolves itself spontaneously at a rate of perhaps 15% for each year of increasing age (Christophersen & Rapoff, 1983).

Enuresis may take the form of day wetting, night wetting, or a combination of the two, although nocturnal enuresis is most common. The disorder may be either a primary or secondary type. Primary enuresis refers to cases in which the child has never developed control, secondary enuresis to instances in which the child developed control but has since resumed wetting.

Etiological Factors

A number of factors have been hypothesized to relate to enuresis. The higher incidence of the disorder in children whose parents also were enuretic has caused some clinicians to emphasize genetic factors. Some researchers have argued that enuretic children are deeper sleepers than nonenuretic children, and thus it is more difficult for them to respond (awaken) to cues associated with a full bladder while asleep. Other re-

---

Table 2.19. DSM-III Criteria for Enuresis

A. Repeated involuntary voiding of urine during the day or night.
B. At least two such events per month for children between the ages of 5 and 6, and at least one event per month for older children.
C. Not due to physical disorder, such as diabetes or epilepsy.

Note. From *Diagnostic and Statistical Manual of Mental Disorders* (3rd ed.) by the American Psychiatric Association (1980). Washington, DC: American Psychiatric Press. Copyright 1980 by the American Psychiatric Association. Reprinted by permission.

searchers have implicated an inadequate functional bladder capacity, which may result in the child being able to retain less urine than other children. Still other neurologically oriented researchers have emphasized the importance of delays in the development of cortical control over reflexive voiding. Psychodynamically oriented clinicians have argued that enuresis results from underlying conflict. Those espousing a behavioral orientation emphasize faulty learning experiences, perhaps compounded by stressful approaches to toilet training, and the maintenance of enuresis by environmental contingencies.

Despite research related to each of these factors, findings often have been conflicting and failed to provide clear information regarding the causes of enuresis. The available evidence, however, suggests that the majority of enuretic children show no signs of significant emotional problems (Shaffer, 1985). When psychological problems are present, they often are secondary to the enuresis rather than causal. See Doleys (1983) and Schaefer (1979) for an overview of research findings regarding etiological factors.

Treatment of Enuresis

The most widely used treatment methods involve drugs, conditioning approaches, and psychodynamic psychotherapy. The drug most commonly used is Tofranil® (imipramine), which is a tricyclic antidepressant. This drug has been shown to be superior to a placebo and to result in a remission rate of 10 to 20%, with about 50 to 65% of tested cases showing a significant reduction in the frequency of bedwetting (Shaffer & Ambrosini, 1985). A major problem, however, is that most children go back to bedwetting when the drug is discontinued.

The most common behavioral treatment is the bell-and-pad approach. In this method, originally developed by Mowrer and Mowrer (1938), the child sleeps on a urine-sensitive pad, constructed so that when the child wets a circuit is completed, activating a buzzer or bell loud enough to awaken the child. The rationale for this approach is that if the bell that wakes up the child can be paired over time with the sensations associated with a distended bladder, the child—due to classical conditioning—will learn to awaken and inhibit urination in response to these sensations (Schaefer, 1979). This method has been found to be quite effective in dealing with bedwetting, with success rates of 70 to 90% being reported (Doleys, 1983; Faschingbauer, 1975).

Another behavioral approach includes retention control training (Kimmel & Kimmel, 1970), in which the child is reinforced for inhibiting urination for longer and longer periods of time. Although research suggests that this approach is less effective than the bell and pad with bedwetting, it does seem to be useful with daytime enuresis (Doleys, 1983).

An additional behavioral approach is dry-bed training (Azrin, Sneed, & Foxx, 1974). This intense training program includes nighttime awakening, practice in appropriate toileting, retention control training as described above, positive reinforcement for appropriate toileting behaviors, and cleanliness training. These procedures are combined in an intensive treatment package that usually is carried out in one evening, with followup maintenance procedures employed until the child has 14 dry nights. Although there are studies supporting the effectiveness of dry-bed training (see Christophersen & Rapoff, 1983), there is some suggestion that use of this approach may elicit strong emotional responses on the part of the parents and child and that temper tantrums and parental upset are not uncommon side effects (Matson & Ollendick, 1977). This aspect, along with findings that treatment is not successful without the simultaneous use of an alarm apparatus, has led some (Shaffer, 1985) to favor the use of the more standard bell-and-pad approach.

Some attempts have been made to assess the effectiveness of traditional psychotherapy in treating enuresis. In this regard DeLeon and Mandell (1966) compared response to treatment in 5- to 14-year-old children who were given bell-and-pad treatment, psychotherapy, or no treatment (control group). Respective improvement rates of 86.3, 18.2, and 11.1% were found for these three groups. The results clearly question the effectiveness of psychotherapy in treating this particular disorder.

ENCOPRESIS

DSM-III criteria for encopresis are presented in Table 2.20. As these criteria indicate, this disorder involves voluntary or involuntary soiling, not resulting from a physical disorder, that occurs past the age when control over defecation is expected. The age at which the diagnosis is considered appropriate has varied. Some authors suggest that a lack of control at age 3 warrants such a diagnosis (Doleys, 1980), and others reserve the diagnosis for children a bit older. As Table 2.20 indicates, DSM-III criteria suggest that the diagnosis be reserved for children aged 4 years or older.

Table 2.20. DSM-III Criteria for Encopresis

A. Repeated voluntary or involuntary passage of feces of normal or near-normal consistency into places not appropriate for that purpose in the individual's sociocultural setting.
B. At least one such event a month after the age of 4.
C. Not due to physical disorder such as aganglionic megacolon.

Note. From *Diagnostic and Statistical Manual of Mental Disorders* (3rd ed.) by the American Psychiatric Association (1980). Washington, DC: American Psychiatric Press. Copyright 1980 by the American Psychiatric Association. Reprinted by permission.

The prevalence of encopresis is difficult to estimate, as the figures obtained vary depending on the age range of the sample. Doleys (1983), in reviewing a number of studies, cited figures as high as 8.1% for 3-year-olds and as low as 1% in children age 10 to 12.

As with enuresis, encopresis may take various forms. The most common distinctions are the continuous type (analogous to primary enuresis) in which the child has never become toilet trained, and the discontinuous type (analogous to secondary enuresis) in which the child was initially toilet trained and has since become incontinent.

Etiological Factors

Anthony (1957) suggested that continuous encopresis is associated with a lax approach to toilet training, and the discontinuous type is more likely a result of rigid and stressful approaches to toilet training. Thus, toilet training may result in encopresis if it is either too casual, where the child may fail to learn appropriate toileting skills and develop little motivation to be trained, or too coercive, where the child develops excessive anxiety over toileting, fears of the toilet, or has significant conflicts with parents over the issue of toilet training.

The development of discontinuous encopresis sometimes begins with the child's retention of feces because of painful defecation associated with anal fissures or hard stools, because of constipation, or for other reasons such as refusal to go to the toilet. In such cases the child's stools may become impacted, and the child may adapt to the sensations of fullness in the rectum and become unaware of the need to defecate. Soiling occurs as feces gradually are expelled without the child's control. Such factors contribute to encopresis in the absence of any physiological disorder that would account for soiling. For an overview of etiological factors, see Schaefer (1979).

Treatment of Encopresis

There are few well-controlled studies dealing with treatment. Although some studies have reported fairly high remission rates with psychotherapy and play therapy, it is not clear whether these rates are higher than those found for children not receiving treatment (Doleys, 1983).

Behavioral approaches usually are of the operant variety, in which the child is either positively reinforced for sitting on the toilet and for defecating, or where mild punishment (e.g., loss of TV) is made contingent on soiling. Extinction procedures also have been employed, whereby the reinforcers that typically follow soiling episodes are removed. Most often a combination of these procedures is employed. In some instances these procedures are supplemented by the use of suppositories to stimulate bowel movements for which the child can then be rewarded. For an excellent example of this type of approach see Wright (1975). Although there are few examples of well-controlled research in this area, a number of case studies have provided reasonably strong support for a behavioral approach to treatment.

CONDUCT DISORDERS

Edward: A Conduct-Disordered Child

Edward's parents reported that their difficulties with him began as early as age 3 or 4, when they first became concerned that he would not listen to them. Initially he simply failed to respond when asked to do things like leave the TV and come to dinner or to come inside after playing outdoors. Both parents noted that this problem had become worse during the past 3 years and that Edward had become increasingly argumentative and aggressive with his younger brother and older sister. Edward's mother reported that he frequently was verbally abusive toward her, often responding to requests with statements such as "I don't have to if I don't want to," "You can't make me," and even "I hate you." She indicated that these behaviors were exacerbated by Edward's high activity level, which caused him always to be involved in something that necessitated reprimanding him and starting the conflict all over again.

In addition to these problems at home, Edward's third-grade teacher recommended that he be referred to the school psychologist, as his behavior in the classroom was so out of control that he was learning very little and interfering with other children in the class. Edward's teacher stated that he was not only disruptive in class, but aggressive on the playground, and on several occasions he had stolen pencils and other small items from other children's desks.

The term "conduct disorder" refers to a constellation of child behaviors, ranging from nondelinquent behaviors of a coercive or oppositional nature, such as aggressiveness, demandingness, noncompliance, screaming, crying, pestering, and throwing temper tantrums, to frankly delinquent activities (Herbert, 1982). The validity of such a category is supported by numerous multivariate (factor analytic) studies that have found these behaviors to occur together with a fairly high frequency in child and adolescent samples.

DSM-III includes two broad categories of conduct disorders: "Socialized" and "Undersocialized." A child with a socialized conduct disorder typically has friends and displays some degree of social attachment toward others, whereas the child with an unsocialized conduct disorder is more often a loner and frequently in conflict with peers and adults. These categories are subdivided further into aggressive and nonaggressive types. Thus, four types of conduct disorder can be diagnosed: socialized aggressive, socialized nonaggressive, undersocialized aggressive, and undersocialized nonaggressive. DSM-III criteria for undersocialized aggressive conduct disorder are presented in Table 2.21. The format for the remaining categories, although similar, varies with respect to degree of socialization and aggressive behavior.

It may be noted that DSM-III includes an additional category, "Oppositional Disorder" (see Table 2.6), which covers a range of somewhat less severe problem behaviors. Problems listed here would be seen as associated with the general heading of conduct disorder as the term is often used. Whether multivariate studies assessing criteria relevant to the DSM-III conduct and oppositional disorder categories will support the view that they represent two distinct syndromes, as opposed to one general category, is open to question.

However defined, conduct disorder refers to a rather heterogeneous group of problem behaviors. Some are merely aversive and disruptive for parents and teachers, and others involve violations of the law and fall within the category of delinquent behavior. As Herbert (1982, pp. 96–97) has indicated, "The common theme running through this rather heterogeneous collection of problems is antisocial disruptiveness and the social disapproval they [conduct-disordered children] earn because they flout society's sensibilities and rules, and because their consequences are so disturbing or explicitly harmful to others."

Table 2.21. DSM-III Criteria for Conduct Disorder, Undersocialized Aggressive Type

---

A. A repetitive and persistent pattern of aggressive conduct in which the basic rights of others are violated, as manifested by either of the following:
  1. Physical violence against persons or property (other than to defend someone else or oneself), e.g., vandalism, rape, breaking and entering, fire setting, mugging, and assault.
  2. Thefts outside the home involving confrontation with the victim, e.g., extortion, purse-snatching, and armed robbery.
B. Failure to establish a normal degree of affection, empathy, or bonds with others as evidenced by no more than one of the following indications of social attachment:
  1. Has one or more peer-group friendships that have lasted over 6 months.
  2. Extends himself or herself for others even when no immediate advantage is likely.
  3. Apparently feels guilt or remorse when such a reaction is appropriate (not just when caught or in difficulty).
  4. Avoids blaming or informing on companions.
  5. Shares concern for the welfare of friends or companions.
C. Duration of pattern of aggressive conduct of at least 6 months.
D. If age 18 or older, does not meet the criteria for antisocial personality disorder.

Note. From *Diagnostic and Statistical Manual of Mental Disorders* (3rd ed.) by the American Psychiatric Association (1980). Washington, DC: American Psychiatric Press. Copyright 1980 by the American Psychiatric Association. Reprinted by permission.

Prevalence

Estimates of prevalence are difficult because of the heterogeneous nature of this category and the fact that the term "conduct disorder" is used in different ways by investigators, for example, in some cases to refer to nondelinquent conduct problems and in others to refer to patterns of delinquent behavior. However, a prevalence rate of 4 to 8% in the general population is one estimate (Yule, 1981). This figure refers to children and adolescents who display a broad pattern of conduct problems, rather than to those who might legally be characterized as delinquent. Accurate estimates of the frequency of delinquent behavior are similarly difficult to make, as figures based on arrest rates, court appearances, or incarceration are influenced by prevailing law enforcement practices and may be correlated with social variables (Johnson & Fennell, 1983). Studies of "normal" children and adolescents responding to anonymous questionnaires have suggested that as many as 75% have engaged in behaviors that could have resulted in arrest if caught (Johnson & Fennell, 1983).

Prognosis

Although it is often possible to deal with mild conduct problems within the home (and children vary markedly in the extent to which they show such problems) there appears to be a degree of continuity between severe early conduct problems and later delinquency. In this regard, Herbert (1982) cites the research of West and Farrington (1973) in London, which showed troublesome, difficult, and aggressive behaviors of 8- to 10-year-old boys to be a strong predictor of delinquency that persisted into adulthood. Studies conducted in this country by Robins (1966) also have found extremeness and variety of early antisocial behavior to predict antisocial behavior in adulthood. Although most conduct-disordered children do not become antisocial adults, a pattern of early conduct problems not infrequently is associated with later difficulties in social behavior (Herbert, 1982).

Etiological Factors

Given the broad nature of this category, a detailed consideration of etiological factors is beyond the scope of the present chapter. Reviews of these factors have been provided by Herbert (1978, 1982) and by Johnson and Fennell (1983). As a brief overview, Herbert (1982) cites several factors suggested by research studies as important. He notes that conduct disorders are significantly related to such variables as temperament characteristics (e.g., high activity level, intense reactivity, low threshold of responsiveness), lower levels of moral development, broken homes, dysfunctional and rejecting family environments, and negative social learning experiences, for example, vicariously learning problem behaviors through observation, or the reinforcement of conduct problems by parents, siblings, and peers.

In addition to these variables cited by Herbert (1982), others that have been implicated in the development of conduct disorders and delinquent behaviors include genetic factors, biologically-based arousal deficits that result in stimulation-seeking behaviors, and chromosomal abnormalities (Johnson & Fennell, 1983). Other studies suggest some relationship between indices of neurological impairment and conduct problems.

Treatment of Conduct Disorders

Although both insight-oriented and client-centered approaches have been employed with conduct-disordered children, the current most popular treatment method is behavioral in nature. The work of Patterson and his colleagues (see Chamberlain & Patterson, 1985, for an overview) is representative. This approach involves training parents to pinpoint problem behaviors such as aggressive responses, noncompliant responses, and destructiveness, as well as more appropriate modes of responding, and to utilize a variety of child management techniques in coping with the problem behaviors. Included among these child management procedures are the reinforcement of appropriate behaviors, and the use of extinction (i.e., withdrawal of reinforcement) and of time out for dealing with undesirable behaviors. School personnel also are involved in the treatment process. This multifaceted approach has been shown to be highly effective in dealing with conduct problems (Patterson, 1974). Other behavioral approaches have been employed to deal with specific behaviors or classes of behaviors displayed by conduct-disordered children. In this regard the work of Forehand & McMahon (1981), who have used a somewhat similar approach in dealing with noncompliance, is especially worthy of note.

Treatment of children and adolescents who have been arrested for delinquent activities frequently takes place in institutions or within community-based programs. It appears that treatment in standard institutional programs is often unsuccessful, with as many as 70 to 80% rearrested within a year or so after release (Gibbons, 1976). Despite these generally discouraging results associated with traditional institutional treatment, other data suggest that well conceived, behaviorally-based programs within this setting can result in positive outcomes. Illustrative of such an approach is the Cascadia Project conducted in Tacoma, Washington by Sarason (1978) and his colleagues. In this program residents were provided with modeling and role-playing experiences in which they were taught a variety of adaptive skills that might decrease the likelihood of future delinquency. Among these skills were learning how to resist temptation from peers, delay gratification, apply for a job, and behave appropriately when stopped by police. This skills-based treatment was found to be highly successful; at 5-year follow-up, the recidivism rate for treated subjects was less than half of that for residents who did not receive treatment. Another example of a community-based program is Achievement Place. Residents in this program live in a homelike setting with seven or eight other residents and houseparents who are trained in behavior management skills. Residents in the program attend school and have a variety of work responsibilities. Within a token economy program, which serves as the basic focus of treatment, they are rewarded for engaging in appropriate behaviors (e.g., completing homework assignments, improved academic performance, practicing conversational skills with adults, modifying aggressive statements, improving problem-solving skills) or fined for inappropriate behaviors. Reinforcement is in the form of points that can be cashed in for back-up reinforcers such as small amounts of cash, snacks, TV viewing or permission to go to town or to stay up later than usual. The overall focus is on using the token economy to increase nondelinquent modes of response. Ample attention is given to insuring that these behaviors generalize to the environment at large, so that they will be maintained after release from the program. A number of controlled studies have provided support for the effectiveness of this program (Hoefler & Bornstein, 1975). Still other community-based programs have been conducted within a similar setting, but with greater emphasis on group treatment approaches in modifying delinquent behaviors. Less research related to these programs has been done and their effectiveness is not as well documented (Johnson & Fennell, 1983).

SUMMARY

We have considered a range of childhood problems that are seen clinically. Despite the focus on abnormal child behavior, it was suggested that the distinction between normal and abnormal is not always an easy one, especially in the case of children, who frequently display problems such as fears, temper tantrums, aggressiveness, noncompliance, problems with toilet training, and heightened activity levels as part of normal development. These behaviors usually occur in mild forms and tend to decline as the child becomes older. Several developmental criteria were suggested as potentially useful in distinguishing between these common developmental problems and behaviors suggestive of psychopathology.

Also considered were attempts to classify childhood disorders. Because of its widespread acceptance in mental health settings, emphasis was placed on DSM-III. DSM-III represents a significant advance over earlier versions of the DSM system in terms of the larger number of child and adolescent categories and the more objective nature of the diagnostic criteria. Nevertheless, there are still unanswered questions concerning the reliability and the validity of many of the diagnostic categories in this system.

Most of the chapter reviewed childhood disorders that frequently require treatment. Included were problems of inattention and activity level, child anxiety disorders, childhood depression, eating disorders, eliminative disturbances, conduct problems, and pervasive developmental disorders. Although it is most often found in adults, the problem of schizophrenia in childhood also was discussed. Attention was given to the prevalence of each disorder, presumed etiological factors, and methods of treatment.

Regarding the issue of treatment, it should be noted that although some of the research presented here suggests that certain approaches to treatment are superior to others in treating specific types of child psychopathology, no treatment has been found to be uniformly superior in dealing with all types of child psychopathology. Thus, drug treatments may have much to offer in the treatment of some problems, behavioral treatments may be effective with other types, and more traditional approaches may be of value in dealing with others. In instances where family variables are significantly related to the nature of the child's presenting problem, family therapies may be preferable to those that concentrate on the individual child. Although research findings may eventually provide guidelines for choosing the most effective treatment for a particular disorder, at present there are no such guidelines for selecting the optimal treatment method in most instances. Given our limited state of knowledge in this area, it is important for the child clinician to be familiar with a range of treatment approaches considered useful by clinicians of differing theoretical orientations. These methods of treatment are discussed throughout the remaining chapters of the book.

REFERENCES

Achenbach, T. M. (1978). Developmental aspects of psychopathology in children and adolescents. In M. E. Lamb (Ed.), *Social and personality development*. New York: Holt, Rinehart & Winston.

Agras, W., Chapin, H., & Oliveau, D. (1972). The natural history of phobia. *Archives of General Psychiatry, 26*, 315–317.

Ambrosini, P. J., & Puig-Antich, J. (1985). Major depression in children and adolescence. In D. Shaffer, A. A. Ehrhardt, & L. L. Greenhill (Eds.), *The clinical guide to child psychiatry*. New York: Free Press.

American Psychiatric Association. (1968). *Diagnostic and statistical manual of mental disorders* (2nd ed.). Washington, DC: American Psychiatric Association.

American Psychiatric Association. (1980). *Diagnostic and statistical manual of mental disorders* (3rd ed.). Washington, DC: Author.

Andersen, A. E. (1984). Anorexia nervosa and bulimia: Biological, psychological and sociocultural aspects. In J. R. Galler (Ed.), *Human nutrition*. New York: Plenum.

Ando, H., & Tsuda, K. (1975). Intrafamilial incidence of autism, cerebral palsy, and mongolism. *Journal of Autism and Childhood Schizophrenia, 5*, 267–274.

Anthony, E. J. (1957). An experimental approach to the psychopathology of childhood: Encopresis. *British Journal of Medical Psychology, 30*, 146–175.

Azrin, N., Sneed, T. J., & Foxx, R. M. (1974). Dry-bed training: Rapid elimination of childhood enuresis. *Behavior Research and Therapy, 12*, 147–156.

Bettelheim, B. (1967). *The empty fortress.* New York: Free Press.

Borland, B. L., & Heckman, H. K. (1976). Hyperactive boys and their brothers: A 25-year follow-up study. *Archives of General Psychiatry, 33*, 669–675.

Bruch, H. (1978). *The golden cage: The enigma of anorexia nervosa.* Cambridge, MA: Harvard University Press.

Buchsbaum, M. S., & Haier, R. J. (1982). Psychopathology: Biological approaches. *Annual Review of Psychology, 34*, 401–430.

Campbell, M., Anderson, L. T., Small, A. M., Perry, R., Green, W. H., & Caplan, R. (1982). The effects of haloperidol on learning and behavior in autistic children. *Journal of Autism and Developmental Disorders, 12*, 167–175.

Cantwell, D. P. (1975). Genetic studies of hyperactive children. In R. R. Fieve, D. Rosenthal, & H. Brill (Eds.), *Genetic research in psychiatry.* Baltimore: Johns Hopkins University Press.

Cantwell, D. P. (1982). Childhood depression: A review of current research. In B. Lahey & A. Kazdin (Eds.), *Advances in clinical child psychology* (Vol. 5). New York: Plenum.

Cantwell, D. P. (1985). Organization and use of DSM-III. In D. Shaffer, A. A. Ehrhard, & L. L. Greenhill (Eds.), *The clinical guide to child psychiatry.* New York: Free Press.

Carlson, G. A., & Cantwell, D. P. (1980). A survey of depressive symptoms, syndrome, and disorder in a child psychiatric population. *Journal of Child Psychology and Psychiatry, 21*, 19–25.

Carson, R. C. (1984). The schizophrenias. In H. E. Adams & P. B. Sutker (Eds.), *Comprehensive handbook of psychopathology.* New York: Plenum.

Carson, T. P., & Carson, R. C. (1984). The affective disorders. In H. E. Adams & P. B. Sutker (Eds.), *Comprehensive handbook of psychopathology.* New York: Plenum.

Casper, R. C., Eckert, E. D., Halmi, K. A., Goldberg, S. C., & Davis, J. M. (1980). Bulimia: Its incidence and clinical importance in patients with anorexia nervosa. *Archives of General Psychiatry, 37*, 1030–1035.

Chamberlain, P., & Patterson, G. R. (1985). Aggressive behavior in middle childhood. In D. Shaffer, A. A. Ehrhardt, & L. L. Greenhill (Eds.), *The clinical guide to child psychiatry.* New York: Free Press.

Christophersen, E. R., & Rapoff, M. A. (1983). Toileting problems in children. In E. Walker & M. Roberts (Eds.), *Handbook of clinical child psychology.* New York: Wiley.

Conners, C. K. (1969). A teacher's rating scale for use in drug studies with children. *American Journal of Psychiatry, 126*, 152–156.

Crisp, A. H. (1982). Anorexia nervosa at normal body weight: The abnormal–normal weight control syndrome. *International Journal of Psychiatry in Medicine, 11*, 203–233.

Crisp, A. H., Kalucy, R. S., Lacey, J. H., & Harding, V. (1977). The long-term prognosis in anorexia nervosa: Some factors predictive of outcome. In R. A. Vigersky (Ed.), *Anorexia nervosa.* New York: Raven.

Crisp, A. H., Palmer, R. L., & Kalucy, R. S. (1976). How common is anorexia nervosa? A prevalence study. *British Journal of Psychiatry, 128*, 549–554.

Crowther, J. H., Bond, L. A., & Rolf, J. E. (1981). The incidence, prevalence, and severity of behavior disorders among preschool-age children in day care. *Journal of Abnormal Child Psychology, 9*, 23–42.

Dally, P. J. (1969). *Anorexia nervosa.* New York: Grune & Stratton.

David, O. J., Hoffman, S. P., Sverd, J., & Clark, J. (1977). Lead and hyperactivity: Lead levels among hyperactive children. *Journal of Abnormal Child Psychology, 5*, 405–410.

Dawson, G., & Mesibov, G. B. (1983). Childhood psychoses. In E. Walker & M. Roberts (Eds.), *Handbook of clinical child psychology.* New York: Wiley.

DeLeon, G., & Mandell, W. A. (1966). A comparison of conditioning and psychotherapy in the treatment of functional enuresis. *Journal of Clinical Psychology, 22*, 326–330.

Delprato, D. J. (1980). Hereditary determinants of fears and phobias: A critical review. *Behavior Therapy, 11*, 79–103.

DeMyer, M. K., Hingtgen, J. N., & Jackson, R. K. (1981). Infantile autism reviewed: A decade of research. *Schizophrenia Bulletin, 7*, 388–351.

Doleys, D. M. (1980). Encopresis. In J. Ferguson & C. B. Taylor (Eds.), *Advances in behavioral medicine.* New York: Spectrum.

Doleys, D. M. (1983). Enuresis and encopresis. In T. Ollendick & M. Hersen (Eds.), *Handbook of child psychopathology.* New York: Plenum.

Dubey, D. T. (1976). Organic factors in hyperkinesis: A critical evaluation. *American Journal of Orthopsychiatry, 46*, 353–366.

Eggers, C. (1978). Course and prognosis of childhood schizophrenia. *Journal of Autism and Childhood Schizophrenia, 8*, 21–36.

Emmelkamp, P. M. (1982). *Phobic and obsessive-compulsive disorders.* New York: Plenum.

Faschingbauer, T. F. (1975). Enuresis: Its nature, etiology and treatment. *JSAS: Catalog of Selected Documents in Psychology, 5*, 194.

Firestone, P., & Prabhu, A. N. (1983). Minor physical anomalies and obstetrical complications: Their relationship to hyperactive and normal children and their families. *Journal of Abnormal Child Psychology, 11*, 207–216.

Forehand, R., & McMahon, R. J. (1981). *Helping the noncompliant child.* New York: Guilford.

Freud, S. (1909). Analysis of a phobia in a five-year-old boy. In *Collected papers* (vol. x), London: Hogarth Press, 1955.

Gardner, R. A. (1985). *Separation anxiety disorder.* Cresskill, NJ: Creative Therapeutics.

Garfinkle, P. E., & Garner, D. M. (1982). *Anorexia nervosa: A multidimensional perspective.* New York: Brunner/Mazel.

Geller, E., Ritvo, E. R., Freeman, B. J., & Yuwiler, A. (1982). Preliminary observations on the effects of fenfluramine on blood seratonin and symptoms in three autistic boys. *New England Journal of Medicine, 307*, 165–169.

Gibbons, D. C. (1976). *Delinquent behavior* (2nd ed.). Englewood Cliffs, NJ: Prentice-Hall.

Gittelman, R. (1985). Anxiety disorders in children. In B. Lahey & A. Kazdin (Eds.), *Advances in clinical child psychology* (Vol. 8). New York: Plenum.

Gold, M. S., Pottash, A. L., Sweeny, A. R., Martin, D. M., & Davies, R. V. (1980). Further evidence of a hypothalamic-pituitary dysfunction in anorexia nervosa. *American Journal of Psychiatry, 137*, 101–102.

Greenhill, L. J. (1985). Pediatric psychopharmacology. In D. Shaffer, A. Ehrhardt, & L. Greenhill (Eds.), *Clinical guide to child psychiatry.* New York: Free Press.

Halmi, K. A. (1985). The diagnosis and treatment of anorexia nervosa. In D. Shaffer, A. A. Ehrhardt, & L. L. Greenhill (Eds.), *The clinical guide to child psychiatry.* New York: Free Press.

Hastings, J. E., & Barkley, R. A. (1978). A review of psychophysiological research with hyperkinetic children. *Journal of Abnormal Child Psychology, 6,* 413–447.

Herbert, M. (1978). *Conduct disorders of childhood and adolescence.* New York: Wiley.

Herbert, M. (1982). Conduct disorders. In B. Lahey and A. Kazdin (Eds.), *Advances in clinical child psychology* (Vol. 5). New York: Plenum.

Hoefler, S. A., & Bornstein, P. H. (1975). Achievement Place: An evaluative review. *Criminal Justice and Behavior, 2,* 146–167.

Howells, J., & Guirguis, E. (1984). *The family and schizophrenia.* New York: International Universities Press.

Johnson, S. B. (1985). Situational fears and object phobias. In D. Shaffer, A. A. Ehrhardt, & L. L. Greenhill (Eds.), *The clinical guide to child psychiatry.* New York: Free Press.

Johnson, J. H., & Fennell, E. (1983). Aggressive and delinquent behavior in childhood and adolescence. In E. Walker & M. Roberts (Eds.), *Handbook of clinical child psychology.* New York: Wiley.

Johnson, J. H., & McCutcheon, S. (1980). Assessing life stress in older children and adolescents: Preliminary findings with the life events checklist. In I. G. Sarason & C. D. Spielberger (Eds.), *Stress and anxiety* (Vol. 7). Washington, DC: Hemisphere.

Kanner, L. (1943). Autistic disturbances of affective contact. *Nervous Child, 2,* 217–250. Reprinted in Kanner, L. (1973). *Childhood psychosis: Initial studies and new insights.* Silver Springs, MD: V. H. Winston & Sons.

Kanner, L. (1973). How far can autistic children go in matters of social adaptation? In L. Kanner (Ed.), *Childhood psychosis: Initial studies and new insights.* Silver Springs, MD: Winston.

Kashani, J., & Simonds, J. F. (1979). The incidence of depression in children. *American Journal of Psychiatry, 136,* 1203–1204.

Kendall, P. C. (1981). Cognitive behavioral interventions with children. In B. Lahey & A. Kazdin (Eds.), *Advances in clinical child psychology* (Vol. 4). New York: Plenum.

Kendall, P. C. (1984). Cognitive behavioral self-control therapy for children. *Journal of Child Psychology and Psychiatry, 25,* 173–179.

Kendall, P. C., & Braswell, L. (1985). *Cognitive-behavioral therapy for impulsive children.* New York: Plenum.

Kennedy, W. A. (1983). Obsessive-compulsive and phobic reactions. In T. Ollendick & M. Hersen (Eds.), *Handbook of child psychopathology.* New York: Plenum.

Kerasotes, D., & Walker, C. E. (1983). Hyperactive behavior in children. In E. Walker & M. Roberts (Eds.), *Handbook of clinical child psychology.* New York: Wiley.

Kimmel, H. D., & Kimmel, E. (1970). An instrumental conditioning method for the treatment of enuresis. *Journal of Behavior Therapy and Experimental Psychiatry, 6,* 121–123.

Kolvin, I. (1971). Psychoses in childhood—A comparative study. In M. Rutter (Ed.), *Infantile autism: Concepts, characteristics and treatment.* London: Churchill.

Kraepelin, E. (1883). *Compendium of psychiatry.* Leipzig: Verlag Von Ambr. Abel.

Langer, E. J., & Abelson, R. P. (1974). A patient by any other name . . . Clinician group differences in labeling bias. *Journal of Consulting and Clinical Psychology, 42,* 4–9.

Lapouse, R., & Monk, M. (1958). An epidemiologic study of behavior characteristics in children. *American Journal of Public Health, 48,* 1134–1144.

Lapouse, R., & Monk, M. (1959). Fears and worries in a representative sample of children. *American Journal of Orthopsychiatry, 29,* 803–818.

Lefkowitz, M. M., & Burton, N. (1978). Childhood depression: A critique of the concept. *Psychological Bulletin, 85,* 716–726.

Leon, G., & Dinklage, D. (1983). Childhood obesity and anorexia nervosa. In T. Ollendick & M. Hersen (Eds.), *Handbook of child psychopathology.* New York: Plenum.

Leon, G. R., & Phelan, P. W. (1985). Anorexia nervosa. In B. Lahey & A. Kazdin (Eds.), *Advances in clinical child psychology* (Vol. 8). New York: Plenum.

Lotter, V. (1966). Epidemiology of autistic conditions in young children: Prevalence. *Social Psychiatry, 1,* 124–137.

Lovaas, O. I. (1977). *The autistic child: Language development through behavior modification.* New York: Irvington.

Lupton, M., Simon, L., Barry, V., & Klawans, H. L. (1976). Biological aspects of anorexia nervosa. *Life Sciences, 18,* 1241–1348.

MacFarlane, J. W., Allen, L., & Honzik, M. P. (1954). *A developmental study of the behavior problems of normal children between 21 months and 14 years.* Berkeley: University of California Press.

Maloney, M., & Klykylo, W. M. (1983). An overview of anorexia nervosa, bulimia, and obesity in children and adolescents. *Journal of the American Academy of Child Psychiatry, 22,* 99–107.

Matson, J. L., & Ollendick, T. H. (1977). Issues in toilet training normal children. *Behavior Therapy, 8,* 549–553.

Mattison, R., Cantwell, D. P., Russell, A. T., & Will, L. (1979). A comparison of DSM-II and DSM-III in the diagnosis of childhood disorders. *Archives of General Psychiatry, 36,* 1217–1222.

McKnew, D. H., & Cytryn, L. (1979). Urinary metabolites in chronically depressed children. *Journal of the American Academy of Child Psychiatry, 18,* 608–615.

Meichenbaum, D. (1979). *Cognitive behavior modification: An integrative approach.* New York: Plenum.

Miller, L. C. (1983). Fears and anxieties in children. In E. Walker & M. Roberts (Eds.), *Handbook of clinical child psychology.* New York: Wiley.

Miller, L. C., Barrett, C. L., & Hampe, E. (1974). Phobias of childhood in a prescientific era. In A. Davids (Ed.), *Child personality and psychopathology* (Vol. 1). New York: Wiley.

Morris, R. J., & Kratochwill, T. R. (1983). *Treating children's fears and phobias.* New York: Pergamon.

Mowrer, O. H., & Mowrer, W. M. (1983). Enuresis: A method of its study and treatment. *American Journal of Orthopsychiatry, 8,* 436–459.

Mullins, L. L., Siegel, L. J., & Hodges, K. K. (1985). Cognitive and life-event correlates of depressive symptoms in children. *Journal of Abnormal Child Psychology, 13,* 305–314.

NIMH (1975). *Research in the service of mental health.* Rockville, MD: National Institute of Mental Health.

Patterson, G. R. (1974). Interventions for boys with conduct problems: Multiple settings, treatments, and criteria. *Journal of Consulting and Clinical Psychology, 42,* 471–481.

Poznanski, E. O., Krahenbuhl, U., & Zrull, J. P. (1976). Childhood depression:

a longitudinal perspective. *Journal of the American Academy of Child Psychiatry, 15,* 491–501.

Puig-Antich, J. (1982). Major depression and conduct disorder in prepuberty. *Journal of the American Academy of Child Psychiatry, 21,* 118–128.

Puig-Antich, J., Perel, J., Lupatkin, W., Chambers, W. J., Tabrizi, M., & Stiller, R. (1979). Plasma levels of imipramine and desmethyl imipramine and clinical response in prepubertal major depressive disorder: A preliminary report. *Journal of the American Academy of Child Psychiatry, 18,* 616–627.

Quay, H. C. (1986). A critical analysis of DSM-III as a taxonomy of psychopathology in childhood and adolescence. In T. Millon & G. Klerman (Eds.), *Contemporary directions in psychopathology.* New York: Guilford.

Ritvo, E. R., Freeman, B. J., Geller, E., & Yuwiler, A. (1983). Effects of fenfluramine on 14 outpatients with the syndrome of autism. *Journal of the American Academy of Child Psychiatry, 22,* 549–558.

Robins, L. (1966). *Deviant children grown up.* Baltimore: Williams & Wilkins.

Ross, D. M., & Ross, D. (1982). *Hyperactivity: Research, theory and action.* New York: Wiley.

Rutter, M. (1985). Infantile autism. In D. Shaffer, A. L. Ehrhardt, & L. L. Greenhill (Eds.), *The clinical guide to child psychiatry.* New York: Free Press.

Safer, D. J., & Allen, R. P. (1976). *Hyperactive children: Diagnosis and management.* Baltimore: University Park Press.

Sandifer, M. G., Pettus, C., & Quade, D. (1964). A study of psychiatric diagnosis. *Journal of Nervous and Mental Disease, 139,* 350–356.

Sarason, I. G. (1978). A cognitive social-learning approach to juvenile delinquency. In R. D. Hare & D. Shalling (Eds.), *Psychopathic behavior: Approaches to research.* New York: Wiley.

Schaefer, C. E. (1979). *Childhood enuresis and encopresis.* New York: Van Nostrand Reinhold.

Schmidt, H. O., & Fonda, C. P. (1956). The reliability of psychiatric diagnosis: A new look. *Journal of Abnormal and Social Psychology, 52,* 262–267.

Schopler, E., & Mesibov, G. B. (1985). *Communication problems in autism.* New York: Plenum.

Schwartz, S., & Johnson, J. H. (1985). *Psychopathology of childhood: A clinical-experimental approach.* New York: Pergamon.

Shaffer, D. (1985). Nocturnal enuresis. In D. Shaffer, A. Ehrhardt, & L. Greenhill (Eds.), *The clinical guide to child psychiatry.* New York: Free Press.

Shaffer, D., & Ambrosini, P. J. (1985). Enuresis and sleep disorders. In J. M. Wiener (Ed.), *Diagnosis and psychopharmacology of childhood and adolescent disorders.* New York: Wiley.

Shaffer, D., Ehrhardt, A. A., & Greenhill, L. L. (1985). *The clinical guide to child psychiatry.* New York: Free Press.

Spitzer, R. L., Forman, J. B., & Nee, J. (1979). DSM-III field trials: I. Intitial interrater diagnostic reliability. *American Journal of Psychiatry, 136,* 815–820.

Stevens-Long, J., & Lovaas, O. I. (1974). Research and treatment with autistic children in a program of behavior therapy. In A. Davids (Ed.), *Child personality and psychopathology* (Vol. 1). New York: Wiley.

Temerlin, M. K. (1968). Suggestion effects in psychiatric diagnosis. *Journal of Nervous and Mental Disease, 147,* 349–353.

Ullmann, L. P., & Krasner, L. (1975). *A psychological approach to abnormal behavior* (2nd ed.). Englewood Cliffs, NJ: Prentice-Hall.

Van Buskirk, S. S. (1977). A two-phase perspective in the treatment of anorexia nervosa. *Psychological Bulletin, 84,* 529–538.

Waldrop, M. F., & Goering, J. D. (1971). Hyperactivity and minor physical anomalies in elementary school children. *American Journal of Orthopsychiatry, 41,* 602–607.

Wallander, J. L., & Hubert, N. C. (1985). Long-term prognosis for children with attention deficit disorder with hyperactivity. In B. Lahey & A. Kazdin (Eds.), *Advances in clinical child psychology* (Vol. 8). New York: Plenum.

Watson, J. B., & Raynor, R. (1920). Conditioned emotional reactions. *Journal of Experimental Psychology, 3,* 1–14.

Weiner, I. (1982). *Child and adolescent psychopathology.* New York: Wiley.

Weiss, G., Minde, K., Werry, J. S., Douglas, V. I., & Nemeth, E. (1971). Studies on the hyperactive child, VIII: 5-year follow-up. *Archives of General Psychiatry, 24,* 409–414.

Wenar, C. (1982). Developmental psychopathology: Its nature and models. *Journal of Clinical Child Psychology, 11,* 192–201.

Werry, J. S., Methven, R. J., Fitzpatrick, J., & Dixon, H. (1983). The inter-rater reliability of DSM-III in children. *Journal of Abnormal Child Psychology, 11,* 341–354.

Werry, J. S., & Quay, H. C. (1971). The prevalence of behavior symptoms in younger elementary school children. *American Journal of Orthopsychiatry, 41,* 136–143.

West, D. J., & Farrington, D. P. (1973). *Who becomes delinquent?* London: Heinemann.

Whalen, C. K. (1983). Hyperactivity, learning problems, and the attention deficit disorders. In T. H. Ollendick & M. Hersen (Eds.), *Handbook of child psychopathology.* New York: Plenum.

Wing. L., Yeates, S. R., Brierly, L. M., & Gould, J. (1976). Prevalence of early childhood autism: Comparison of administrative and epidemiological studies. *Psychological Medicine, 6,* 89–100.

Wright, L. (1975). Outcome of a standardized program for treating psychogenic encopresis. *Professional Psychology, 6,* 453–456.

Yule, W. (1981). The epidemiology of child psychopathology. In B. Lahey and A. Kazdin (Eds.), *Advances in clinical child psychology* (Vol. 4). New York: Plenum.

3

GENERAL ISSUES IN INDIVIDUAL TREATMENT

As previously noted, there are numerous approaches to the treatment of child psychopathology. Examples alluded to in previous chapters include those that rely heavily on the application of learning principles, typically referred to as behavior modification or behavior therapy; psychopharmacological approaches or drug therapy; a range of family therapies that focus on the modification of family variables presumed to contribute to childhood problems; and methods of group therapy and residential treatment. In addition to these methods, others traditionally associated with the term "child psychotherapy" are of special significance, because for many years they represented the primary nonbiologically oriented methods for treating child psychopathology. Due to the development of competing methods of intervention, recent years have witnessed a renewed interest in these approaches (Tuma & Sobotka, 1983).

Although the term child psychotherapy often has been associated with particular treatment approaches, any designation of treatments as examples of child psychotherapy must be viewed as somewhat arbitrary. No one definition of psychotherapy has gained universal acceptance (Hersen, Michelson, & Bellack, 1984), and clinicians would disagree on which approaches should be included under this heading. Indeed, all of the treatments considered in this book may be viewed as "psychotherapeutic" in a general sense. Nevertheless, there do seem to be some general characteristics of approaches usually referred to by this label. Psychotherapy, for example, commonly is thought of as an interpersonal process involving verbal and nonverbal interchanges between a patient who exhibits psychological problems (usually assumed to be of an intrapsychic nature) and a professional who wishes to be of help.

Within this context the therapist gains an understanding of the patient's problems and utilizes the nature of the relationship and various therapeutic techniques to facilitate constructive personality change. The psychoanalytic and client-centered approaches discussed in the next chapter are among the methods most often considered within this category. To place these approaches in perspective, it is useful at this point to consider several issues relevant to these more traditional methods of treatment. Although our discussion will deal with topics of special relevance to child psychotherapy, several of the issues considered, such as ethics of treatment, are also pertinent to other treatment methods.

CHILDREN VERSUS ADULTS IN PSYCHOTHERAPY

Although there are special considerations that must be taken into account in treating children with psychological problems, it has been argued that the basic principles involved are quite similar to those used in treating adults (Reisman, 1973).

It has been suggested that the major difference between working with adults and children lies in the need to alter therapy techniques to accommodate the child's level of cognitive and emotional development. Children, for example, are conceptually more concrete, linguistically less competent, and less introspective than adults. This means that although the basic principles of psychotherapy may be the same for adults and children (Clarizio & McCoy, 1983; Reisman, 1973), the immaturity and dependent status of the child may require modifications in the application of these principles (Clarizio & McCoy, 1983). An overview of the important differences between children and adults with respect to psychotherapy are presented in Table 3.1.

Among the factors to be considered in working with children (Table 3.1), the child's level of cognitive development and his or her dependence on the parents are worthy of special comment. The child's immature cognitive and linguistic skills require placing a much greater emphasis on nonverbal communication than with adults. Thus, child psychotherapy often is carried out within the context of play activities, rather than involving the level of verbal interchange characteristic of adult psychotherapy. The child's dependence on others may also require that the therapist deal with the patient's family to a much greater degree than is usually the case in working with adults, because child psychopathology is often intimately related to factors within the family.

The ways in which developmental factors influence the conduct of child psychotherapy will become clearer as we consider specific approaches to child psychotherapy in the next chapter. (For a related discussion of issues that must be confronted when adult therapists work with children, see Goggins and Goggins, 1979.)

Table 3.1. Summary of Differences Between Adults and Children with Implications for Child Therapy

FACTOR	ADULT	CHILD	TREATMENT IMPLICATION FOR CHILD
Motivation for treatment	Often self-referred; better motivated to work on own difficulties.	Referred by others; lacks motivation to work on own problems.	Some therapists feel the need for initial sessions to develop a therapeutic relationship upon which to base later, more intensive therapy.
Insight into treatment objectives	More likely to share common goals with therapist and to be aware of his or her own role in therapy.	More apt to lack common goals with therapist.	The child must find therapy intrinsically interesting; his or her needs for exploration and manipulation should be utilized.
Linguistic development	Satisfactory verbal facility.	Limited verbal facility; greater use of nonverbal communication.	Speech-mediated interactions are minimized, with more emphasis on nonverbal communication and experiencing of consequences.
Cognitive development	Greater cognitive sophistication; better able to engage in verbal, abstract problem solving.	More dependent on concrete events and objects in efforts to reason logically.	Child needs tangible aids to better express, understand, and integrate complex feelings and beliefs.
Dependence on environmental forces	More independent of environment.	Very dependent on environment and significant others.	Treatment must accord more attention to dealing with significant others in the child's life and to external reality pressures.
Plasticity of personality	More "set" in his or her ways; defenses are better established.	More pliable and open to therapeutic influence; less integration and internal consistency in personality.	Intervention procedures should be undertaken before personality becomes stabilized; less need for depth-therapy techniques, as the child is more susceptible to environmental influences.

Note. From *Behavior Disorders in Children* (3rd ed.) by H. F. Clarizio and G. F. McCoy (1983). p. 420. New York: Harper & Row. Copyright 1983 by Harper & Row, Publishers, Inc. Reprinted by permission.

ELEMENTS OF CHANGE IN CHILD PSYCHOTHERAPY

Child psychotherapy usually is undertaken with at least two goals in mind. One of these goals is to resolve the problem behaviors that resulted in the child being referred for treatment. The second goal is to bring about a general personality change that will reduce the likelihood of the child developing problems in the future. What goes on in psychotherapy to bring about such changes? In an especially thoughtful discussion of traditional approaches to child psychotherapy, Tuma and Sobotka (1983) have suggested that therapeutic changes are attributable to the therapeutic relationship (general factors) as well as to therapeutic techniques (specific factors) employed within the context of this relationship.

Tuma and Sobotka note that general factors include the opportunity to talk about one's problems with a therapist (opportunity for catharsis) who listens and communicates an attitude of acceptance (attention from the therapist), and who reinforces appropriate in-therapy behavior (reinforcement effects) and creates positive expectations for change (expectancy effects). In commenting on the important role of therapist attention, these authors give special consideration to several "therapist-offered conditions" described by Rogers (1942, 1951). They suggest that change in therapy is enhanced not simply by giving the child undivided attention, but through responding in a way that communicates empathy, warmth and genuineness. Here empathy relates to the therapist's communications that he or she cares for the child and is able to understand the child's problems from the child's perspective. Genuineness refers to characteristics of openness, honesty, and authenticity that lead the child to believe the therapist can be trusted. Warmth involves the ability of the therapist to communicate an atmosphere of nonjudgmental acceptance in which the child can feel secure in dealing with sensitive and anxiety-arousing topics through play or verbalization. Tuma and Sobotka emphasize the importance of these characteristics by citing the results of numerous research studies linking these variables with positive therapy outcome (see Truax & Mitchell, 1971). Indeed, it often has been suggested that empathy, genuineness, and warmth are necessary (although not in themselves sufficient) conditions for therapeutic change. We will have more to say about these factors in the next chapter, when client-centered approaches to treatment are discussed.

Specific therapeutic communications that contribute to change include questions designed to elicit information or encourage the child to continue talking; exclamations (e.g., "Mm-hmm," "I see what you mean," or "That is interesting") to facilitate further discussion or communicate the importance of a particular topic; and confrontations, which encourage the child to deal with some therapy-related issue (e.g., pointing out that the patient may have played some role in a problem he or she had with another child). Therapists also frequently use clarifications to help the child understand the significance of certain behaviors. At one level a clarification may simply involve descriptions of the patient's behavior or a repetition of the child's statements to get the child to elaborate on what he or she is doing (e.g., "It looks like you spanked that doll really hard"). In other instances clarifications are designed to help the child understand and label feelings of which he or she may be unaware. In this respect clarification is similar to the technique of "reflection of feeling" used by client-centered therapists (see chapter 4), in which the therapist comments on the child's feeling state, as reflected in his or her behavior. One example of such a reflection is the statement "That made you really mad" in response to a child clenching his fist and becoming flushed while talking about getting blamed for something done by a younger sibling. Reflective statements are useful in helping the child label feelings, thus making them less confusing and overwhelming (Freedheim & Russ, 1983).

An additional technique used by child therapists in varying degrees is interpretation of the child's play or verbal statements. Interpretations are the therapist's comments regarding the relationships between thoughts, feelings, and behaviors or the posing of tentative hypotheses to increase the child's understanding of the causes of his or her behavior. Interpretations may vary from those that deal with material close to consciousness to those designed to bring unconscious material into awareness. As an example, consider the interpretation "I wonder if not going to school is one way of making sure your mother is safe during the day" as it might be used with a child who is refusing to go to school due to separation anxiety (see chapter 2).

As Tuma and Sobotka (1983, p. 408) have suggested, the timing of interpretations is essential. They note that:

> Questions, clarifications, exclamations, and confrontations prepare the way for the interpretive process. . . . Typically, early comments by the therapist are centered on empathic and accepting comments. . . . Later, as certain areas are pursued, questions (or their equivalent) and clarifications are used to gain a fuller understanding of the child's feelings and attitudes. Once they are understood, confrontations are used, and finally, when the child appears ready to accept them, interpretations are offered.

By using techniques like the ones described here within the context of a good therapeutic relationship, the therapist helps the child to develop a better awareness of his or her feelings, as well as insight into the causes of problem behaviors. This increased understanding lays the foundation for the child to work through significant conflicts and develop alternative and more adaptive ways of relating and behaving. It should be emphasized that none of the general or specific factors considered here are in themselves sufficient to accomplish the goals of psychotherapy. Constructive change results from the combined effects of these variables (Tuma & Sobotka, 1983).

THE INTERVENTION PROCESS: FROM REFERRAL TO PSYCHOTHERAPY

REFERRAL FOR TREATMENT

Only rarely does a child request treatment. In most cases the child is referred by some adult. Parents, teachers, and pediatricians are the most common referral sources. Referrals also frequently are made by juvenile courts and by youth and family service agencies. Referral for treatment almost always is based on an adult's perception of the child's behavior as abnormal. This perception may be due to a host of variables. For example, some parents, perhaps because of poor coping abilities or experiencing high levels of stress, have little tolerance for child behaviors seen as normal by most other parents and child experts. Thus, they may view certain "normal" behaviors as pathological or at least troublesome enough to warrant seeking help in dealing with them. Such situations suggest the need for parents to be involved in treatment as well as the child, or even instead of the child. In other cases children display genuine adjustment problems that may relate to intrapsychic conflicts or the child's intrinsic emotional makeup or temperament. Some children display behavior problems due to disturbed home and social environments. Others display emotional problems and act out secondary to learning disabilities or physical impairment. The range of factors that can result in referral necessitates a thorough assessment of each child in order to determine the nature of his or her problems and the proper approach to treatment.

ASSESSING THE APPROPRIATENESS OF PSYCHOTHERAPY

Though clinicians may differ in clinical technique, most would agree that assessment is a necessary prerequisite for treatment. Assessment is directed toward determining whether the child displays evidence of psychopathology and the factors that contribute to this pathology, and whether the problem is amenable to psychotherapy or must be dealt with in some other way.

As indicated in chapter 1, the assessment process often begins with a parent interview. The clinician obtains information regarding the specific nature of the child's problem behaviors, the duration of these problems, any precipitating events, the situations in which the problem behaviors occur, how these problems are responded to by others, and previous attempts to deal with the child's difficulties. Additionally, the clinician may inquire about the child's developmental history (e.g., age at which developmental milestones were met), medical history (e.g., pregnancy and birth complications, illnesses or injuries that might contribute to the child's problems), school performance (e.g., grades, teacher reports of behavior), peer and family relationships, and any other factors that might impact on the child and family and contribute to the child's problems. An assessment usually also is made of the parents' expectations regarding child behavior, disciplinary methods used, and the degree to which the parents may actually contribute to the child's difficulties. In general, an attempt is made to get a description of the presenting problems and preliminary information regarding contributing factors.

The parent interview frequently is supplemented by an interview with the child. With very young children this interview may take place in a playroom where the clinician can interact with the child and observe the appropriateness of his or her behavior (see chapter 1). With an older child the interview may focus more on talking than on play behaviors. The emphasis is on obtaining certain types of information similar to that solicited in the parent interview, as well as information regarding the child's perceptions of his or her difficulties and life circumstances. Examples of areas the therapist might wish to inquire about in the child interview are presented in Table 3.2.

This interview process plus a detailed history may be sufficient to make a clinical disposition regarding treatment, or it may suggest the need for psychological testing or the use of other assessment methods (as described in chapter 1) to delineate more clearly the nature of the child's problems.

A major assessment-related question is whether the child is likely to benefit from a psychotherapeutic approach, such as psychoanalytic or client-centered therapy, or from some alternative approach to treatment. As Reisman (1973) has pointed out (see also chapter 2), children can display a range of problems that result in distress and are a source of concern to their parents. Only some of these problems are amenable to psychotherapy. To illustrate, Reisman notes that many children with serious behavioral problems come from chaotic homes and social environments that may contribute to their behavior. Modification of the child's environment may be a more effective treatment approach than psychotherapy. Also cited is the child with infantile autism. Reisman indicates that because psychotherapy depends on a level of communication that autistic children do not possess, the appropriateness of treating such children in this manner is questionable. Other forms of treatment, however, may be of value.

Table 3.2. Content Areas Frequently Assessed in Child Interviews

AREA (ALL AGES)	EXAMPLES OF SPECIFIC CONTENT
Referral problem	What does the child think the main problem is? Does the child see the referral problem as a problem? What does the child think will help?
Interests	What does the child like to do (in spare time)? What does the child like to do alone? With friends? With family members?
School	What does the child like best about school? Least? How does the child feel about his or her teachers? What kinds of grades does the child get in school?
Peers	Who does the child like to play with? Who are the child's friends? What do they like to do together? Who does the child dislike?
Family	How does the child get along with his or her parents? What do they do that the child likes? That makes the child angry? How does the child get along with his or her brothers and sisters? What do they do that the child likes or dislikes?
Fears/worries	What kinds of things is the child afraid of? What kinds of things make the child nervous and jumpy? What kinds of things does the child worry about?
Self-image	What does the child like or dislike about himself or herself? What can the child do well, relative to peers? How would the child describe himself or herself?
Mood/feelings	What kinds of things make the child feel sad or happy? How often do these feelings happen? What kinds of things make the child feel mad? What does he or she do when mad?
Somatic concerns	Does the child have any headaches or stomachaches? Any other kinds of body pains? How often does this happen? What does the child usually do?
Thought disorder	Does the child hear things or see things that seem funny or unusual? Describe them.
Aspirations	What would the child like to do for a living when he or she gets older? What are other things the child would like to do when older?
Fantasy	What kinds of things does the child daydream about? What kinds of things does the child dream about? If the child could have any three wishes, what would they be?

Note. From Interviewing and behavioral observation by A. LeGreca (1983). In E. Walker & M. C. Roberts (Eds.) *Handbook of Clinical Child Psychology.* New York: Wiley. Copyright 1983 by John Wiley & Sons, Inc. Reprinted by permission.

According to Reisman, one should only involve the child in psychotherapy after the appropriateness of other approaches has been considered. Among those children seen as most suitable for traditional forms of psychotherapy Reisman lists those "who experience fears, unhappiness, inhibitions, immature habits or behaviors, difficulties in getting along with others, and failures in school, as well as their involved parents" (1973, p. 16). He notes (p. 16) ". . . These kinds of disturbances constitute the majority of those that occur in childhood."

These statements suggest that although traditional child psychotherapy may be the preferred approach for treating certain childhood problems, there are conditions for which it is neither useful nor desirable. Proper pretherapy assessment that focuses on intrapsychic as well as environmental and family variables that contribute to the child's difficulties is essential to determine when psychotherapy is appropriate.

THE SETTING

Unlike therapy with adults, which usually is conducted in the therapist's office, the setting for child psychotherapy is most often a playroom. The choice of this setting is based on the proposition that whereas adults and adolescents communicate best through the use of language, children communicate more effectively through the medium of play. Although the specific role of play and the meanings ascribed to it vary depending on the therapist's orientation, play is seen by most as an important vehicle for patient–therapist interaction.

To facilitate the therapeutic process, the playroom is equipped with materials that are suitable for children of different ages and backgrounds and that encourage different types of behavior. Play materials are described as being unstructured or structured. Unstructured materials include items such as sand, water, clay, and paints, and allow the child maximum freedom of expression and release for tension and pent-up feelings (Moustakas, 1959). Moustakas suggests that unstructured play materials are especially valuable early in therapy, as they allow the child an opportunity to express feelings in an indirect manner at a time when he or she may not be able to deal with these feelings more openly. Structured materials include toy guns, punching bags, cars, and trucks. Also included are puppets or dolls that vary in apparent age, race, and sex. These materials elicit themes that deal with feelings, attitudes, and conflicts in the areas of family and peer relationships. Play with both structured and unstructured materials encourages expression of the child's thoughts, feelings, and emotions. Freedom of expression through play is thought to be therapeutic in itself, but it also provides information to help the therapist chart the course of treatment.

The structure of psychotherapy is defined not only by the physical setting, but also by the frequency and duration of therapy sessions, which vary depending on the nature of the child's difficulties and practical considerations (e.g., the number of times per week the parents can bring their child to treatment as well as the cost involved in multiple weekly sessions). It is most common, however, for sessions to be 45 to 60 minutes and to be scheduled once or twice per week (Freedheim & Russ, 1983). Whatever the decision regarding session length and frequency, this information is discussed with the child to provide guidelines regarding the extent and nature of the therapeutic involvement. As Dare (1977) has suggested, the regularity and punctuality of the therapeutic contact suggest to the child that the psychotherapist views the treatment as important. This structure, in terms of the defined frequency and length of therapy sessions, along with the provision of appropriate play materials, provides the primary context in which the therapist and child engage in the process of psychotherapy.

STAGES OF PSYCHOTHERAPY

The Initial Stage of Therapy

In this phase the foundation is laid for later stages of treatment. In the early sessions the therapist is likely to continue the assessment process. Through additional contact with the parents, interactions with the child, and observations of his or her play, the therapist comes to know the child better and gains additional information concerning important areas of conflict and the specific factors that contribute to the problem behavior. This information is used in determining treatment goals and the direction therapy should take in order to meet these goals.

A second characteristic of the beginning stage of therapy has to do with the development of a patient–therapist (and parent–therapist) relationship. Successful treatment depends on a good working relationship with the child in which he or she feels comfortable in talking and interacting with the therapist. Although therapists with a client-centered orientation place greatest emphasis on the patient–therapist relationship, and indeed see the relationship as the primary vehicle through which personality change occurs, developing adequate rapport with the patient (and parents) is viewed as necessary by most therapists, regardless of orientation.

Along with continued assessment, the determination of goals, and the development of a therapeutic relationship, another important feature of the early stage of treatment is the structuring of the therapeutic process. The patient not only becomes familiar with the setting and the frequency and length of sessions, but also learns about limits that may be imposed on his or her behavior within the therapy sessions.

It is usually suggested to patients that in therapy they can speak of anything they wish, and they are encouraged to express themselves freely. Most therapists accept a range of behaviors exhibited by the child; however, certain behaviors may be viewed as unacceptable and demand a response from the therapist. For example, most therapists would agree that limits should be set against hitting or otherwise behaving in a physically aggressive manner toward the therapist. Most therapists would prohibit the child from behaving in a manner that might result in harm to himself or herself. Most would not allow the child to destroy materials in the playroom. Other less serious situations that might require limit setting could include the child insisting on multiple trips to the bathroom during sessions in the absence of a physical need, the inappropriate demonstration of physical affection, or other behaviors that might interfere with treatment. Setting limits may range from simple statements that certain behaviors are unacceptable to physical restraint in extreme cases, such as when the child poses a threat of hurting himself or herself or someone else.

In most instances relatively few limits are needed, and therapists only invoke them when necessary. For example, children are not routinely told that they cannot hit the therapist or tear up play materials if these behaviors have not appeared spontaneously. The setting of limits is most often a response to specific inappropriate behaviors rather than a strict laying down of rules. It should be done in such a way that the therapist conveys continued acceptance of the child as a person, at the same time stating the unacceptability of certain behaviors. It is assumed that limit setting is therapeutic in addition to reducing the immediate problem, because it provides a lesson in self control, gives the child a sense of security, and reassures the child that certain, possibly threatening fantasies cannot be carried out in behavior (Reisman, 1973).

Finally, limit setting is one example of why dividing therapy into stages is at best arbitrary. Although providing guidelines for acceptable behavior in therapy often occurs during the early stages, it may also be necessary and appropriate to set limits at any time in the treatment process.

The Middle Phase of Treatment

The process of resolving conflict and of bringing about constructive personality change is something that occurs throughout therapy, but this process is most evident during the middle phase of treatment. The focus is on using assessment information and the evolving patient–

therapist relationship to effect patient change through the application of various treatment methods, such as those described earlier. The treatment methods depend on the orientation of the therapist and the nature of the child's problem. Thus, an analytically oriented therapist may interpret the child's play behaviors or verbalizations in an attempt to bring unconscious conflicts into the open so they can be dealt with in an emotionally constructive manner. A client-centered therapist may use a technique such as reflection of feeling to clarify the nature of the child's feelings, and provide a therapy atmosphere that facilitates personal growth. To avoid oversimplification, it should be noted that the activities of the therapist during this phase of treatment involve more than the application of interpretation and reflection of feeling. Although their use is often characteristic of this stage of therapy, these techniques would almost certainly be accompanied by the use of additional treatment methods. The extent to which all of these methods are employed would depend on the nature of the patient–therapist interactions in a given session and the therapist's view as to what needs to be accomplished to move the patient toward treatment goals.

The Termination Phase

As treatment progresses toward the goals set earlier, the issue of termination arises. This phase involves dealing with several questions. First, although the initial goals of therapy may largely have been accomplished, other issues might have developed during the course of treatment that the child and his or her parents or the therapist feel the need to deal with. A second question has to do with the criteria that should be adopted in judging the appropriateness of termination. Finally, given that a decision to terminate is made, one must ask how it can be best accomplished; for example, how many sessions it is likely to take to deal with remaining issues.

There are many complexities surrounding the process of termination that necessitate a certain degree of tact and skill on the part of the therapist. The topic of termination must be raised so that the patient, along with his or her parents, and the therapist can discuss it without eliciting feelings of rejection in the child, who may have developed a strong attachment to the therapist. Reisman (1973, p. 73) suggests that the topic can best be introduced by general statements such as, "It sounds as though things are going a lot better for you, is that right? Well, I wonder if you've given any thought as to what that might mean as far as your coming down here to see me goes," or alternatively, "We've been seeing each other for some time now, and I wonder how you feel about it." It is noted that statements of this type need to be presented "slowly, deliberately, and matter of factly, so that the client does not feel compelled to respond to them in a certain way. There should be room for the client to express his opinions and for the therapist to modify his."

Timing is crucial in discussing termination. Ideally, it should be approached at a time when maximal gains have been accomplished. This is not to imply that the child must be a paragon of mental health for termination to be considered, because this criterion would often necessitate an indefinite therapeutic involvement. It is more appropriate that the issue be considered when most of the original goals or later goals delineated during treatment generally have been achieved and the patient, parents, and therapist together feel that the child is better equipped to handle future problems as they arise. As Reisman (p. 74) suggests, "It is clear that for many clients psychotherapy ends, not with a giddy rush into a bright new day, but with a sober appraisal of accomplishments and a resolve to deal with problems as they come."

After a decision to terminate has been made, some time usually transpires before the actual end of therapy. The length of time is determined jointly by the therapist, the child, and the parents. It may vary from weeks to months, during which time loose ends are tied up, separation issues are dealt with, and plans for the future are made. It also provides time for the child to lessen his or her dependency on the therapist and begin to function more independently. Sessions may be spaced further apart to decrease the child's reliance on the therapist and to make a final assessment as to whether the child is really ready for termination or further work is necessary. One aspect of termination is to make the child and parents aware that the therapist is available if unexpected problems arise at a later date. Some therapists also will set a specific time for a follow-up visit or other sort of contact with the patient and parents to assess how the child is doing post-treatment. Although follow-up is not always done, due to time pressures and other factors, it is important for two reasons. First, it provides an opportunity for the patient to report any problems that may have developed since termination so that these can be treated if necessary. Second, follow-up information provides the therapist with data concerning the effectiveness of the treatment procedures employed with the patient. Although patient and parent feedback is subjective and cannot take the place of objective research, it does provide useful clinical data that the therapist can use in a self-corrective manner.

The Process of Therapy: A Final Note

As suggested earlier, one cannot really divide psychotherapy into specific phases as we have done here, except in an arbitrary manner for didactic purposes. While it is possible to speak of what typically transpires at various stages in a very general way, these descriptions fail to capture the fluid nature of patient–therapist interactions, the degree to which the therapist's behavior varies depending on the specific case, and the very essence of the therapeutic "process." It is hoped that the nature of this process will become clearer as we discuss specific approaches to psychotherapy.

ETHICAL ISSUES IN CHILD TREATMENT

Despite the lack of attention given to the topic in the literature, nowhere is the need to consider ethical issues more obvious than in the realm of child treatment. Ross (1980, p. 62) has suggested that "the ethical implications of treating an individual's psychological problems increase in magnitude as an inverse function of that individual's freedom of choice." When it is considered that children usually enter therapy not because of their desire for help, but because their behavior is judged problematic by adults, and that their continued involvement in treatment may relate more to parental commitment than their own, the need to consider the rights of the child becomes apparent.

In the sections that follow we will briefly consider several ethical issues that may arise in the process of child psychotherapy, as well as in other types of child treatment. As ethical questions typically do not lend themselves to simple, straightforward answers, our purpose is simply to consider a number of the issues involved in seeing children in treatment, rather than attempting to pose solutions.

THE ISSUE OF COMPETENCE

Standards for ethical conduct, such as the American Psychological Association's *Ethical Standards of Psychologists* (1977), are quite explicit regarding the issue of competence. These standards state that practitioners must be responsible for maintaining high standards of conduct, recognize the boundaries of their competence, and only provide services in areas in which they are skilled. For example, if a professional receives a referral for child treatment and is unqualified in this area, he or she is ethically bound to refer the child to someone who is competent in child treatment. It must be emphasized that general training in clinical psychology, psychiatry, or social work does not necessarily qualify one to offer psychological services to children, as many training programs do not provide didactic and clinical experience in working with younger age groups (Johnson & Tuma, 1983; Tuma, 1986). When one considers the role of developmental factors as they relate to the assessment, understanding, and treatment of child behavior problems (Achenbach,

1982; Gelfand & Peterson, 1985), and that adult-oriented clinical methods are not always translatable into clinical work with children, it is apparent that specific training is necessary for those providing child treatment.

CHILD OR PARENT AS CLIENT?

A very real and at times perplexing problem encountered in child treatment is: Who is the client? At first it obviously appears to be the child. After all, it is the child whose behavior is of concern, who is seen in therapy sessions, and whose welfare is our main concern. But what about the parents? One usually assumes that they have the child's best interests in mind, and certainly they are legally responsible for the welfare of the child. In most cases they also pay for the child's treatment. Most therapists attempt to work with the child and also attend to the wishes and concerns of the parents, but there are times where considering the rights of both parents and child results in conflict.

Frequently the child is brought to treatment against his or her wishes. The problem may involve behaviors that pose a problem for parents but cause no distress in the child. The child sees no need for therapy and has no desire for treatment. Ross (1980) suggests that this situation poses a significant conflict in values, because respecting the child's rights may violate the parents' right to seek and obtain help for their child. Ross (p. 66) asks, "Does a 7-year-old really have the right to refuse treatment? Are we not entitled, maybe indeed required, to have mature adult judgment override the immature judgment of a child? But at what point does a child's judgment cease to be immature? At 10, 13, 16, 18? And is it really determined by chronological age?" We cannot arbitrarily judge whose wishes should be given greater weight in such cases. The decision depends on the age and level of cognitive development of the child, the child's degree of disturbance, the degree of disturbance noted in the parents, and the degree to which the therapist feels treatment is warranted.

Ethical dilemmas may occur throughout the treatment process. For example, one might ask whose concerns should be emphasized in setting the goals for treatment. In most instances determining treatment goals is accomplished through the therapist's thoughtful discussions with both the child and the parents. When the parents and child have similar goals that are reasonably consistent with what the therapist feels can be accomplished, there is no problem. The situation is quite different, however, when the client is a preadolescent whose parents desire greater compliance, respect, and interaction with a "more acceptable" group of friends, and the youth's goals center on "finding himself" and developing greater independence, or on simply rejecting the parents' goals. Likewise, the child and parents may have different opinions concerning the desirability of continuing therapy. As Ross (1980) has noted, "The involuntary status of the child client may . . . play a role at every stage of treatment, from beginning to end." He agrees with Gelfand and Hartmann (1975, p. 67) that the clinician "is not simply an agent of the parents or the child but must determine how best to serve all concerned." In order to accomplish this task, it is important to involve the child as well as the parents in the decision-making process.

CHILDREN'S COMPETENCE IN TREATMENT DECISION MAKING

Many of the issues raised in the preceding section are related to the child's competence to participate in treatment decision making. Although ethical considerations argue for the child's involvement in making decisions regarding his or her treatment whenever possible, this does not always happen. To illustrate, in a recent study by Adelman, Kaser-Boyd, and Taylor (1984) of children and adolescents (median age 15 years) who were referred for therapy as a result of an Individual Education Plan (IEP) completed by school personnel (35 cases), it was found that 80% of the children were excluded from participating in the referral decision. This failure to include the children in the decision-making process occurred in spite of the fact that the majority of children (27 of 35) were rated as having an adequate understanding of what therapy involved and were judged competent to participate in such decisions. Although the reasons for excluding the children from the decision-making process are not clear, it seems that it was not due to their inability to participate, but rather from the view that only adults were capable of making informed decisions regarding the children's need for treatment.

Although there are instances in which it is in fact inappropriate for the child to be brought into the decision-making process (e.g., when the child is very young, seriously disturbed, or severely mentally retarded), there is little reason to assume that most children are incapable of actively participating in making decisions regarding their treatment. Data that are especially relevant to children's competence to participate in this role have been provided by Weithorn (1980). In this study Weithorn presented groups of normal children aged 9 to 21 years with a number of vignettes specifically related to problems of both a psychological and physical nature. In assessing the ability of children of different ages to deal with treatment issues, the results suggested that at age 14 children were as capable as adults in understanding and reasoning about treatment decisions. Although their reasoning was more immature, even 9-year-olds were found to generally reach the same treatment decisions as older groups. These findings, along with other studies of children's competence to consent, suggest that older adolescents are quite capable of making adequate treatment decisions and that even elementary school children can participate in decisions regarding routine treatment issues (Ehrenreich & Melton, 1983). Thus, it is important to include at least older children and adolescents in making decisions regarding treatment whenever possible and to actively involve them in discussing the goals of treatment. Not only is their participation appropriate from an ethical standpoint, but it may have other positive effects in terms of decreasing the resistance to treatment that sometimes comes with being excluded, and of enhancing motivation (Adelman et al., 1984).

THE ISSUE OF CONFIDENTIALITY

An additional topic addressed by the APA ethical standards (American Psychological Association, 1977) has to do with confidentiality. The APA *Ethical Standards* (p. 4) state that, "Confidentiality of professional communications about individuals is maintained. Only when the originator and other persons involved give their express permission is a confidential professional communication shown to the individual concerned. The psychologist is responsible for informing the client of the limits of confidentiality." Thus, information obtained from a patient must be treated as confidential unless the patient gives permission for the information to be divulged. This principle not only protects the client's right to privacy, but also facilitates treatment, as it insures that even sensitive material can be dealt with in confidence. It should be noted that it is common for reports to be shared among several professionals who may be working with a child in different capacities. But even then the sharing of information is done only with the consent of the child's legal guardian, and permission of the child should be obtained as well whenever possible.

Several points can be raised regarding confidentiality in child psychotherapy. The first of these touches on the previously discussed topic of parent versus child rights. Do children in treatment have the right to assume that what transpires in therapy sessions is truly confidential, or do parents have a right to be informed about the process of their child's treatment? There are no simple answers to this question, especially when it is considered that in most states parents have a legal right to see their child's records if they desire (Ehrenreich & Melton, 1983), but it is appropriate to attempt to strike a balance between the rights of the parents and child. Parents may be informed in a general way as to what is happening in therapy but without discussing specific topics dealt with during treatment sessions. Again, the guiding principle is to adopt a course of action that in the therapist's view serves the best interests of all concerned.

A second issue has to do with certain limits that must be placed on confidentiality. For example, statutes in most states require professionals who suspect child abuse to report these suspicions to an appropriate protective services agency. By law, if a child in therapy reports having been abused or neglected, the therapist must report the incident. Likewise, most therapists would feel obligated to respond to situations in which the child was at risk for harming himself or herself or others, even if this action resulted in a breach of confidentiality. In cases where the treatment of a child has been ordered by the courts, the therapist may be required to inform the judge or the child's probation officer if therapy sessions are missed. For both therapeutic and ethical reasons the therapist is obligated to inform the child (to the extent possible, given the child's age and level of understanding) of any limitations on the extent to which material considered in therapy can be kept confidential.

ETHICAL ISSUES: A SUMMARY STATEMENT

Regarding the potential ethical issues that may confront the child psychotherapist, Koocher (1976), following the lead of Ross (1974), has suggested a children's "Bill of Rights", which, if taken seriously, may serve as guidelines in dealing with problems like the ones discussed here. These rights include (a) the right of the child to be told the truth, (b) the right to be treated as a person, (c) the right to be taken seriously, and (d) the right to participate in decision making (Koocher, 1976). It is clear that they simply involve treating the child with the same degree of respect that would be given to an adult seen in clinical practice. For a checklist of ethical issues to be considered in offering clinical services, see Table 3.3.

THE ISSUE OF EFFECTIVENESS

To what extent is individual psychotherapy effective in resolving the psychological problems of childhood? A survey of practitioners would almost certainly yield claims of effectiveness, with many clinicians seeing therapy as being so obviously of value that formal evaluation is unnecessary. Others, however, would argue that a determination of effectiveness should be made by conducting objective investigations instead

Table 3.3. Ethical Issues for Human Services

A. Have the goals of treatment been adequately considered?
  1. To insure that the goals are explicit, are they written?
  2. Has the client's understanding of the goals been assured by having the client restate them orally or in writing?
  3. Have the therapist and client agreed on the goals of therapy?
  4. Will serving the client's interests be contrary to the interests of other persons?
  5. Will serving the client's immediate interests be contrary to the client's long-term interest?
B. Has the choice of treatment methods been adequately considered?
  1. Does the published literature show the procedure to be the best one available for that problem?
  2. If no literature exists regarding the treatment method, is the method consistent with generally accepted practice?
  3. Has the client been told of alternative procedures that might be preferred by the client on the basis of significant differences in discomfort, treatment time, cost, or degree of demonstrated effectiveness?
  4. If a treatment procedure is publicly, legally, or professionally controversial, has formal professional consultation been obtained, has the reaction of the affected segment of the public been adequately considered, and have the alternative treatment methods been more closely reexamined and reconsidered?
C. Is the client's participation voluntary?
  1. Have possible sources of coercion on the client's participation been considered?
  2. If treatment is legally mandated, has the available range of treatments and therapists been offered?
  3. Can the client withdraw from treatment without a penalty or financial loss that exceeds actual clinical costs?
D. When another person or an agency is empowered to arrange for therapy, have the interests of the subordinated client been sufficiently considered?
  1. Has the subordinated client been informed of the treatment objectives and participated in the choice of treatment procedures?
  2. Where the subordinated client's competence to decide is limited, have the client as well as the guardian participated in the treatment discussions to the extent that the client's abilities permit?
  3. If the interests of the subordinated person and the superordinate persons or agency conflict, have attempts been made to reduce the conflict by dealing with both interests?
E. Has the adequacy of treatment been evaluated?
  1. Have quantitative measures of the problem and its progress been obtained?
  2. Have the measures of the problem and its progress been made available to the client during treatment?
F. Has the confidentiality of the treatment relationship been protected?
  1. Has the client been told who has access to the records?
  2. Are records available only to authorized persons?
G. Does the therapist refer the clients to other therapists when necessary?
  1. If treatment is unsuccessful, is the client referred to other therapists?
  2. Has the client been told that if dissatisfied with the treatment, referral will be made?
H. Is the therapist qualified to provide treatment?
  1. Has the therapist had training or experience in treating problems like the client's?
  2. If deficits exist in the therapist's qualifications, has the client been informed?
  3. If the therapist is not adequately qualified, is the client referred to other therapists, or has supervision by a qualified therapist been provided? Is the client informed of the supervisory relation?
  4. If the treatment is administered by mediators, have the mediators been adequately supervised by a qualified therapist?

Note. From Ethical issues in human service by The Association for the Advancement of Behavior Therapy, 1977, *Behavior Therapy*, 8, v–vi. Copyright 1977 by the Association for the Advancement of Behavior Therapy. Reprinted by permission.

of relying only on the subjective impressions of clinicians who employ such procedures.

In a widely cited study Levitt (1957) reviewed a number of previously published reports of child treatment that provided information regarding improvement assessed at termination (18 studies) or at follow-up (17 studies). Treatment methods employed in these studies included (p. 194): "counseling, guidance, placement recommendations to schools and parents, as well as deeper-level therapies." Children treated in the studies displayed problems that could loosely be termed neurotic in nature. Taken together, Levitt found the overall improvement rate for children receiving treatment to be 67.05% at the close of treatment and 78.22% at follow-up.

Given that patients often show spontaneous remission in the absence of formal treatment, perhaps due to developmental factors or as the result of a supportive environment, Levitt attempted to obtain a comparison group against which he could judge the effectiveness of therapy. In selecting this comparison group he reasoned that it should be composed of children as similar as possible to those receiving treatment, that is, children who had been referred for treatment, evaluated, or judged to be in need of treatment, but who had not actually participated in psychotherapy. Based on these criteria, Levitt chose "clinic defectors" for comparison. These were children who had been referred to mental health professionals and offered treatment but who had not followed up on treatment recommendations. Levitt assumed that for psychotherapy to be considered effective, the rates of improvement found for treated children should be significantly higher than for defectors, whose improvement should reflect only spontaneous remission.

Levitt found two studies that provided follow-up data on defectors (Witmer & Keller, 1942; Lehrman, Sirluck, Black, & Glick, 1949). Considered together, these studies suggested an overall improvement rate of 72.5%. Comparing these figures with the 67.05% improvement rate for treated children assessed at the close of therapy, Levitt concluded that the findings provided little support for the effectiveness of child psychotherapy. Although the improvement rates for treated children who were evaluated at follow-up compared more favorably, they may be seen as reflecting the effects of nonspecific factors operating after the termination of therapy (Levitt, 1957). Other findings by Levitt (1963) arrived at similar conclusions.

These findings have been used by many researchers to argue against the effectiveness of child psychotherapy. Although the results are certainly not supportive of child therapy, several points have been raised regarding this study that make an argument of therapy ineffectiveness questionable (see Barrett, Hampe, & Miller, 1978, for an overview). Criticisms have centered around the fact that it is unclear whether children in the treatment and defector groups were similar in terms of initial degree of disturbance, the argument being that the defectors may have been less disturbed, or whether similar criteria were used to rate improvement. Further, cases in the two groups may not have been assessed over a similar time period. For example, in the Witmer and Kellner study, defectors were assessed 8 to 13 years after clinic contact. This time period is much longer than the average duration of therapy experienced by children in treatment, thus allowing more time for spontaneous remission to occur and possibly inflating the improvement rates for defectors. To the extent that the treatment and control groups differed on such variables, comparisons between the groups become difficult to interpret. Findings that support the use of defectors in comparison studies notwithstanding (Levitt, 1963), the conclusions that can be drawn from this research are limited. However, the difficulty in finding a comparison group for a study of this kind that would not be open to similar criticisms must be acknowledged.

Putting aside methodological issues, an additional point may be made concerning Levitt's findings. Although there were no overall differences between rates of improvement for treated and nontreated children, there was a significant degree of variability among studies. In considering improvement figures at the close of therapy for the various treatment studies, one finds that the figures vary from a low of 43% improvement in one study to a high of 86% in another. Rather than suggesting that child psychotherapy is ineffective, these results indicate that sometimes it is quite effective and in other cases it is not.

Levitt, Beiser, and Robertson (1959) conducted a study to check on Levitt's earlier (1957) findings. They compared 327 children who had received treatment at the Institute for Juvenile Research in Chicago with a group of 142 clinic defectors who were similar to the treatment group on a range of variables, including degree of disturbance and level of motivation for therapy. Improvement in both groups was assessed through psychological tests, clinician judgments, and parent evaluations, and no significant differences between the groups were found.

Other studies on the effectiveness of traditional child psychotherapy have been provided by Shepherd, Oppenheim, and Mitchell (1971). Their research, which was conducted as part of a larger epidemiological study, sought to assess the outcome of therapy for a random sample of 50 neurotic children (aged 5–15) drawn from a child guidance-clinic population over a 4-year period. A control group consisted of an equal number of children from the general population, who were matched with the treatment cases for age, sex, and problem behavior. Children in this group had never been referred for treatment, but had been found in a previous survey to show behaviors similar to those of the children in the treatment group. Interview and checklist data from parents were evaluated for degree of improvement. Of the children receiving treatment, only 65% were judged as having improved at the end of therapy, 16% were considered worse, and the remainder were unchanged. In the control group 61% of the children were rated as improved, 9% were considered worse, and the remaining 30% were unchanged. These findings are similar to others that have been discussed in failing to provide support for the effectiveness of child psychotherapy, even when controls other than defectors are employed.

To put these findings in perspective, it should be noted that none of these studies represent examples of well controlled experimental investigations, and each may be faulted on methodological grounds. Even more significant is the nature of the question addressed in these studies. Each was designed to provide information concerning the general issue of psychotherapy effectiveness, with "psychotherapy" being very broadly defined. For example, it can be recalled from the Levitt (1957) study that the "psychotherapy" received by children sometimes consisted of deeper-level (e.g., psychoanalytic) therapies, sometimes counseling, and in some cases only recommendations to schools and parents concerning ways of dealing with the child's problems. Further, treatment was provided by therapists who differed in theoretical orientation and professional training, and the children displayed a range of problem behaviors. Somewhat similar statements would also describe the other studies presented here. Commenting on these studies, Schwartz and Johnson (1981, p. 330) suggest that they simply indicate, "to the extent that it is appropriate to ignore important variables such as the characteristics of the therapist and their orientation, the nature of the patient's problems, and the specific nature of the intervention procedures employed, 'psychotherapy' may be judged *on the average* [italics added] to be ineffective." As indicated earlier, however, this conclusion does not preclude the fact that some types of psychotherapy may be effective for some types of problems.*

---

*Casey and Berman (1985) recently reviewed 75 child psychotherapy studies that compared treated children drawn from clinical and nonclinical settings with children who did not receive treatment but were drawn from the same population. In comparing treatment and control groups with regard to standardized measures of treatment effect, based on data provided in the studies, the authors concluded that children receiving therapy benefited more than untreated children. Although this review is more supportive of child psychotherapy effectiveness than previous reviews (e.g., Barrett et al., 1978; Levitt, 1957), its

The value of studies like those reported here have come to be seriously questioned. It is becoming increasingly obvious that such studies do not take into account variations in therapeutic approaches, therapist characteristics, and patients. In a widely cited paper, Kiesler (1966) commented on this problem by referring to the prevalence of several myths that were reflected in much of the existing psychotherapy research. Among these was the myth of therapist uniformity, which refers to the implicit assumption in many studies that therapists are more alike than different and that whatever they do with the patient can be considered psychotherapy. Likewise, there was a patient uniformity myth that all patients are more alike than different. Although Kiesler's paper focused on adult psychotherapy and was written some 20 years ago, these myths are well represented in the existing child psychotherapy research. Kiesler challenged these myths and suggested that studies characterized by an adherence to them are likely to obscure important information and not provide meaningful findings.

To illustrate, it may be that some approaches to therapy are generally more effective than others. It may also be that, independent of therapeutic approach, some therapists display characteristics that make them more effective than other therapists. It has been suggested that therapists displaying high levels of empathy, genuineness, and unconditional positive regard tend to be effective, and therapists who lack these qualities have patients who not only fail to improve, but get worse (Mitchell, Bozarth, & Krauft, 1977). It is also likely that clients with some types of disorders are more likely to show improvement as a result of therapy than clients with other types of disorders (Levitt, 1963). Further, these variables may interact with one another, so that a particular approach to therapy is effective with one disorder but not another, and a therapist may be successful with some patients but not with others.

When these possibilities are considered, it becomes obvious that simple treatment-versus-control group comparisons are unlikely to yield data strongly supportive of psychotherapy. In such studies, some patients are likely to improve while others become worse (Bergin, 1966) or show little

positive findings are tempered by the fact that in 57% of the studies considered, the children receiving treatment had not been referred to a clinic, 15% of the studies employed community volunteers as treatment subjects, and in another 4% of the studies the source of the subjects was not known. Thus, in less than 25% of the studies those receiving treatment were known to be clinic cases. Given this preponderance of studies involving nonclinic cases, it is difficult to draw firm conclusions regarding the effectiveness of psychotherapy as practiced with children displaying more severe problems such as those seen in an actual clinic setting.

change, with the overall effect indicating no difference between treated and nontreated individuals. These negative findings may mask the fact that therapy was very effective with some patients, some therapists showed a high success rate, or a particular approach was quite successful. These considerations have led psychotherapy researchers to suggest that rather than attempting to ascertain whether psychotherapy is effective, a more useful area of investigation might be the combination of methods, patients, therapists, and conditions that result in positive treatment outcome (Barrett et al., 1978; Heinieke & Strassman, 1976; Kiesler, 1966, 1971). Attempts to explore these areas, however, necessitate more complex approaches to research than typically have been found in the child psychotherapy literature. Rather than employing simple treatment-versus-control group designs, factorial designs are needed in which the interaction of treatment method and relevant therapist and patient variables can be assessed, as well as overall treatment effects. Unfortunately, whereas recent years have seen significant advances in research on the effects of adult psychotherapy (Hersen, Michelson, & Bellack, 1984), child treatment research has not kept pace with work in the adult area. Some studies have attempted to evaluate the effectiveness of specific approaches to treatment rather than the effects of psychotherapy generally, but few of these even have approximated the factorial approach to assessment suggested by Kiesler (1966, 1971).

ETHICAL ISSUES AND TREATMENT EFFECTIVENESS

Considering research on the effectiveness of child psychotherapy raises a significant question regarding the ethics of clinical practice. Most would agree that clinicians should offer only treatments that are likely to result in positive personality and behavior change. If this general premise is accepted, however, questions arise regarding the appropriateness of methods such as child psychotherapy, as well as other treatment approaches.

The question is whether, in the absence of research data providing support for the effectiveness of child psychotherapy, this approach may be used by the clinician who is sensitive to ethical issues and at the same time wishes to offer help to children and parents in distress. The answer is complex: Certainly to offer a treatment that has been well researched and demonstrated to be ineffective would be unethical, but this is not the case with most of the treatments considered in this text. Because of methodological issues and other problems inherent in the research, most studies have been inconclusive rather than provided evidence of ineffectiveness. Although the research presented here does not generally support the efficacy of psychotherapy, it leads one to conclude not that therapy is ineffective, but that its effectiveness has been inadequately tested within the clinical setting. As has been suggested, more sophisticated research is needed to assess the effectiveness of these approaches.

Faced with a child referred for treatment and in obvious need of help, and being aware of the findings in the treatment literature, what is one to do? First, ethical considerations demand that a child be offered the best available treatment for the problem he or she displays. In some instances treatment may be suggested by the research literature. In the case of enuresis, for example, the bell-and-pad procedure has been demonstrated to be useful in adequately controlled experimental studies. Further, research suggests that behavioral treatment is significantly more effective than traditional child psychotherapy in dealing with this problem (DeLeon & Mandell, 1966). Thus, a behavioral approach would be not only the most effective, but the approach dictated by ethical considerations. This is not to imply, however, that behavioral approaches are necessarily the treatment of choice for all problems. It should be emphasized that this position implies that the type of treatment offered should not simply be the one suggested by the therapist's theoretical orientation, but one that at a given point in time is most likely to be useful based on available research findings—if such guidelines are available. It is necessary for the clinician to be familiar with many treatment methods, not just one approach dictated by past training or theoretical preference and to give adequate consideration to research findings pertinent to one's clinical activities.

Unlike the case of enuresis, there are other child problems for which the research literature yields few hints regarding effective treatment. Rather than refusing to see the child until the needed research is done, the clinician must rely on his or her theoretical orientation, knowledge of normal and abnormal child development, past training in child treatment, and perhaps consultation with other professionals concerning the most appropriate treatment method. Thus, in such instances the clinician must rely on reasoned judgment, based on a thorough consideration of all factors involved. As suggested earlier in Table 3.3, the approach finally taken should be consistent with general clinical practice and offer, in the view of the clinician, a high probability of a favorable outcome. For each case it is essential that careful measurement of behavior change be done to assess the efficacy of whatever treatment is employed. Assessment provides clinical data for determining the treatment approach to be taken with future cases of a similar nature, as well as feedback concerning the effectiveness of a particular treatment with a specific childhood problem.

SUMMARY

We have considered briefly the general nature of psychotherapy, the ways in which psychotherapy with children differs from that with adults, and the general and specific factors contributing to psychotherapeutic change.

It was noted that the intervention process most often begins with a parent or other adult's concern about a child's allegedly problematic behaviors. This concern may result in a referral of the child being made, followed by a careful assessment to determine the nature of the child's psychopathology (if it exists); the environmental, social, and intrapsychic factors that most likely are contributing to the child's problem; and general guidelines for treatment. Special attention should be given to assessing whether the child is a suitable candidate for psychotherapies like those considered in this chapter, or whether some other form of intervention is called for.

When psychotherapy is determined to be the treatment of choice, the treatment process involves three stages. Although what goes on in each of these stages may vary, depending on the orientation of the therapist and the particular nature of the child's problems, one can generally speak of a beginning, middle, and termination phase. The initial phase involves further assessment, the setting of goals for therapy, possibly the delineation of limits, and the development of a therapeutic relationship. The middle phase primarily consists of the therapist and child actively working through the problems experienced by the child. Therapeutic techniques that differ according to the therapist's orientation are employed in an effort to reach the therapeutic goals set earlier in the intervention process. The final phase is characterized by an assessment of the degree to which the goals have been achieved; by discussions between therapist, child, and parents regarding the desirability of termination; and, if it is judged to be appropriate, working toward termination. It is also desirable that the therapist consider a fourth stage, that of follow-up, to determine that the child is functioning adequately some time after the end of treatment.

In addition to considering the nature and process of child psychotherapy, several studies on the effectiveness of psychotherapy with children were reviewed. Such studies generally have provided less support for treatment effectiveness than is desirable, due to inherent methodological problems. The ethical issue of offering treatments that have not been well validated (such as child psychotherapy) was discussed, as were other ethical issues of maintaining confidentiality and determining whether the parent or child is the client. Regarding matters of ethics in psychotherapy, it is important, as far as possible, to work in the best interests of both the parents and child.

REFERENCES

Achenbach, T. M. (1982). *Developmental psychopathology* (2nd ed.). New York: Wiley.

Adelman, H. S., Kaser-Boyd, N., & Taylor, L. (1984). Children's participation in consent for psychotherapy and their subsequent response to treatment. *Journal of Clinical Child Psychology, 13,* 170–178.

American Psychological Association (1977). *Ethical standards of psychologists.* Washington, DC: Author.

Association for Advancement of Behavior Therapy. (1977). Ethical issues in human service. *Behavior Therapy, 8,* v–vi.

Barrett, C. L., Hampe, E., & Miller, L. C. (1978). Research on psychotherapy with children. In S. L. Garfield & A. E. Bergin (Eds.), *Handbook of psychotherapy and behavior change* (2nd ed.). New York: Wiley.

Bergin, A. E. (1966). Some implications of psychotherapy research for therapeutic practice. *Journal of Abnormal Psychology, 71,* 235–246.

Casey, R. J., & Berman, J. S. (1985). The outcome of psychotherapy with children. *Psychological Bulletin, 98,* 388–400.

Clarizio, H. F., & McCoy, G. F. (1983). *Behavior disorders in children* (3rd ed.). New York: Crowell.

Dare, C. (1977). Psychoanalytic theories. In M. Rutter & L. Herson (Eds.), *Child psychiatry: Modern approaches.* Oxford: Blackwell Scientific.

DeLeon, G., & Mandell, W. A. (1966). A comparison of conditioning and psychotherapy in the treatment of functional enuresis. *Journal of Clinical Psychology, 22,* 326–330.

Ehrenreich, N. S., & Melton, G. B. (1983). Ethical and legal issues in the treatment of children. In E. Walker & M. Roberts (Eds.), *Handbook of clinical child psychology.* New York: Wiley.

Freedheim, D. K., & Russ, S. R. (1983). Psychotherapy with children. In E. Walker & M. Roberts (Eds.), *Handbook of clinical child psychology.* New York: Wiley.

Gelfand, D. M., & Hartmann, D. P. (1975). *Child behavior analysis and therapy.* New York: Pergamon.

Gelfand, D. M., & Peterson, L. (1985). *Child development and psychopathology.* Beverly Hills, CA: Sage.

Goggins, J. E., & Goggins, E. B. (1979). When adult therapists work with children: Differential treatment considerations. *Professional Psychology, 10,* 330–337.

Heinieke, C. M., & Strassmann, L. H. (1976). Toward more effective research on child psychotherapy. *Journal of the American Academy of Child Psychiatry, 15,* 561–576.

Hersen, M., Michelson, L., & Bellack, A. S. (1984). *Issues in psychotherapy research.* New York: Plenum.

Johnson, J. H., & Tuma, J. M. (1983). Training in clinical child psychology: A brief overview of selected issues. *Journal of Clinical Child Psychology, 12,* 365–368.

Kiesler, D. J. (1966). Some myths of psychotherapy research and the search for a paradigm. *Psychological Bulletin, 65,* 110–136.

Kiesler, D. J. (1971). Experimental designs in psychotherapy research. In A. E. Bergin & S. L. Garfield (Eds.), *Handbook of psychotherapy and behavior change*. New York: Wiley.

Koocher, G. P. (1976). A "bill of rights" for children in psychotherapy. In G. P. Koocher (Ed.), *Children's rights and the mental health professions*. New York: Wiley.

LaGreca, A. (1983). Interviewing and behavioral observation. In E. Walker & M. C. Roberts (Eds.), *Handbook of clinical child psychology*. New York: Wiley.

Lehrman, L. J., Sirluck, H., Black, B. J., & Glick, S. J. (1949). Success and failure of treatment of children in the child guidance clinics of the Jewish Board of Guardians. *Research Monograph* (Whole No. 1).

Levitt, E. E. (1957). The results of psychotherapy with children: An evaluation. *Journal of Consulting Psychology, 21,* 189–196.

Levitt, E. E. (1963). Psychotherapy with children: A further evaluation. *Behavior Research and Therapy, 1,* 45–51.

Levitt, E. E., Beiser, H. R., & Robertson, R. E. (1959). A follow-up evaluation of cases treated at a community child guidance clinic. *American Journal of Psychiatry, 29,* 337–347.

Mitchell, K. M., Bozarth, J. D., & Krauft, C. C. (1977). A reappraisal of the therapeutic effectiveness of accurate empathy, nonpossessive warmth, and genuineness. In A. S. Gurman & A. M. Razin (Eds.), *Effective psychotherapy: A handbook of research*. New York: Pergamon.

Moustakas, C. (1959). *Psychotherapy with children: The living relationship*. New York: Ballantine.

Reisman, J. (1973). *Principles of psychotherapy with children*. New York: Wiley.

Rogers, C. (1942). *Counseling and psychotherapy*. Boston: Houghton Mifflin.

Rogers, C. (1951). *Client-centered therapy*. Boston: Houghton Mifflin.

Ross, A. O. (1974). *Psychological disorders of children: A behavioral approach to theory, research and therapy*. New York: McGraw-Hill.

Ross, A. O. (1980). *Psychological disorders of children: A behavioral approach to theory, research and therapy* (2nd ed.). New York: McGraw-Hill.

Schwartz, S., & Johnson, J. H. (1981). *Psychopathology of childhood: A clinical-experimental approach*. New York: Pergamon.

Shepherd, M., Oppenheim, B., & Mitchell, S. (1971). *Childhood behavior and mental health*. New York: Grune & Stratton.

Truax, C. B., & Mitchell, K. M. (1971). Research on certain therapist interpersonal skills in relation to process and outcome. In A. E. Bergin & S. L. Garfield (Eds.), *Handbook of psychotherapy and behavior change*. New York: Wiley.

Tuma, J. M. (1986). The Hilton Head conference on training clinical child psychologists: History and background. *The Clinical Psychologist, 39,* 4–7.

Tuma, J. M., & Sobotka, K. R. (1983). Traditional therapies with children. In T. Ollendick & M. Hersen (Eds.), *Handbook of child psychopathology*. New York: Plenum.

Weithorn, L. A. (1980). *Competency to render informed treatment decisions: A comparison of certain minors and adults*. Unpublished doctoral dissertation, University of Pittsburgh.

Witmer, H. L., & Keller, J. (1942). Outgrowing childhood problems: A study of the value of child guidance treatment. *Smith College Studies in Social Work, 13,* 74–90.

4

PSYCHOANALYTIC AND CLIENT-CENTERED THERAPY

Relatively few of the psychotherapeutic approaches used in the treatment of adults (Herink, 1980; Parloff, 1980; Harper, 1974; Corsini, 1979) have been widely applied to child treatment. Apart from behavioral approaches, which will be considered in chapter 5, the psychodynamic and client-centered models of psychopathology have provided the theoretical foundation for much of the clinical work with children during the past 3 decades (Axline, 1947; Guerney, 1983; Moustakas, 1973; Sandler, Kennedy, & Tyson, 1980; Schaefer & O'Conner, 1983). Because of the popularity of these approaches and their contributions to the area of child treatment, they provide the focus for this chapter.

THE PSYCHOANALYTIC MODEL OF PERSONALITY DEVELOPMENT

Freud initially placed central importance on the division of the mind into conscious and unconscious regions. He assumed individuals are motivated more by unconscious than conscious processes and that self-awareness and the resolution of psychological conflicts are accomplished partly by bringing unconscious material into consciousness, where it can be dealt with in therapy. Freud (1949, 1953) developed two techniques for exploring unconscious material: free association and dream analysis. Through the use of these techniques, hypotheses were formulated regarding the nature of the patient's unconscious conflicts.

Freud's later formulations, beginning around 1920, deemphasized the role of the unconscious (Hall, 1954). He conceptualized personality as being organized into three components: the id, ego, and superego (Freud, 1933, 1961). As Hall (p. 54) stated, ''Much of what had formerly been assigned to the unconscious became the id, and the structural distinction between consciousness and unconsciousness was replaced by the three-part organization of the id, ego, and superego."

The id was thought by Freud to be the primary source of all psychic energy. Its sole function is the gratification of basic biological needs—survival and perpetuation of the species. Freud called the id the "true psychic reality" because it represents the inner world of subjective experience, with no knowledge of objective reality (Hall & Lindzey, 1970, p. 32). The id seeks immediate gratification without regard to personal or social consequences or to external reality in general, and therefore is said to be governed by the pleasure principle. However, the id is limited in its capacity to gratify the individual's needs, and as a result a new psychological structure called the ego evolves out of the id's energy system.

The ego operates according to the reality principle; it mediates between the objective reality of the external world and the subjective reality of the id. The aim of the reality principle is to find a logical or realistic way to gratify the needs of the organism, since this is not possible through id processes. The ego accomplishes this aim by formulating and implementing a plan. Thus, thinking, problem solving, memory, and all higher-order cognitive processes are considered ego functions.

The final structure to develop is the superego, the internal representative of the traditional values of society as conveyed to the developing child by his or her parents. The superego develops out of the psychic energy of the ego, and its fundamental purpose is to regulate the expression of impulses that otherwise would endanger the stability and survival of society. It is the moral and ethical realm of the personality. As Hall and Lindzey (1970, p. 35) stated "The main functions of the superego are 1) to inhibit the impulses of the id, particularly those of a sexual or aggressive nature, since these are the impulses whose expression is most highly condemned by society, 2) to persuade the ego to substitute moralistic goals for realistic ones, and 3) to strive for perfection." The superego's drive toward perfection is nonrational, and in this respect it is like the id. Conversely, it is like the ego in its efforts to control the impulses of the id.

In summary, the id, ego, and superego may be thought of as the biological, psychological, and social components of personality. As Hall (1954, p. 22) stated:

> In the mentally healthy person these three systems form a unified and harmonious organization. By working together cooperatively they enable the individual to carry on efficient and satisfying transactions with the environment. The purpose of these transactions is the fulfillment of man's basic needs and desires. Conversely, when the three systems of personal-

ity are at odds with one another the person is said to be maladjusted. He is dissatisfied with himself and with the world, and his efficiency is reduced.

Finally, as noted above, these three structures are hypothetical in nature and there is no sharp boundary between them. They are simply convenient labels to conceptualize dynamic processes that, according to Freud, govern personality.

Freud conceptualized personality as a developmental process. The human infant is viewed as a primitive organism controlled primarily by the id and totally dependent on its parents for survival. Despite the best efforts of the parents and the processes of the id, the infant's needs are not always gratified immediately; hence ego processes develop in an effort to obtain more effective and efficient need gratification. As the ego develops in the service of the id, a new problem arises. Although the ego is governed by the "reality principle," it does so without regard to the welfare of others or society in general. The principles necessary for people to coexist within society must become part of the evolving personality structure of the child. As we know from the foregoing discussion, Freud referred to this evolving structure as the superego.

The dynamic interrelationship of these three structures and the evolution of the ego and superego occurs within the context of five developmental stages (Cameron, 1963) as postulated by Freud: the oral, anal, phallic, latency, and genital stages. Freud specified, however, that basic personality is formulated during the first 5 years of life, which covers only the oral, anal, and phallic stages. The latency period, as its name infers, represents a period of quiescence relative to the dynamics of the three previous stages. Finally, adolescence signals the onset of the genital stage and social, emotional, and sexual maturity. To be fully mature depends on the adequate development and integration of the id, ego, and superego in the pregenital stages.

The oral stage covers the period from birth to 12 to 18 months of life. The focus is on the mouth as a primary source of gratification with this stage marking the onset of ego development. Through experiences centered around oral gratification, the infant begins to differentiate the reality of the external world from the subjective reality of its own being. The anal stage begins between 12 and 18 months of age, with the child's developing control of bowel and bladder functions and parental efforts to regulate these functions. Freud believed that toilet training marks the first major effort of the child's parents to foster social compliance and to convey to the child a sense of "good" and "bad." Thus, this phase marks the onset of superego development. The phallic stage begins around the 3rd year of life and is characterized by the child's increasing interest in his or her genitals and by issues of sexual identification, which are played out through the Oedipus complex. Simply stated, the Oedipal complex represents the child's unconscious sexual desire for the parent of the opposite sex. These feelings are expressed in the child's fantasies and in the alternation of loving and rebellious behaviors directed toward the parents (Hall & Lindzey, 1970). The male child's incestuous cravings for his mother and his fear of retaliation by his father give rise to castration anxiety. This anxiety produces a repression of the child's sexual desires and subsequent identification with the father. A somewhat analogous, but more complex, process occurs in the female child. In contrast to the castration complex, the female experiences penis envy. She feels she has lost something of value, blames her mother, and attempts to possess her father in order to regain what she has lost. Hall and Lindzey (1970, pp. 52–53) state that,

> Unlike the boy's Oedipus complex, which is repressed or otherwise changed by castration anxiety, the girl's Oedipus complex tends to persist, although it undergoes some modification due to the realistic barriers that prevent her from gratifying her sexual desire for the father.

Differences of gender notwithstanding, resolution of the Oedipus complex between the child's 5th and 6th year of life marks the end of the phallic stage and the emergence of the latency stage.

Psychopathology emerges when imbalances occur between the id, ego, and superego as the dynamic interrelationship of these structures evolves across the five developmental stages. The ego is the pivotal structure that mediates between the demands of the id and superego. An imbalance gives rise to anxiety. If the ego cannot use conscious processes to resolve the imbalance logically and rationally, then unconscious processes called defense mechanisms of the ego emerge. These mechanisms consist of repression, fixation, regression, reaction formation, and projection (Cameron, 1963) and are used to some extent by everyone; but extensive reliance on them signifies the ego's inability to deal consciously and more effectively with internal conflicts. Although defense mechanisms protect the individual from anxiety, they do not resolve the fundamental imbalance between the id and superego structures. Therefore, the individual continues to be subject to further anxiety and maladaptive functioning. Psychoanalytic therapy attempts to resolve imbalances in the postulated structures of personality through analysis of the patient's developmental experiences, especially those during the oral, anal, and phallic stages, as well as analysis of his or her current difficulties and the defense mechanisms used to cope with them.

HISTORICAL DEVELOPMENT OF PSYCHOANALYTIC TREATMENT OF CHILDREN

As Melanie Klein (1932) indicated, it was Freud's 1909 classic analysis of "Little Hans," a child with a phobia, that represented the beginning of child analysis. She noted that this initial analysis was of major importance because it demonstrated that psychoanalysis could be applied to children, and suggested that children actually exhibit the impulses and drives Freud had inferred from the analysis of adults. However, Freud was never identified significantly with the subsequent development of child psychoanalytic treatment. It was 10 to 15 years after the analysis of Little Hans that the foundation of child analysis began in the writings and lectures of Anna Freud and her colleagues at the Vienna Institute of Psychoanalysis (A. Freud, 1946, 1966), and in the work of Melanie Klein (1932) and Hug-Hellmuth (1921) in Berlin. Initially, child analysis was conceived as a basic modification of adult analysis (Freud, 1966).

In classical psychoanalytic theory it is assumed that the patient's social and emotional development was arrested as a result of an imbalance of the id, ego, and superego that occurred due to unresolved problems or conflicts at the oral, anal, or phallic stages of development. Treatment occurs within the context of a therapist–patient relationship in which the therapist remains relatively passive, neutral, and nondirective. This therapeutic posture minimizes distortions of the patient's thought processes and enhances the development of a transference neurosis. By analyzing the patient's spontaneously expressed thoughts and feelings—technically referred to as "free association"—and dreams, the therapist gains insight into the patient's areas of conflict and resistance. Through the judicious use of interpretation the therapist can help the patient gain insight and subsequently resolve his or her problems.

The patient's problems and conflicts are thought to be most clearly reflected in the transference neurosis, which is literally a transfer of the patient's childhood conflicts and problems with early object relationships (i.e., with the parents) onto the therapist. The development of a transference neurosis is facilitated by the therapist's basically passive and neutral role. The transference neurosis is crucial to the success of therapy because the patient, as an adult, no longer has an intense relationship with those individuals, usually parents, who were fundamental in the development of the patient's personality. Working through the transference neurosis marks the resolution of the patient's maladjustment.

There was basic agreement among early analysts that changes in psychoanalytic technique were necessary for the analysis of children. Children could not be dealt with in the passive fashion of the adult. The therapist had to be more actively involved with the child to facilitate a treatment alliance and to guide the child through the treatment process. Because children vary greatly in their cognitive and linguistic development, there needed to be greater latitude in modes of self-expression. Young children commonly express their thoughts and emotions through play, and pre-adolescent and adolescent patients rely more on verbal expression. Despite agreement among analysts that children vary in their level and mode of expression, controversy arose over the relationship between play and free association, the nature of interpretation of conflicts, and whether or not children form a transference neurosis. These controversies were reflected in two major schools of thought: one represented by Melanie Klein (1932) and the other by Anna Freud (1946).

Although Klein's conceptualization of child analysis was initially popular in England and America, most of her ideas are given limited credence in contemporary psychoanalytic thought. Her early popularity seemed to stem from her innovative use of play as a mode of expression in child analysis. In fact, Klein and Hug-Hellmuth (1921) were the first analysts to emphasize the role of play in the treatment of children. The term "play therapy" originally was used by Klein to refer to a therapeutic process that involved the psychoanalytic interpretation of the child's play as the equivalent of free association. Today, play therapy is thought of more commonly as a form of child treatment in which play is the major mode of expression regardless of the specific school of thought.

Anna Freud and the Vienna group disagreed with the significance placed on the role of play in child analysis by Klein and her associates. The Vienna group viewed play as one of several modes of expression and did not agree that play could be equated with the cognitively purposeful act of free association in adult analysis. Although the child expresses thoughts, feelings, and emotions through play, the behavior is not motivated to provide the therapist with material for analysis and interpretation. Conversely, Klein (1932, p. 29) stated,

> The child expresses its phantasies, its wishes, and its actual experiences in a symbolic way through play and games . . . for play is the child's most important medium of expression. If we make use of this play technique, we soon find that the child brings as many associations to the separate elements of its play as adults do to the separate elements of their dreams.

The controversy over the role of play naturally extended itself to controversy over the role of interpretation. Klein advocated interpretation based on the child's play behavior and suggested that interpretation begin early in the psychoanalytic process. In contrast, Anna Freud believed there was no justification for early interpretation and that the child's play behavior was not always symbolic of conflict, and hence of little interpretative value with respect to the child's specific emotional conflicts or maladjustment. She stated (1946, p. 29):

> Instead of being invested with symbolic meaning it [play] may sometimes admit of a harmless expression. The child who upsets a toy lamppost may on its walk the day before have come across some incident in connection with such an object; the car collision may be reproducing some happening in the street; and the child who runs toward a lady visitor and opens her handbag is not necessarily, as Mrs. Klein maintains, thereby symbolically expressing its curiosity as to whether its mother's womb conceals another little brother or sister, but may be connecting some experience of the previous day when someone brought it a little present in a similar receptacle.

A third controversy arose over the role of the transference neurosis. As previously noted, in the analysis of adults the patient transfers the focus of conflicts that developed in early childhood from their original source (typically the parents) to the therapist. Transference occurs in part as a response to the therapist's passive and emotionally neutral stance and derives its impetus from the fact that the patient was not able to resolve his or her original conflicts through interaction with the parents. Klein suggested that children develop a transference neurosis; Anna Freud and her colleagues disagreed. Anna Freud argued that the transference neurosis does not develop in child treatment for two major reasons. First, the child is not dysfunctional because of old unresolved conflicts, but is still engaged in conflicts with primary relationship figures such as the parents. Second, because the therapist is not neutral in child analysis, but often actively engages in the child's play, it is difficult, if not impossible, for the child to produce a transference that can be interpreted clearly.

Although many issues are still debated regarding the classical psychoanalytic treatment of children, it is fair to state that Anna Freud's position on the nature of free association, interpretation, and transference neurosis is largely accepted in contemporary psychoanalytic thought. The way in which this theoretical position translates into therapist behavior during child analysis is discussed by Achenbach (1974). He asserted that the goal of child analysis, like that of adult analysis, is to alter the relationship among the basic structures of personality so that they work in harmony (p. 283):

> In child analysis, however, the patient's immature ego, his inability to use introspection as free association, and his tendency to deal with conflict through action rather than thought often cause other elements of the analytic relationship to play a larger role than is the case with adults. These elements include verbalization and clarification of unrepressed thoughts, direct suggestion by the analyst, corrective emotional experience resulting from the child's relationship with the analyst as an understanding adult, and manipulation of the child's environment through the analyst's advice to the parents.

CONTEMPORARY PSYCHOANALYTIC POSITION

Psychoanalytic thought regarding child treatment has developed and matured greatly over the years. Contemporary thought is less rigidly devoted to libidinal theory, although sexual and aggressive impulses continue to play a central role. Greater consideration is given to the range of constitutional, cultural, interpersonal, social, cognitive, and general developmental influences in the formation of personality and development of psychopathology. In general, contemporary thought reflects the basic views of Anna Freud and her colleagues regarding free association, interpretation, and the transference neurosis. Consistent with adult analysis, child analysis is seen as reconstructive in nature. That is, its purpose is to modify the patient's basic personality organization so that id, ego, and superego function in harmony. Treatment involves the traditional 50-minute session, four to five times per week, over an extended period of time, usually 1 to 3 years.

How frequently is traditional child psychoanalysis used as a technique? According to Finch and Cain (1968), it is rarely taught in this country, and hence there are few practitioners. One reason for this state of affairs is that psychoanalysis is prohibitively expensive and does not appear to be applicable to many forms of child psychopathology (A. Freud, 1968). A widely used alternative is psychoanalytically oriented child psychotherapy, which emerged out of developments in psychoanalytic treatment and from the influence of neoanalytic schools of thought (Munroe, 1955). The psychoanalytically oriented approach is characterized by a marked reduction in the number of sessions, usually one or two a week, and it is more symptom or problem oriented, although unconscious processes are still important. In addition, a broader range of psychopathology is treated than in classical child analysis. It is important, however, to note that psychoanalytic psychotherapy is guided by the same general theoretical principles as child psychoanalysis.

Developmental Considerations

Unlike the adult, the child is in a process of cognitive and emotional development independent of treatment, and the child's level of development has significant implications for treatment (Harter, 1983). For example, Harter noted that the child's understanding of emotions progresses from being singular to sequential, and finally to simultaneous (p. 101):

> Our initial studies revealed a three-stage sequence. In the first stage, children simply deny that two feelings can co-occur. Our youngest subjects were quite vehement on this issue. Some merely asserted that this was not possible . . . others attempted to document their statement: "You can't have two feelings at the same time because you only have one mind!", or "I've never

had two feelings at the same time, I've only lived 6 years you know!'' The second stage marks the ability to think about the co-occurrence of two feelings; however, they can only be experienced sequentially, not simultaneously. Examples are: "I was happy we were going to see *Star Wars* again, but sad when we got there late"; "I was scared in the haunted house and then happy going on the merry-go-round." The ability to conceptualize two emotions simultaneously defines the third stage. Examples of such responses are: "I get angry and upset when my brother messes up my stuff"; "I was happy that I was watching TV, but scared my mom was going to punish me for not cleaning my room."

Harter's (1980, 1981) work suggests that the conceptualization of several emotions simultaneously does not develop before 8 or 9 years of age. Her observations have obvious implications for the child's ability to profit from specific interpretations and clarifications made by the therapist. Harter and Barnes (1980) also noted that the child's capacity to understand his or her parents' feelings varies according to developmental age. For example, children in the 4- to 6-year age range have difficulty differentiating their emotional states from those of their parents, and some emotions are more difficult to differentiate than others.

Children also vary developmentally in their capacity to understand the motives and causes of their own behavior. Piaget (1965) addressed the issue of intentionality of behavior in his studies on the moral judgment of children. He noted that the young child's judgment of the moral rightness or wrongness of an act is based on the objective outcome, while the older child becomes concerned with the underlying motivation of the act. For example, to the young child stealing five cookies from the store is worse than stealing one. The older child focuses on the more fundamental issue of stealing. The capacity to understand intentionality is important within the context of therapy, since the therapist is concerned with helping the child understand the motivations underlying his or her behavior.

These are only a few examples of developmental differences that must be considered by the child therapist, and these considerations are not unique to psychoanalytically oriented treatment. Harter (1983) provides an excellent introduction to the importance of developmental issues in child psychotherapy.

Types of Psychopathology

Anna Freud (1968) delineated three broad categories of child psychopathology, one of which is treatable by child psychoanalysis, and the other two by psychoanalytic psychotherapy. The three types are infantile or classical neurosis, developmental phase problems, and problems that arise as a result of environmental interference with normal development. The infantile or classical neurosis is considered by Anna Freud and most contemporary analysts to be the only form of psychopathology strictly amenable to child psychoanalysis (Pearson, 1968; Finch & Cain, 1968; Sandler et al., 1980). This psychopathological condition arises from internalized conflicts between the evolving psychic structures of the id, ego, and superego and is characterized by excessive use of ego defense mechanisms and anxiety. Childhood phobias, hysterical conversion reactions, and obsessive-compulsive neuroses are examples of classical neurosis from a psychoanalytic perspective. Pearson (1968) noted that classical neurosis in childhood manifests itself most often during the latency period. The following adaptation by Schaefer and Millman (1977, pp. 51–52) of Kaufman's (1962) case study of a hysterical conversion reaction illustrates the psychoanalytic conceptualization and treatment of this problem.

At the age of 8½ years, Catherine was referred for psychoanalysis because of hysterical blindness. She had two older sisters and two younger brothers. The analyst viewed Catherine's mother as feeling like a failure for not having a boy (instead of Catherine) and as seeing her daughter as a rival sibling. In treatment, Catherine's major problems were viewed as sibling rivalry and difficulty accepting a feminine role, a difficulty that was associated with castration anxiety.

Preceding the onset of hysterical blindness, two old women caught Catherine investigating a 6-year-old boy's genitals and she was made to feel guilty about this forbidden activity. In the first few sessions, Catherine and the therapist conversed and drew pictures. A quick transference cure developed; she simultaneously gave the analyst lollipops and gave up her symptoms. Her drawings were of houses, with much concern over the safety of the structures and the openings. In games with the analyst, she always wanted to be first and discussed her feelings that her brothers and sisters were always first. The analyst interpreted her playing Chinese checkers as symbolical expression of her castration anxiety and penis envy. Her wish for a phallus was transformed during therapy into a wish for Santa Claus to bring her a baby. Playing checkers and Monopoly was seen by the analyst as revealing her wish to be first, her not wanting to give unless getting something, and her guilt about her aggressive feelings. Catherine expressed castration anxiety in various ways—she saw the feet of a duck as too small; a doll lacked a nose; and she told the analyst she would pinch his finger off. Concern was expressed about the difference between boys and girls, about things being damaged, and about where babies come from.

In psychoanalytic terms, her unresolved wish for a penis from her father was expressed symbolically as a gift from Santa Claus. She felt damaged and castrated and wanted the analyst's finger as a substitute phallus. She expressed both hostility toward her mother and the accompanying fear of retaliation by being starved by her mother. The conflict aroused by repressed oedipal material was displaced to her eyes, resulting in the symptom of hysterical blindness. Neurotic conflict and the problems of sexual identity were resolved by analyzing the transference. Resolving the unconscious oedipal conflict (guilt and castration anxiety) furthered her process of developing a feminine identity.

The second type of psychopathology, developmental phase problems, is similar to the first in that the child's conflicts also are assumed to be intrapsychic; however, the conflicts are related to the present rather than the past and are acute and ongoing. The acute nature of these problems makes them unsuitable for formal analysis, since so much of the child's conscious energy (ego) is bound up with the problem that little energy is left for the child to engage in the self-examining process of child analysis. Anna Freud (1968) related developmental phase conflicts to external events exerted on the child at particular stages of development. For example, the death of a parent or sibling, trauma, or disease can trigger acute adjustment problems. In such cases the usual psychoanalytic format does not work very effectively. Instead, the therapist places emphasis on helping the patient learn to cope with external events more adaptively and, where appropriate, works with significant members of the child's family. The following example by Terr (1983, pp. 310–311) illustrates a developmental phase problem treated with brief therapy.

> A therapist who learns from a child, other children, a parent, or a teacher about a repeated, monotonous, atypical, strange play must suspect a past psychic trauma. . . . I had just recently begun seeing Andrew (age 7) for a short course of once-weekly sessions because of negative behavior, whining, and unhappiness at school, when his mother phoned me. "He's been putting little Tony [his 2-year-old brother] in a box!" When I asked Andrew about it, he reluctantly corroborated his mother's story. He could think of no reason for his behavior other than that it was fun. I then asked Andrew if anyone had put him in a box and frightened him. "Not a box, a clothes dryer," Andrew answered. "Jeremy and his friends bet me 5 bucks that I could get into a dryer. When I got in they banged the door shut and left. I thought I would die in there. I punched and punched the door. Almost broke my hand. I screamed. Nobody came. Finally I got out. And they never paid me the 5 bucks!" Andrew and I spent two psychotherapy sessions talking about his anxiety in the clothes dryer. His play did not recur, nor did he complain of repeated dreams. The trauma had been fairly recent and short-lived. According to his mother, there had been no sign of further post-traumatic behavior in the 4 years following the interpretation of Andrew's play episodes.

The third type of psychopathology, environmental interference with normal psychosexual development, occurs when the child's normal course of development is interfered with by external forces. Anna Freud (1968) identified at least two types of interference. First, deprivation of the child's basic developmental needs may occur when parents have little or no parenting skills as a result of ignorance or emotional problems of their own. Second (and certainly not mutually exclusive of the first type), parents or other caretakers may interfere with the child's psychosexual development by fostering dependency, by over-aggressive or hostile control, or by being sexually seductive. The following case example by Willock (1983, pp. 400–401) of an aggressive, acting-out child illustrates this third category of psychopathology.

Sean was referred for psychiatric evaluation at the age of 10, shortly after he and some friends had been apprehended by the police for breaking into a building, kicking holes in the walls, and setting a number of fires with cigarette lighters stolen from a nearby store. This particularly alarming incident occurred within a context of generally problematic functioning. Sean's academic performance had been deteriorating over the past year. School personnel reported that he would not follow directions and he had been expelled from the school lunchroom because he was always fighting with other children. His mother also reported that Sean would not listen to her and that he was given to violent outbursts during which he would slam doors and smash toys. She was also worried about Sean's fantasies of stealing a gun from a relative in order to shoot his mother, his 8-year-old brother, and himself. It also appeared that Sean's mother was inappropriately seductive with him and was having difficulties setting appropriate limits around the nature of his physical contact with her.

Sean's mother had become pregnant, and therefore married, in her mid-teens. Several months later her husband was drafted and sent to Vietnam. He reacted to this stressful turn of events by sexually acting out in a manner that strained the marriage. After his tour of duty, Sean's mother and father lived together for a few months until Sean's mother decided to leave her husband and stay with her parents. One reason Sean's mother left her husband was that he had spanked Sean so hard for wetting his pants that he bruised his buttocks. Sean was 1½ years old and he had a brother who was 3 months old at the time of this separation.

Sean formed a strong positive attachment with his grandfather, but this was frequently stressed by separations. Sean's living situation was repeatedly disrupted by his being shuttled back and forth between his grandparents' and his mother's home. Sometimes the reason Sean's mother sent the boys off to their grandparents was her fear of her own abusive potential and, indeed, she had hit Sean a number of times. When Sean was 7, his mother remarried, but a year later Sean lost his stepfather through another divorce. Babysitters played a large role in Sean's upbringing, although the boys inevitably managed to drive all sitters away with their unruly behavior. Thus Sean's life prior to treatment had consisted of many separations and losses, harsh physical punishment, and inadequate parenting from an immature, overwhelmed mother.

Although it is relatively easy to delineate these three broad psychopathological categories theoretically, they often overlap in any given patient. For example, the last case illustration certainly contained elements of the second and third categories as outlined by Anna Freud (1968). In addition, there are many other ways of conceptualizing child psychopathology. Finch and Cain (1968), Pearson (1968), and Anna Freud (1965) provide expanded coverage of the various psychoanalytic conceptualizations.

When to Treat

For the psychoanalytic therapist, any child falling into one of the three categories above would potentially be in need of treatment. However, the decision to implement psychoanalysis or psychoanalytic psychotherapy is based on the therapist's clinical judgment of the severity of the problem, the environmental resources or support systems available to the child, and the likelihood that the child may have the necessary personal resources to resolve the problem on his or her own. Much of the psychoanalytic literature attempts to provide guidelines for deciding whether or not to treat a child (e.g., Sandler et al., 1980), but the decision most often is based on experience and clinical judgment. It would appear that there are no universally accepted objective indices by which therapists, psychoanalytic or otherwise, make decisions to treat potential child patients.

The Role of Parents

In general, contemporary practitioners are not opposed to working with the parents of their child patients, especially if the therapist views the child's problem as resulting from factors other than a classical neurosis. Even in the case of classical neurosis, however, many psychoanalytic therapists will have some form of contact with the parents. There also tends to be much greater involvement with the parents of prelatency children than with parents of the adolescent or genital-stage patient. In some prelatency-age children, treatment is conducted almost exclusively with the parents, whereas with adolescent patients the parents may be seen only for the initial intake process, with subsequent meetings occurring only at the request of the patient.

An Overview

Contemporary psychoanalytic treatment is characterized more frequently by a "psychoanalytically oriented" approach than by classical psychoanalysis. That is, the overall duration of treatment is shorter than psychoanalysis, the patient is seen only once or twice a week, the approach is more problem oriented, and there is a greater tendency to involve the parents in the treatment process. Treatment takes place in the context of play sessions in the case of young children, with increasing emphasis on verbal or "talk therapy" with older children. Following the pioneering work of Anna Freud, contemporary psychoanalytic thought rejects the notion of a free-association equivalent in play therapy and suggests a cautious approach to the interpretation of the child's play behavior, as it may reflect situational as well as intrapsychic factors. Because the occurrence of a childhood transference neurosis is considered unlikely, less attention is focused on transference-related issues in child than adult treatment. Psychoanalytic psychotherapy is applicable to a broad spectrum of childhood psychopathology, but classical child psychoanalysis appears to work best only for the treatment of infantile or classical neurosis. Psychoanalytic treatment may be used with children of all ages, but it is more common with latency-age chilren. Frequent involvement of the parents in the therapeutic process is more typical with young children and gradually diminishes in the treatment of older children and adolescents.

A Psychoanalytically Oriented Treatment Case

An example of psychoanalytic psychotherapy rather than one of classical child psychoanalysis is presented here, because the former treatment approach is more common in clinical practice. The case study is from Finell (1980, pp. 97–99) and deals with a 6-year-old boy who was seen for 15 therapy sessions. The parents sought therapy for their son because of his frequent nightmares, timid behavior, and excessive fears.

John, aged 6, was brought to the clinic by his mother. . . . John could not bear to hear the news on radio or television, because the frequent broadcasts of stories of war and violence sent him into a panic. In addition, he allowed himself to be intimidated by his peers and made no attempt to defend himself even against children who were smaller than himself.

Although John was prepared for his visit to the therapist by his mother, he was visibly frightened and uncomfortable in the strange situation and wanted to leave at once. After a few short visits in which no attempt was made to discuss his problems, he relaxed to the point that he began to look forward to the visits. Since his confidence was gained, the time seemed ripe to begin the discussion of his problems. The reason for his being in therapy was discussed, and his cooperation was sought. Being an intelligent and serious youngster, John had no difficulty in grasping the therapist's communication. In fact, he expressed pleasure at the chance he was given to obtain help in overcoming his fears.

During the introductory sessions John had played with many of the toys. However, no particular pattern was observed in his play. Once the "therapeutic pact" was established, a change occurred in his play. He began to create scenes with a doll family that turned out to be quite repetitive. In practically each scene, the smaller boy doll was repeatedly injured; he fell from his fathers's shoulders, was hit by a car, etc. At other times, when the family was on an outing, the doll was accidentally left behind. The therapist suggested to John that the boy doll was really John, and that for some reason, as yet unknown to both of them, he saw himself as being hurt or left behind. Perhaps John felt he should be punished for something.

John showed that he understood these communications by responding in subsequent sessions with a change in the script. Now it was the father rather than the boy doll who was run over, fell out of the car, etc. This play continued repetitively, and provided some understanding into the meaning of John's fears.

It was now feasible to understand John's fear of physical harm as a wish for punishment. He apparently harbored resentful and hostile feelings towards his father, and hoped that his father would be hurt. However, since the father was so much stronger than John, retaliation, abandonment, and destruction were feared as the consequence for his wishes. For the child whose sense of reality testing is only partially developed, hostile feelings often seem like real acts. In the immature mind, thoughts are magically powerful and are indistinguishable from deeds. They are, therefore, subject to punishment.

Play provided the means through which these interpretations were made to John. Just as John had used dolls to communicate his feelings and fears, the therapist now used the dolls to illustrate her interpretations. However, although progress was made in terms of the understanding of John's doll play, the reason for John's intense hostility toward his father was not yet known.

Fortunately, John's mother, Mrs. D., was extremely cooperative and readily accepted an appointment to see the therapist. The basic ground rule for the therapeutic encounter was discussed—confidentiality. In spite of this, Mrs. D. was somewhat reluctant to offer any information concerning intimate family matters. It was not until the third interview that she offered some insight into a home situation that was volatile and was undoubtedly intensifying feelings in John that, according to Freudian theory, are universally present in children of his age.

Mother and father were engaged in bitter fights that had become so intense that on occasion the father would storm out of the house, threatening never to return. On the evenings of his absences, Mrs. D. reported that John would stay up late with her, watching TV. It would seem then, as a result of John's experiences in the home, his oedipal feelings were intensified and left him with an acute sense of guilt. John's guilt over his rivalrous feelings towards his father, as well as his fear of punishment by him, left him in a state of panic and confusion. The broadcast of violent news reawakened his inner terror. John anticipated attacks from others and presented a picture of a child whose inner life was one of turmoil and disaster.

Once again, the therapist interpreted the reconstruction of John's psychic life in simple language, illustrating all interpretations with the dolls. Along with this interpretative work, John was assured that his wishes could in no way actually hurt his father, and that it was not his fault that his parents were fighting. Even if they separated, John was not to blame in any way.

The proof that John understood these interpretations was evident 3 weeks later in a telephone interview, when Mrs. D. reported that John's general panic had begun to subside. John no longer insisted that news broadcasts be shut off. Even more impressive was her observation that, for the first time as far as she could remember, John had pushed another boy in self-defense.

Therapy was discontinued after the 15th session, and a follow-up conversation with the mother 1 year later revealed that John had sustained the gains he had made through therapy despite the fact that his father had permanently left the home. Mrs. D. informed the therapist that after the separation she had decided to seek therapy for herself. She now felt more secure in her role as an independent woman than she had ever felt previously and believed that she communicated a greater sense of stability to her son as a result. The fact that she was now building a new life for herself and had become involved in activities outside of the home made her less dependent on John as husband substitute. Thus, it would seem that the psychic separation between parent and child—so necessary for emotional maturity to be achieved—was now available to John.

This example illustrates the therapist's initial conceptualization of a specific set of problem behaviors that brought the child to treatment. There was a recognition of the child's fearfulness, and the need to establish a relationship with the child before the more central process of therapy could begin. The relationship was established in a few sessions, although it can take much longer. Once the child was comfortable with the therapist, the real purpose of therapy was discussed. This "therapeutic pact" provided the basis for the child's joint cooperation with the therapist. The next phase of treatment was characterized by the therapist's attempts to relate repetitive themes in the child's play to the child's underlying fears. Consistent with Anna Freud's position on free association and interpretation, the therapist realized that many aspects of the child's behavior were innocuous and made interpretations with caution, treating them as hypotheses to be empirically tested. Parental involvement was crucial to the delineation of the child's problems and validation of the hypotheses. As the underlying nature of the child's problems became apparent, the therapist was able to help him understand and work through his fears. Finally, in line with the principles of psychoanalytic psychotherapy, treatment focused on the resolution of a specific set of problems, and when they were resolved treatment was terminated.

THE CLIENT-CENTERED MODEL

Like the psychoanalytic theory of personality development, client-centered theory evolved out of clinical experience. Whereas psychoanalytic theory represented a new and bold conceptualization of personality development, client-centered theory has drawn on many previous schools of personality theory, including psychoanalysis, to formulate an integrated theory of personality and psychopathology. Carl Rogers (1951) is recognized as the founder of this approach, which he most clearly articulated in his book *Client-Centered Therapy* and later elaborated (1959, 1961).

In contrast to Freud, Rogers did not place much emphasis on structures of personality. He did, however, delineate two entities: the "organism" and the "self." The organism is the focus of all experience, both somatic and psychological. Experience is defined as everything the organism responds or reacts to at any given moment in time. Consciously experienced phenomena are said to be symbolized, which simply means the person is capable of recognizing, articulating, and reacting to the experience. Experiences may not be consciously perceived, even though the organism reacts to them. These unconsciously experienced events are said to be unsymbolized. Together, the consciously and unconsciously experienced events constitute the phenomenal field, which can be thought of as the person's subjective reality—a personal or idiosyncratic view that may or may not be congruent with the "true reality" of the surrounding world. A sense of self develops out of this phenomenal field as a result of the organism's experiences. The self or "self-concept" is the person's view of what he or she is as an individual. As Rogers (1959, p. 200) stated, the self is "the organized, consistent conceptual gestalt composed of perceptions of the characteristics of the 'I' or 'me' and the perceptions of the relationships of the 'I' or 'me' to others and to various aspects of life, together with the values attached to these perceptions."

As in psychoanalytic theory, client-centered theory postulates a primary motivational system: the organism's inherent tendency toward "self-actualization". This is defined as the individual's tendency to develop all of his or her capacities in ways that serve to maintain and enhance growth. Self-actualization is a rational and constructive process. Regarding the concept of self-actualization Rogers (1961, p. 195) has suggested

> I have little sympathy with the rather prevalent concept that man is basically irrational, and that his impulses, if not controlled, will lead to destruction of others and self. Man's behavior is exquisitely rational, moving with subtle and ordered complexity toward the goals his organism is endeavoring to achieve.

In the context of this tendency toward self-actualization, the individual learns to experience fundamental needs for positive regard from others, and for self-regard. The need for positive regard from others develops as a result of the infant being loved and cared for by its parents, and the need for self-regard develops when the child receives acceptance from parents and others. How do these needs affect self-actualization? As Rogers (1959, p. 224) noted,

> If an individual should experience only unconditional positive regard, then no conditions of worth would develop, self-regard would be unconditional, the needs for positive regard and self-regard would never be at variance with organismic evaluation, and the individual would continue to be psychologically adjusted, and would be fully functioning.

However, no individual ever experiences total unconditional positive regard; therefore the developing child learns to differentiate between behaviors that are approved, or have worth, and those that are unacceptable. "Unworthy" behaviors tend to be excluded from the self-concept even if they are organismically valid, which results in a self-concept that is incongruent with organismic experience. This incongruence creates a corresponding distortion in the development of the child's self-concept. The distortion is experienced as threat that evokes anxiety and subsequent psychopathology, as illustrated in the following example from Hall and Lindzey (1970, p. 532).

A boy has a self-picture of being a good boy and of being loved by his parents, but he also enjoys tormenting his little sister, for which he is punished. As a result of this punishment he is called upon to revise his self-image and his values in one of the following ways: (a) "I am a bad boy," (b) "My parents don't like me," (c) "I don't like to tease my sister." Each of these self-attitudes may contain a distortion of the truth. Let us suppose that he adopts the attitude "I don't like to tease my sister," thereby denying his real feelings. Denial does not mean that the feelings cease to exist; they will still influence his behavior in various ways even though they are not conscious. A conflict will then exist between the introjected and spurious conscious values and the genuine unconscious ones. If more and more of the "true" values of a person are replaced by values taken over or borrowed from others, yet which are perceived as being his own, the self will become a house divided against itself. Such a person will feel tense, uncomfortable, and out of sorts. He will feel as if he does not really know what he is and what he wants.

Optimal personality development is achieved when the organism's inherent tendency toward self-actualization is not markedly interfered with by experiences that force the individual to deny his or her thoughts, feelings, and emotions. Rogers asserts that the denial of one's true self, as a result of experiences that do not contribute to positive regard, produces conflict and tension within the individual, and between the individual and others. To continue on the path toward self-actualization, the person must reconcile the breach between what he or she is organismically and his or her distorted self-concept. Client-centered therapy attempts to provide an environment characterized by unconditional positive regard as expressed through the therapist's emotional support, acceptance, and concern for the patient. This process allows the patient to develop a positive self-concept and to establish a foundation for the experience of self-actualization.

HISTORICAL DEVELOPMENT OF CLIENT-CENTERED TREATMENT

The development of client-centered child therapy as an alternative to psychoanalytic treatment can be traced from Alfred Adler's (1927) rejection of orthodox psychoanalytic thought to the conceptualizations of Otto

Rank (1936), the works of Taft (1933), Allen (1942), and Axline (1947), and finally to the work of Carl Rogers (1939, 1942, 1951, 1959, 1961). Munroe's (1955) classic text, *Schools of Psychoanalytic Thought,* presents an excellent account of the variations in psychoanalytic thought that began to occur as early as 1920. These neoanalytic schools of thought could be differentiated from orthodox psychoanalytic theory on the basis of their acceptance or rejection of Sigmund Freud's primary emphasis on the biological nature of man, with its focus on sexual and aggressive instinctual drives. A prominent group of theorists who rejected Freud's emphasis were more concerned with the individual in terms of self-concept and interpersonal relationships. As Munroe indicates, this was not to imply that strict Freudians considered these factors to be irrelevant; rather, it was a matter of emphasis. This shift in emphasis, however, provided the impetus for variations in psychoanalytic thought and treatment.

Adler (1927), one of Freud's early students and colleagues, was the first to rebel against orthodox psychoanalytic thought. He was followed by Karen Horney (1937), Eric Fromm (1947), and Harry Stack Sullivan (1953). These four theorists often are grouped together because of their mutual concern for the role of the self and the importance of interpersonal and social dynamics in the development of personality and psychopathology. Each theorist, however, placed a different emphasis on the self (Adler, Horney), the role of the individual in society and culture (Fromm), and interpersonal dynamics (Sullivan). Although these theorists provided the basis for variations in psychoanalytic treatment, many common elements remained. In general, though, their treatment methods involved more active interaction with the patient, less interest in unconscious processes, more concern with the patient's present than past situation, and interpretation based on their particular theoretical focus.

Despite the emphasis by Adler and Horney on the self, the lectures and writings of Otto Rank (1936) come closer to being the therapeutic forerunner of client-centered therapy. Rank, also one of Freud's friends and students, placed great emphasis on the therapeutic relationship as a means of helping the individual come to know and differentiate himself or herself from the therapist and others in the environment. Rank's work had particular impact on the field of social work. He frequently lectured at major social work schools in New York and Philadelphia, and his notion of how the individual develops a differentiated self or self-concept had a marked influence on the development of client-centered therapy. Equally important was the emphasis he placed on the patient's ability to direct the course of treatment and resolve his or her own problems within the context of a relationship with a supportive, but minimally intrusive therapist.

Rank's therapeutic notions, with some variation as related to child treatment, first emerged in the writings of Taft (1933) and later in those of Allen (1942). During the same decade Carl Rogers began to formulate his own ideas of treatment, influenced by Rank's notions regarding the central role of the therapeutic relationship. In 1939 Rogers published *The Clinical Treatment of the Problem Child*, which made reference to Rank and "passive therapy." Rogers' first formalized statements on client-centered theory appeared in *Counseling and Psychotherapy* (1942). Over the next decade he developed the theory and in 1951 published his most highly formalized version of it in his now classic book *Client-Centered Therapy*. The term "client-centered" emphasized Rogers' notion that the patient possesses the inherent ability to solve his or her own problems. He believed that the therapeutic process should occur in an environment in which the therapist exhibits the three essential characteristics of genuineness, empathic understanding, and positive regard or acceptance of the patient (Rogers, 1951).

Like Freud, Rogers is not primarily identified with child psychotherapy. There is no question, however, that his work over the past 5 decades has greatly influenced the development of client-centered child psychotherapy. Axline (1947) is the most well-known advocate of client-centered therapy for children. In 1959 Moustakas propounded essentially the same set of concepts as those offered by Axline. Finally, Allen's (1942) client-centered work on psychotherapy with children is still relevant for those interested in this technique.

CONTEMPORARY CLIENT-CENTERED POSITION

Unlike the development of child psychoanalysis, the history of client-centered psychotherapy is not marked by rival schools of thought that struggled to evolve an appropriate treatment method. The basic client-centered methodology appears to be as applicable to children as to adults. The only modifications necessary have been those related to the child's developmental age and varying modes of expression.

The client-centered approach with children as outlined by Axline (1947) remains essentially unchanged today and is characterized by the following points:

1. The therapist must establish a warm rapport with the child as soon as possible.
2. The therapist accepts the child exactly as he or she is.
3. The therapist establishes a feeling of permissiveness in the relationship, so that the child feels free to express his or her feelings completely.
4. The therapist recognizes the feelings the child is expressing and reflects

those feelings back to the child in such a manner that the child gains insight into his or her behavior.

5. The therapist maintains a deep respect for the child's ability to solve his or her own problems. The responsibility to make choices and to institute change is the child's.

6. The therapist does not attempt to direct the child's actions or conversation in any manner; the child leads the way and the therapist follows.

7. The therapist does not attempt to hurry the therapy along. It is a gradual process and is recognized as such by the therapist.

8. The therapist only establishes limitations that are necessary to anchor the therapy to the world of reality and make the child aware of his or her responsibility in the relationship.

Only points 4 and 6 differ in any significant manner from the psychoanalytic model of child treatment. Point 4 indicates that interpretation within the client-centered model is almost exclusively reflective. Although psychoanalysts employ reflective interpretations, they also interpret unconscious processes, as noted in the Finell (1980) transcript quoted earlier. In addition, the psychoanalytic therapist is much more directive than the client-centered therapist in helping the child through the therapeutic process.

Developmental Considerations

As in the psychoanalytic model, the client-centered therapist is sensitive to variations in the child's development. Unlike psychoanalysis, however, conceptualizing the child into psychosexual stages of development is viewed as essentially irrelevant. Primary consideration is given to the child's general level of cognitive and language development, but only insofar as the therapist needs to plan the therapeutic environment and understand the child's modes of communication and capacity to understand and conceptualize his or her thoughts, feelings, and emotions.

Types of Psychopathology

In categorizing types of psychopathology, client-centered theory is very straightforward compared to psychoanalysis. In general, client-centered theory is opposed to diagnostic classification, but does acknowledge broad classes of problems. Children are seen in treatment because they are experiencing emotional discomfort and may be in conflict with those around them. The therapist accepts the child as he or she is and begins to help the child know and to understand his or her problems. Client-centered and psychoanalytic therapists basically treat the same types of child psychopathology.

When to Treat

The decision to treat a child via the client-centered model is not significantly different than that for the psychoanalytic model. The therapist's clinical judgment as to the child's level of discomfort is used to determine the need for treatment, along with the therapist's impressions regarding the child's potential for resolving the problems without treatment.

Role of Parents

As in the psychoanalytic treatment of children, client-centered therapy also involves the parents. The therapist attempts to deal with the parents and accept them in the same manner as he does the child. The client-centered therapist also has a somewhat more positive attitude toward the intentions of the child's parents than is seen in the psychoanalytic model. As Moustakas (1959, p. 250) stated:

> Parents realize the significance of their participation and are eager to explore their relationship with the child. . . . Parents cannot be blamed for the emotional difficulties of the child. The problems which are created arise in living, in relations. They grow out of experiences in the family. Thus, parents are seen because the child's problem has emerged in the context of the parent–child relationship, therefore, they need assistance as much as the child.

Moustakas further commented that "nearly every parent relates himself to the child's difficulty, recognizes his own part in it, and wants to help." However, as in the psychoanalytic model, the degree of parent involvement varies as a function of the child's age.

An Overview

Client-centered psychotherapy with children has changed very little over the past 30 years. The theory is straightforward; there are few treatment principles, and client-centered treatment is easier to understand and implement than psychoanalytic psychotherapy, although neither model is highly amenable to empirical testing. Axline's (1947) text continues to be the single best guide for client-centered psychotherapy with children. Like psychoanalytic psychotherapy, client-centered treatment is used with a broad range of psychopathology. There appears to be little difference between these treatment models with respect to parent involvement; both support varying degrees of contact, depending on the individual case. Despite significant theoretical differences regarding the nature of child psychopathology and the capacity of the child for change, the two systems have a number of common features with respect to the treatment process.

A Client-Centered Treatment Case

The following case study from Moustakas (1959, pp. 115–137) illustrates the basic aspects of client-centered therapy. Although this case study was published nearly 3 decades ago, it is indicative of current client-centered treatment with children. The case deals with a 4-year-old girl who was seen in treatment for 21 sessions. The parents originally sought treatment because the child had frequent stomachaches and was constantly pulling at her hair, which resulted in partial baldness.

Carol, an only child, 4 years old, was referred to the play therapist. . . . Carol's mother was considerably worried about Carol's recent complaints of stomachaches during mealtimes. Also, Carol's habit of twisting and pulling her hair had become so serious that she was partially bald.

Family background data included the following: the mother's repeated statement that Carol looked and acted like a stepsister who the mother hated; the mother's strong emphasis on cleanliness, and the degradation she felt in her own family experiences, where her stepparents were alcoholic and her home was usually littered with scraps of food and dirt; the parent's belief that Carol was incapable of loving them or anyone; and the crowded conditions in the family's seven-room house, where they lived with three other families. . . .

Carol's mother saw her as a selfish, inconsiderate, disagreeable, unruly child with stomachaches and hair-twisting symptoms. The therapist found her to be a frightened, lonely, love hungry, confused, and hostile child. . . . During therapy, Carol expressed her attitudes of resentment, hatred, loneliness, and fear. She explored these feelings and attitudes, expressed them again and again, and re-explored them.

During the 1st session, Carol chattered incessantly. She pointed to the toys but did not play with them, and in other ways showed diffuse anxiety. At the end of the 1st session, she expressed hostile feelings toward adults rather tentatively but directly, saying that people who bring children to the playroom (in Carol's case, her mother) break the toys first and "then let the kids play with them."

Direct Excerpt from Session 2

During the 2nd session, Carol conveys the attitude that her home is filled with troubles and shows her fear of her mother. She becomes immature in her play, drinks from the nursing bottle and chews the nipple. She shows hostility toward her mother and implies that her mother is responsible for her immaturity.

Carol's negative expressions become more generalized. In her play, she shoots all the humanlike figures in the room except one doll, which she identifies as her girlfriend. She is especially vehement against the therapist, shooting him and telling him to die and never get up. At the end of the 2nd session she shoots off all the lights, so that no one will see the "crimes" she has committed in her fantasy.

C: I'm gonna use this stick to paint with.
T: You are?

C: Mm-hm. I'm not messing up my hands. I'm gonna use all these.

T: All the colors, hm?

C: That's what I'm gonna do. Use all of them. That's what I always do. (Pause) We have much troubles. Much troubles.

T: You really have troubles, don't you?

C: Mm-hm. I'm gonna wash my hands.

T: You don't like to have your hands dirty.

C: I don't much. No, I won't wash my hands now. I'll wait before I go upstairs.

T: You're going to wash them before you go upstairs, hm?

C: I don't want my mommy to see them dirty.

T: You don't want her to know about it.

C: (Picks up nursing bottle and chews on the nipple. Drinks for a while and then starts chewing again.) Looks like I'll have to stay here 19 years.

T: A long, long time, isn't it?

C: Just for this old bottle.

T: That will keep you here if nothing else does.

C: Yes. (Laughs and continues to drink. Chews nipple for quite a while.)

T: Just keep working and working and working on it, hm?

C: My mommy is going to have to wait until I get to be 4 years old.

T: She'll have to wait until you grow up to be 4, hm?

C: Yes. (Sighs heavily and continues to chew nipple.)

C: I'm gonna shoot up this whole place.

T: Just shoot everything, hm?

C: Yeah. (Laughs shrilly)

T: Shooting all over.

C: (Laughs) I'm shooting everybody in the place.

T: Everybody is being shot down, hm?

C: Everybody except my girlfriend.

T: She's the only one you won't shoot.

C: Yeah, I'm gonna shoot you now. (Laughs) Why don't you fall down?

T: You'd like me to just fall.

C: Uh-huh. After I shoot you, you can stay up just 1 minute. Then you be dead. (Shoots at therapist and laughs.) You don't get up.

T: Not ever to get up.

C: You never get up. Nobody's gonna see. I'm gonna shoot the lights off.

In the 4th session, Carol's anger becomes direct and she shows . . . how her mother has always deceived her and cheated her. Her feelings are severe and intense as her sarcasm mounts. She reveals hatred for her mother, who has always tricked her and withheld her love. In the play situation Carol retaliates, expresses hostility toward her mother, and poisons her. Later in the session, Carol shows the positive side of her feelings toward her mother in her desire to be loved. She takes "all that bad food out" and gives the mother good food. . . .

[Moustakas' comments on sessions 5 through 15, followed by comments on sessions 16 to 21, illustrate further changes in the child's behavior during therapy.]

Carol again expresses feelings of anger and resentment against her parents. In her play she refers to their constant quarreling and indicates their frequent criticism of her. She retaliates with "Squawk. Squawk. Squawk. That's all they'll get back."

Later, Carol removes the clothing from all the doll figures and implies that if all people were "naked" we could see each other as we really are.

Hostility toward the mother reappears. Carol wishes to escape her mother's persistent admonitions. In a whisper she says, "It's so quiet around here today. That's what I want. Just so much peace and quiet." She indicates the tragedy of her home situation, telling the therapist that she has no home at all, not like other kids.

As the sessions continue, Carol becomes more relaxed and spontaneous in her play. There is even a childishness about her. In previous sessions, she acted more like a miniature adult. Now she acts silly and laughs continually.

Carol recognizes her selfishness but justifies it, indicating that she has never had good "food" but "now I'm having good things to eat." When her feelings of selfishness are accepted, she offers to share her "food" with the therapist. . . .

These sessions (16 through 21) are characterized mainly by Carol's exploration of the positive feelings in herself toward herself and other people. She builds a music house with blocks, where people are close to their parents, play games with them, and have fun with them. She makes the house a spacious one, and "the kids are gonna have a good time."

In the 20th session, Carol creates a village in the sand. She decides not to destroy the home this time and realizes that "If I help them, then they'd like me." She makes a huge cake in the sand and decides at first to eat it all up as her "selfish" feelings momentarily return, but later she says, "I'll divide it up with them (all the people), because they're my friends." She now sees herself as a friend, someone people care about and regard as important. And in the play experiences, Carol indicates that it is not too late, the dreams can still come true.

Finally, Carol expresses a positive friendly attitude toward people, saying, "I'm gonna make a pie so big, it's gonna cover the whole place . . . and now I'm gonna cut it up in little pieces and share it with all the people."

During the therapy experience, Carol expressed her deep resentments and fears in the relationship with her mother, using clay and sand to symbolize these attitudes. As Carol clarified and reorganized these attitudes . . . she became more accepting of herself and her mother. Acceptance of herself and her mother enabled Carol, then, to move out of her inner world and express feelings of affection and friendliness toward others. Many of these positive feelings and explorations were dramatized in her play in sand. Following the 15th play session, these socialized attitudes were most clearly revealed. In her play, Carol expressed a desire to help people, to do things for them and with them, and to win their friendship and their love. Carol's perceptions of herself and others were now both more positive and more realistic. Her mother's perceptions of Carol were also different. . . . "It is not very difficult to see Carol's growth. For a long time now, we have had to punish her very little. Her manners are improving. She just seems to do things much better. She seems to just get along better with everyone. . . . My husband says she's been acting a lot smarter and has noticed lately that she's using big words when she speaks. . . . I think sometimes when I look at some other people's children that Carol is almost perfect. . . . For 4 years of her life, Carol showed us very little affection, but in the last 6 months she has begun to kiss us and to hug us. My husband is much warmer to her now and he spends much more time with her . . .

Although Moustakas offers many clinical impressions and interpretations of the patient's play activities and verbalizations, at no time throughout treatment, as indicated from the 2nd-session excerpts, are they expressed or offered as hypotheses to the child as possible underlying causes for her distress. Specific comments made by the therapist were reflective in nature and simply reiterated the child's feelings, thoughts, and emotional reactions. Therapy provided the child a nonthreatening environment in which all feelings could be expressed without fear of retaliation by the therapist. The therapist's reflections helped the child to clarify her feelings and attitudes. As a result, the child's behavior improved markedly, and she gained a sense of security and self-confidence. While the child was in treatment, the parents were seen by a social worker. As this experience helped them, they in turn aided the child's progress in therapy.

OUTCOME RESEARCH: PSYCHOANALYTIC AND CLIENT-CENTERED APPROACHES

There are few research studies on psychoanalytic and client-centered treatments of children, and those that exist are poor in quality. Although hundreds of articles and books have been written on these two models of therapy, a recent review of child psychotherapy research by Barrett, Hampe, and Miller (1978) reported only two psychoanalytic research projects (Heinieke, 1969; Heinieke & Strassman, 1975), and six client-centered studies over the past 30 years (Bills, 1950a, 1950b; Cox, 1953; Moustakas & Schlalock, 1955; Dorfman, 1958; Seeman, Barry, & Ellinwood, 1964).

The psychoanalytic studies of Heinieke and colleagues focused on "dosage" or number of sessions per week. Their results showed that children benefited more from an intense, long-term regimen of treatment than from fewer sessions over a shorter period of time. The client-centered studies examined process (Moustakas & Schlalock, 1955) and outcome (Bills, 1950a, 1950b; Cox, 1953; Dorfman, 1958; Seeman, Barry, & Ellinwood, 1964). In general, the outcome studies have shown a modest improvement of treatment over comparison groups, but the methodology of all these studies is inadequate. Moustakas and Schlalock's process study simply pointed out that the client-centered therapist behaves in a manner consistent with the client-centered philosophy, and that the more disturbed children in the study were more likely to engage in nondirective play.

It should be evident from these meager findings that there is insufficient evidence either to support or reject the efficacy of individual child psychotherapy of the type described in this chapter. Continued use of these methods suggests that they have some practical value, and there are many case illustrations in the literature that attest to their success. There is a need, however, to determine their usefulness empirically.

SUMMARY

The history of individual child psychotherapy, as distinct from behavior therapy, reveals the development of two major schools of thought: psychoanalytic and client-centered. Client-centered child psychotherapy has remained essentially unchanged since its inception in the 1940s and early 1950s. Psychoanalytic child psychotherapy, on the other hand, evolved from an adult model of treatment to one in which rival schools of thought debated over certain key issues. A model of child psychoanalysis emerged during the 1920s and 1930s, followed by the delineation of psychoanalytic child psychotherapy, which has been applied to a much broader range of psychopathology than child analysis. A comparison of the psychoanalytic and client-centered models of psychotherapy reveals some common aspects, but there are differences with respect to (a) motivational parameters underlying behavior, (b) the relevance of unconscious processes, and (c) the nature and use of interpretations of the child's behavior.

Although both psychoanalytic and client-centered theory and treatment flourish, there is insufficient research data to support or refute their efficacy. In essence, these approaches continue to thrive because clinicians are convinced that their respective approaches can help children resolve adjustment problems.

REFERENCES

Achenbach, T. M. (1974). *Developmental psychopathology.* New York: Wiley.

Adler, A. (1927). *Understanding human nature.* New York: Greenberg.

Allen, F. H. (1942). *Psychotherapy with children.* New York: Norton.

Axline, V. (1947). *Play therapy.* Boston: Houghton Mifflin.

Barrett, C. L., Hampe, E. I., & Miller, L. C. (1978). Research on child psychotherapy. In S. L. Garfield & A. E. Bergin (Eds.), *Handbook of psychotherapy and behavior change* (2nd ed.). New York: Wiley.

Bills, R. E. (1950a). Nondirective play therapy with retarded readers. *Journal of Consulting Psychology, 14,* 140–149.

Bills, R. E. (1950b). Play therapy with well adjusted retarded readers. *Journal of Consulting Psychology, 14,* 246–249.

Cameron, N. (1963). *Personality development and psychopathology.* Boston: Houghton Mifflin.

Corsini, R. (Ed.). (1979). *Current psychotherapies.* Itasca, IL: F. E. Peacock.

Cox, P. N. (1953). Sociometric status and individual adjustment before and after play therapy. *Journal of Abnormal and Social Psychology, 48,* 354–356.

Dorfman, E. (1958). Personality outcomes of client-centered child therapy. *Psychological Monographs, 72* (3 Whole No. 456).

Finch, S. M., & Cain, A. C. (1968). Psychoanalysis of children: Problems of etiology and treatment. In J. Marmor (Ed.), *Modern psychoanalysis.* New York: Basic Books.

Finell, J. (1980). Psychoanalytic play therapy. In G. S. Belkin (Ed.), *Contemporary psychotherapies.* Chicago: Rand McNally.

Freud, A. (1946). *The psycho-analytical treatment of children.* London: Imago.

Freud, A. (1965). *Normality and pathology in childhood.* New York: International Universities Press.

Freud, A. (1966). A short history of child analysis. *Psychoanalytic Study of the Child, 21,* 7-14.

Freud, A. (1968). Indications and contraindications for child analysis. *Psychoanalytic Study of the Child, 23,* 37-46.

Freud, S. (1933). *New introductory lectures on psychoanalysis.* New York: Norton.

Freud, S. (1949). *An outline of psychoanalysis.* New York: Norton.

Freud, S. (1953). The interpretation of dreams. In *Standard edition of the complete psychological works of Sigmund Freud* (Vol. 4). London: Hogarth Press.

Freud, S. (1961). The ego and the id. In *Standard edition of the complete psychological works of Sigmund Freud* (Vol. 19). London: Hogarth Press.

Fromm, E. (1947). *Man for himself.* New York: Rinehart.

Guerney, L. F. (1983). Client-centered (nondirective) play therapy. In C. E. Schaefer & K. J. O'Connor (Eds.), *Handbook of play therapy.* New York: Wiley.

Hall, C. S. (1954). *A primer of freudian psychology.* New York: Mentor.

Hall, C. S., & Lindzey, G. (1970). *Theories of personality* (2nd ed.). New York: Wiley.

Harper, R. A. (1974). *Psychoanalysis and psychotherapy: 36 systems.* New York: Jason Aronson.

Harter, S. (1980). Children's understanding of multiple emotions: Cognitive-developmental approach. In *Proceedings of the Jean Piaget Society.* Hillsdale, NJ: Lawrence Erlbaum, 1980.

Harter, S. (1981). A model of intrinsic mastery motivation in children: Individual differences and developmental change. In W. A. Collins (Ed.), *Minnesota Symposium on Child Psychology* (Vol. 14). Hillsdale, NJ: Lawrence Erlbaum.

Harter, S. (1983). Cognitive-developmental considerations in the conduct of play therapy. In C. E. Schaefer & K. J. O'Connor (Eds.), *Handbook of play therapy.* New York: Wiley.

Harter, S., & Barnes, R. (1980). *Children's understanding of parental emotions.* Unpublished manuscript, University of Denver.

Heinieke, C. M. (1969). Frequency of psychotherapeutic session as a factor affecting outcome: Analysis of clinical ratings and test results. *Journal of Abnormal Psychology, 74,* 533-560.

Heinieke, C. M., & Strassman, L. H. (1975). Toward more effective research on child psychotherapy. *American Academy of Child Psychiatry, 14,* 561-588.

Herink, R. (Ed.). (1980). *The psychotherapy handbook: The A to Z guide to more than 250 different therapies in use today.* New York: New American Library.

Horney, K. (1937). *The neurotic personality of our time.* New York: Norton.

Hug-Hellmuth, H. V. (1921). On the technique of child analysis. *International Journal of Psychoanalysis, 2,* 287-305.

Kaufman, I. (1962). Conversion hysteria in latency. *American Academy of Child Psychiatry Journal, 1,* 385-396.

Klein, M. (1932). *The Psycho-analysis of children.* London: Hogarth Press.

Moustakas, C. (1959). *Psychotherapy with children.* New York: Harper & Row.

Moustakas, C. (1973). *Children in play therapy,* (rev. ed.). New York: Aronson.

Moustakas, C., & Schlalock, H. B. (1955). An analysis of therapist–child interaction in play therapy. *Child Development, 26,* 143–157.

Munroe, R. L. (1955). *Schools of psychoanalytic thought: An exposition, critique, and attempt at integration.* New York: Holt, Rinehart & Winston.

Parloff, M. B. (1980). Psychotherapy and research: An anaclitic depression. *Psychiatry, 43,* 279–293.

Pearson, G. H. (1968). *A handbook of child psychoanalysis.* New York: Basic Books.

Piaget, J. (1965). *The moral judgment of children.* New York: Free Press.

Rank, O. (1936). *Truth and reality and will therapy.* New York: Knopf.

Rogers, C. R. (1939). *The clinical treatment of the problem child.* Boston: Houghton Mifflin.

Rogers, C. R. (1942). Counseling and psychotherapy. Boston: Houghton Mifflin.

Rogers, C. R. (1951). *Client-centered therapy.* Boston: Houghton Mifflin.

Rogers, C. R. (1959). A theory of therapy, personality, and interpersonal relationships, as developed in the client-centered framework. In S. Koch (Ed.), *Psychology: A study of a science* (Vol. 3). New York: McGraw-Hill.

Rogers, C. R. (1961). *On becoming a person.* Boston: Houghton Mifflin.

Sandler, J., Kennedy, H., & Tyson, R. L. (1980). *The technique of child psychoanalysis.* Cambridge, MA: Harvard University Press.

Schaefer, C. E., & Millman, H. L. (1977). *Therapies for children.* San Francisco: Jossey-Bass.

Schaefer, C. E., & O'Connor, K. (1983). *Handbook of play therapy.* New York: Wiley.

Seeman, J., Barry, E., & Ellinwood, C. (1964). Interpersonal assessment of play therapy outcome. *Psychotherapy: Theory, Research and Practice, 1,* 64–66.

Sullivan, H. S. (1953). *The interpersonal theory of psychiatry.* New York: Norton.

Taft, J. (1933). *The dynamics of therapy in a controlled relationship.* New York: Macmillan.

Terr, L. C. (1983). Play therapy and psychic trauma: A preliminary report. In C. E. Schaefer & K. J. O'Connor (Eds.), *Handbook of play therapy.* New York: Wiley.

Willock, B. (1983). Play therapy with the aggressive, acting-out child. In C. E. Schaefer & K. J. O'Connor (Eds.), *Handbook of play therapy.* New York: Wiley.

5

BEHAVIORAL APPROACHES

Scott is a 9-year-old boy with a history of severe dog phobia. At the age of 6 Scott observed his younger sister being knocked down by a large dog and subsequently began to display extreme fear reactions when confronted by even the most friendly animal. His avoidance of dogs resulted in a withdrawal from all outdoor activities and a refusal to play with friends outside the house. In addition, he refused to walk to school, making it necessary for his parents to drive him each day.

A behavioral treatment program was undertaken to help reduce Scott's dog phobia and enable him to resume normal activities for a child his age. Scott first was trained to relax so that he would not become overwhelmed by fear when confronted with dog-related stimuli. After learning to relax, he was exposed to a series of activities that were graded in order of their fear-evoking characteristics. For example, when Scott was able to look at a picture book of dogs without reporting any fear, he then was asked to watch other children play with dogs of various sizes while he observed them behind a one-way mirror. Later in the treatment program, Scott was assisted in gradually approaching a small dog and eventually larger dogs by watching the therapist pet the dog and then imitating the therapist's behavior. Through this process of gradual exposure, first through imaginary procedures and later by contact with dogs in real-life situations, Scott was able to overcome his debilitating fears and to play outside, both at home and school, without worrying about the presence of dogs.

This chapter presents a number of behavioral approaches to the treatment of child behavior problems, such as that displayed by Scott. In this context we will consider the theoretical foundations of behavior therapy and also examine the research evidence regarding the effectiveness of behavioral approaches as they are used with children.

DEFINITION AND SCOPE OF BEHAVIOR THERAPY

Behavior therapy is an approach to therapeutic change that attempts to modify current responses that interfere with an individual's adaptive functioning. The approach focuses attention on observable behavioral manifestations of the person's cognitive self-report statements, overt behaviors, and/or physiological responses. Many diverse approaches are subsumed under the general heading of behavior therapy. However, all behavioral methods are similar in that they involve the application of empirically derived psychological principles, such as learning principles, in changing dysfunctional patterns of behavior. From this perspective the acquisition, maintenance, and alteration of maladaptive behaviors are presumed to follow the same general principles as more appropriate and functional behaviors. Thus, maladaptive behaviors are viewed as bad habits or faulty learning patterns. The goal of the behavior therapist is to help the person change these troublesome habits and develop new, more adaptive ways of behaving.

Unlike their more psychodynamically-oriented colleagues, behavior therapists make no assumptions regarding unconscious or intrapsychic causes of problem behaviors. The individual's past history is considered important only insofar as previous experiences provide information about current events that might maintain the maladaptive behaviors. Rather, the major emphasis of a behavioral perspective is on the relationship between problem behaviors and environmental events that elicit and maintain these behaviors, and the ways in which environmental factors can be modified to produce adaptive behavioral change. While behavior therapists acknowledge the contribution of genetic and other biological variables to both adaptive and maladaptive behavior, intervention is directed at environmental factors, which are more readily accessible to change.

Behavior therapy can also be seen as a system for collecting, organizing, and evaluating clinical data so as to enable the therapist to design a treatment program tailored to the specific needs of the client. A distinctive feature, therefore, is the command it gives the therapist in implementing therapy and evaluating the progress of treatment. When one carefully considered treatment approach fails to result in the desired behavior change, another approach is implemented according to objective indicators, each variation being an application of experimentally established principles.

BEHAVIORAL ASSESSMENT

As with other approaches to treatment, a careful assessment of the presenting problem and the current determinants of problem behaviors is a prerequisite to developing an effective treatment program. Although this general goal is not dissimilar from that of other orientations, behavioral approaches to assessment differ from other more traditional methods in several respects.

Traditional forms of assessment typically take a "sign" approach to the interpretation of test behavior; the person's responses are viewed as a sign of underlying personality traits or unconscious conflict. It is usually assumed that behavior is determined by inferred personality traits that are relatively stable over time and across situations. Thus, traditional assessment is only minimally concerned with the setting in which the individual is assessed.

In contrast, approaches to behavioral assessment focus on what the client is doing, the content validity of the test items, and a sampling interpretation of test responses (Goldfried & Kent, 1972; O'Leary, 1972; Ollendick & Hersen, 1984). Behavioral assessment assumes limited cross-situational consistency and considers the situational context of behavior as important. Therefore, there is an effort to sample how the individual responds in various real-life situations. Furthermore, behavior therapists do not rely exclusively on information provided by verbal reports of the child and significant others, such as parents and teachers; they may also attempt to assess behaviors as they occur in the natural environment. The theoretical and conceptual differences between traditional and behavioral assessment are summarized by Hartmann, Roper, & Bradford (1979) in Table 5.1.

The behavioral assessment process represents a *functional analysis of behavior* as it attempts to determine the relationships between problem behaviors and the environmental stimuli that elicit and maintain those behaviors. Once the relationships between environmental events and the problem behavior have been determined, these events can be systematically altered to produce the desired behavior change.

As noted in chapter 1, Kanfer and Saslow (1969) have introduced a useful model for behavioral assessment. Within this SORKC framework stimulus events (S) refer to external stimuli, such as dogs, or internal stimuli, such as fearful thoughts, that systematically precede the maladaptive behavior. These stimuli may elicit the behavior's occurrence or serve as discriminative events for the behavior. Organismic variables (O) include such factors as biological conditions or physical handicaps that may influence the individual's behavior. Responses (R) occur in one or more of the three basic response systems: motor, cognitive, and physiological. These responses can be problematic on the basis of characteristics of frequency, duration, and intensity. Contingency relationships (K) describe the association between the behavior and its consequences, and specify the likelihood that a response will be reinforced. Finally, consequences (C) are the positive and negative events that follow the behav-

Table 5.1. Differences Between Behavioral and Traditional Approaches to Assessment

ASSESSMENT	BEHAVIORAL	TRADITIONAL
Assumptions		
• Conception of personality	Personality constructs mainly employed to summarize specific behavior patterns, if at all.	Personality is a reflection of enduring underlying states or traits.
• Causes of behavior	Maintaining conditions sought in current environment.	Intrapsychic or within the individual.
Implications		
• Role of behavior	Important as a sample of a person's repertoire in a specific situation.	Behavior assumes importance only insofar as it indexes underlying causes.
• Role of history	Relatively unimportant, with some exceptions, e.g., to provide a retrospective baseline.	Crucial in that present conditions are seen as a product of the past.
• Consistency of behavior	Behavior thought to be specific to the situation.	Behavior expected to be consistent across time and settings.
Uses of Data	Describe target behaviors and maintaining conditions. Select the appropriate treatment. Evaluate and revise treatment.	Describe personality functioning and etiology. Diagnose or classify. Make a prognosis; predict.
Other Characteristics		
• Level of inferences	Low.	Medium to high.
• Comparisons	Intraindividual or idiographic.	Interindividual or nomothetic.
• Methods of assessment	Direct, e.g., observations of behavior in the natural environment.	Indirect, e.g., interviews and self-reports.
• Timing of assessment	Ongoing: prior, during, and after treatment.	Pre- and perhaps post-treatment, or strictly to diagnose.
• Scope of assessment	Specific and including many variables, e.g., of target behaviors in various situations; of side effects, context, and strengths as well as deficiencies.	Global, e.g., of cure or improvement, but only of the individual.

Note. Adapted from "Some Relationships Between Behavioral and Traditional Assessment" by D. P. Hartmann, B. L. Roper, and D. C. Bradford, 1979, *Journal of Behavioral Assessment, 1*, pp. 3–21. Copyright 1979 by Plenum Publishing Co. Adapted with permission.

ior. The consequences can be physical, social, or self-generated events, such as a self-administered reward.

A number of methods are used to obtain information within the functional analysis framework. The interview represents one of the most commonly used assessment procedures. Important information about the child's problem is obtained from the child and significant informants, such as parents and teachers. Behavioral interviews attempt to obtain information about the problem behavior and events in the child's environment that contribute to its instigation and maintenance. A behavioral interview typically focuses on the following information (Gelfand & Hartmann, 1984): How often does the problem behavior occur? How does the problem interfere with the child's daily functioning? When and in what situations does it occur? What events precede and follow the behavior? What things have been tried to change the behavior? The interview also explores information pertaining to the child's and family's assets and resources and level of motivation for change (Evans & Nelson, 1977; Linehan, 1977; Gross, 1984).

In addition to the clinical interview, the child and his or her parents and teachers may be asked to complete a variety of specialized questionnaires and rating scales (Humphreys & Ciminero, 1979; Mash & Terdal, 1981; McMahon, 1984). These measures provide information about the severity and nature of the problem behaviors, as well as identifying factors associated with them. These checklists and rating scales may be designed to assess highly specific problem areas, such as fears or social skills, or they may provide a global assessment of the child's behavioral adjustment across a diverse range of areas.

Behavioral assessment also emphasizes the collection of objective information in the natural environment through behavioral observations. Naturalistic observations are presumed to provide a more objective method for directly sampling the child's behavior than can be obtained from self-report or interview procedures (Goldfried & Kent, 1972). The problem behavior must be carefully defined, so that it can be observed and recorded in a systematic manner in the natural setting, such as the child's home or school. Depending on the observation system used, a number of child behaviors, as well as behaviors of significant others, such as parents and teachers, also might be observed to determine their relationship to the problem behavior.

A wide range of observational procedures have been developed. Some have focused on discrete behaviors, such as tics or physical aggression (e.g., Firestone, 1976; Ollendick, 1981). Other procedures involve complex coding systems that record multiple behaviors and interactions between several or more persons (e.g., Patterson, Ray, Shaw, & Cobb, 1969; Wahler, House, & Stambaugh, 1976). An excellent discussion of behavioral observation procedures and related clinical and methodological issues has been presented by Barton and Ascione (1984).

Physiological measures also have been used in the assessment of behavioral problems in children. Numerous indices of autonomic nervous system activity, such as heart rate, blood pressure, muscle tension, skin conductance, and respiration, have been used in the assessment of somatic disorders and stress and fear-related problems (e.g., Kallman & Feuerstein, 1977). Physiological measurement has had considerable application in the area of biofeedback, in which physiological responses are modified directly by means of highly sophisticated, psychophysiological monitoring equipment.

Evaluation of Treatment Effectiveness

Assessment in behavior therapy is an ongoing process that begins with the identification of the problem behavior and continues until the goals of the treatment program have been reached. Assessment and treatment in behavior therapy are interrelated. Since behavior tends to change in a gradual manner, continuous measurement of the problem behavior provides feedback on the extent to which the behavior has changed since the last assessment period.

Continuous monitoring of the problem behavior provides the therapist with information about whether or not the behavior has, in fact, changed. However, it does not permit the therapist to specify clearly what has caused the change in the behavior. Although the behavior may have changed coincidentally with the introduction of the treatment program, it is also possible that uncontrolled and extraneous events in the patient's environment effected the change. In order to demonstrate a causal relationship between the treatment program and a change in the problem behavior, therapists often use single-subject experimental designs. These designs permit the therapist to rule out the influence of factors other than the treatment procedures that may have produced the observed change in the child's behavior. Barlow and Hersen (1984), Gelfand and Hartmann (1984), and Kazdin (1984) provide detailed discussions of the various research designs used in the evaluation of behavioral intervention programs. Two of these single-subject designs are briefly reviewed below.

Reversal or ABAB Design

One method of demonstrating the efficacy of a particular treatment procedure is a reversal or ABAB design, which involves the alternate application and withdrawal of the treatment program over time. The strategy followed in the reversal design involves:

1. Measurement of the baseline level of the target behavior (A phase).
2. Introduction of the treatment procedure (B phase).

3. Withdrawal of treatment and return to baseline conditions (A phase).
4. Reinstatement of the treatment procedure (B phase).

If the target behavior returns to near baseline levels when the treatment program is discontinued temporarily and changes in the predicted direction when the treatment program is reinstated, it is highly probable that the behavior changes can be attributed to the treatment program. The use of a behavioral procedure to reduce the aggressive and destructive behavior of a young child was evaluated in an ABAB design illustrated in Figure 5.1.

Multiple-Baseline Design

For practical or ethical reasons, it may be undesirable to use a reversal design once the problem behavior has been modified effectively by the treatment program. For example, one would not want to jeopardize desired changes obtained with highly aggressive or self-injurious behaviors. A multiple-baseline design may be used to evaluate treatment programs in which reversal to baseline conditions would be undesirable or not possible. In the multiple-baseline design, comparisons are based on the effect of treatment across several individuals, or across several behaviors in the same individual. In essence, several baselines are established at the same time. The individual program is sequentially applied to each behavior or to each individual. Baseline measures of the remaining behaviors continue until the treatment procedure eventually is applied to all behaviors or individuals. If behavior change is observed only when the treatment program is introduced sequentially across each behavior or individual, it is possible to conclude that the treatment was responsible for the behavior change. Figure 5.2 illustrates a multiple-baseline design in the evaluation of a behavioral treatment program for distractibility and short attention span in three overactive preschool boys.

THEORETICAL FOUNDATIONS

Several theoretical models have had a primary influence on behavior therapy and provide a systematic framework for understanding the mechanisms through which behaviors are learned. Behavior therapists acknowledge that no one model is sufficient to predict all types of learning. The models briefly reviewed below are not necessarily mutually exclusive, nor are they intended to be exhaustive of the theoretical approaches that have contributed to the development of behavior therapy.

RESPONDENT CONDITIONING

Respondent behaviors are involuntary, elicited, or autonomic, such as salivating in the presence of food or being startled at a loud or sudden noise. In respondent conditioning, also called classical conditioning, a

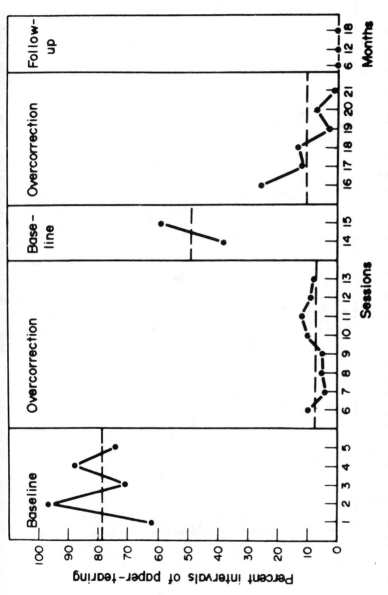

Figure 5.1. Percentage of intervals in which paper tearing was observed. From "Restitution and Positive Practice Overcorrection in Reducing Aggressive-Disruptive Behavior: A Long-Term Follow-Up" by E. S. Shapiro, 1979, *Journal of Behavior Therapy and Experimental Psychiatry, 10,* pp. 131–134. Copyright 1979 by Pergamon Press, Ltd. Reprinted by permission.

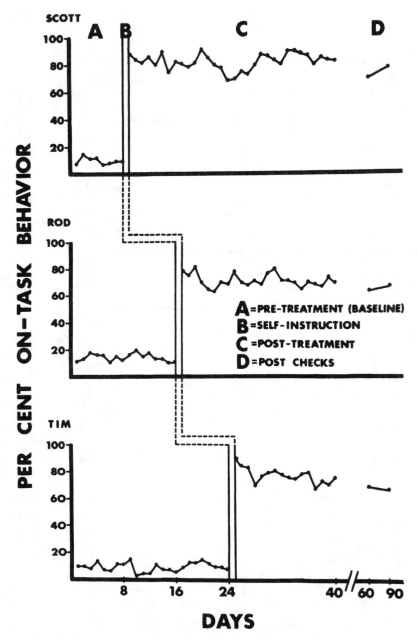

Figure 5.2. Daily percentages of on-task behaviors across experimental conditions for three overactive preschool boys. From ''The Effects of a Self-Instructional Package on Overactive Preschool Boys'' by P. H. Bornstein and R. P. Quevillon, 1976, *Journal of Applied Behavior Analysis, 9,* pp. 179–188. Copyright 1976 by the Society for the Experimental Analysis of Behavior, Inc. Reprinted by permission.

previously neutral stimulus eventually comes to elicit autonomic or reflex responses. This model of learning first was described in detail by the Russian psychologist Pavlov (1927), who trained dogs to salivate as a conditioned response when a bell was sounded. Watson and Raynor (1920) presented one of the earliest demonstrations of respondent conditioning in humans by developing a conditioned emotional response (i.e., fear) in Albert, an 11-month-old child. They first demonstrated that Albert was totally unafraid of furry animals, such as a white rat. When presented with a loud noise (unconditioned stimulus), however, Albert reacted with a startle and began to cry and shake (unconditioned response). When the loud noise was presented at the same time the child reached for the white rat, he began to react to the animal with the same fearful response. Thus, a previously neutral stimulus (white rat) became a conditioned stimulus capable of eliciting a fearful (conditioned) response in the child. Respondent conditioning provides the behavior therapist with several procedures for modifying maladaptive behaviors that have been acquired in this manner.

OPERANT CONDITIONING

Behaviors that are modified or maintained by their consequences are called operants, because they operate on or influence the environment, which results in additional consequences that strengthen or weaken the behavior. Operants constitute what a person does or says as he or she interacts with the environment.

Operant or instrumental conditioning occurs in a learning situation in which certain events or consequences are made contingent on specified behaviors. Every response made by an individual has some consequences. The operant conditioning procedures that are based on the laboratory investigations of Skinner (1953) suggest that it is more important to explore the effect of consequences on behavior than to know what caused the behavior in the first place. Consequences may be either positive or aversive for an individual. In operant conditioning, positive or reinforcing consequences are used to increase the frequency of desired behaviors, and negative or aversive consequences are used to decrease the frequency of undesirable behaviors.

Until recently it was believed that responses of the autonomic nervous system could be modified only through respondent conditioning. Clinical and research evidence suggests, however, that autonomic responses such as heart rate and skin temperature are subject to voluntary control through operant conditioning (Blanchard & Epstein, 1978).

SOCIAL LEARNING THEORY

In 1969 Bandura published a book that outlined a comprehensive model of behavior that attempted to integrate conditioning theory with cognitive processes. Bandura called this integrated approach social learning theory. According to him (1969, 1977), all behavior is acquired and maintained by one or more of three separate regulatory systems. These systems include the learning models specified by operant and respondent conditioning and in addition involve the influence of cognitive mediational processes on behavior.

Social learning theory suggests that much behavior is learned and modified through symbolic processes, particularly observational learning. Through observational learning, also referred to as vicarious learning or modeling, an individual may acquire a response without having previously performed the behavior. Learning by observing or by imitating the behavior of others is an important process in the acquisition of many skills.

In observational learning, the individual (or observer) is exposed to a model's behavior and the consequences that may accrue to it. It is not essential that the observer actually engage in any overt responses, or that he or she receive direct consequences for the behavior. The model may be physically present or be presented to the observer through filmed or imaginal (i.e., symbolic) procedures.

Bandura (1971) makes a distinction between the acquisition and performance of a response. According to him, a response is learned by observing the model's behavior. The observer forms symbolic responses (imaginal representations) similar to the responses performed by the model; these symbolic mediators have cue-producing properties that modify and guide the observer's behavior (Bandura, 1969). Whether an individual actually performs the modeled behavior depends on a number of factors, such as the consequences to the model's behavior and the availability of incentives.

Observational learning can produce a number of behavioral changes (Rimm & Masters, 1972, pp. 103–104). Through observing a model's behavior, an individual

> may learn new, appropriate behavior patterns, and modeling may thus serve an *acquisition* function. More likely, the observation of a model's behavior in various situations may provide social *facilitation* of appropriate behaviors by inducing the client to perform these behaviors, of which he was previously capable, at more appropriate times, in more appropriate ways, or toward more appropriate people. Modeling may lead to *disinhibition* of behaviors that the client has avoided because of fear or anxiety. And while disinhibiting behaviors, modeling may promote *vicarious* and *direct extinction* of the fear associated with person, animals, or object toward which the behavior was directed.

COGNITIVE BEHAVIOR MODIFICATION

The role of cognitive processes in the acquisition and modification of behavior represents a recent theoretical advance within behavior therapy (Mahoney, 1974; Meichenbaum, 1977). Behavior therapists recognize that cognitive processes, such as thought patterns, expectations, attributions of one's own behavior, and attitudes and beliefs, can affect how an individual behaves. It is presumed that maladaptive or faulty thoughts, such as irrational beliefs or self-defeating statements, can lead to maladaptive behavior patterns. This emphasis on cognitive processes has resulted in the recent development of cognitive therapy procedures such as restructuring and self-instructional training (see Kendall & Braswell, 1985).

CLINICAL APPLICATIONS OF CHILD BEHAVIOR THERAPY

This section presents some of the behavioral procedures most frequently used in the treatment of childhood behavior problems. The treatment techniques are organized according to the theoretical perspectives reviewed above. Each procedure is briefly described, and case examples are provided.

PROCEDURES BASED ON RESPONDENT CONDITIONING

Several behavior change procedures are based primarily on respondent conditioning principles. The two that are most frequently used are systematic desensitization, and the bell-and-pad method for treating enuresis.

Systematic Desensitization
This behavioral technique, based on the principle of counterconditioning, is widely used for the treatment of anxiety-related disorders. It can be traced to some of the earliest accounts of the application of learning-based techniques in the treatment of fear in young children (Jones, 1924).
Wolpe (1958) is primarily associated with the development of systematic desensitization. He assumed that the process underlying this procedure was reciprocal inhibition. Essentially he proposed that anxiety or fear could be reduced or inhibited by replacing the maladaptive anxiety response with an adaptive one. According to Wolpe (1958, p. 71), "If a response antagonistic to anxiety can be made to occur in the presence of anxiety-evoking stimuli so that it is accompanied by a complete or partial suppression of the anxiety responses, the bond between these stimuli and the anxiety responses will be weakened." Thus, the association between a particular stimulus and the anxiety response that it elicits can be broken or counterconditioned by presenting the stimulus while the anxiety response is prevented from occurring. Although muscle relaxation training (Jacobson, 1938) is the most frequently used anxiety-inhibiting response, other responses also have been identified as incompatible with anxiety, including eating, assertion, and sexual arousal (Wolpe, 1958). The

exact mechanisms underlying the effects of desensitization procedures remain open to empirical validation (Davison & Wilson, 1973; Goldfried, 1971), but there is considerable evidence for the effectiveness of systematic desensitization as a method for reducing anxiety-related responses. Systematic desensitization involves three basic components:

1. Training in a response that is incompatible with anxiety, such as deep muscle relaxation.
2. Construction of a hierarchy of anxiety-evoking situations.
3. Having the child relax while being exposed to anxiety-evoking stimuli, either imaginally or in vivo.

The most common method of relaxation training is the procedure developed by Jacobson (1938) to induce deep muscle relaxation. After the child is placed in a comfortable position in a recliner chair, he or she is instructed to alternately tense and relax various muscle groups (i.e., face, neck, arms, and legs) and to concentrate on feelings of tension and relaxation. Each muscle group is tensed for approximately 10 seconds and relaxed for about 30 seconds. The therapist enhances sensations of relaxation with suggestions of warmth and safety. The muscle groups are alternately tensed and relaxed a minimum of two times, or until the child reports complete relaxation.

Deep muscle relaxation training takes approximately three sessions to complete. The child is encouraged to practice relaxation at home briefly at least twice each day. Following sufficient practice, the child is usually capable of inducing total relaxation in just a few minutes. Variations of muscle relaxation training procedures with children are outlined in detail by Cautela and Groden (1978) and by Koeppen (1974). One example of relaxation instructions developed by Koeppen for use with young children is presented in Table 5.2.

An anxiety hierarchy consists of a number of statements about specific situations that relate to the child's fears. Each item or statement is elaborated upon in sufficient detail to enable the child to imagine vividly the event or experience. Necessary information about the specific components of the child's fear and its unique stimulus characteristics are obtained from data gathered during the assessment process. With the assistance of the child and significant others, such as parents and teachers, a series of situations that result in increasing amounts of anxiety or discomfort for the child are ordered from least to most anxiety arousing. Each item in the hierarchy is arranged in such a way that the child perceives only a small increase in anxiety over the previous item when the scene is imagined.

The length of a hierarchy for a particular child depends on a number of factors, such as the range of stimuli involved and the intensity of the child's fear. In addition, hierarchies can vary across several dimensions.

Table 5.2. Excerpts from a Relaxation Training Script

Hands and Arms. Pretend you have a whole lemon in your left hand. Now squeeze it hard. Try to squeeze all the juice out. Feel the tightness in your hand and arm as you squeeze. Now drop the lemon. Notice how your muscles feel when they are relaxed. Take another lemon and squeeze it. Try to squeeze this one harder than you did the first one. That's right. Real hard. Now drop your lemon and relax. See how much better your hand and arm feel when they are relaxed. Once again, take a lemon in your left hand and squeeze all the juice out. Don't leave a single drop. Squeeze hard. Good. Now relax and let the lemon fall from your hand. (Repeat the process for the right hand and arm.)

Arms and Shoulders. Pretend you are a furry, lazy cat. You want to stretch. Stretch your arms out in front of you. Raise them up high over your head. Way back. Feel the pull in your shoulders. Stretch higher. Now just let your arms drop back to your side. Okay, kitten, stretch again. Stretch your arms out in front of you. Raise them over your head. Pull them back, way back. Pull hard. Now let them drop quickly. Good. Notice how your shoulders feel more relaxed. This time let's have a great big stretch. Try to touch the ceiling. Stretch your arms way out in front of you. Raise them way up high over your head. Push them way, way back. Notice the tension and pull in your arms and shoulders. Hold tight, now. Great. Let them drop very quickly and feel how good it is to be relaxed. It feels good and warm and lazy.

Shoulder and Neck. Now pretend you are a turtle. You're sitting out on a rock by a nice, peaceful pond, just relaxing in the warm sun. It feels nice and warm and safe here. Oh-oh! You sense danger. Pull your head into your house. Try to pull your shoulders up to your ears and push your head down into your shoulders. Hold it tight. It isn't easy to be a turtle in a shell. The danger is past now. You can come out and once again relax and feel the warm sunshine. Watch out now! More danger. Hurry, pull your head back into your house and hold it tight. You have to be closed in tight to protect yourself. Okay, you can relax now. Bring your head out and let your shoulders relax. Notice how much better it feels to be relaxed than to be all tight. One more time, now. Danger! Pull your head in. Push your shoulders way up to your ears and hold tight. Don't let even a tiny piece of your head show outside your shell. Hold it. Feel the tenseness in your neck and shoulders. Okay. You can come out now. It's safe again. Relax and feel comfortable in your safety. There's no more danger. Nothing to worry about. Nothing to be afraid of. You feel good.

*Jaw.*You have a giant jawbreaker bubble gum in your mouth. It's very hard to chew. Bite down on it. Hard! Let your neck muscles help you. Now relax. Just let your jaw hang loose. Notice how good it feels just to let your jaw drop. Okay, let's tackle that jawbreaker again now. Bite down. Hard! Try to squeeze it out between your teeth. That's good. You're really tearing that gum up. Now relax again. Just let your jaw drop off your face. It feels so good just to let go and not have to fight that bubble gum. Okay, one more time. We're really going to tear it up this time. Bite down. Hard as you can. Harder. Oh, you're really working hard. Good. Now relax. Try to relax your whole body. You've beaten the bubble gum. Let yourself go as loose as you can.

Note. From "Relaxation Training for Children" by A. S. Koeppen, 1974, *Elementary School Guidance and Counseling, 9,* pp. 14–21. Copyright 1974 by American Association for Counseling and Development. Reprinted by permission.

Some hierarchies are spacial–temporal and vary along space and/or time dimensions. Thematic hierarchies, on the other hand, involve items that have a similar theme but differ in the extent to which they are anxiety arousing. Many hierarchies represent a combination of these two forms (Paul & Bernstein, 1973). A hierarchy used in the treatment of test-anxious children is presented in Table 5.3.

Once the child has learned to achieve a state of deep relaxation and the anxiety hierarchy has been developed, desensitization can begin. Typically, the child is instructed to relax, and then the therapist presents the scenes from the hierarchy, one at a time, for the child to vividly imagine. The child is asked to remain as relaxed as possible while visualizing each scene. If the child experiences even the slightest anxiety, he or she is instructed to signal the therapist by raising a finger. At that point the child is told to stop imagining and to continue relaxing. After the child is relaxed, the same scene is attempted again. If anxiety is not signaled, a second opportunity to visualize the scene is provided. Following three consecutive successes, the next scene in the hierarchy is then presented. This process is followed until the most anxiety-evoking scene can be imagined without experiencing anxiety. Three to four items usually are presented during each therapy session.

The stepwise progression of substituting relaxation for anxiety generalizes from low-anxiety situations to higher-anxiety situations, so that even-

Table 5.3. Desensitization Hierarchy for Test Anxiety

You are attending a regular class session.
You hear about someone else who has a test.
You are studying at home. You are reading a normal assignment.
You are in class. The teacher announces a major exam in 2 weeks.
You are at home studying. You are beginning to review and study for a test that is a week away.
You are at home studying, and you are studying for the important test. It is now Tuesday and 3 days before the test on Friday.
You are at home studying and preparing for the upcoming exam. It is now Wednesday, 2 days before the test on Friday.
It's Thursday night, the night before the exam on Friday. You are talking with another student about the exam tomorrow.
It's the night before the exam, and you are home studying for it.
It's the day of the exam, and you have 1 hour left to study.
It's the day of the exam. You have been studying. You are now walking on your way to the test.
You are standing outside the test room talking with other students about the upcoming test.
You are sitting in the testing room waiting for the test to be passed out.
You are leaving the exam room, and you are talking with other students about the test. Many of their answers do not agree with yours.
You are sitting in the classroom waiting for the graded test to be passed back by the teacher.
It's right before the test, and you hear a student ask a possible test question that you cannot answer.

Table 5.3. (*Continued*)

You are taking the important test. While trying to think of an answer, you notice everyone around you writing rapidly.
While taking the test, you come to a question you are unable to answer. You draw a blank.
You are in the important exam. The teacher announces 30 minutes remaining, but you have an hour's work left.
You are in the important exam. The teacher announces 15 minutes remaining, but you have an hour's work left.

Note. From "Systematic Desensitization of Test Anxiety in Junior High Students" by J. L. Deffenbacher and C. C. Kemper, 1974, *The School Counselor, 12,* pp. 216–222. Copyright 1974 by American Association for Counseling and Development. Reprinted by permission.

tually the child can imagine the most feared activity with little distress. Generalization to real-life fear situations is facilitated by assigning tasks between sessions involving the performance of those items that were imagined without anxiety.

A number of variations of systematic desensitization have been developed (Morris & Kratochwill, 1983). One of the most frequently used is in vivo desensitization. This procedure is similar to imagery-based desensitization approaches, except that hierarchy items are presented in the actual situation rather than in imagery.

Another procedural modification, developed specifically for use with children, is emotive imagery. As Lazarus and Abramovitz (1962) have noted, this approach is designed to "arouse feelings of self-assertion, pride, affection, mirth, and similar anxiety-inhibiting responses," the assumption being that such feelings are capable of inhibiting anxiety in the same way as relaxation in standard systematic desensitization. They describe the steps in this procedure as follows:

1. Develop a graduated hierarchy of the child's fears.
2. Determine the child's hero image, such as Superman.
3. Have the child imagine a series of credible events, within which a story about his or her favorite hero is woven.
4. Carefully arouse the child's affective responses with the story.
5. When the child's positive emotions have been aroused, introduce each hierarchy item until the entire hierarchy has been completed without distress.

Several reports suggest that this procedure may be useful in cases in which systematic desensitization is inappropriate (see Elliot & Ozolins, 1983).

The clinical application of desensitization techniques can be illustrated by the following example provided by Stedman (1976), who used these procedures with a 9-year-old school phobic child. This girl became extremely anxious in any school situation that required her to perform a new or poorly mastered academic task in front of the class. Two situations in which this was a problem were her reading and music classes, where she attempted to avoid the anxiety-producing situations by leaving school before the classes began.

Behavioral intervention included two forms of desensitization, a standard systematic desensitization program using an imagined hierarchy, and an in vivo desensitization program implemented by a teacher in the school setting. A contingency contracting system also was implemented, in which the girl's parents reinforced her school attendance. Treatment involved 16 sessions with the child and her parents, and two meetings with school personnel.

The systematic desensitization program followed the procedures outlined earlier and focused on the main precipitant of the child's school avoidance—music class. She was trained in deep muscle relaxation, and a hierarchy was developed that focused on music class and had as a general theme performance of unfamiliar or complex school-related tasks in front of peers and teachers. Systematic desensitization began in the 3rd therapy session and continued through the 14th session, with the child progressing through the hierarchy while deeply relaxed and reporting continuing anxiety reduction.

Starting with the 8th therapy session, her music teacher was incorporated into an in vivo desensitization program that was carried out in or near the school setting and included the following steps: (a) her teacher would tutor her outside school until she reached a level of skill similar to that of her class; (b) she would reenter music class for 10-minute periods, but would not be required to play her recorder; and (c) she would remain in music class for the full time and would play the recorder (Stedman, 1976, p. 285).

This multifaceted treatment program was successful in that the child began attending class regularly and reported little anxiety in doing so. A 2-year follow-up indicated that the treatment gains had been maintained, and she was even leading her classmates in singing at school.

Another example of desensitization is illustrated by Wish, Hasazi, and Jurgela (1973), who have reported on the treatment of an 11-year-old boy with a fear of loud noises that centered around firecrackers, thunder, or jet engines. The child was able to learn muscle relaxation techniques and assisted in the construction of a fear hierarchy, which consisted of a list of the fear-provoking sounds arranged in order of their anxiety-evoking properties. An audiotape was made of the sounds from the hierarchy, with his favorite music superimposed. The child was instructed to relax in a dark room and to listen to the tape with the volume gradually increased during the 8-day (three sessions per day) treatment period. Following treatment he could listen comfortably to the previously feared sounds. A 9-month follow-up showed that his tolerance for previously feared noises was maintained. Such methods also have been successful in the clinical treatment of a wide range of other childhood fears and phobias (Morris & Kratochwill, 1983).

Systematic desensitization with adults has received considerable research attention, and its effectiveness has been well demonstrated. Although the procedure enjoys considerable case-study support for use with anxious and fearful children, there have been few controlled experimental studies with this population (Graziano, DeGiovanni, & Garcia, 1979; Hatzenbuehler & Schroeder, 1978). The few controlled studies that exist with children do not argue strongly for the superiority of systematic desensitization over other behavioral treatment procedures (Richards & Siegel, 1978). However, the findings from case studies and controlled experimental investigations do suggest that systematic desensitization, when combined with other techniques such as positive reinforcement, and when tied to eventual in vivo practice with the feared situation, can be a potentially useful method for reducing a variety of anxiety-based problems in children (Cayton & Russo, 1985; Morris & Kratochwill, 1983; Ollendick, 1979).

Bell-and-Pad Procedure

The most frequently used behavioral method for treating enuresis is the bell-and-pad or urine-alarm conditioning procedure. This device was first used by Mowrer and Mowrer (1938) to assist children in learning nocturnal bladder control. Although the bell-and-pad procedure originally was based on a respondent conditioning paradigm, the exact mechanism by which this device works remains to be clearly determined (Lovibond, 1963). The systematic use of this procedure in the treatment of enuresis did not occur until 30 years after it was initially developed.

In the procedure the child sleeps on a specially constructed pad of two foil outersheets, the top one having holes that are separated by an absorbent paper connected to a buzzer. As soon as the child begins to urinate, the wet paper sheet completes an electric circuit that activates a bell or buzzer. The noise from the buzzer is presumed to inhibit further urination by causing the bladder muscles to reflexively (automatically) contract. Because the noise awakens the child at the time his or her bladder is full, after a number of pairings of the noise with the full bladder the child learns to respond to his or her bladder cues without the assistance of the bell and pad. Thus, bladder distension automatically elicits contraction of the sphincter muscles and awakening of the child. Most children eventually learn to sleep through the night without wetting the bed.

Despite misconceptions that drinking before bedtime should be curtailed, in this procedure the child may be encouraged to drink fluids before bedtime to ensure that sufficient pairings of the bell and the act of micturition will occur. The child is asked to sleep without pajama bottoms or in light underclothing so that the alarm is triggered at the exact moment urination begins. When the alarm is activated, the child is instructed to turn it off and go immediately to the bathroom to finish urinating. If the child has difficulty awakening, the parents are asked to arouse him or her, making sure the child is completely awake before going to the bathroom by washing the child's face with cold water. After returning to the bedroom, the device is reset, the pad is washed off, and a dry sheet is placed on the pad. The child typically is given primary responsibility to remake the bed before going back to sleep.

The parents are asked to keep a record of the number of times that the bell rings each night and the diameter of the wet spot on the sheet. As the procedure begins to take effect, the size of the spot and the number of times that the bell rings should decrease. The child is rewarded with praise and sometimes with tangible reinforcers for each dry night, and parents are instructed not to make negative comments about any wetting incidents.

To maintain parental motivation and to ensure that the procedure is followed correctly, weekly contact with the parents and child is essential, particularly during the first weeks of treatment. Use of the bell-and-pad typically is discontinued following 2 weeks of consecutive dry nights. Parents are told that relapses (typically defined as 2 or more wet nights in a week) may occur and are asked to reinstate the bell-and-pad procedure if this happens. Most enuretic children require 4 to 8 weeks with the bell-and-pad method before treatment can be terminated. More detailed descriptions of this procedure are presented by Lovibond and Coote (1970), Schaefer (1979), and Walker (1978).

Research had revealed a high degree of effectiveness for the bell-and-pad procedure for children who remain in treatment. Bell-and-pad conditioning has been found superior to traditional psychotherapy (DeLeon & Mandell, 1966; Werry & Cohressen, 1965) and drug therapy (Forrester, Stein, & Susser, 1964; Young & Turner, 1965) for the treatment of childhood enuresis. This procedure has demonstrated an initial success rate of 70 to 90% (Doleys, 1983; Faschingbauer, 1975).

One problem in the use of the procedure is the relapse rate, which has been suggested to be as high as 35% (Doleys, 1983; Shaffer, 1985). Several procedural modifications of the bell-and-pad method have been found to effectively reduce the relapse rate, however. One of these involves the reintroduction of the bell and pad immediately after relapse occurs. An overlearning procedure, in which the child increases fluid intake before bedtime and the bell-and-pad apparatus is used beyond the criterion point at which it is normally withdrawn, also has been effective in reducing relapses (Jehu, Morgan, Turner, & Jones, 1977; Young & Morgan, 1972). Doleys (1983), however, has cautioned that excessive fluid intake prior to bedtime might result in renewed bedwetting and therefore discourage the parents and child. He suggests that some children may benefit from a delay in the use of the overlearning technique for several weeks after the initial training period, and that a gradual increase in the amount of liquids be used.

A final method for reducing the rate of relapse is intermittent reinforcement, in which the alarm is activated during a variable number of wetting incidents (usually 50–70%) rather than after each wetting has occurred. According to learning theory, this procedure should be effective in reducing the relapse rate because an intermittent schedule of reinforcement makes the trained response (i.e., bladder control) more resistant to extinction. The use of an intermittent reinforcement schedule has shown promise as a technique for reducing the relapse rate with the bell and pad (Finley, Besserman, Bennett, Clapp, & Finley, 1973; Finley & Wansley, 1976).

To date, few therapeutic interventions can claim as dramatically positive results as the bell-and-pad procedure. In fact, it is the best researched and most commonly used approach for the treatment of enuresis (Doleys, 1983).

PROCEDURES BASED ON OPERANT CONDITIONING

Treatment techniques derived from principles of operant conditioning are the most frequently used behavior therapy procedures with children (Phillips & Ray, 1980). All operant approaches to treatment involve the manipulation of environmental events that precede or follow the target behavior. Operant treatment procedures are used to teach new behaviors not in the child's repertoire, to increase the frequency of desirable behaviors occurring at a low rate, and to decrease the frequency of undesirable behaviors occurring at an excessive rate or at inappropriate times or in inappropriate settings. For an excellent general discussion of the clinical application of operant methods, see Kazdin (1984).

Positive Reinforcement

A behavioral procedure in which a positive event contingently follows a behavior and increases the frequency of that behavior is called positive reinforcement. An event is a positive reinforcer only if it has the effect of increasing the frequency of the behavior that it follows. Positive reinforcement is probably the most frequently used operant conditioning procedure in behavioral intervention programs and often is used in conjunction with other operant procedures.

Allen, Hart, Buell, Harris, and Wolf (1964) used positive reinforcement to increase the peer interaction of a socially isolated 4-year-old girl. The child spent almost no time playing with other children at her preschool and instead engaged in numerous behaviors that resulted in considerable attention from the teachers. Because classroom observations indicated that adult attention was reinforcing for the child, it was decided to make adult attention contingent on her interaction with other children. Therefore, the teachers were instructed initially to give attention to the child when she was exhibiting any form of social behavior with other children. Solitary activities or interactions solely with adults were to be given little or no attention from the teachers. When she was interacting regularly with other children for extended periods of time, adult reinforcement of her interactions gradually was made more intermittent, until she received the same attention from teachers as her classmates. Observations at the end of the treatment program indicated that she was spending approximately 60% of her time interacting with other children, in contrast to less than 20% during the pretreatment period.

Bernal (1972) describes the treatment of a 5-year-old girl who insisted on eating only strained baby foods and refused any of her mother's efforts to feed her regular table foods. The problem developed when the child choked on a piece of solid food, and her mother responded by feeding her strained baby foods. When the mother attempted to reintroduce solid food the child refused, and a pattern of mealtime conflicts ensued. Earlier attempts by the mother to treat the problem, some as extreme as withholding baby food until the child became hungry enough to eat solid foods, had failed. A medical examination completed prior to treatment indicated that there were no physical causes for the eating problem.

Observations of mother–child interactions during mealtimes revealed that the mother inadvertently was reinforcing the child for undesirable eating habits by providing attention contingent on solid food refusal and numerous noneating-related behaviors. Therefore, the mother was instructed to reinforce the child with praise and smiles only when the child took a bite of table food and to ignore all other behaviors. Treatment consisted of a gradual shaping procedure in which preferred foods were used to reinforce the eating of foods she disliked. Table foods were gradually introduced, and eating small quantities was reinforced by praise and access to the baby food. As previously nonpreferred foods acquired desirable properties and were accepted readily by the child, they too were used as reinforcers for new table foods. Television viewing also was made contingent on eating greater quantities of table food. Within a period of 4 months the girl added 50 table foods to her diet that she previously had refused to eat.

Closely related to positive reinforcement is the technique of shaping, which entails reinforcing successive approximations to some desired response, with each approximation slightly closer to the final target behavior. Many positive reinforcement programs utilize shaping. Hence, rather than demanding that the child display a perfectly performed desired behavior immediately, successive approximations to it are reinforced. Semenoff, Park, and Smith (1976) provide a good example of shaping in the treatment of a 6-year-old electively mute child. He only talked with his parents and a few close relatives and peers, and he would not talk at all in the classroom. The child was cooperative and followed directions in the classroom, but instead of asking for help if he had a problem, he would become frustrated and cry. Teachers and speech therapists in the school collaborated in a behavioral treatment program which entailed several facets. The major component was a shaping procedure that moved all the way from imitating actions and simple sounds in a speech therapy room with several children present to speaking in whispers, in spoken words, to his teacher alone in class, and, after several more successive approximations, to speaking spontaneously in front of the whole class. The child continued to show progress through the rest of the first-grade school year, with no deterioration in his behavior during the summer. Bimonthly follow-up during second grade indicated that he was responding orally to 100% of the questions directed to him, and the frequency of his spontaneous remarks equaled the class average. His parents also reported that he was considerably more comfortable with strangers at home and was talking to a wide variety of people.

Extinction

In this procedure reinforcement is withheld from a behavior that was previously reinforced, resulting in a decrease in the frequency of that behavior. Although extinction can be an effective technique for reducing or eliminating the frequency of a behavior, its effect on behavior is often a gradual process (Kazdin, 1984). As a result, extinction may not be appropriate with destructive or highly disruptive behaviors that necessitate a more rapid reduction in the behavior's occurrence. Because extinction does not teach new behaviors, it typically is used in conjunction with a reinforcement program. Desirable behaviors are reinforced that are incompatible with the behavior to be eliminated. In essence, the patient is taught alternative methods for obtaining reinforcement in a more acceptable manner.

The modification of severe tantrums in a 21-month-old child using an extinction procedure was reported by Williams (1959). When the parents left the room after putting the child to bed, he would scream until they returned. As a result, the parents often had to spend as much as 2 hours in the room until the child fell asleep. Based on the assumption that parental attention was serving as a reinforcer for tantrum behavior, an extinction procedure was implemented in which the parents were instructed to put the child to bed and not return to the room when the tantrum occurred. Initially, the duration of screaming after the child was put to bed was 45 minutes. By the second night, the screaming had dropped to 15 minutes, and by the 10th night the child no longer exhibited tantrum behavior when his parents left the room. No further tantrums were reported by the parents at a 2-year follow-up.

An extinction procedure was used by Wolf, Brinbrauer, Williams, and Lawler (1965) to eliminate the daily vomiting behavior of a 9-year-old mentally retarded girl. Observations suggested that the vomiting was being reinforced and maintained by the contingencies of permitting her to leave the classroom and return to her dormitory when the vomiting occurred. The teacher was instructed to ignore the vomiting and to keep the child in the classroom until school ended. A reversal procedure, in which pretreatment conditions temporarily were reinstated, demonstrated that the vomiting behavior was maintained by allowing the child to leave the classroom after each episode. Using this treatment approach, the vomiting behavior was completely eliminated within 30 class days.

Alford, Blanchard, and Buckley (1972) also used contingent withdrawal of social attention (i.e., an extinction procedure) in the treatment of a hospitalized 17-year-old girl. She had started to vomit after every meal when she was 7 years old and continued to do so since that time. As a result of this problem, she was severely depressed. No physical cause for the vomiting could be identified, and medication failed to alleviate the problem. In the hospital it was observed that the girl often sought attention from the hospital staff and other patients, suggesting that the attention she received from others for her vomiting may have served as an effective positive reinforcer. Therefore, during the first phase of treatment two hospital staff members sat alone with her in her room and interacted with her in a pleasant manner as she ate each of her daily meals. If she vomited, however, the staff members immediately left the room and did not return during the meal. During the second phase of treatment the girl was permitted to eat with the other patients in the dining room. With the girl's knowledge, the other patients were instructed to ignore any of her discussions about nausea or vomiting and to move away from her table if she actually vomited. By the fourth meal following the initiation of the treatment program, the girl ceased to vomit. After 12 consecutive meals with no episodes of vomiting, she was discharged from the hospital. Only one incident of vomiting was reported at a 7-month follow-up.

Punishment

A procedure is defined as punishment when the presentation of an aversive event or the removal of a positive event is made contingent on the appearance of a behavior and when it decreases the frequency of that behavior. When it is considered that punishment is defined empirically in terms of the ability of a procedure to bring about reduction in behavior, it is clear that not all procedures *assumed* to be punishers are punishers in all cases. As but one example, spanking a child, which is assumed by most parents to be "punishment," may not necessarily decrease the frequency of the undesirable behavior; for some children it may serve as a positive reinforcer by providing negative attention.

One form of punishment involves the presentation of aversive events contingent on the occurrence of a given behavior. Two kinds of aversive events may serve as punishers for an individual. Primary aversive stimuli are naturally aversive to an organism and include electric shock, loud noises, and physical pain. Secondary (conditioned) aversive stimuli, on the other hand, acquire their aversive properties through repeated associations with events that are already aversive to the individual. Fines, reprimands, and statements of disapproval from significant others are all examples of secondary or learned aversive stimuli.

The second form of punishment involves the removal of positive events contingent on the performance of the undesirable behavior. For example, a child might lose an opportunity to watch television or to play outside for fighting with other children. There are basically two behavioral procedures that involve the removal of positive events. Time out (also referred to as time out from positive reinforcement) is a procedure in which the individual is removed, for a short period of time, to an area where reinforcing events, including interaction with others, are not available. Time out can be an effective strategy for decreasing undesirable behaviors, because it removes the individual from situations or events that may be reinforcing and which therefore maintain the problem behavior. In response cost, a penalty or fine is imposed or reinforcers are removed; for example, losing privileges or forfeiting tokens earned.

As with extinction, punishment should not be used as the only intervention strategy. Punishment provides the patient with feedback about what he or she is doing wrong. It does not teach the individual how to behave in a desirable manner. The application of punishment should be concurrent with the reinforcement of alternative, adaptive behaviors. There is some evidence that punishment suppresses rather than eliminates a response. This provides the therapist with an opportunity to condition other responses that are more desirable. If the desirable responses are also incompatible with the punished response, the likelihood that the maladaptive behavior will recur in the future is decreased.

Punishment techniques have been effective in decreasing a number of undesirable behaviors (Azrin & Holz, 1966; Kazdin, 1984; Matson & DiLorenzo, 1984). Because punishment procedures tend to produce a rapid decrease in the frequency of behavior, they are particularly useful in the management of self-injurious behaviors and behaviors that are highly dangerous or disruptive to others. Unless one is dealing with such problematic behaviors, however, it is best to try other intervention strategies first. Unpredictable side effects may result from the injudicious use of punishment procedures (Kazdin, 1984; Johnston, 1972). Potential side effects include:

1. Punishment may elicit motor and emotional responses, such as fear, that become conditioned to the situation or punishing agent and thereby interfere with the performance of desirable behaviors.
2. Termination of punishment reinforces escape behaviors, such as withdrawal.
3. The individual may learn to avoid the aversive situation and thus have no opportunity to be reinforced for desirable behaviors.
4. If the problem behavior is already an avoidance response (e.g., school phobia), punishment may increase its frequency.
5. Attempted punishment may be a reinforcer for the individual (e.g., negative attention).
6. Punishment may result in the modeling of an undesirable behavior (e.g., a child hit by parents may exhibit aggressive behavior when frustrated).

A dramatic demonstration of the use of contingent aversive stimulation with a young child exhibiting chronic ruminative vomiting was presented by Lang and Melamed (1969). Four months prior to behavioral intervention, this 9-month-old boy had begun to vomit shortly after each feeding. Three previous hospitalizations, extensive medical tests, and exploratory surgery failed to reveal any organic basis for the vomiting. A number of medical procedures, such as changes in the diet and feeding positions, antiemetic medications, and individualized nursing care, were attempted without success. At the time behavioral treatment was started, the child was in critical physical condition. He weighed only 12 pounds and was being fed by means of a tube inserted through his nose into his stomach. Behavioral treatment consisted of delivery of a brief and mild electric shock to the child's leg as soon as there was evidence of reverse paristalsis. Physiological recordings of muscular activity in the child's neck and throat were taken during treatment to determine with greater accuracy when reverse paristalsis was starting. These recordings enabled the therapists to deliver temporally precise punishment contingencies, and they insured that the aversive stimulus would be made to follow the vomiting behaviors and not normal sucking and feeding behaviors. A loud tone also was paired with the shock, so that the tone acquired aversive properties and eventually could be used by itself. To facilitate generalization, sessions were conducted at different times throughout the day and when the child was engaged in different activities. The shock was needed only infrequently after the first two feeding sessions in which it was used. By the sixth feeding session, vomiting no longer occurred after eating. Five days after treatment had been initiated, the child was discharged from the hospital and was continuing to eat without vomiting.

Assessments at 1 and 5 months following discharge from the hospital indicated that the child weighed 21 pounds and 26 pounds, respectively. At a 1-year follow-up the child showed continued weight gain, with no recurrence of the vomiting. In addition, he was more responsive to his environment, and social development was significantly improved.

Creer (1970) demonstrated the use of time out in the case of two 10-year-old boys who had a history of repeated admissions to the hospital because of frequent asthmatic attacks. Preliminary assessment suggested that the hospital setting had become very reinforcing for the boys, because it afforded an opportunity for special activities and attention from the hospital staff. It was discovered that the children intentionally exacerbated their asthmatic symptoms by hyperventilation and by not seeking medical assistance during the early stages of the attacks, presumably to seek admission to the hospital and avoid unpleasant social situations. Treatment involved a time-out procedure in which positive reinforcement was removed upon their entering the hospital. They were placed in a private room and permitted to leave only for eating and to go to the bathroom. Contacts with people other than the hospital staff were highly restricted and privileges, such as access to television and comic books, were removed. This procedure resulted in a significant reduction in subsequent asthma-related admissions and the length of time the boys remained in the hospital. Similar findings are reported by Creer, Weinberg, and Molk (1974).

A response-cost program was used by Burchard and Barrera (1972) to reduce the frequency of swearing, noncompliance, and aggressive behaviors in 11 mildly mentally retarded adolescents. When a child engaged in one of these undesirable behaviors, he or she was required to give up either 5 or 30 tokens that previously had been earned, or to take 5 or 30 minutes of time out. The results indicated that both response cost and time out were effective in considerably reducing the frequency of the target behaviors. Furthermore, the higher response cost and longer time-out period were more effective than the lower response cost and shorter time-out period.

An alternative procedure for reducing the frequency of undesirable behavior which includes a punishment component is overcorrection. Overcorrection teaches the consequences of inappropriate behavior and provides the opportunity to learn more appropriate behavior through restitution and positive practice, respectively (Foxx & Bechtel, 1982; Ollendick & Matson, 1978). In one type of overcorrection (restitutional overcorrection) the child is required to restore the environment to the state it was in prior to engaging in some inappropriate behavior and to subsequently improve the environment over its original condition. Thus, a child who throws food on the floor might be required to first clean up the mess and perhaps clean the entire floor and replace the food that has been ruined. The rationale for this restitutional approach is that the offender must assume responsibility for the disruption caused by his or her behavior by being required to restore the environment to a greatly improved state. Central to this approach is the identification of the effects of the child's inappropriate behavior on the environment, the implementation of procedures that improve this situation and, beyond this, teaching the child appropriate rather than inappropriate behaviors. A second type of overcorrection (positive practice overcorrection) can be used in those situations where behaviors may have little effect on the environment and a restitutional approach would be inappropriate. Here, for example, an autistic child engaging in repetitive rocking might be required to practice sitting appropriately in a chair for extended periods of time without rocking. Or, the autistic child who engages in stereotyped hand movements might be required to engage in behaviors involving more appropriate use of the hands.

In both types of overcorrection, compliance with the required activities is encouraged through verbal instructions if possible or with the degree of physical assistance necessary to ensure compliance if verbal instruction is not enough. It should be noted that in overcorrection the behaviors required of the child are to be practiced for an extended period of time, with no reinforcement being given by the therapist. This, combined with the fact that the child may be physically assisted in the performance of these behaviors, contributes to the aversiveness of the procedures (Schwartz & Johnson, 1985).

Azrin, Sneed, and Foxx (1974) have incorporated overcorrection into their dry-bed training program for enuresis. In addition to the bell-and-pad method described earlier, other procedures used in the training program include hourly awakenings and positive practice in going to the toilet. If the child wets the bed, he or she receives cleanliness training and positive practice. In positive practice, the child is required to engage in 20 consecutive trials, during which all responses involved in using the toilet are rehearsed. Cleanliness training consists of having the child change his or her wet clothes and bed sheets, and dispose of the wet ones. Several studies have suggested that this procedure significantly reduces or eliminates bed wetting (Azrin et. al., 1974; Doleys, 1983).

Overcorrection also has been used effectively in the treatment of self-stimulatory behaviors in autistic and mentally retarded children (Azrin, Kaplan, & Foxx, 1973; Foxx & Azrin, 1973; Harris & Wolchick, 1979). This procedure involves terminating the child's ongoing self-stimulatory behavior by verbal instruction or physical prompting and then having the child engage in incompatible behavior for a given time period. For example, an autistic child who engaged in frequent repetitive hand clapping was instructed to move his hand in several positions upon exhibiting the stereotypic behavior, including putting his hands above his head or in his pockets, or holding them together in front of him. His hands were manually guided by the teacher whenever he failed to follow her verbal commands. This technique was effective in virtually eliminating the child's inappropriate hand-clapping behavior (Foxx & Azrin, 1973).

Token Economy Programs

A systematic and highly complex reinforcement program in which tokens are used as reinforcers is referred to as a token economy. Tokens are conditioned reinforcers such as money, points, or stars. The individual is directly reinforced with the tokens for desirable behavior, and these tokens are later exchanged for desired backup reinforcers such as food, toys, and activities.

An effective token economy requires that the target behaviors on which the tokens are made contingent and the number of tokens that are administered for performing each behavior, as well as the exchange rate of tokens for backup reinforcers, be made explicit.

Token economy programs have been used in a wide range of settings and are particularly useful in motivating individuals with longstanding behavior problems (Kazdin, 1977). Such programs have been effective in teaching appropriate behaviors and reducing maladaptive behaviors with predelinquent youths in group homes (Phillips, 1968), children in special education classrooms (O'Leary & Drabman, 1971), and institutionalized retarded individuals (Girardeau & Spradlin, 1964).

There are a number of advantages of token programs over other types of reinforcement systems (Kazdin & Bootzin, 1972; Kazdin, 1977).

1. Tokens can be given immediately, without undue concern as to what each person will buy with them.
2. The therapist can individualize reinforcers, which is particularly important when working with more than one individual in the treatment program.
3. Tokens may be used anywhere and at any time, without satiation. They do not lose their reinforcing value through repeated use, because a variety of backup reinforcers are available.
4. With tokens, no delay in reinforcement is required. They can be delivered without interfering with ongoing desirable behaviors.
5. Token systems are particularly effective when social reinforcement such

as praise and attention are not adequate incentives for the individual to respond in appropriate ways.

Token programs usually are regarded as a temporary method for promoting behavior change when other procedures have been ineffective. Because token reinforcers are an artificial modification of the natural environment, it is important to begin gradually weaning the individual from the program once the desirable behaviors occur at an acceptable rate. The token program gradually is withdrawn and replaced with more natural reinforcers such as praise, attention, and approval.

An excellent example of a token economy system is a residential treatment program for predelinquent and delinquent youth referred to as Achievement Place (Phillips, 1968; Phillips, Phillips, Fixsen, & Wolf, 1971), a community-based group home for adjudicated youth. The treatment program is carried out by teaching parents (a professionally trained married couple) in a small family-style setting located in a home in the youths' own community. The role of the teaching parents is to develop in the youths a number of adaptive behaviors, such as social, academic (i.e., study), self-care, and prevocational skills, to enable them to find work in their community.

The treatment program at Achievement Place is based on a flexible motivational point system in which a broad range of target behaviors (e.g., reading books, doing homework, stealing, being aggressive, disobeying) are followed immediately by either positive or negative consequences in the form of earned and lost points for appropriate and inappropriate behaviors, respectively. Points earned can be cashed in for a range of privileges such as getting an allowance, watching TV, and being able to stay up late. When a youth has maintained an acceptable level of performance in the token economy system, he or she can graduate to a merit system in which points are no longer used and all privileges are free. Evaluations of this treatment program have indicated that it is effective in reducing the recidivism rate of delinquency and in improving school attendance and academic performance (Fixsen, Phillips, Phillips, & Wolf, 1972; Kirgin, Braukmann, Fixsen, Phillips, & Wolf, 1975).

Biofeedback

There have been a number of reports of the use of biofeedback in the treatment of somatic disorders in children (e.g., Siegel, 1983; Varni, 1983). Biofeedback teaches an individual to become aware of internal body sensations so that he or she can control certain basic physiological responses. This is accomplished by means of highly specialized equipment that converts physiological activity into bioelectric signals, which in turn provide the individual with continuous external feedback regarding a particular visceral response such as heart rate, muscle activity, and skin temperature.

When the individual has modified his or her physiological response so that it matches a given criterion, positive visual or auditory feedback is immediately provided. This feedback serves as a reinforcer for the physiological response that precedes it. Although the reasons why this method works are not entirely understood, it is clear that people can learn to alter certain visceral responses by receiving precise information from biofeedback monitoring.

Biofeedback techniques have been applied directly to the respiratory tract to improve lung functioning and increase the amount of airflow in children with asthma. Kahn, Staerk, and Bonk (1973) treated asthmatic children between the ages of 8 and 15 by using "counterconditioning" via biofeedback. That is, the children were trained to give responses that were incompatible with asthmatic constriction of the airways. Following experimentally induced constriction of the airways, respiratory function was electronically monitored by the biofeedback apparatus. A red light was activated and praise was delivered when the child responded with relaxed and dilated bronchial airways. Following 15 training sessions, there was a significant improvement in the experimental group compared to the no-treatment control group. Follow-up 8 to 10 months after treatment indicated that the control group had significantly more asthmatic attacks, used more medication, and had more visits to the hospital emergency room than the treated children. Using a similar biofeedback procedure, Feldman (1976) reported an improvement in airway obstruction (equivalent to that produced by medication) for four chronically asthmatic children.

Diamond and Franklin (1976) reported the use of a biofeedback treatment program for children with migraine headaches. Thirty-two children between the ages of 9 and 18 years who were diagnosed as having migraine headaches were treated with the following procedures: (a) skin temperature biofeedback (i.e., hand warming) with autogenic phrases involving suggestions of warmth and relaxation, (b) progressive muscle relaxation training, and (c) electromyographic (EMG) biofeedback using the frontalis (forehead) muscle, which was presumed to be an indicator of overall bodily muscle tension. Twenty-six of the 32 children were found to respond favorably to this treatment package, as reflected by a decrease in both the frequency and severity of the migraine headaches. For an in-depth review of the literature on biofeedback treatments of children, see Finley (1983).

MODELING PROCEDURES

Learning by observing or imitating the behavior of others is an important process in the acquisition of a range of child behaviors. Extensive research has shown that modeling is an effective way for children to acquire, strengthen, and weaken behaviors. Modeling techniques are based primarily on the principles of observational learning.

There is currently substantial literature regarding the use of modeling procedures in the treatment of children's anxiety and fear-related behaviors. Modeling techniques have been used most often with common childhood fears, such as fear of animals and water, and medical and dental fears. The usual procedure is to have the child observe one or several models approach and interact with the feared stimulus with no adverse consequences or with positive consequences resulting from the model's behavior. In addition, approach behavior usually occurs in a graduated manner, so that the model engages in increasingly more anxiety-arousing interactions with the feared stimulus (Perry & Furukawa, 1980). Thus, the model teaches new response patterns to the child or disinhibits the performance of previously established behaviors by reducing the fear-evoking capacity of the situation (Bandura, 1969).

Three variations of modeling have been used in treating anxiety and fears in children: live modeling, symbolic modeling, and participant modeling (Ollendick & Cerny, 1981). Each type of procedure varies in the extent to which the model's behavior is presented in the presence of the fearful child, and in the model's interaction with the child.

In live modeling, the model performs graduated approach behavior to the fear-related stimulus in the child's presence; however, the child is not required to interact with the feared object. This approach was used in a classic study by Bandura, Grusec, and Menlove (1967) to increase the approach behaviors of young children who had demonstrated a fear of dogs. The models were two 4-year-old males who were not fearful of dogs. Fearful children were assigned to one of four groups. In the first group (modeling plus positive context), the children observed as a model fearlessly approached and interacted with a dog in a highly enjoyable partylike atmosphere. In another group (modeling plus neutral context) children watched the model simply approach the dog. The third group (exposure plus positive context) attended a party with the dog present; however, no approach behavior was modeled. In the fourth group (positive context only), the children participated in a party in which neither the dog nor the model was present.

Children in each group were exposed to eight 10-minute treatment sessions over 4 consecutive days. In the two modeling conditions, the model performed a series of interactions with the dog that included a gradual change in the physical restraints on the dog, the closeness of the model's approach behaviors, and the duration of the model's contact with the dog. For example, during the first treatment session, the dog was confined to a playpen and the model periodically talked to and petted the dog. By the fifth session, the model walked the dog on a leash outside the playpen.

In the last session, the model climbed into the playpen and fed, hugged, and petted the dog. The effectiveness of treatment was assessed by a behavioral avoidance test before and after treatment and at a follow-up session. Children in the two modeling groups demonstrated significantly more approach behaviors after treatment and follow-up than the children in the two control groups. In addition, children in the two modeling conditions were able to perform the terminal task in the behavioral avoidance test (remaining alone in the room with the dog) significantly more often than the other two groups.

White and Davis (1974) investigated the relative effectiveness of (a) live modeling, (b) familiarization with dental equipment (without modeling), and (c) no treatment on children who exhibited fears that interfered with dental treatment. The subjects were 15 children between 4 and 8 years of age. In the live modeling group, 5 children observed, behind a one-way mirror, a child-model undergoing dental treatment. Children in the familiarization group observed the dentist and his assistant name and handle the same dental equipment used in the modeling condition, without the model present. Children in the control group participated in neither activity. The children in the first two conditions received the experimental interventions during six sessions over a 3-week period. The results indicated that approach behaviors, ranging from "walking down the hall" to "allowing of restoration," were not different between the live model and familiarization groups. Both of these treatments produced significantly greater approach behavior than was found in the no-exposure group, both at the immediate dental treatment session and at a 6-month follow-up. However, children in the modeling group did exhibit fewer hiding and refusal of treatment behaviors than the exposure-only group. Children in the exposure-only group also requested that a significant other (i.e., mother, sibling) be present during dental treatment, whereas no such requests were made by children in the modeling group.

Symbolic modeling typically involves the presentation of a model on film or videotape. Another type of symbolic modeling, called covert modeling, consists of an individual picturing in imagery himself or herself engaging in various approach behaviors with the feared event. Although covert modeling procedures have been investigated with adults, there have been relatively few reports of the use of this technique with children (Rosenthal, 1980).

The use of filmed modeling in the treatment of childhood fears is illustrated in a report by Bandura and Menlove (1968). This study was similar to the Bandura et al. (1967) one described above, except that the model was presented on film. One group of children observed a film that depicted a fearless 5-year-old boy engaging in increasingly greater contacts with a dog. A second group watched a film showing several male and female peer-models interacting with dogs of different sizes. A control group viewed a film about Disneyland that was similar in length to those observed by the other two groups. Children in both film-modeling groups were found to increase their approach behavior ratings significantly on a behavioral avoidance test, as compared to the control group. No significant differences were observed on approach behaviors between the two experimental groups. Children in the multiple-model condition, however, were somewhat more successful than those in the single-model group in remaining alone in the room with the dog.

In an attempt to assist children in their efforts to cope with normal and realistic fears of hospitalization and surgery, Melamed and Siegel (1975) explored the effectiveness of filmed modeling. Participants in this study were 60 children, aged 4 to 12, who had been admitted to a pediatric hospital for elective surgery. These children had no prior history of hospitalization and were scheduled for tonsillectomies, hernia operations, or urinary-genital tract surgery. Thirty children each, matched for age, sex, race, and type of operation, were assigned to the experimental and control groups. Numerous self-report, physiological, and behavioral outcome measures were used to assess state and trait anxiety in the children. These measures were given before and after the children viewed the film, the evening before surgery, and 1 month following discharge from the hospital. In addition, parents completed a measure of the children's behavior problems prior to hospitalization and again at follow-up.

Prior to admission to the hospital, children in the experimental and control groups viewed one of the two films described as follows (Melamed & Siegel, 1975, pp. 514–515):

The experimental film, entitled *Ethan Has an Operation*, depicts a 7-year-old white male who has been hospitalized for a hernia operation. This film is 16 minutes in length and consists of 15 scenes showing various events that most children encounter when hospitalized for elective surgery from time of admission to time of discharge, including the child's orientation to the hospital ward and medical personnel such as the surgeon and anesthesiologist, having a blood test and exposure to the standard hospital equipment, separation from the mother, and scenes in the operating and recovery rooms. In addition to explanations of the hospital procedures provided by the medical staff, various scenes are narrated by the child, who describes his feelings and concerns that he had at each stage of the hospital experience. Both the child's behavior and verbal remarks exemplify the behavior of a coping model so that while he exhibits some anxiety and apprehension, he is able to overcome his initial fears and complete each event in a successful and nonanxious manner. . . . The subjects in the control group were shown a 12-minute film entitled *Living Things Are Everywhere*. The control film was similar in interest value to the experimental film in maintaining the children's attention but was unrelated in content to the hospitalization. It presents the experiences of a white preadolescent male who is followed on a nature trip in the country.

The results indicated a significant reduction in preoperative and postoperative anxiety in children who observed the peer-modeling film, but no reduction in anxiety for the children who observed the control film. Children in the filmed modeling group evidenced lower sweat-gland activity, fewer self-reported medical fears, and less anxiety-related behaviors than those in the control group. These results were obtained both the night before surgery and at a 1-month postsurgical examination. Moreover, only children in the control group were reported by their parents to have exhibited an increase in the frequency of behavior problems following hospitalization. These findings suggest that filmed modeling may help children to cope more effectively with potentially stressful experiences and actually prevent fearful reactions from occurring.

Bandura (1976) has stated that participant modeling, which involves a combination of modeling and guided reinforced practice, is a particularly effective procedure. Participant modeling provides an opportunity for the fearful child to observe a model demonstrating approach behaviors to the feared object and then, after observing the model, to make direct contact with the feared object. In a carefully structured and graduated process, modeled performances by the therapist (or some other model) immediately are imitated and practiced by the child under gradually more difficult and real-life conditions. The therapist initially provides extensive encouragement, physical or verbal prompts, information feedback, and positive reinforcement for the child's practice attempts, gradually phasing out his or her involvement as the child learns to engage in the previously feared activity independently (Bandura, 1976; Rosenthal & Bandura, 1978). Bandura and his associates also have found that behavior change can be accelerated and generalization enhanced in participant modeling by the use of (a) adjunctive procedures or so-called response-induction aids, such as prompts, joint performance with the therapist, or gradually increasing time of exposure to the feared object; and (b) self-directed performance, that is, independent practice with a variety of situations following the initial participant-modeling session (Bandura, Jeffrey, & Gajdos, 1975; Bandura, Jeffrey, & Wright, 1974).

Lewis (1974) examined the effectiveness of a participant-modeling procedure in reducing children's fear of the water. The relative effectiveness of participation plus filmed modeling, filmed modeling alone, participation alone, and no treatment were investigated with 40 children who exhibited a fear of swimming at a summer camp. The children, who were between 5 and 12 years of age, were administered a 16-item behavioral avoidance test that required increasingly difficult swimming behaviors, including climbing into a pool 3 feet deep and putting one's face in the water. Based on their performance on this test, they were matched for levels of avoidance and assigned to one of the four groups. In the modeling-plus-participation group, each child was shown an 8-minute film of three peer-models performing graded tasks in the swimming pool similar to those in the behavioral avoidance test. The film included a narration in which the models described their performance and how they were feeling, and praised themselves for their activities in the water. Immediately after they viewed this film, an experimenter accompanied the children to the pool and for 10 minutes physically assisted them in practicing the items on the avoidance test, praising them for any activity that was attempted or completed. Children in the modeling-alone condition saw the 8-minute film, but instead of practicing in the pool with the experimenter, played a 10-minute game of checkers. The children in the participation-only group saw an 8-minute cartoon with no themes of water activity and then were taken to the pool, where they attempted the items on the avoidance test with the physical assistance and encouragement of the experimenter. Finally, children in the control group viewed the cartoon and then played checkers with the experimenter for 10 minutes. The results demonstrated that all three treatment groups exhibited less fear and engaged in more water activities than the control group. Children in the modeling-plus-participation group, however, exhibited a greater reduction in fear of the water and more improvement in swimming ability than any other group.

Finally, the use of participant modeling with several patients having severe needle phobias is illustrated in a study by Taylor, Ferguson, and Wermuth (1977). The patients were hospitalized for diagnostic tests or surgery that necessitated the withdrawal of blood samples or the injection of medication. Because of their intense fear of needles, however, the patients fainted or refused to cooperate with the medical procedures.

A participant-modeling approach was used in which the patients were given an instrument tray containing intravenous equipment including syringes, covered needles, and alcohol swabs. When the patient was able to tolerate having the tray in the room the therapist identified and handled each item and gave it to the patient. The patient was instructed to handle the equipment until he or she felt comfortable in doing so. In addition, the patient was asked to handle increasingly larger covered needles. This exercise was continued until the patient reported no longer feeling anxious, at which time the covers were removed from the needles. When the patient was able to hold the syringe and exposed needle comfortably, the therapist demonstrated touching the needle to his own skin, moving the needle up and down his arm. The patient was asked to imitate this behavior. A syringe was then filled with liquid, and the patient was asked to copy the therapist's behavior of injecting the liquid into an orange. The patient continued to practice this activity until any anxiety in doing it ceased. Finally, the therapist stuck the needle into his own arm to demonstrate that there were no adverse consequences. The treatment session culminated in the therapist drawing blood from the patient's arm. The whole procedure, which lasted approximately an hour, significantly reduced the patients' anxiety and distress and enabled them to engage in the previously feared medical procedures.

There is currently substantial literature regarding controlled investigations of modeling in the treatment of childhood fears and anxiety-related behaviors (Gelfand, 1978; Graziano et al., 1979; Melamed & Siegel, 1980; Richards & Siegel, 1978; Thelen, Fry, Fehrenbach, & Frautschi, 1979). Some investigators have suggested that modeling approaches may be the most effective means of fear reduction in children (Bandura, 1976; Gelfand, 1978). Ollendick (1979) has summarized the research literature in this area by noting that the short-term efficacy of modeling procedures has been demonstrated adequately in the treatment of circumscribed fears. Participant modeling in particular appears to be a rather powerful treatment procedure that induces rapid behavior change (Gelfand & Hartmann, 1984).

In addition to the treatment of fear-related behaviors, modeling procedures have been used successfully to reduce social isolation with nursery school children. For example, O'Connor (1969) showed preselected socially isolated children 11 filmed scenes depicting a child who initially observed social interactions and then joined in the activities with positive consequences. Behavioral measures revealed that social withdrawal was sharply reduced as a result of viewing the film, compared with no change for the control children.

Evers and Schwarz (1973) treated 13 socially withdrawn nursery school children with either exposure to a modeling tape or exposure to the modeling tape plus teacher reward for classroom interaction. Results showed that exposure to a film modeling appropriate social behavior reduced social isolation with or without praise, and improvement was maintained at a 4-week follow-up.

Likewise, Keller and Carlson (1974) exposed a group of socially isolated preschool children to videotapes depicting children engaged in socially rewarding behaviors. Children in the control group viewed a nature film. Results showed that children in the modeling group increased the amount of social rewards that they gave to and received from peers. Their level of social interaction also increased more than that of the control children.

Sarason and Ganzer (1973) used modeling to reduce antisocial behavior and teach new, adaptive ways of dealing with common problem situations. A group of delinquent boys observed models who demonstrated social skills such as how to apply for a job, resist peer pressure, and delay gratification. The boys practiced imitating the modeled behavior and received feedback regarding their performance. A second group of delinquents attended group meetings in which the same topics were discussed but no modeling or imitation occurred. Boys in the control group received no special treatment. Both the modeling and the discussion treatment groups showed positive changes in attitudes and behavior, as well as less recidivism than the control group.

A number of researchers have demonstrated the efficacy of modeling and adjunctive techniques to teach self-care skills to mentally retarded children. Modeling tends to be an excellent teaching method, particularly with children who have difficulty learning via more traditional techniques. For example, Eaton and Brown (1974) used modeling and reward to train 13 mentally retarded youths in appropriate mealtime behavior. Using verbal instruction, modeling, and manual guidance, O'Brien and Azrin (1972) trained 12 institutionalized mental retardates in the use of proper table manners. Finally, Horner and Keilitz (1975) have also used verbal instructions, modeling, and prompts with social rewards to teach 8 mentally retarded adolescents tooth brushing skills.

COGNITIVE BEHAVIORAL TECHNIQUES

Cognitive behavior therapy with children is a relatively new development within the area of behavior therapy, and a diverse set of procedures are subsumed under the general label of cognitive behavioral techniques. These procedures, including self-instruction training and training in problem solving, teach children alternative methods of responding to problem situations by modifying their patterns of thinking (for overviews see Hobbs, Moguin, Tyroller, & Lahey, 1980; Kendall, 1981, 1984; Kendall & Braswell, 1985). The general goal of these cognitive behavioral treatment strategies is the development of mediating cognitive skills that guide the child's problem-solving behaviors and facilitate his or her performance on tasks that require careful planning prior to responding.

Illustrative of the basic approach, Meichenbaum and Goodman (1971) used a self-instructional program to help 7- to 9-year-old "impulsive" children gain control over their behavior through self-verbalization. The training program was conducted over a 2-week period and consisted of four half-hour individual sessions. The children learned self-instructional procedures as they performed a variety of perceptual-motor tasks. The training program involved the following functions: (a) the therapist performed the task and verbalized aloud, as the child observed, (b) the child performed the same task as the therapist instructed aloud, (c) the child performed the task and verbalized the instructions aloud, (d) the child performed the task while whispering the instructions, and finally (e) the child performed the task while mentally repeating the instructions.

The following example illustrates the instructions that the child was taught to say aloud and then repeat mentally during a particular task (Meichenbaum & Goodman, 1971, p. 117).

Okay, what is it that I have to do? You want me to copy the picture with the different lines. I have to go slow and be careful. Okay, draw the line down, down, good; then to the right, that's it; now down some more and to the left. Good, I'm doing fine so far. Now back up again, no, I was supposed to go down. That's okay. Just erase the line carefully . . . Good. Even if I make an error I can go slowly and carefully. Okay, I have to go down now. Finished. I did it.

This brief training program resulted in considerable improvement in the children's performance on a number of tasks. Furthermore, these improvements were maintained at a 4-week follow-up assessment.

Kanfer, Karoly, and Newman (1975) investigated the effectiveness of verbal self-control procedures for reducing children's fear of the dark. Forty-five children, 5 to 6 years of age, who evidenced strong fear of the dark participated in the study. The program was conducted in a classroom equipped with rheostat illumination controls, covered windows, and an intercom system. The children were randomly assigned to one of three groups and taught one of three sets of verbal cues: (a) sentences that emphasized the child's active control or competence in the dark such as "I can take care of myself in the dark" (competence group), (b) sentences that focused on reducing the aversive qualities of the dark such as "the dark is a fun place to be" (stimulus group), and (c) sentences that had a neutral content such as portions from "Mary Had a Little Lamb" (control group). The children were trained in a well-lit room and then were tested in a totally dark room, with duration of darkness tolerance and terminal light intensity (children could increase the illumination) serving as outcome measures.

Children were trained individually, with the trainer communicating to them from another room via an intercom. They were instructed to listen to and repeat the self-instructional sentences exactly as presented. They were then provided with additional instructions for elaborating statements that were to accompany the initial sentences. For example, the competence group children were told (Kanfer et al., 1975, p. 253): "When you are in the dark, you know that you can turn on the light when you feel like it. In your room when it's dark, you know exactly where everything is— your bed, your dressers, your toys. When you are in the dark, if you felt like talking to someone you could always talk to your parents, and they could hear you."

As can be seen in Figure 5.3, the effect of the competence-focused treatment condition was superior to the other groups. Self-instructional sentences that emphasized the child's competence to cope with the anxiety-inducing experience of being in a dark room resulted in the longest

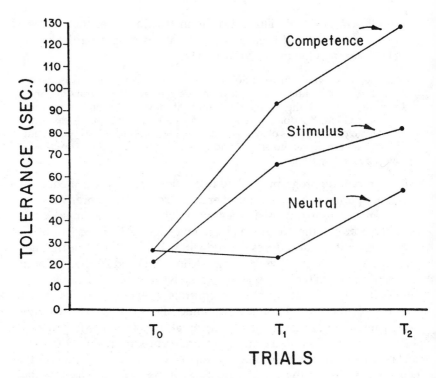

Figure 5.3. Mean time for tolerance of the dark in the competence, stimulus, and neutral verbalization groups during pretest baseline (T_0) and two test trials (T_1 and T_2). From "Reduction of Children's Fear of the Dark by Competence-Related and Situational Threat-Related Verbal Cues" by F. H. Kanfer, P. Karoly, and A. Newman, 1975, *Journal of Consulting and Clinical Psychology, 43*, p. 254. Copyright 1975 by the American Psychological Association. Reprinted by permission.

tolerance times. Self-instructional sentences that emphasized the positive aspects of the dark were less effective, whereas neutral sentences had no appreciable effect. Hence, self-instructions related to active coping and competence with the feared stimulus may be an important component in enabling children to confront anxiety-arousing experiences.

Siegel and Peterson (1980) examined the effectiveness of a self-control treatment package on anxiety reduction in preschool children undergoing dental treatment. Forty-two children were assigned to one of three conditions. In a self-control coping skills group, the children were taught cue-controlled muscle relaxation in which they repeated the words "calm and nice," which were paired with relaxation. Each child also was taught to use imagery of a pleasant scene or favorite place that he or she selected with the assistance of the experimenter. Finally, each child was instructed to use calming self-talk by repeating the phrase, "I will be all right in just a little while. Everything is going to be all right." Children assigned to a sensory information group were presented with the typical sights, sounds, and sensations that they would experience during restorative dental treatment. Finally, children in a control group were read a story that was unrelated to the dental experience. The results indicated that both self-control coping skills training and sensory information were significantly more effective than the control condition in reducing disruptive behaviors, ratings of anxiety and discomfort, and physiological arousal, and in increasing the children's cooperation during the dental procedures. There were no significant differences between the two treatment groups. These treatment effects were maintained at a second dental treatment session approximately 1 week after exposure to the experimental conditions (Siegel & Peterson, 1981).

Russell and Thoresen (1976) taught problem-solving skills to neglected, predelinquent, and acting-out children at a residential family-style treatment program. The children were found to be deficient in effective problem-solving skills, and when describing troublesome situations from their past, they often made statements such as "It was the first thing I thought to do, so I did it," "I didn't know what else I could do," and "I didn't know that [result] would happen" (Russell & Thoresen, 1976, p. 377). Russell and Thoresen referred to problem solving as "decision making" and attempted to teach decision making to these children, viewing it as an important self-control skill. Steps in their decision-making process included identifying the problem, collecting information, generating alternatives, recognizing personal values, anticipating probable consequences, making the best possible decision, and evaluating the decision at a later time. These self-management skills would presumably help the children cope with problems at the residential program and later with problems occurring at home. These skills might also give the children practice in maintaining the appropriate behaviors taught at the treatment program and allow them to contend effectively with relapses and new problems that inevitably would arise.

Russell and Thoresen incorporated what they believed to be the critical steps in decision making into a self-contained program of written materials, integrated with an audiotape, that was aimed at children 8 to 12 years old. One component of the program was a decision chart (Fig. 5.4) that included all components of the decision-making process. The child had to learn and complete each step in sequence and then fill out several charts correctly for both simulated and real personal problem situations before completing the training program. The teaching strategy and format used with the program are described as follows (Russell & Thoresen, 1976, p. 379):

> To allow maximum individualization with minimal staff monitoring, the [program] uses an informal, programmed text structure. First, the child reads a simple explanation for each step of the problem-solving process with ex-

Name_____

Date _____

DECISION CHART

My problem is: I don't know what to do _____

_____

1. I could _____
    good point _____
    bad point _____
2. I could _____
    good point _____
    bad point _____
3. I could _____
    good point _____
    bad point _____

Before I decide I will need to know _____

_____

My decision is # _____, because I value_____

THE NEXT DAY....
after I carried out my decision.

A GOOD result of my decision was: _____
A BAD result of my decision was: _____

NEXT TIME I have the same problem I think I will: _____

_____

Figure 5.4. A decision chart used in teaching decision-making and problem-solving skills to children. From "Teaching Decision-Making Skills to Children" by M. L. Russell and C. E. Thoresen, in *Counseling Methods* (p. 379), edited by J. D. Krumboltz and C. E. Thoresen, 1976, New York: Holt, Rinehart & Winston. Reprinted by permission.

amples, pictures, and a cartoon character who "thinks out loud" for the reader. The child then listens to a story on the audiotape demonstrating an application of the step by another child or posing a problem for the listener to solve. In this way the child listens to a social model using the decision process and then obtains practice in applying each of the decision steps to a problem situation himself. At the conclusion of each section the child completes a brief quiz requiring knowledge of all the steps taught in previous sections.

The results of Russell and Thoresen's skills development program were tentative but encouraging. First, five children participating in a preliminary treatment outcome study clearly learned the decision-making steps. On the average, they were able to recall 90% of the decision-making sequence and reproduce 90% of the decision chart from memory. Second, following training these children demonstrated significant improvement in their ability to generate possible alternative solutions and to anticipate probable consequences of their actions when presented with simulated problem situations. The average number of alternative solutions given by the children almost doubled from pre- to post-treatment, going from 4.8 to 7.6 solutions.

Spivack and Shure (1974, 1982) have developed a comprehensive cognitive behavioral program for teaching interpersonal problem-solving skills to young children. Their previous research had determined that age-appropriate, interpersonal problem-solving skills were related to behavioral and social adjustment. They identified several skills that were important for effective interpersonal problem solving, including: (a) an awareness of potential problems that may occur when people interact; (b) generation of alternative solutions to problems; (c) means-ends thinking, or identifying the steps necessary to carry out solutions to a problem; (d) consequential thinking, or understanding the consequences of behavior for oneself and for others; and (e) cause-effect thinking, or understanding that social interactions may be a reciprocal-interactive process influenced by the feelings and actions of the people involved.

Based on these research findings, the investigators have developed a treatment program that attempts to teach young children the skills necessary to solve interpersonal problems and conflicts. The training program consists of a series of daily lessons that are presented to the children for a period of almost 3 months. The first series of lessons are intended to teach prerequisite language skills, the appreciation and expression of emotion, and the importance of taking another person's perspective. The remaining lessons teach specific problem-solving skills through elaborate training scripts that consist of structured games and dialogues between the children and trainer, who is usually the classroom teacher. In these lessons the children are exposed to hypothetical interpersonal problem situations. They are encouraged to generate alternative solutions to these situations and to consider the possible consequences of the solutions. The emphasis throughout training is not to teach the children what to think in interpersonal problem situations, but rather how to think. That is, they are not taught specific solutions to problems but rather a general problem-solving skill, which they can apply to many conflict situations. An example of a dialogue between a teacher and child during a problem in the classroom is presented in Table 5.4 to illustrate how the teacher helps the child practice problem-solving skills in real-life situations.

Table 5.4. A Dialogue Used to Teach Problem-Solving Skills

Teacher: What's the matter? What happened? (*Elicits child's view of the problem*)
Child: Robert won't give me the clay!
Teacher: What can you do or say so he will let you have the clay? (*Elicits a problem solution*)
Child: I could ask him.
Teacher: That's one way. And what might happen next when you ask him? (*Guides consequential thinking*)
Child: He might say no.
Teacher: He might say no. What else could you try? (*Guides child to think of an alternative solution*)
Child: I could snatch it.
Teacher: That's another idea. What might happen if you do that? (*Does not belittle the child's solution; continues to guide consequential thinking*)
Child: He might hit me.
Teacher: How would that make you feel? (*Asks the child to consider his own feelings*)
Child: Mad.
Teacher: How would Robert feel if you grabbed the clay? (*Asks the child to consider the feelings of another*)
Child: Mad.
Teacher: Can you think of something different you can do or say so Robert won't hit you and you both won't be mad? (*Guides the child to think of further solutions*)
Child: I could say, "You keep some and give me some."
Teacher: That's a different idea. (*Reinforces the idea as "different," not as "good," avoiding adult judgments*)

Note. Adapted from "The Cognition of Social Adjustment: Interpersonal Cognitive Problem-Solving Training" by G. Spivack and M. B. Shure, in *Advances in Clinical Child Psychology,* Vol. 5 (pp. 323–372) edited by B. B. Lahey and A. E. Kazdin, 1982, New York: Plenum. Copyright 1982 by Plenum Publishing Corp. Reprinted by permission.

Evaluations of this program have indicated that development of problem-solving skills as a function of the training have led to enhanced social adjustment, which in turn generalizes over time and place. The degree of cognitive change in relation to behavioral adjustment has been found to be highly correlated, in that children who have improved the most in cognitive skills also demonstrate the greatest teacher-rated behavioral adjustment. The treatment program has been particularly effective in controlling impulsivity and increasing social interactions in withdrawn and inhibited children (Shure & Spivack, 1972).

OUTCOME RESEARCH

There has been more research evaluating the effectiveness of child behavior therapy than is available on any other approach to the treatment of child behavior disorders. This extensive research on treatment outcome in behavior therapy is due, in large part, to the emphasis that behavior therapy places on the scientific method and the continuous evaluation of progress in therapy (Kazdin, 1984).

Considerable research evidence is available supporting the efficacy of numerous behavioral intervention techniques with a diverse range of populations and problems. Behavior therapy procedures have been used effectively in the home, at school, and in institutional and community settings. In addition, parents, teachers, and numerous paraprofessionals have been trained to use a variety of behavioral techniques with children directly in the settings where the behavior problems occur. In many instances, behavioral treatment programs have resulted in rapid and dramatic changes in problem behaviors that were resistant to other forms of treatment. Among the problem areas that have been treated successfully with child behavior therapy are academic and school difficulties (Hallahan, Lloyd, Kauffman, & Loper, 1983; Lahey & Drabman, 1981; O'Leary & O'Leary, 1976), hyperactivity and attentional disorders (Barkley, 1983; Mash & Dalby, 1979), conduct disorders and juvenile delinquency (Kazdin & Frame, 1983; Patterson & Reid, 1973; Redner, Snellman, & Davidson, 1983), social skills deficits (Bornstein, Bellack, & Hersen, 1980; Combs & Slaby, 1977; Kendall & Morison, 1984; Gottman, Gonso, & Schuler, 1976), fears and phobic disorders (Graziano et al., 1979; Hatzenbuehler & Schroeder, 1978; Morris & Kratochwill, 1983; Siegel & Ridley-Johnson, 1985), numerous problems exhibited by autistic and retarded children (Brinbrauer, 1976; Forehand & Baumeister, 1976; Lovaas & Newsom, 1976; Schreibman, Koegel, Charlop, & Egel, 1982), and a variety of somatic disorders (Russo & Varni, 1982; Siegel, 1983).

There is much variability in the amount and quality of research that exists on the various behavioral techniques, with some approaches having more supporting research evidence than others. Some procedures have been investigated in well controlled experimental studies, and others have been explored primarily through single-case studies. Single-case studies using within-subject research methodologies can provide useful information about a treatment procedure (cf. Barlow & Hersen, 1984); however, they do not always permit a clear evaluation of the comparative effectiveness of several treatment procedures. In addition, their results tend to be more heuristic and suggestive than definitive regarding the effects of a procedure across a broad population of children. It is important to make a distinction between uncontrolled case studies without systematic assessment and well controlled single-subject experimental designs. The latter experimental procedures enable the investigator to evaluate whether a change in the child's behavior can be attributed to the treatment program rather than to some other events that might have occurred contiguous in time with treatment (cf. Barlow & Hersen, 1984; Kazdin, 1982). Unfortunately, many behavior problems are not readily amenable to group research designs that assess the comparative effects of various treatment approaches. For example, some disorders do not occur with sufficient frequency in children to permit group studies. Furthermore, some disorders are highly disruptive or present serious life-threatening conditions for the child. As a result, many of these disorders require immediate and complete intervention, often at the expense of an adequate experimental design. Notably lacking are long-term follow-up studies of the behavioral treatment of childhood disorders. Such research is needed to evaluate the extent to which treatment gains are maintained following termination of the formal treatment program.

Finally, there are few comparative outcome studies that have investigated the relative efficacy of behavior therapy techniques and other approaches to the treatment of childhood disorders. Notable exceptions include studies suggesting that the bell-and-pad treatment of enuresis is superior to traditional psychotherapy (DeLeon & Mandell, 1966; Werry & Cohressen, 1965) and drug therapies (Forrester et al., 1964; Young & Turner, 1965), and comparative studies of pharmacotherapy and behavioral procedures in treating hyperactive children that have indicated behavioral techniques to be either equally effective or superior in dealing with such problems as disruptive behavior and excessive activity levels (Ayllon, Layman, & Kandel, 1975; Christensen & Sprague, 1973). Additional comparative outcome studies are needed.

ISSUES AND TRENDS IN
CHILD BEHAVIOR THERAPY

MISCONCEPTIONS ABOUT BEHAVIOR THERAPY

There has been some criticism of behavior therapy on the grounds that it is a superficial form of treatment, does not deal with underlying causes, and focuses only on the symptoms of the person's disorder. Furthermore, it has been suggested that other symptomatic behaviors will appear following behavioral treatment (symptom substitution), because the underlying difficulties have not been resolved. Despite these concerns, there is considerable research evidence that symptom substitution does not occur automatically with behavior therapy if the appropriate controlling events are addressed in treatment (Kazdin & Wilson, 1978; Sloan, Staples, Cristol, Yorkston, & Whipple, 1975). Additionally, proponents of behavior therapy note that it is not a superficial treatment approach, as it takes into consideration a broad array of complex environmental and cognitive factors that contribute to and maintain the individual's current behavior problems.

Concerns also have been expressed regarding what some have suggested is behavior therapy's use of "bribery" in the form of tangible reinforcers such as candy, prizes, privileges, and other incentives that are often used in behavioral treatment programs with children. Some individuals have objected to such reinforcement programs on the basis that children are rewarded for activities that they should be expected to do anyway, or because the activities should be intrinsically rewarding without the need for external incentives.

Behavior therapists have responded by noting that bribery is typically defined as rewarding someone for engaging in immoral or illicit behavior and that it involves the "rewarding" of such behaviors before they have been performed. Reinforcement in behavioral treatment programs, on the other hand, is used to teach positive behaviors and is provided only after the child performs the behavior in question. Furthermore, some children function at a level that initially requires tangible reinforcers to initiate the learning of new behaviors. This is particularly true in the case of children with severe behavior disorders such as autism, or children with significant cognitive deficits who are not responsive to naturally occurring reinforcers in the environment. Behavior therapists also point out that the ultimate goal of treatment is to withdraw the use of tangible reinforcers so that social reinforcers, such as praise and affection, can be used as the primary means of maintaining desirable behaviors (O'Leary, Poulous, & Devine, 1972).

A final objection to behavior therapy is that it is mechanistic and dehumanizing. Behavior therapists note that this concern reflects a rather simplistic understanding of behavior theory as this approach involves more than the use of specific techniques. Behavior therapists, like therapists of other theoretical orientations, acknowledge the importance of the client–therapist relationship as essential to the therapy process (Wilson & Evans, 1977). In addition, behavior therapy often has been associated with a form of treatment in which the client has little or no control over what transpires in therapy. However, practitioners of this approach respond to this concern by noting that the client, whenever possible, is actively involved in setting the goals of treatment and in developing the treatment program. Furthermore, behavioral procedures attempt to maximize personal competence by teaching adaptive behaviors such as problem-solving and self-control skills to enable the client to have maximal control over his or her own behavior and the environment.

MAINTENANCE AND GENERALIZATION OF TREATMENT EFFECTS

As noted above, behavioral approaches have been used effectively with a broad range of child behavior problems and in diverse settings (Bijou & Redd, 1975; Gelfand and Hartmann, 1984; Ollendick & Cerny, 1981; Ross, 1981). However, the efficacy of any treatment must be judged not only for its ability to initiate behavior change but also for its potential in promoting the maintenance of behavior change following termination of the formal treatment program. Anyone trying to change maladaptive behaviors in children is faced with the problem of maintaining the treatment effects when the child returns to his or her natural environment. Available evidence indicates that the effective transfer and maintenance of behavior change does not occur automatically after the termination of treatment (Marholin, Siegel, & Phillips, 1976; Stokes & Baer, 1977), an observation that earlier led Baer, Wolf, and Risley (1968) to conclude that transfer of newly acquired behaviors must be specifically programmed into the therapeutic process and not left to chance.

Behavior therapists have proposed a number of strategies to facilitate the maintenance and generalization of treatment effects, including insuring that the contingencies of reinforcement are similar in both the treatment setting and natural environment, and teaching the child to control the antecedents and consequences of his or her own behavior (Goldstein & Kanfer, 1979; Marholin & Siegel, 1978; Stokes & Baer, 1977). Further research is clearly needed to identify factors that contribute to the most effective maintenance and generalization of therapeutic gains produced by behavior therapy procedures.

SIGNIFICANT OTHERS AS THERAPEUTIC AGENTS

Given the complex nature of behavior problems displayed by children, it is interesting to note the extent to which significant others, like parents and teachers, have been used as primary change agents in behavioral treatment programs. Under the professional guidance of behavior therapists, parents and teachers have been trained to successfully modify a variety of behavior problems in the child's natural environment. Because in many instances social contingencies maintain undesirable behaviors in children, the success of behavioral procedures is often highly dependent on the direct participation of significant members of the child's environment in the treatment program. This model of intervention, based on natural change agents in the child's environment, has received considerable attention in the behavioral literature (e.g., Berkowitz & Graziano, 1972; Dangel & Polster, 1984; O'Dell, 1974; O'Leary & O'Leary, 1976; Patterson, 1971). Outcome research on the effectiveness of parent behavior management programs has demonstrated positive behavioral changes in both child and parent that appear to be maintained following completion of the training programs (Gordon & Davidson, 1981; Forehand & King, 1977; Forehand & Peed, 1979).

In part because behavior therapy provides explicit and systematic treatment procedures, a treatment program designed by a therapist can be implemented effectively by people who have little previous experience with the techniques. This is not to say, of course, that regular supervision and evaluation by the therapist will not be needed in such cases. Training significant members of the child's environment to serve as "co-therapists" with the behavior therapist in a consultant-mediator model of treatment (Tharp & Wetzel, 1969) has important implications for the maintenance of behavior change following treatment termination, as well as the potential for preventing the development of further behavior problems.

SUMMARY

We have presented a number of behavior therapy techniques that are used in the treatment of numerous childhood problems. It was noted that these methods are based largely on empirically derived principles of learning, and that the goal of therapy is to employ these principles in modifying maladaptive behaviors and in helping the child learn more effective ways of responding to his or her environment.

A behavioral approach to assessment, involving a functional analysis of behavior, was reviewed, and differences between traditional and behavioral assessment methods were considered. Behavioral assessment focuses on the relationship between the problem behaviors and environmental events that elicit and maintain these behaviors. It is only after the relationship between the environmental events that the problem behavior has been determined that these events can be altered systematically to produce a desired change in behavior. Environmental events of particular interest to the behavior therapist are those that precede and follow the target behavior in a consistent manner. Behavioral assessment is an ongoing process that begins before treatment is implemented and continues until the treatment goals have been reached. Within this context several single-subject research designs, used to evaluate the effectiveness of behavioral techniques, were presented.

Also reviewed were a number of theoretical models—for example, respondent conditioning, operant conditioning, social learning theory, and cognitive behavior modification—that have influenced the development of behavioral treatment methods. Each of these learning models has provided the behavior therapist with a diverse range of specialized techniques for modifying maladaptive behaviors and teaching desirable and adaptive responses.

Much of the chapter reviewed frequently used behavior therapy procedures with children. Among those considered were systematic desensitization, the bell-and-pad procedure for treating enuresis, positive reinforcement, extinction, punishment, token economy programs, biofeedback training, modeling, and cognitive intervention strategies. In each case the behavioral technique was described, and its use in treating childhood behavior problems was illustrated.

Outcome research has shown behavioral techniques to be useful in treating a variety of child problems and populations in many settings. Research also has shown that parents and teachers can be trained to use behavioral intervention strategies to successfully modify a number of behavior problems in the child's natural environment. Although one should not conclude that behavioral approaches are the treatment of choice for all childhood problems, they do have much to offer in dealing with a broad range of childhood difficulties. Long-term follow-up studies are needed to evaluate whether treatment gains are maintained for extended periods of time after behavior therapy programs have been discontinued.

Finally, several misconceptions and objections to the use of behavior therapy techniques with children were analyzed. Among the issues addressed were symptom substitution, the use of "bribery" in token economy programs, and the supposedly mechanistic and dehumanizing nature of behavioral treatment procedures. Many of these concerns are unfounded; behavioral procedures, if applied appropriately and in a professional manner, represent an effective approach to dealing with many childhood problems and ultimately result in children having increased rather than decreased control over their environment and lives.

REFERENCES

Alford, G. S., Blanchard, E. B., & Buckley, T. M. (1972). Treatment of hysterical vomiting by modification of social contingencies: A case study. *Journal of Behavior Therapy and Experimental Psychiatry, 3,* 209–212.

Allen, K., Hart, B., Buell, S., Harris, R., & Wolf, M. (1964). Effects of social reinforcement on isolate behavior of a nursery school child. *Child Development, 35,* 511–518.

Ayllon, T., Layman, D., & Kandel, H. J. (1975). A behavioral-educational alternative to drug control of hyperactive children. *Journal of Applied Behavior Analysis, 8,* 137–146.

Azrin, N. H., & Holz, W. (1966). Punishment. In W. N. Honig (Ed.), *Operant behavior: Areas of research and application.* New York: Appleton-Century-Crofts.

Azrin, N. H., Kaplan, S. J., & Foxx, R. M. (1973). Autism reversal: Eliminating stereotyped self-stimulation of retarded individuals. *American Journal of Mental Deficiency, 18,* 241–248.

Azrin, N. H., Sneed, T. J., & Foxx, R. M. (1974). Dry-bed training: Rapid elimination of childhood enuresis. *Behaviour Research and Therapy, 12,* 147–156.

Baer, D. M., Wolf, M. M., & Risley, T. R. (1968). Some current dimensions of applied behavior analysis. *Journal of Applied Behavior Analysis, 1,* 91–97.

Bandura, A. (1969). *Principles of behavior modification.* New York: Holt, Rinehart & Winston.

Bandura, A. (1971). *Psychological modeling: Conflicting theories.* Chicago: Aldine-Atherton.

Bandura, A. (1976). Effective change through participant modeling. In J. D. Krumboltz & C. E. Thoresen (Eds.), *Counseling methods.* New York: Holt, Rinehart & Winston.

Bandura, A. (1977). *Social learning theory.* Englewood Cliffs, NJ: Prentice-Hall.

Bandura, A., Grusec, J., & Menlove, F. (1967). Vicarious extinction of avoidance behavior. *Journal of Personality and Social Psychology, 5,* 16–23.

Bandura, A., Jeffrey, R., & Gadjos, E. (1975). Generalizing change through self-directed performance. *Behaviour Research and Therapy, 13,* 141–152.

Bandura, A., Jeffrey, R., & Wright, C. (1974). Efficacy of participant modeling as a function of response induction aids. *Journal of Abnormal Psychology, 83,* 56–64.

Bandura, A., & Menlove, F. (1968). Factors determining vicarious extinction of avoidance behavior through symbolic modeling. *Journal of Personality and Social Psychology, 8,* 99–108.

Barkley, R. A. (1983). Hyperactivity. In R. J. Morris & T. R. Kratochwill (Eds.), *The practice of child therapy.* New York: Pergamon.

Barlow, D. H., & Hersen, M. (1984). *Single-case experimental designs: Strategies for studying behavior change.* New York: Pergamon.

Barton, E. J., & Ascione, F. R. (1984). Direct observation. In T. Ollendick & M. Hersen (Eds.), *Child behavioral assessment.* New York: Pergamon.

Berkowitz, B. P., & Graziano, A. M. (1972). Training parents as behavior therapists: A review. *Behaviour Research and Therapy, 10,* 297–317.

Bernal, M. E. (1972). Behavioral treatment of a child's eating problem. *Journal of Behavior Therapy and Experimental Psychiatry, 3,* 43–50.

Bijou, S. W., & Redd, W. H. (1975). Child behavior therapy. In S. Arieti (Ed.), *American handbook of psychiatry* (Vol. 5). New York: Basic Books.

Blanchard, E. B., & Epstein, L. H. (1978). *A biofeedback primer.* Boston: Addison-Wesley.

Bornstein, M. R., Bellack, A. S., & Hersen, M. (1980). Social skills training for highly aggressive children. *Behavior Modification, 4,* 173–186.

Bornstein, P. H., & Quevillon, R. P. (1976). The effects of a self-instructional package on overactive preschool boys. *Journal of Applied Behavior Analysis, 9,* 179–188.

Brinbrauer, J. S. (1976). Mental retardation. In H. L. Leitenberg (Ed.), *Handbook of behavior modification and behavior therapy.* Englewood Cliffs, NJ: Prentice-Hall.

Burchard, J. D., & Barrera, F. (1972). An analysis of time out and response cost in a programmed environment. *Journal of Applied Behavior Analysis, 5,* 271–282.

Cautela, J. R., & Groden, J. (1978). *Relaxation: A comprehensive manual for adults, children, and children with special needs.* Champaign, IL: Research Press.

Cayton, T. G., & Russo, D. C. (1985). The behavior therapies. In D. Shaffer, A. Ehrhardt, & L. Greenhill (Eds.), *The clinical guide to child psychiatry.* New York: Free Press.

Christensen, D. E., & Sprague, R.L. (1973). Reduction of hyperactive behavior by conditioning procedures alone and combined with methylphenidate (Ritalin). *Behavior Research and Therapy, 11,* 331–334.

Combs, M. L., & Slaby, D. A. (1977). Social skills training with children. In B. B. Lahey & A. E. Kazdin (Eds.), *Advances in clinical child psychology* (Vol. 1). New York: Plenum.

Creer, T. L. (1970). The use of time-out from positive reinforcement procedure with asthmatic children. *Journal of Psychosomatic Research, 14,* 117–120.

Creer, T. L., Weinberg, E., & Molk, L. (1974). Managing a hospital behavior problem: Malingering. *Journal of Behavior Therapy and Experimental Psychiatry, 5,* 259–262.

Dangel, R. F., & Polster, R. A. (1984). *Parent training.* New York: Guilford.

Davison, G. C., & Wilson, G. T. (1973). Processes of fear reduction in systematic desensitization: Cognitive and social reinforcement factors in humans. *Behavior Therapy, 4,* 1–21.

Deffenbacher, J. L., & Kemper, C. C. (1974). Systematic desensitization of test anxiety in junior high students. *The School Counselor, 12,* 216–222.

DeLeon, G., & Mandell, W. A. (1966). A comparison of conditioning and psychotherapy in the treatment of functional enuresis. *Journal of Clinical Psychology, 22,* 326–330.

Diamond, S., & Franklin, M. (1976). Biofeedback—choice of treatment in childhood migraine. *Biofeedback and Self-Regulation, 1,* 349–350.

Doleys, D. M. (1983). Enuresis and encopresis. In T. Ollendick & M. Hersen (Eds.), *Handbook of child psychopathology.* New York: Plenum.

Eaton, P., & Brown, R. I. (1974). The training of mealtime behavior in the subnormal. *British Journal of Mental Subnormality, 20,* 78–85.

Elliott, C., & Ozolins, M. (1983). Use of imagery and imagination in treatment of children. In E. Walker & M. Roberts (Eds.), *Handbook of clinical child psychology.* New York: Wiley.

Evans, I. M., & Nelson, R. O. (1977). Assessment of child behavior problems. In A. R. Ciminero, K. D. Calhoun, & H. E. Adams (Eds.), *Handbook of behavioral assessment.* New York: Wiley.

Evers, W. L., & Schwarz, J. C. (1973). Modifying social withdrawal in preschoolers: The effects of filmed modeling and teacher praise. *Journal of Abnormal Child Psychology, 1,* 248–256.

Faschingbauer, T. F. (1975). Enuresis: Its nature, etiology and treatment. *JSAS: Catalog of Selected Documents in Psychology, 5,* 194.

Feldman, G. M. (1976). The effects of biofeedback training on respiratory resistance in asthmatic children. *Psychosomatic Medicine, 38,* 27–34.

Finley, W. W. (1983). Biofeedback with children. In E. Walker & M. Roberts (Eds.), *Handbook of clinical child psychology.* New York: Wiley.

Finley, W. W., Besserman, R. L., Bennett, L. F., Clapp, R. K., & Finley, P. M. (1973). The effect of continuous, intermittent, and "placebo" reinforcement on the effectiveness of the conditioning treatment of enuresis nocturna. *Behaviour Research and Therapy, 11,* 289–297.

Finley, W. W., & Wansley, R. A. (1976). Use of intermittent reinforcement in a clinical-research program for the treatment of enuresis nocturna. *Journal of Pediatric Psychology, 4,* 24–27.

Firestone, P. (1976). The effects and side effects of time out on an aggressive nursery school child. *Journal of Behavior Therapy and Experimental Psychiatry, 6,* 79–81.

Fixsen, D. L., Phillips, E. L., Phillips, E. A., & Wolf, M. M. (1972). *The teaching-family model of group home treatment.* Paper presented at the annual meeting of the American Psychological Association, Honolulu.

Forehand, R., & Baumeister, A. A. (1976). Deceleration of aberrant behavior among retarded individuals. In M. Hersen, R. M. Eisler, & P. M. Miller (Eds.), *Progress in behavior modification* (Vol. 2). New York: Academic Press.

Forehand, R., & King, H. E. (1977). Noncompliant children: Effects of parent training on behavior and attitude change. *Behavior Modification, 1,* 93–108.

Forehand, R., & Peed, S. (1979). Training parents to modify noncompliant behavior of their children. In A. J. Finch, Jr., & P. C. Kendall (Eds.), *Clinical treatment and research in child psychopathology.* New York: Spectrum.

Forrester, R., Stein, Z., & Susser, M. A. (1964). A trial of conditioning therapy in nocturnal enuresis. *Developmental Medicine and Child Neurology, 6,* 158–166.

Foxx, R. M., & Azrin, N. H. (1973). The elimination of autistic self-stimulatory behavior by overcorrection. *Journal of Applied Behavior Analysis, 6,* 1–14.

Foxx, R. M. & Bechtel, D. R. (1982). Overcorrection. In M. Hersen, R. Eisler, & P. Miller (Eds.), *Progress in behavior modification* (Volume 13). New York: Academic Press.

Gelfand, D. M. (1978). Behavioral treatment of avoidance, social withdrawal and negative emotional states. In B. B. Wolman, J. Egan, & A. O. Ross (Eds.), *Handbook of treatment of mental disorders in childhood and adolescence*. Englewood Cliffs, NJ: Prentice-Hall.

Gelfand, D. M., & Hartmann, D. P. (1984). *Child behavior analysis and therapy* (2nd ed). New York: Pergamon.

Girardeau, F. L., & Spradlin, J. E. (1964). Token rewards in a cottage program. *Mental Retardation, 2*, 345–351.

Goldfried, M. (1971). Systematic desensitization as training in self-control. *Journal of Consulting and Clinical Psychology, 37*, 228–234.

Goldfried, M. R., & Kent, R. N. (1972). Traditional versus behavioral assessment: A comparison of methodological and theoretical assumptions. *Psychological Bulletin, 77*, 409–420.

Goldstein, A. P., & Kanfer, F. H. (1979). *Maximizing treatment gains: Transfer enhancement in psychotherapy*. New York: Academic Press.

Gordon, S. B., & Davidson, N. P. (1981). Behavioral parent training. In A. S. Gurman & D. P. Kniskern (Eds.), *Handbook of family therapy*. New York: Brunner/Mazel.

Gottman, J. M., Gonso, J., & Schuler, P. (1976). Teaching social skills to isolated children. *Journal of Abnormal Child Psychology, 4*, 179–197.

Graziano, A. M. (1971). *Behavior therapy with children* (Vol. 1). Chicago: Aldine-Atherton.

Graziano, A. M., DeGiovanni, I. S., & Garcia, K. A. (1979). Behavioral treatment of children's fears: A review. *Psychological Bulletin, 86*, 804–830.

Gross, A. M. (1984). Behavioral interviewing. In T. Ollendick & M. Hersen (Eds.), *Child behavioral assessment*. New York: Pergamon.

Hallahan, D. P., Lloyd, J. W., Kauffman, J. M., & Loper, A. B. (1983). Academic problems. In R. J. Morris & T. R. Kratochwill (Eds.), *The practice of child therapy*. New York: Pergamon.

Harris, S. L., & Wolchik, S. A. (1979). Suppression of self-stimulation: Three alternative strategies. *Journal of Applied Behavior Analysis, 12*, 185–198.

Hartmann, D. P., Roper, B. L., & Bradford, D. C. (1979). Some relationships between behavioral and traditional assessment. *Journal of Behavioral Assessment, 1*, 3–21.

Hatzenbuehler, L. C., & Schroeder, H. E. (1978). Desensitization procedures in the treatment of childhood disorders. *Psychological Bulletin, 85*, 831–844.

Hobbs, S., Moguin, L., Tyroller, M., & Lahey, B. (1980). Cognitive behavior therapy with children: Has clinical utility been demonstrated? *Psychological Bulletin, 87*, 147–165.

Horner, R. D., & Keilitz, I. (1975). Training mentally retarded adolescents to brush their teeth. *Journal of Applied Behavior Analysis, 8*, 301–309.

Humphreys, L. E., & Ciminero, A. R. (1979). Parent report measures of child behavior: A review. *Journal of Clinical Child Psychology, 5*, 56–63.

Jacobson, E. (1938). *Progressive relaxation*. Chicago: University of Chicago Press.

Jehu, D., Morgan, R. T. T., Turner, A., & Jones, A. A. (1977). A controlled trial of the treatment of nocturnal enuresis in residential homes for children. *Behaviour Research and Therapy, 15*, 1–16.

Johnston, J. M. (1972). Punishment of human behavior. *American Psychologist, 27*, 1033–1054.

Jones, M. C. (1924). The elimination of children's fears. *Journal of Genetic Psychology, 7*, 382–390.

Kahn, A. V., Staerk, M., & Bonk, C. (1973). Role of counter conditioning in the treatment of asthma. *Journal of Psychosomatic Research, 17,* 389–392.

Kallman, W. M., & Feuerstein, M. (1977). Psychophysiological procedures. In A. R. Ciminero, K. S. Calhoun, & H. E. Adams (Eds.), *Handbook of behavioral assessment.* New York: Wiley.

Kanfer, F. H., Karoly, P., & Newman, A. (1975). Reduction of children's fear of the dark by competence-related and situational threat-related verbal cues. *Journal of Consulting and Clinical Psychology, 43,* 251–258.

Kanfer, F. H., & Saslow, G. (1969). Behavioral diagnosis. In C. M. Franks (Ed.), *Behavior therapy: Appraisal and status.* New York: McGraw-Hill.

Kazdin, A. E. (1977). *The token economy: A review and evaluation.* New York: Plenum.

Kazdin, A. E. (1984). *Behavior modification in applied settings* (3rd ed.). Homewood, IL: Dorsey.

Kazdin, A. E., & Bootzin, R. R. (1972). The token economy: An evaluative review. *Journal of Applied Behavior Analysis, 5,* 343–372.

Kazdin, A. E., & Frame, C. (1983). Aggressive behavior and conduct disorder. In R. J. Morris & T. R. Kratochwill (Eds.), *The practice of child therapy.* New York: Pergamon.

Kazdin, A. E., & Wilson, G. T. (1978). *Evaluation of behavior therapy: Issues, evidence, and research strategies.* Cambridge, MA: Ballinger.

Keller, M. F., & Carlson, P. M. (1974). The use of the symbolic modeling to promote social skills in preschool children with low levels of social responsiveness. *Child Development, 45,* 912–919.

Kendall, P. C. (1981). Cognitive behavioral interventions with children. In B. Lahey & A. Kazdin (Eds.), *Advances in clinical child psychology* (Vol. 4). New York: Plenum.

Kendall, P. C. (1984). Cognitive behavioral self-control therapy for children. *Journal of Child Psychology and Psychiatry, 25,* 173–179.

Kendall, P. C., and Braswell, L. (1985). *Cognitive behavioral therapy for impulsive children.* New York: Plenum.

Kendall, P. C., & Morison, P. (1984). Integrating cognitive and behavioral procedures for the treatment of socially isolated children. In A. W. Meyers & W. E. Craighead (Eds.), *Cognitive behavior therapy with children.* New York: Plenum.

Kirgin, K. A., Braukmann, C. J., Fixsen, D. L., Phillips, E. L., & Wolf, M. M. (1975). *Is community-based correction effective? An evaluation of Achievement Place.* Paper presented at the annual meeting of the American Psychological Association, Chicago.

Koeppen, A. S. (1974). Relaxation training for children. *Elementary School Guidance and Counseling, 9,* 14–21.

Lahey, B. B., & Drabman, R. S. (1981). Behavior modification in the classroom. In W. E. Craighead, A. E. Kazdin, & M. J. Mahoney (Eds.), *Behavior modification: Principles and applications.* Boston: Houghton Mifflin.

Lang, P. J., & Melamed, B. G. (1969). Avoidance conditioning therapy of an infant with chronic ruminative vomiting. *Journal of Abnormal Psychology, 74,* 1–8.

Lazarus, A. A., & Abramovitz, A. (1962). The use of emotive imagery in the treatment of children's phobias. *Journal of Mental Science, 108,* 191–195.

Lewis, S. A. (1974). A comparison of behavior therapy techniques in the reduction of fearful avoidance behavior. *Behavior Therapy, 5,* 648–655.

Linehan, M. M. (1977). Issues in behavioral interviewing. In J. D. Cone & R. P. Hawkins (Eds.), *Behavioral assessment: New directions in clinical psychology.* New York: Brunner/Mazel.

Lovaas, O. I., & Newsom, C. D. (1976). Behavior modification with psychotic children. In H. Leitenberg (Ed.), *Handbook of behavior modification and behavior therapy*. Englewood Cliffs, NJ: Prentice-Hall.

Lovibond, S. H. (1963). The mechanisms of conditioning treatment of enuresis. *Behaviour Research and Therapy, 1*, 17–21.

Lovibond, S. H., & Coote, M. A. (1970). Enuresis. In C. G. Costello (Ed.), *Symptoms of psychopathology*. New York: Wiley.

Mahoney, M. J. (1974). *Cognition and behavior modification*. Cambridge, MA: Ballinger.

Marholin, D., & Siegel, L. J. (1978). Beyond the law of effect: Programming for the maintenance of behavior change. In D. Marholin (Ed.), *Child behavior therapy*. New York: Gardner.

Marholin, D., Siegel, L. J., & Phillips, D. (1976). Treatment and transfer: A search for empirical procedures. In M. Hersen, R. M. Eisler, & P. M. Miller (Eds.), *Progress in behavior modification* (Vol. 3). New York: Academic Press.

Mash, E. J., & Dalby, T. (1979). Behavioral interventions for hyperactivity. In R. Trites (Ed.), *Hyperactivity in children*. Baltimore, MD: University Park Press.

Mash, E. J., & Terdal, L. G. (1981). *Behavioral assessment of childhood disorders*. New York: Guilford.

Matson, J. L., & DiLorenzo, T. M. (1984). *Punishment and its alternatives*. New York: Springer.

McMahon, R. J. (1984). Behavioral checklists and rating scales. In T. Ollendick & M. Hersen (Eds.), *Child behavioral assessment*. New York: Pergamon.

Meichenbaum, D. H. (1977). *Cognitive behavior modification*. New York: Plenum.

Meichenbaum, D., & Goodman, J. (1971). Training impulsive children to talk to themselves: A means of developing self-control. *Journal of Abnormal Psychology, 77*, 115–126.

Melamed, B. G., & Siegel, L. J. (1975). Reduction of anxiety in children facing hospitalization and surgery by use of filmed modeling. *Journal of Consulting and Clinical Psychology, 43*, 511–521.

Melamed, B. G., & Siegel, L. J. (1980). *Behavioral medicine: Practical applications in health care*. New York: Springer.

Morris, R. J., & Kratochwill, T. R. (1983). *Treating children's fears and phobias: A behavioral approach*. New York: Pergamon.

Mowrer, O. H., & Mowrer, W. M. (1938). Enuresis: A method for its study and treatment. *American Journal of Orthopsychiatry, 8*, 436–459.

O'Brien, F., & Azrin, N. H. (1972). Training and maintaining a retarded child's proper eating. *Journal of Applied Behavior Analysis, 5*, 67–72.

O'Connor, R. D. (1969). Modification of social withdrawal through symbolic modeling. *Journal of Applied Behavior Analysis, 2*, 15–22.

O'Dell, S. (1974). Training parents in behavior modification: A review. *Psychological Bulletin, 81*, 418–433.

O'Leary, K. D. (1972). The assessment of psychopathology in children. In H. C. Quay & J. S. Werry (Eds.), *Psychopathological disorders of childhood*. New York: Wiley.

O'Leary, K. D., & Drabman, R. (1971). Token reinforcement programs in the classroom: A review. *Psychological Bulletin, 75*, 379–398.

O'Leary, S. G., & O'Leary, K. D. (1976). Behavior modification in the school. In H. Leitenberg (Ed.), *Handbook of behavior modification and behavior therapy*. Englewood Cliffs, NJ: Prentice-Hall.

O'Leary, K. D., Poulos, R. W., & Devine, V. T. (1972). Tangible reinforcers: Bonuses or bribes? *Journal of Consulting and Clinical Psychology, 38*, 1–8.

Ollendick, T. H. (1979). Fear reduction techniques with children. In M. Hersen, R. M. Eisler, & P. M. Miller (Eds.), *Progress in behavior modification* (Vol. 8). New York: Academic Press.

Ollendick, T. H. (1981). Self-monitoring and self-administered overcorrection: The modification of nervous tics in children. *Behavior Modification, 5,* 75–84.

Ollendick, T. H., & Cerny, J. A. (1981). *Clinical behavior therapy with children.* New York: Plenum.

Ollendick, T. H., & Hersen, M. (1984). *Child behavioral assessment.* New York: Pergamon.

Ollendick, T. H., & Matson, J. L. (1978). Overcorrection: An overview. *Behavior Therapy, 9,* 830–843.

Patterson, G. R. (1971). *Families: Application of social learning to family life.* Champaign, IL: Research Press.

Patterson, G. R., Ray, R. S., Shaw, D. A., & Cobb, J. A. (1969). *Manual for coding of family interactions* (Document No. 01234). New York, NY: ASIS/NAPS Microfiche Publications.

Patterson, G. R., & Reid, J. B. (1973). Intervention for families of aggressive boys: A replication study. *Behaviour Research and Therapy, 11,* 383–394.

Paul, G. L., & Bernstein, D. A. (1973). *Anxiety and clinical problems: Systematic desensitization and related techniques.* Morristown, NJ: General Learning Press.

Pavlov, I. P. (1927). *Conditioned reflexes.* (G. V. Ansep, Trans.). London: Oxford University Press.

Perry, M. A., & Furukawa, M. J. (1980). Modeling methods. In F. H. Kanfer & A. P. Goldstein (Eds.), *Helping people change* (2nd ed.). New York: Pergamon.

Phillips, E. L. (1968). Achievement place: Token reinforcement procedures in a home-style rehabilitation setting for ''pre-delinquent'' boys. *Journal of Applied Behavior Analysis, 1,* 213–223.

Phillips, E. L., Phillips, E. A., Fixsen, D. L., & Wolf, M. M. (1971). Achievement Place: Modification of the behaviors of predelinquent boys within a token economy. *Journal of Applied Behavior Analysis, 4,* 45–59.

Phillips, J. S., & Ray, R. S. (1980). Behavioral approaches to childhood disorders. *Behavior Modification, 4,* 3–34.

Redner, R., Snellman, L., & Davidson, W. S. (1983). Juvenile delinquency. In R. Morris & T. R. Kratochwill (Eds.), *The practice of child therapy.* New York: Pergamon.

Richards, C. S., & Siegel, L. J. (1978). Behavioral treatment of anxiety states and avoidance behaviors in children. In D. Marholin (Ed.), *Child behavior therapy.* New York: Gardner.

Rimm, D. C., & Masters, J. C. (1972). *Behavior therapy: Techniques and empirical findings.* New York: Academic Press.

Rosenthal, T. L. (1980). Modeling approaches to test anxiety and related performance problems. In I. G. Sarason (Ed.), *Test anxiety: Theory, research, and applications.* New York: Lawrence Erlbaum.

Rosenthal, T. L., & Bandura, A. (1978). Psychological modeling: Theory and practice. In S. L. Garfield & A. E. Bergin (Eds.), *Handbook of psychotherapy and behavior change* (2nd ed.). New York: Wiley.

Ross, A. O. (1981). *Child behavior therapy: Principles, procedures and empirical basis.* New York: Wiley.

Russel, M. L., & Thoresen, C. E. (1976). Teaching decision-making skills to children. In J. D. Krumboltz & C. E. Thoresen (Eds.), *Counseling methods.* New York: Holt, Rinehart & Winston.

Russo, D. C., & Varni, J. W. (Eds.). (1982). *Behavioral pediatrics: Research and practice.* New York: Plenum.

Sarason, I. G., & Ganzer, V. J. (1973). Modeling and group discussion in the rehabilitation of juvenile delinquents. *Journal of Counseling Psychology, 20,* 442–449.

Schaefer, C. E. (1979). *Childhood enuresis and encopresis.* New York: Van Nostrand.

Schreibman, L., Koegel, R. L., Charlop, M. H., & Egel, A. (1982). Autism and childhood schizophrenia. In A. S. Bellack, M. Hersen, & A. E. Kazdin (Eds.), *International handbook of behavior modification and therapy.* New York: Plenum.

Schwartz, S., & Johnson, J. H. (1985). *Psychopathology of childhood.* Elmsford, NY: Pergamon.

Semenoff, B., Park, C., & Smith, E. (1976). Behavioral interventions with a 6-year-old elective mute. In J. D. Krumbaltz & C. E. Thoresen (Eds.), *Counseling methods.* New York: Holt, Rinehart & Winston.

Shaffer, D. (1985). Nocturnal enuresis: Its investigation and treatment. In D. Shaffer, A. Ehrhardt, & L. Greenhill (Eds.), *The clinical guide to child psychiatry.* New York: Free Press.

Shapiro, E. S. (1979). Restitution and positive practice overcorrection in reducing aggressive-disruptive behavior: A long-term follow-up. *Journal of Behavior Therapy and Experimental Psychiatry, 10,* 131–134.

Shure, M. B., & Spivack, G. (1972). Means-ends thinking, adjustment and social class among elementary school-aged children. *Journal of Consulting and Clinical Psychology, 38,* 348–353.

Siegel, L. J. (1983). Psychosomatic and psychophysiological disorders. In R. J. Morris & T. R. Kratochwill (Eds.), *The practice of child therapy.* New York: Pergamon.

Siegel, L. J., & Peterson, L. (1980). Stress reduction in young dental patients through coping skills and sensory information. *Journal of Consulting and Clinical Psychology, 48,* 785–787.

Siegel, L. J., & Peterson, L. (1981). Maintenance effects of coping skills and sensory information on young children's response to repeated dental procedures. *Behavior Therapy, 12,* 530–535.

Siegel, L. J., & Ridley-Johnson, R. (1985). Anxiety disorders of childhood and adolescence. In P. H. Bornstein & A. E. Kazdin (Eds.), *Handbook of clinical behavior therapy with children.* Homewood, IL: Dorsey.

Skinner, B. F. (1953). *Science and human behavior.* New York: Macmillan.

Sloane, R. B., Staples, F. R., Cristol, A. H., Yorkston, N. H., & Whipple, K. (1975). *Psychotherapy versus behavior therapy.* Cambridge, MA: Harvard University Press.

Spivack, G., & Shure, M. B. (1974). *Social adjustment of young children: A cognitive approach to solving real-life problems.* San Francisco: Jossey-Bass.

Spivack, G., & Shure, M. B. (1982). The cognition of social adjustment: Interpersonal cognitive problem-solving training. In B. B. Lahey & A. E. Kazdin (Eds.), *Advances in clinical child psychology* (Vol. 5). New York: Plenum.

Stedman, J. M. (1976). Family counseling with a school-phobic child. In J. D. Krumboltz & C. E. Thoresen (Eds.), *Counseling methods.* New York: Holt, Rinehart & Winston.

Stokes, T. F., & Baer, D. M. (1977). An implicit technology of generalization. *Journal of Applied Behavior Analysis, 10,* 349–367.

Taylor, C. B., Ferguson, J. M., & Wermuth, B. M. (1977). Simple techniques to treat medical phobias. *Postgraduate Medical Journal, 53,* 28–32.

Tharp, R. G., & Wetzel, R. J. (1969). *Behavior modification in the natural environment.* New York: Academic Press.

Thelen, M., Fry, R. A., Fehrenbach, P. A., & Frautschi, N. (1979). Therapeutic videotape and film modeling: A review. *Psychological Bulletin, 86,* 701–720.

Varni, J. W. (1983). *Clinical behavioral pediatrics: An interdisciplinary biobehavioral approach.* New York: Pergamon.

Wahler, R. G., House, A. E., & Stambaugh, E. E. (1976). *Ecological assessment of child problem behavior.* New York: Pergamon.

Walker, C. E. (1978). Toilet training, enuresis, encopresis. In P. R. Magrab (Ed.), *Psychological management of pediatric problems* (Vol. 1). Baltimore, MD: University Park Press.

Ward, M. H., & Baker, B. L. (1968). Reinforcement therapy in the classroom. *Journal of Applied Behavior Analysis, 1,* 323–328.

Watson, J. B., & Raynor, R. (1920). Conditioned emotional reactions. *Journal of Experimental Psychology, 3,* 1–14.

Werry, J., & Cohressen, J. (1965). Enuresis—An etiological and therapeutic study. *Journal of Pediatrics, 67,* 423–431.

White, W. C., & Davis, M. T. (1974). Vicarious extinction of phobic behavior in early childhood. *Journal of Abnormal Child Psychology, 2,* 25–37.

Williams, C. (1959). The elimination of tantrum behavior by extinction procedures. *Journal of Abnormal and Social Psychology, 59,* 269.

Wilson, G. T., & Evans, I. M. (1977). The therapist–client relationship in behavior therapy. In R. S. Gurman & A. M. Razin (Eds.), *The therapist's contribution to effective psychotherapy: An empirical approach.* New York: Pergamon.

Wish, P. A., Hasazi, J. E., & Jurgela, A. R. (1973). Automated direct deconditioning of a childhood phobia. *Journal of Behavior Therapy and Experimental Psychiatry, 4,* 279–283.

Wolf, M. M., Brinbrauer, J. S., Williams, T., & Lawler, J. A. (1965). A note on apparent extinction of the vomiting of a retarded child. In L. P. Uillmann & L. Krasner (Eds.), *Case studies in behavior modification.* New York: Holt, Rinehart & Winston.

Wolpe, J. (1958). *Reciprocal inhibition therapy.* Stanford, CA: Stanford University Press.

Young, G. C., & Morgan, R. T. T. (1972). Overlearning in the conditioning treatment of enuresis: A long-term follow-up study. *Behaviour Research and Therapy, 10,* 419–420.

Young, G. C., & Turner, R. (1965). CNS Stimulant drugs and conditioning treatment of nocturnal enuresis. *Behaviour Research and Therapy, 3,* 93–101.

6

BIOLOGICAL APPROACHES
TO THE TREATMENT OF
BEHAVIOR PROBLEMS

A review of the literature reveals two major biological treatment approaches to child psychopathology: psychotropic medications and alterations in diet. The use of psychotropic medications began in the 1930s with Charles Bradley's use of stimulants to treat behaviorally disturbed children. Beginning in the 1940s, anticonvulsant medications were used for the treatment of behavioral disturbances thought to have a neurological basis. The major tranquilizers, or antipsychotic medications, were first synthesized in the 1950s and were used for the treatment of a broad range of nonpsychotic conditions in children, as well as for the management of psychosis. Antianxiety drugs, typically sedatives, were introduced in the treatment of sleep disturbances and anxiety states. In the 1960s antidepressant medications were developed and used in the treatment of enuresis, phobias, and other behavioral disturbances. It was not until the mid 1970s that antidepressant medications were also used for the treatment of preadolescent depression. Although some clinical studies were reported before this time, there was no real agreement as to the symptoms characteristic of childhood depression. In fact, some professionals did not believe in the concept of childhood depression, and others felt it was rare. Lithium carbonate, an antimanic medication, was introduced in the late 1960s for the treatment of aggressive and hyperactive states, especially in children or adolescents with a family history of manic depressive illness. Thus, by 1970 five major classes of psychotropic medications had been delineated: stimulants, antipsychotics, antidepressants, antianxiety drugs, and antimanics.

From the 1930s there has been a marked increase in the use of drugs to treat a wide variety of emotional and behavioral disturbances in children. Antipsychotic medications have been used extensively in residential treatment centers, and stimulant drugs have been used widely in the outpatient treatment of attention deficit disorders. The other classes of medications have been used less extensively, with the exception of the antidepressant drug imipramine for the symptomatic treatment of nocturnal enuresis. The 1970s marked the beginning of an antidrug movement in this country that was to some extent a reaction to the increased use of illicit drugs across the nation. There was also concern that drugs, such as the stimulants and antipsychotics, were being used to overcontrol the behavior of children and adolescents, while more time consuming and costly behavioral and educational methods were ignored (Schrag & Divoky, 1975). As a result of this antidrug movement, described by Sprague (1978), new federal agencies and guidelines have been instituted to optimize the safe and ethical use of psychotropic medications in clinical research and practice.

In light of the general antidrug atmosphere of the 1970s, it is not surprising that alternatives to medication were sought. Feingold (1974) proposed that many behavioral and learning disturbances in children were the result of adverse reactions to artificial substances in foods, and that elimination of these substances would result in marked improvement in functioning. His proposal was greeted with much hope and enthusiasm by parents and educators and is still very popular today. As Conners (1980, p. 12) has stated,

> The idea that "natural is best" is something most parents accept readily. Every day the newspapers provide fresh awareness of the growing hazards of pesticides, heavy metals in food and water, radiation, and other offshoots of industrial and scientific technology.

Although the dietary control of behavior and learning problems has become popular recently, this approach has been around for a long time in many forms, from the inclusion to exclusion of specific foods, to the advocacy of increased ingestion of vitamins. Using dietary control to treat behavior disorders was first undertaken by the allergist Shannon (1922), who felt that allergies, especially to foods, could affect central nervous system (CNS) tissue and subsequently give rise to the behavioral disturbances. Treatment involved elimination of the allergenic food substances from the patient's diet. This position is still advocated today, but differs significantly from the position popularized by the allergist Feingold (1974) that behavioral disturbances are the result of "adverse systemic reactions" to pollutants in foods, rather than immunologically mediated allergic reactions. Although the distinction between adverse systemic reactions and immunologically mediated ones is important from a pathophysiological point of view, it is typically overlooked; thus, the public and many professionals mistakenly assume that Feingold believed in the allergenic or immunologic mediation of behavioral disturbances. The most outspoken advocate of allergenically mediated behavioral disturbances is Rapp (1980), an allergist at the University of Buffalo School of Medicine.

Others have been concerned with the effect of sucrose (sugar) on behavior and learning. Despite the common belief that excessive ingestion of sugar produces hyperactivity, there has been almost no scientific research on this issue. Finally, brief consideration is given to megavitamin therapy, which has been advocated primarily for the treatment of severe behavior disturbances. This area is conspicuous for its lack of quality research and abundance of clinical testimonial.

PSYCHOPHARMACOLOGICAL TREATMENT
HISTORICAL OVERVIEW

1930–1950
Pediatric psychopharmacology began in the mid 1930s with the research of Bradley and his colleagues at the Emma Pendleton Bradley Home in Providence, Rhode Island. Bradley was particularly interested in the possible psychotherapeutic effects of Benzedrine, a CNS stimulant, as the result of a series of studies on the effects of Benzedrine in adults (Peoples & Guttmann, 1936; Myerson, 1936; Davidoff, 1936; Sargant & Blackburn, 1936; Carlisle, 1937; Nathanson, 1937; Wilbur, MacLean, & Allen, 1937).

Bradley's first study was reported in 1937 in the *American Journal of Psychiatry*. Thirty patients (21 boys and 9 girls) from 5 to 14 years in age were studied. As Bradley noted, the group was heterogeneous with respect to psychopathology, including children displaying both seriously withdrawn and aggressive behavior as well as those exhibiting school problems and evidence of brain damage. Observations of the patients were made daily by the staff for 3 consecutive weeks. Benzedrine sulfate was administered to all patients during the 2nd week of observation.

Fourteen of the children showed striking improvement in school performance, as suggested by the following statement (p. 578).

> There appeared a definite "drive" to accomplish as much as possible during the school period, and often to spend extra time completing additional work. Speed of comprehension and accuracy of performance were increased in most cases. Insight into school improvement was generally present, though few of the children attributed it to the medication they had received earlier in the day. The improvement was noted in all school subjects. It appeared promptly the first day Benzedrine was given and disappeared on the first day it was discontinued.

Fifteen of the children responded to the Benzedrine by becoming emotionally subdued, calm, and generally less emotionally labile. The effect was not sedative in nature, for the children appeared to have plenty of energy. Their behavior and emotional energy was simply more purposeful and adaptive. Seven of the children experienced a sense of well being or euphoria. Spontaneous comments by some of the children reflected their observed changes in affect and behavior (p. 579): ''I have joy in my stomach.'' ''I feel fine and can't seem to do things fast enough today.'' ''I feel peppy.'' ''I start to make my bed and before I know it, it is done.'' In contrast to these euphoric or positive-affect observations, three of the children were noted to have become hypersensitive and prone to crying episodes, two other children appeared tense and worried, one hyperactive child became more hyperactive, aggressive, and irritable than before, and three children not showing previous excess motor activity exhibited marked increases to the point of agitation.

These initial results led to continued study of the efficacy of benzedrine sulfate in the treatment of emotionally and behaviorally disturbed children for the next 15 years (Molitch & Poliakoff, 1937; Molitch & Sullivan, 1937; Molitch & Eccles, 1937; Cutts & Jasper, 1939; Bradley & Bowen, 1940, 1941; Bradley & Green, 1940; Bender & Cottington, 1942; Bakwin, 1948; Bradley, 1950). Bradley (1950, p. 35) summarized 12 years of experience with the amphetamines Benzedrine and Dexedrine sulfate:

> Specific behavior responses to both drugs approximated one another both in quality and frequency, with 50 to 60% of the children becoming more subdued, 15 to 25% showing no change, 20% showing increased activity, and 5% showing an acceleration of school progress only. Clinically these reactions indicated 60 to 75% symptomatic improvement, 15 to 25% no change, and 10 to 15% unfavorable responses. Children with a variety of clinical diagnoses were benefited, with no evidence of tolerance or addiction following prolonged administration.

Claims were made that the amphetamines were useful in the treatment of a wide variety of emotional and behavior problems (Bradley, 1950; Bender & Cottington, 1942), improved cognitive performance (Molitch & Sullivan, 1937; Molitch & Eccles, 1937), and were helpful in the treatment of enuresis. Conversely, Bender and Cottington (1942) and Bender and Nichtern (1956) noted that the amphetamines were contraindicated in the treatment of schizophrenia, psychopathic personalities, and children with organic brain disease, and worked best with children who exhibited neurotic behavior patterns. In the past 10 years subsequent research, characterized by improved methodology and greater precision in diagnostic classification, has narrowed the use of the amphetamines and other CNS stimulants, notably Ritalin® and Cylert®, to the treatment of the attention deficit disorders as defined by DSM-III (American Psychiatric Association, 1980).

1950–1960

During the 1950s there was a marked reduction of interest in the amphetamines, possibly because of the emergence of the antipsychotic drugs. Ritalin®, the most widely used CNS stimulant for the treatment of attention deficit disorders today, was first synthesized in 1954 but did not come into wide use until the 1960s.

Chlorpromazine (Thorazine®), the first of the phenothiazine derivatives, was synthesized in 1950 in France by Charpentier (Dundee, 1954). It was used initially as an adjunct and supplement to general anesthesia because of its sedative and calming effects. Lehmann and Hanrahan (1954) reported on its usefulness in the treatment of adult psychiatric patients for the symptomatic control of agitation.

Numerous clinical impressionistic studies of the efficacy of chlorpromazine in the treatment of children and adolescents appeared in the mid 1950s (Bair & Herold, 1955; Denhoff & Holden, 1955; Gatski, 1955; Flaherty, 1955; Silver, 1955; Rettig, 1955; Freed & Peifer, 1956; Miksztal, 1956). Collectively, these studies suggested that chlorpromazine was effective in the treatment of schizophrenic and nonschizophrenic disorders in which hyperactivity was a prominent feature. Results were generally more dramatic with schizophrenic patients. There also tended to be improvement in sociability and behavioral compliance.

The first controlled study of antipsychotic drugs with children and adolescents was conducted by Freedman, Effron, and Bender (1955). They reported on 3 years of experience in the treatment of 195 boys, aged 7 to 12 years, with six different medications. The authors concluded that chlorpromazine was the drug of choice in the treatment of schizophrenic and borderline children with hyperactivity. Anxiety states and primary behavior disorders responded best to the antihistamine Benadryl. Amphetamines were not among the six drugs used over the 3-year period.

Surprisingly, the amphetamines, with their previously demonstrated effectiveness in the treatment of primary behavior problems and hyperactivity, were not compared against chlorpromazine in any of the reported studies of the 1950s. A second well-controlled study of chlorpromazine was conducted by Hunt, Frank, and Krush (1956). The authors' conclusions were similar to those of Freedman et al. (1956). They compared schizophrenic, borderline, delinquent, and brain-damaged patients and found the greatest improvement in the schizophrenic-hyperactive children; however, chlorpromazine reduced hyperactivity across all groups. Improved social functioning was most prominent in the schizophrenic and borderline patients.

Freedman (1958) reviewed the literature to that time on psychotropic medications. He concluded that (a) the literature was characterized by clinical impressionistic studies that proclaimed the wonders of chlorpromazine for the effective treatment of a wide variety of disorders, from enuresis to schizophrenia; (b) potential toxicity or side effects of treatment were either downplayed or simply not adequately addressed; (c) results of the few controlled studies did suggest that chlorpromazine might be effective in the treatment of severely disturbed hyperactive children; and (d) limited evidence existed regarding the efficacy of psychotropic drugs beyond chlorpromazine, and possibly Benedryl®, for the treatment of anxiety and behavior problems, and possibly of meprobamate for the treatment of organic brain disorders characterized by hyperactivity.

1960–1970

Wiener and Jaffe (1977) have noted that the 1960s were characterized by (a) marked reinterest in stimulant medications for the treatment of a wide range of problems, with particular emphasis on the treatment of hyperactivity; (b) the synthesis of two additional classes of phenothiazine compounds—the piperazines and piperidines; (c) the introduction of two new antipsychotic compounds—the thioxanthenes and the butyrophenones; (d) the introduction of the antidepressants; and (e) an increased emphasis on research methodology.

Double-blind, placebo-controlled studies by Eisenberg et al. (1963) and by Conners and Eisenberg (1963) provided evidence of the efficacy of dextroamphetamine and methylphenidate (Ritalin®) in the treatment of hyperactivity, distractibility, and impulsivity. Studies by Conners, Eisenberg, and Barcai (1967) and Millichap, Aymat, Sturgis, Larsen, and Egan (1968) provided further support for the use of stimulants in the treatment of hyperactivity. Improvements were noted in general behavior as well as on cognitive tasks that required attention and vigilance. These findings were consistent with the less highly controlled studies of Bradley and others in the 1930s and early 1940s. Some studies, such as Fish's (1960a, 1960b), lauded the use of amphetamines in the treatment of phobic and hypochondriacal patients, but the focus for stimulant medications was narrowed to the treatment of primary hyperkinetic behavior disorders (Cytryn, Gilbert, & Eisenberg, 1960).

Fish (1960a, 1960b) reported on the first comparative use of chlorpromazine with the new antipsychotic medications prochlorperazine (Compazine®), trifluoperazine (Stelazine®), and perphenazine (Trilafon®). All were found to be effective, but differed in their sedative properties and severity of side effects. Several studies appeared, comparing the effectiveness of thioridazine (Mellaril®) with other antipsychotics in the treatment of behavior disorders and hyperkinesis (LeVann, 1961; Shaw, Lockett, Lucas, Lamontagne, & Crimm, 1963; Alderton & Hoddinott, 1964; Alexandris & Lundell, 1968; Ucer & Kreger, 1969). Interest in thioridazine was stimulated because it was effective and had fewer side effects than other antipsychotic medications. As with the stimulants, the antipsychotics were not found to be useful for as broad a range of behavioral disturbances as had been suggested by earlier researchers (Rosenblum, Buoniconto, & Graham, 1960; La Veck, De La Crug, & Simundson, 1960; Garfield, Helper, Wilcott, & Murrly, 1962).

As noted above, two additional classes of antipsychotic medications appeared in the 1960s: the *thioxanthenes*, chlorprothixene (Taractan®) and thiothixene (Navane®), and the *butyrophenones*, haloperidol (Haldol®) and trifluperidol (Triperidol®). These compounds were thought to be more effective and less sedating than the phenothiazines, but to have greater extrapyramidal motor system side effects (DiMascio, 1970, 1971; Werry, 1978). Published studies on the thioxanthenes appeared in the mid 1960s (Oettinger, 1962; Wolpert, Hagamen, & Merlis, 1966, 1967; Wolpert, Quintos, White, & Merlis, 1968). Rogers (1965) published one of the first reports on Haldol® for the treatment of destructive and aggressive behavior in children or adolescents. A somewhat earlier study by Seignot (1961) reported on the effectiveness of Haldol® for the treatment of Gilles de la Tourette syndrome, and many subsequent studies attested to the efficacy of Haldol® for this specific disorder (Shapiro, Shapiro, & Wayne, 1973; Shapiro, Shapiro, Brunn, & Sweet, 1978).

The antidepressants first were used in children for the treatment of enuresis (MacLean, 1960). Here two classes of antidepressants were introduced: the monoamine oxidase (MAO) inhibitors and the tricyclics, but the MAO inhibitors were not used in the pediatric age range because of their toxicity (Byck, 1975). MacLean found that low dosages of imipramine (Tofranil®) gave symptomatic relief of bed wetting. As with other medications, reports of the efficacy of antidepressants were based on clinical impressionistic studies. The first controlled study was conducted by Poussaint and Ditman (1965), who found that imipramine was superior to a placebo in the control of nocturnal enuresis. Subsequent controlled studies supported their results (Bindelglass, Dec, & Enos, 1968; Shaffer, Costello, & Hill, 1968). The use of antidepressants for the treatment of depression, hyperkinesis, and behavior problems revealed equivocal results in controlled studies, and supportive results for their efficacy in uncontrolled clinical studies (Lucas, Lockett, & Grimm, 1965; Rapoport, 1965; Krakowski, 1965; Kurtis, 1966; Frommer, 1967).

1970–Present

The decade of the 1970s was marked by further refinements in methodology and diagnostic classification (Conners & Werry, 1979) and increased public concern over the use of behavior-modifying drugs (Sprague, 1978). Studies dealing with the efficacy of stimulants outnumbered those on antipsychotics and antidepressants, and lithium carbonate (a drug used in adults for the treatment of manic depressive illness) was studied for its usefulness in the treatment of severe psychopathology, cyclic mood changes, and hyperactivity. Lithium carbonate was used most commonly in adolescents with a family history of manic depressive illness. With the exception of lithium, no new major drugs or classes of drugs were studied extensively in the pediatric psychopharmacology literature, although two new classes of antipsychotic medications were introduced, the dihydronindolones and the dibenzoxazepines. The few studies available suggest that both classes have similar potency and side effects to those of the other antipsychotic drugs (Campbell, Fish, Shapiro, & Floyd, 1972; Greenhill, Hirsch, Halpern, & Spalten, 1980).

Stimulants, notably Ritalin®, dextroamphetamine, and Cylert®, became the drugs of choice for the treatment of the attention deficit disorders.* Caffeine was studied, but was not found to be useful as a treatment (Conners, 1975; Garfinkel, Webster, & Sloman, 1975; Huestis, Arnold, & Smeltzer, 1975). Research focused on the specific classes of behavior most affected by the stimulants (Barkley, 1976, 1977; Barkley & Cunningham, 1980). Haldol® became the psychotropic drug of choice for the treatment of Gilles de la Tourette syndrome, although other nonpsychotropics were used (Shapiro et al., 1978). The tricyclic antidepressants continued to be studied for their potential usefulness in the treatment of enuresis and in the treatment of the DSM-III defined anxiety disorders, conduct disorders, and attention deficit disorders. They were found to be beneficial in the treatment of enuresis, but of questionable value in the treatment of other disorders in children and adolescents (Conners & Werry, 1979). In the late 1970s antidepressants were found to be useful with children who met DSM-III criteria for the diagnosis of depression (Puig-Antich, Blau, Marx, Greenhill, & Chambers, 1978; Puig-Antich et al., 1979).

Lithium carbonate was first used with adolescents by van Krevelen and van Voorst (1959), but its use was not subsequently reported in the pediatric psychopharmacology literature until the 1970s (Whitehead & Clark, 1970; Dyson & Barcai, 1970; Campbell et al., 1972; Gram & Rafaelsen, 1972; Feinstein & Wolpert, 1973; Greenhill, Rieder, Wender, Bucksbaum, & Zahn, 1973; Kelly, Koch, & Buegel, 1976). These studies suggest that lithium might be beneficial in the treatment of aggressive and explosive behaviors. However, reviews by Campbell, Schulman, and Rapoport

---

*Prior to DSM-III, children with primary problems of attention, impulsivity, distractibility, and gross hyperactivity were diagnosed as manifesting a hyperkinetic syndrome. As defined by DSM-III, "Attention Deficit Disorders" represents a more refined delineation of this earlier diagnostic category.

(1978), Conners and Werry (1979), and Campbell, Cohen, and Perry (1983) all agree that lithium carbonate has not played a practical or significant role in the treatment of childhood psychopathology, although it deserves greater study (Wiener, 1985).

Anticonvulsants and Sedatives

Two other categories of drugs should be mentioned from a historical perspective: the anticonvulsants and the sedatives. The former have been used since the mid 1930s for treatment of behavior disorders, especially those characterized by severe temper tantrums or aggressiveness. Sedatives have been used to treat acute anxiety states and sleep disturbances.

Jasper, Solomon, and Bradley (1938) found that 83% of a group of behavior problem children manifested EEG abnormalities characterized by epileptiform waves and slowing. The children were described as hyperactive, impulsive, variable, and prone to misbehavior. None of them had seizures, however, despite their epileptiform EEG abnormalities. A number of subsequent studies found similar findings (Pasamanick, 1951; Gibbs & Gibbs, 1951; Gross & Wilson, 1964; Chao, Sexton, & Davis, 1964). The Jasper et al. study (1938) undoubtedly triggered some of the later studies that attempted to assess the usefulness of anticonvulsants for the treatment of children with behavior disorders and EEG abnormalities in the absence of seizures. Dilantin® was the anticonvulsant used in the treatment of behavior-disturbed children and adolescents in the 1930s, and published reports of its use for this purpose emerged in the 1940s (Brown & Solomon, 1942; Lindsley & Henry, 1942; Walker & Kirkpatrick, 1947). Of particular interest were patients who presented with behavior disturbance and an abnormal EEG pattern without the presence of seizures, but studies were not limited to children with abnormal EEG findings. If the patient presented with severe behavior problems like those children who presented with an abnormal EEG, anticonvulsants were considered. It was thought that behavioral outbursts, hyperactivity, or aggressiveness might represent a seizure equivalent and hence be manageable with anticonvulsant medication (Chao et al., 1964; Remschmidt, 1976).

The studies conducted during the 1940s provided equivocal support for the usefulness of Dilantin® in the treatment of behavior disorders with or without evidence of abnormal EEG data or other evidence of damage or dysfunction to the brain. Subsequent studies were conducted over the next 30 years, with similar findings (Pasamanick, 1951; Zimmerman & Burgemeister, 1955; Putnam & Hood, 1964; Chao et al., 1964; Baldwin & Kenny, 1966; Lefkowitz, 1969; Looker & Conners, 1970; Wender, 1971; Conners, Kramer, Rothschild, Schwartz, & Stone, 1971). In summary, Wiener and Jaffe (1977, p. 31) state, "Individual case reports with marked improvement in response to Dilantin® continue to be reported, despite the fact that controlled studies demonstrating positive effects do not exist.'' Despite these observations, anticonvulsants continue to be used on a limited basis for the treatment of behavior disorders, especially if other, more commonly used drugs (stimulants or antipsychotics) fail to be of help. Dilantin®, however, is being replaced by other anticonvulsant medications for the treatment of behavior disorders (Grant, 1974).

Over the years a number of drugs have been used for the treatment of sleep disorders and acute anxiety states in children. These have included the benzodiazepines (Valium®, Librium®, Serepax®, Serax®, Mogadon®, and Dalmane®), the now rarely used propanediols (Equanil® and Miltown®), the barbiturates (phenobarbitol and chloral hydrate), and the antihistamines (notably Benadryl®, Phenergan®, Atarax®, and Vistaril®). Although all three groups of drugs have varied uses, they also have sedation and behavioral disinhibition as a common property. Werry (1978) stated that the relief of anxiety and tension are secondary to the depressant effect these drugs have on the central nervous system, and their role in sleep disturbance stems from this depressant effect as well as from changes induced in the sleep cycle. A review by Gittelman-Klein (1978) indicated that few controlled studies exist on the use of these drugs in the treatment of acute anxiety states or various sleep disturbances. Those studies that do exist question the value of such medications in the treatment of anxiety states (Cytryn et al., 1960; Eisenberg, Gilbert, Cytryn, & Molling, 1961). Werry (1978, p. 346) concluded:

> The role of the sedative or antianxiety drugs is one of the poorest researched areas in pediatric psychopharmacology. These drugs may be occasionally useful in sleep disorder, in acutely disturbed children, and in nonpsychotic anxiety. The antimuscarinic (antihistamine) type of sedatives seem to be the most popular, but their role is no more properly established than that of the virtually unexplored, attractively safe benzodiazepines. . . . In general, anxiety in children is situational rather than sustained and exquisitely sensitive to psychological maneuvers.

DRUG CLASSIFICATION

Historically, psychotropic drugs have been classified by their effect on target behaviors or classes of psychopathology. For example, most of the phenothiazine compounds have been used to alleviate or significantly reduce symptoms of psychosis in adults and subsequently have been classified as antipsychotic drugs. Within this framework drugs are classified by their chemical structure and by a generic name given to the drug by its manufacturer. Thus, the antipsychotic (behavioral classification) phenothiazine (chemical classification), known generically as chlorpromazine, is marketed by Smith-Kline and French Laboratories as Thorazine® (trade name). Although generic names are usually more difficult to pronounce, they are less confusing than trade names because they provide information regarding the chemical classification of the drug. The same drug can be produced by different drug companies and given different trade names; the generic name, however, remains the same regardless of the manufacturer.

Behavioral classification of drugs was derived from adult psychopharmacology research and based on target symptoms the drugs seemed to alleviate. Thus, the terms antipsychotic, antidepressant, antianxiety, and antimanic were affixed to specific drugs that reduced such symptoms. These classifications seem reasonable in adult psychopharmacology, but they are misleading when applied to pediatric psychopharmacology. For example, a group of drugs chemically referred to as tricyclics have been classified as antidepressant agents, yet their primary use in children and adolescents has been for the treatment of nocturnal enuresis. They also have been used in the treatment of childhood phobias. Only recently have they been used to treat depression in children. Lithium carbonate, a drug used for the treatment of manic depressive illness in adults, has been used to treat violent or aggressive behavior in children. Thus, the antipsychotic medications are used to treat psychotic and nonpsychotically disturbed children and to alleviate or reduce different symptomatology in children than in adults.

If this all sounds confusing it is, but it should help to point out that classification by any means is problematic. It reflects the current inadequacy of diagnosis and classification in childhood psychopathology (Achenbach, 1978), as well as the developing nature of pediatric psychopharmacology research (Conners & Werry, 1979; Gittelman-Klein, Spitzer, & Cantwell, 1978).

Consistent with the pediatric psychopharmacology literature, and despite the above-noted problems, we have chosen to use the adult-derived behavioral classification of psychotropic drugs. Specifically, it classifies drugs into the following categories: antipsychotics, commonly referred to as neuroleptics or major tranquilizers; antidepressants; stimulants; antianxiety drugs or minor tranquilizers; and the antimanic medications. Table 6.1 presents the commonly used drugs in each of these categories along with their chemical, generic, and trade names.

Antipsychotic Drugs
Although the term antipsychotic is used widely in the pediatric psychopharmacology literature, it is misleading because the symptoms of the adult psychotic patient, for which the antipsychotics were first found to be useful in reducing, are generally different from the symptoms seen in childhood psychosis or severe behavioral disturbances for which the anti-

Table 6.1. Classification of Psychotropic Drugs Used with Children and Adolescents

CATEGORY	CHEMICAL NAME	GENERIC NAME	TRADE NAME
Antipsychotics	Phenothiazines	Chlorpromazine	Thorazine
		Prochlorperazine	Compazine
		Thioridazine	Mellaril
		Perphenazine	Trilafon
		Trifluoperazine	Stelazine
		Trifluperidol	Triperidol
		Fluphenazine	Prolixin
	Butyrophenones	Haloperidol	Haldol
	Thioxanthenes	Thiothixene	Navane
		Chlorprothixene	Taractan
	Dibenzoxazepine	Loxapine	Loxitane
	Dihydroindolone	Molindone	Lidone
Antidepressants	Tricyclics	Imipramine	Tofranil
		Amitriptyline	Elavil
		Desipramine	Norpramin
Stimulants	Sympathomimetic	Dextroamphetamine	Many (see PDR)
	Amines and other analogs	Methylphenidate	Ritalin
		Pemoline	Cylert
	Xanthines	Caffeine	
	Acetylcholine	Deanol	Deaner
Antianxiety	Barbiturates	Phenobarbitol	
	Benzodiazepines	Diazepam	Valium
		Chlordiazepoxide	Librium
		Oxazepam	Serax
		Nitrazepam	Mogadon
		Flurazepam	Dalmane
		Lorazepam	Ativan
		Clonazepam	Clonapin
	Propanediols	Meprobamate	Miltown
	Antihistamines	Diphenhydramine	Benadryl
		Hydroxyzine	Atarax
Antimanic	Lithium salts	Lithium carbonate	Many (see PDR)

psychotics are effective. As Gittelman-Klein et al. (1978, p. 158) have stated, ''The drugs do not have a normalizing or true antipsychotic action as in adults, nor do they eliminate or reduce significantly much of the children's bizarre interests and inappropriate social interactions, but they may have dramatic beneficial effects on certain disturbing symptoms such as severe hyperactivity and mood lability.''

A review of the literature reveals that antipsychotics are useful in children and adolescents for the reduction of (a) hyperactivity in retarded and nonretarded individuals with or without brain injury, (b) some classes of stereotypic behaviors, such as tics, but not idiosyncratic or learned inappropriate personal or social behaviors, (c) explosive, aggressive, or violent behavior, and (d) hallucinations, delusions, or thought disorders when they occur in the older child or adolescent with acute onset of symptoms. It should be clear that these conditions refer to specific symptoms or behaviors and not to diagnostic categories, and that the use of antipsychotic drugs in children and adolescents is not limited to individuals diagnosed as psychotic. Based on their clinical work and the research literature, Gittelman-Klein et al. (1978) find antipsychotic medications to be useful in three DSM-III conditions: the pervasive developmental disorders, the stereotyped movement disorders, and the attention deficit disorders (although stimulants appear to be the primary drug of choice in this diagnostic category). Antipsychotics appear to be contraindicated in conduct, developmental, and anxiety disorders.

Chemical Classes. There are currently five classes of antipsychotics: the phenothiazines, which are divided into three subgroups called the aliphatics, piperidines, and piperazines; the thioxanthenes; the butyrophenones; the dibenzoxapines; and the dihydroindolones. The phenothiazines were the first compounds to be synthesized, and the dibenzoxapines and dihydroindolones were the most recent. All five classes of antipsychotics appear to be of equivalent potency, but they vary in terms of side effects. For example, sedation appears to be greater in the phenothiazines than in the thioxanthenes or butyrophenones. Extrapyramidal motor-system side effects are most common with the butyrophenones, followed by the phenothiazines, and least prevalent in the thioxanthenes. The dibenzoxazepines appear similar to the phenothiazines.

Treatment-Emergent Side Effects. The spectrum of possible side effects from treatment with antipsychotics is quite broad. A more detailed review can be found in the Physicians Desk Reference (1986), in the chapter on antipsychotics by Winsberg and Yepes (1978), or in Klein, Gittelman, Quitkin, and Rifkin (1980). The most common short-term effects are (a) drowsiness, apathy, and general lethargy; (b) the anticholinergic effects of blurring of vision, dry mouth, urinary retention, constipation, and abdominal pain; (c) extrapyramidal effects, which include dystonias, akinesias, and parkinsonian-type reactions such as mild tremor, pilling, rolling movements of the fingers, masklike face, and stiffness of voluntary movement; and (d) behavior and mood changes, which include irritability, excitability, euphoria, depression, worsening of symptoms, and perceptual distortion. These treatment-emergent side effects are usually eliminated or significantly reduced with adjustments in dosage level or withdrawal from the medication, or with the use of anticholinergic drugs. While most of the above-noted effects are short-term and dose related, there is concern that long-term use of antipsychotics may result in nonreversible changes in functioning. Particular concern has been given to the extrapyramidal side effects, and specifically to the syndrome known as tardive dyskinesia (Gualtieri, 1981). This condition is characterized by persistent stereotyped involuntary movements of a chorea-athetotic nature, especially of the upper extremities and face. The facial movements commonly involve lip smacking and tongue protrusions. Tardive dyskinesia has been reported most frequently in older adults on long-term antipsychotic agents (usually several years or more), but there have been reports of persistent general extrapyramidal side effects, as well as tardive dyskinesia, in children (Angle & McIntire, 1968; Dabbous & Bergman, 1966; Shields & Bray, 1976; McAndrew, Case, & Treffert, 1972; Paulson, Rizvi, & Crane, 1975; Gualtieri, 1981).

Cognition and Learning. The effects of the antipsychotic agents on cognition and learning are also of concern, especially in the pediatric age range. Few controlled studies have been conducted in this area, however, and reviews by Conners and Werry (1979) and Klein et al. (1980) suggest that the results to date are controversial. Thus, there is insufficient data on which to draw any firm conclusions regarding the effects of antipsychotics on cognition and learning, in the laboratory or in naturalistic settings such as the classroom.

Efficacy. Although the general quality of drug studies has improved over the years, Campbell (1985) stated that numerous methodological problems still have made it difficult to make any cogent statement about the effectiveness of antipsychotic medications, despite many clinical claims of their efficacy. Most studies have not controlled crucial variables such as age, disorder, severity, chronicity, and dosage, to name a few. Many studies have lacked adequate assessment of treatment outcome, and experimental design in general has been weak. Given these methodological problems, it would be premature to attempt to provide percentage estimates of the patients who are significantly helped by antipsychotic agents. However, there is some suggestion from the research literature that Haldol® is particularly useful with Gilles de la Tourette's syndrome and severe childhood disturbance such as infantile autism (Campbell et al., 1982; Anderson et al., 1984). This does not imply that other antipsychotic agents are not useful; it simply suggests that research studies with other medications have not been as systematic or methodologically sound, and therefore few practical conclusions can be drawn.

Antidepressant Drugs

As with the antipsychotics, the term antidepressant is somewhat misleading as it applies to the use of these medications in the pediatric age range. In children and adolescents the antidepressants, notably the tricyclic antidepressants, have been used most frequently for the symptomatic control of enuresis (Blackwell & Currah, 1973). The effectiveness of the tricyclic antidepressants in the control of enuresis has lead to speculation that enuresis is a depressive equivalent in children and adolescents, but there has been little support for this notion (Shaffer & Ambrosini, 1985). For example, although the antidepressant effects of the tricyclics require a buildup time in the system of 7 to 14 days, the reduction of enuretic symptoms occurs immediately or within a few days. The tricyclics also are equally effective in reducing enuresis in the presence or absence of psychopathology. At one time it was felt that the antidepressants affected the enuretic process through their anticholinergic and/or possible antiadrenergic effects (Mahony, Laferte, & Mahoney, 1973; Blackwell & Currah, 1973). However, studies have shown that tricyclics with no anticholinergic activity are as effective in controlling enuresis as ones with anticholinergic properties (Petersen, Anderson, & Hansen, 1974). Additionally, primary anticholinergic and antiadrenergic agents do not alter enuretic symptoms (Wallace & Forsythe, 1969; Shaffer, Hedge, & Stephenson, 1978).

The antidepressants have been used frequently in the treatment of the DSM-III conduct and attention-deficit disorders to reduce restless, hyperactive, and antisocial behavior, but generally are less effective than the stimulants (Greenberg, Yellin, Spring, & Metcalf, 1975; Rapoport, Quinn, Bradbard, Riddle, & Brookes, 1974; Waizer, Hoffman, Polizos, & Engelhardt, 1974; Winsberg, Bialer, Kupietz, & Tobias, 1972; Yepes, Balka, Winsberg, & Bialer, 1977). They have been used with some success to treat school phobias and separation anxiety (Gittelman-Klein, 1975).

Numerous reports have appeared in the literature regarding the efficacy of antidepressants in the treatment of childhood depression (Conners, 1976; Schulterbrandt & Raskin, 1977; Klein, Gittelman, Quitkin, & Rifkin, 1980); however, they are of questionable value because the patient populations were generally heterogeneous and not well defined with respect to an operational definition of depression (Campbell et al., 1983). There were no systematic attempts to validate childhood depression, applying criteria used in adults, until the late 1970s (Puig-Antich et al., 1978; Puig-Antich et al., 1979). The studies by these investigators have shown antidepressants to be effective in reducing depressive symptoms in prepubertal children. More recently, Puig-Antich (1982) reported on the successful treatment of preadolescents who met the DSM-III criteria for depression, as well as that of the conduct disorders. This finding again has raised the issue of depressive equivalents in children, but in this case with adequate support of primary depressive symptomatology. Clearly, more research is needed in this area.

Using Gittelman-Klein et al.'s (1978) application of DSM-III criteria, antidepressants appear to be appropriate for use in the developmental disorder of enuresis, the anxiety disorder of separation anxiety, and the attention deficit disorders with hyperactivity and/or conduct problems, although stimulants are the first drugs of choice. When children meet the criteria of childhood depression outlined by Puig-Antich et al. (1978), antidepressants may be helpful. Antidepressants appear to be contraindicated in the DSM-III diagnostic categories of pervasive developmental disorders, stereotyped movement disorders, and conduct disorders in the absence of primary depressive symptomatology.

Chemical Classes. There are three major classes of antidepressants: monoamine oxidase inhibitors, tricyclics, and quadricyclics. Campbell et al. (1983) noted that the MAO inhibitors have been used in Europe to treat presumably depressed children, but there is little evidence of their efficacy, and they have quite serious side effects (Annell, 1972; Byck, 1975). As a result of these findings, they have not been used in the pediatric age range in this country and are used sparingly in adults. The tricyclic antidepressants are the drugs of choice, whereas the newer quadricyclics have not been extensively studied in children. Three tricyclics are commonly used: imipramine, amitriptyline, and desipramine. Imipramine (Tofranil®) has been the tricyclic agent of choice in the symptomatic treatment of enuresis, and generally with the other conditions or symptoms for which antidepressants have been used with children.

Treatment-Emergent Side Effects. Antidepressants originally were thought to be quite safe in children. DiMascio, Solty, and Shader (1970) found the prevalence and severity of the short-term side effects to be like those in adults, namely (a) mild drowsiness and lethargy, (b) tremors, (c) the anticholinergic effects of dry mouth, constipation, urinary retention, and difficulty with visual focusing, (d) insomnia and suppression of appetite, and (e) irritability and tearfulness. More recently there has been concern about the use of tricyclics in children because of their effects on the cardiovascular system. Saraf, Klein, Gittelman-Klein, and Groff (1974) reported on the sudden death of a 6-year-old child who was administered high doses of imipramine (14 mg/kg) for the treatment of school phobia. Electrocardiograph abnormalities have been reported with doses in the 5 mg/kg range (Winsberg, Goldstein, Yepes, & Perel, 1975). Several reports of tricyclic-induced seizures have appeared in the literature with dosages in the 7 to 10 mg/kg range (Brown, Winsberg, Bialer, & Press, 1973). These findings have lead to the strong recommendation that tricyclics should not be given in excess of 5 mg/kg, and dosages near this level should be accompanied by EKG monitoring (Hayes, Panitch, & Barker, 1975). For the treatment of enuresis, the typical dose of the tricyclic imipramine is .5 to 2.5 mg/kg, which is well below levels that have produced cardiovascular abnormalities or seizures. Imipramine and amitriptyline are given in doses of 2 to 5 mg/kg in the treatment of attention deficit disorders and anxiety disorders.

Cognition and Learning. Several studies have found that tricyclics improve performance on attentional or vigilance tasks (Rapoport, Quinn, & Lamprecht, 1974; Kupietz & Balka, 1976; Yepes et al., 1977). This finding, along with tricyclic suppression of appetite, has suggested a similarity in action to the stimulants (Rapoport & Mikkelsen, 1978). Only one study has been reported on the effects of tricyclics on academic functioning. Quinn and Rapoport (1975) found no difference in the academic achievement of patients who were on tricyclics over 1 year when compared with a group of children who had stopped taking the tricyclics in the course of the year. Needless to say, there is insufficient data to draw any conclusions regarding the effects of tricyclics on academic functioning. Research in this area would be particularly meaningful from a theoretical perspective, because problems in learning are in some cases felt to be symptomatic of depression or what has been termed a depressive equivalent (Rapoport, 1976).

Efficacy. Shaffer and Ambrosini (1985) have suggested that antidepressants rarely eliminate enuretic symptomatology. From their review of the literature, they found that complete remission occurs in 10 to 20% of the cases, with an occasional study suggesting 50% complete remission. Roughly 50 to 65% of the subjects in well-controlled studies will show a 50% reduction in frequency of nocturnal wetting. Their findings are consistent with those of Schmitt (1982). Some children show a good initial response, but return to their regular wetting pattern in 1 to 6 weeks despite stable blood plasma levels of medication. A positive response, if it occurs, does so within a week. Discontinuation of medication typically results in recurrence of the enuretic symptoms.

Insufficient research data exists regarding the efficacy of antidepressants in children and adolescents for the treatment of depression, school phobias, separation anxiety, or attention deficit disorders, even though clinical case studies have suggested antidepressants may be useful for these conditions.

Stimulants

As noted in the historical overview, pediatric psychopharmacology began in the mid 1930s with the use of amphetamines (Bradley, 1937). Since that time, several hundred studies have been conducted to assess the efficacy of stimulants for the treatment of behavioral disturbances. These research efforts exceed the investigation of any other psychotropic medication. Stimulants have been found to be effective in facilitating attention and vigilance, reducing distractibility, and reducing impulsivity and motor restlessness, both in laboratory and naturalistic settings (Barkley, 1977; Cantwell & Carlson, 1978; Conners & Werry, 1979; Werry, 1982). Some improvement does occur in social adjustment, but it appears to be secondary to a reduction in the above-noted behaviors that are typically irritating to peers and adults (Barkley & Cunningham, 1980; Whalen, Henker, & Dotemoto, 1980).

In Bradley's studies a wide range of behavioral disturbances were treated with stimulants, but over the years the stimulants have been restricted to a few conditions. They have been found to be the drugs of choice in treatment of the DSM-III-defined attention deficit disorders, with or without hyperactivity. Stimulants have been found useful in the treatment of the conduct disorders. They are contraindicated in the treatment of pervasive developmental disorders and stereotyped movement disorders, because they tend to exacerbate symptoms in these conditions.

Chemical Classes. Five classes of stimulants have been used to treat behavioral disturbances in the pediatric age range: the amphetamines (Dextroamphetamine®); methylphenidate (Ritalin®); magnesium pemoline (Cylert®); the xanthines, namely caffeine; and deanol. The xanthines and deanol have not been effective (Conners, 1975; Klein et al., 1980). Methylphenidate appears to be the stimulant of choice because its side effects are somewhat less than those of Dextroamphetamine®, the only amphetamine currently used for treatment. Magnesium pemoline is somewhat less effective than methylphenidate or Dextroamphetamine®, which are thought to be equivalent (Conners & Taylor, 1980). One advantage of magnesium pemoline is its longer action, essentially twice that of methylphenidate or Dextroamphetamine®, which allows for one convenient daily dose. Within the last year, however, Ciba drug company, the manufacturer of methylphenidate, has developed a long-acting form of methylphenidate that can be given in a single daily dose.

Treatment-Emergent Side Effects. The most common side effects of stimulants are irritability, drowsiness, sadness and crying, and stomachache and loss of appetite. These side effects are dose related and most common at the onset of treatment. Allen and Safer (1973) reported suppression of height and weight with chronic use of stimulants. Subsequent research suggests that such suppression occurs in doses above 1 mg/kg or approximately 20 mg per day with methylphenidate, and at half this level with dextroamphetamine (Gross, 1976; Hechtman, Weiss, & Perlman, 1978; Conners & Werry, 1979). Gross (1976) noted that the suppressive effect is minimal over time and often is followed by a rebound effect when treatment is stopped. In a well-controlled study McNutt, Boileau, and Cohen (1977) found no evidence of suppression in height or weight over 1 year of treatment. Thus, as Campbell et al. (1983) have noted, there is general controversy over the issue of height and weight suppression as a secondary feature to treatment with stimulants. There is no evidence to date that stimulants are addictive, or that they have long-term side effects like the antipsychotics (Beck, Langford, MacKay, & Sum, 1975; Denhoff, 1973; Freedman, 1971; Weiss, 1975).

Cognition and Learning. There has been a great deal of interest in the effects of stimulant medications on academic performance. Based on their research, Sprague and Sleator (1977) stated that cognitive functioning is optimal with a dosage of .3 mg/kg, and optimal social behavior and activity levels are obtained with 1 mg/kg. However, their findings have neither been replicated in other studies nor their own research (Wiener, 1985). Despite the effectiveness of the stimulants to improve behaviors that are felt to be important in learning and problem solving, there is little evidence to date that academic performance is significantly facilitated (Barkley & Cunningham, 1980), although performance improvements have been reported for the specific laboratory tasks of learning, attention, memory, and problem solving (Conners & Werry, 1979; Solanto, 1984). In contrast, our clinical experience suggests that when stimulant medications significantly reduce motor impulsivity and facilitate attention and concentration, there is a marked improvement in the day-to-day academic performance of the child. Pelham (1983) points out that most studies of stimulant medication and academic functioning have too many methodological problems to warrant any conclusions at the present time. Finally, some research has suggested that stimulant medication in combination with behavioral or other therapy programs may facilitate optimal adaptation in the home and school (Christensen & Sprague, 1975; Ross & Ross, 1982).

Efficacy. Cantwell's (1977) review of the literature suggested that stimulant medication results in moderate to good reduction of symptoms in 65 to 75% of those children treated. Symptom exacerbation, or negative side effects, occurs in 5 to 10%, and no change occurs in 15 to 25% of the children treated.

Antianxiety Drugs

The antianxiety drugs have in common an ability to sedate and to disinhibit behavior. Although these medications have been used to treat a broad range of behavioral disturbances, there is little systematic research on their efficacy with children (Klein et al., 1980; Campbell et al., 1983). Conners and Werry (1979) note that pediatricians use antianxiety medications to treat sleep disturbances, but again there is no compelling evidence of their usefulness. According to Werry (1978), insomnia, nightmares, and sleepwalking are common in children and usually have been treated with the antimuscarinic antihistamines (Diphenhydramine® and Hydroxyzine®). When these sleep disturbances are thought to be symptomatic of separation anxiety, the antidepressant imipramine is a more appropriate drug of choice. Night terrors and somnambulism are distinct from the foregoing sleep disturbances in that they are more a function of CNS immaturity than of an emotional disturbance (Guilleminault & Anders, 1976); children seem to outgrow night terrors and somnambulism with age. Pharmacological treatment is usually instituted because of parental distress rather than discomfort to the child. Since these two sleep disturbances occur during stage 4 of the sleep cycle, it has been suggested that a denzodiazepine such as flurazepam be used because it shortens the stage-4 period. There is, however, no empirical data on children to support the efficacy of this choice.

Anxiety is symptomatic to many diagnostic categories, and therefore its presence is not sufficient to recommend the use of an antianxiety agent. Interestingly, almost no systematic research has been conducted on the use of antianxiety drugs with the DSM-III anxiety disorders. Antidepressant drugs have been used most frequently for the treatment of separation anxiety and school phobias. Although it has been suggested that antianxiety drugs might be of value in treating the shy and withdrawn child because of their ability to disinhibit behavior, there is no systematic research on this issue.

From the available literature it is evident that the antianxiety drugs have been used primarily for treatment of specific symptoms. They have not been recommended for treatment of any specific DSM-III childhood disorder and may exacerbate attention deficit disorders or other conditions in which behavioral disinhibition is undesirable.

Chemical Classes. The antianxiety drugs are composed of (a) general depressants, such as the barbiturates, chloral hydrate, and opiates; (b) selective depressants, such as the benzodiazepines and propanediols; and (c) the antimuscarinics, such as the antihistamines (Werry, 1978). Although all of these drugs have varied clinical uses, their common aspects of sedation and behavioral disinhibition account for their potential usefulness in

the symptomatic treatment of sleep disturbances and anxiety. Drug tolerance develops rapidly with all of these agents with respect to their antianxiety properties; thus, increasingly higher doses are required to obtain
symptomatic relief. Because tolerance develops quickly and treatment-
emergent side effects are significant with increasing dosages, most physicians will not use these agents for long periods of time.

Treatment-Emergent Side Effects. The most common side effects are drowsiness and excessive sedation, excessive behavioral disinhibition, psychological and/or physical dependence, and withdrawal seizures.

Cognition and Learning. Virtually no experimental research has been conducted in this area, but clinical evidence clearly suggests that cognitive
functioning and learning are interfered with due to the sedative effects
of these drugs. To the extent that anxiety interferes with performance, it
is possible that an antianxiety agent might enhance performance (Levitt,
1968).

Efficacy. There is virtually no systematic or reliable research data regarding the usefulness of antianxiety agents with children or adolescents.
Clearly, work in this area is needed.

Antimanic Drugs

Lithium carbonate is the only antimanic drug used in the pediatric age
range. It has been a very useful drug for the treatment of manic depressive illness in adults, but has been used sparingly in children and adolescents. Campbell, Schulman, and Rapoport (1978) reviewed the literature
on the use of lithium in the pediatric age range and found few controlled
studies. In children and adolescents, lithium has been used to control aggressive behavior and emotional explosiveness with some success (Werry,
1982). Lithium does not appear to be useful in the treatment of the attention deficit disorders. Campbell et al. (1983) suggest that it may be useful
in the treatment of aggressive and self-injurious behavior of severely retarded children and adolescents.

Werry (1982) suggests that lithium, although deserving of more systematic research, cannot be recommended for the treatment of any specific
childhood disorder as delineated by DSM-III. Additionally, it is a drug
that must be used with caution since it has significant short- and long-
term side effects (Rapoport, Mikkelsen, & Werry, 1978).

Chemical Classes. There are a variety of lithium salts, but lithium carbonate and lithium chloride have been most commonly used for their psychotropic properties.

Treatment-Emergent Side Effects. Lithium is a fairly toxic substance that must be monitored closely. Mild to moderate side effects are common with nontoxic doses. The most frequent side effects are nausea, diarrhea, muscular weakness, tremor, blurred vision, drowsiness, polyuria, and polydipsia. Long-term side effects are typically metabolic and endocrine in nature and include euthyroid goiter, hypothyroidism, and diabetes insipidus-like symptoms. These symptoms, however, are reversible when the drug is discontinued. Lithium toxicity typically occurs gradually and primarily affects the central nervous system. Symptoms include depressed functioning, slurred speech, vomiting, and eventual loss of consciousness and coma.

Cognition and Learning. There are no systematic studies or clinical case reports of the effect of lithium treatment on learning and cognition.

Efficacy. Lithium is not widely used in the pediatric age range, but it is prescribed for the control of aggressive and explosive behavior, and with conduct disorders in which there might be an underlying bipolar illness (O'Donnell, 1985). There is, however, insufficient research data regarding the efficacy of lithium with such conditions. Successful treatment has been reported, but generally in less than 50% of the cases, with a range of less than 20 to over 90% of the cases showing improvement across studies. The general problem, as with so many pharmacological studies, is that the methodology is poor.

PSYCHOSOCIAL CONSIDERATIONS

Most psychopharmacology research papers do not address the potential negative psychological effects of psychotropic medications on children. It is fair to state that medication can significantly reduce behavior problems and, in turn, social and personal functioning often is improved. However, we must keep in mind that medication is not requested by the child, but by significant adults in his or her life. Many children view medication as an imposition and loss of self-control that undoubtedly affects their self-esteem. Other children, with the help of well-meaning adults, feel they cannot function without the medication and often abdicate any sense of personal responsibility for their behavior. It is not uncommon to hear children state there is something wrong with their body or brain, so that they must take the medication. Although drug-induced behavioral improvement undoubtedly occurs, it should not be overemphasized at the expense of potential negative psychological effects. As Valins and Nisbett (1971) have suggested, the long-term outcome of treatment might be enhanced by underselling rather than overselling medication when it is used in the treatment of behavior disorders. These issues have been discussed at length by Whalen and Henker (1976).

SUMMARY

The past 40 years have been marked by a gradual increase in the variety and use of psychotropic medications in the pediatric age range. The stimulants and anticonvulsants were the first medications to be used for their possible psychotherapeutic value, followed by the development of the antipsychotic drugs in the 1950s, and by the antidepressants and antimanic medications in the 1960s. While stimulant medications were found to be useful, there has been little support for the use of anticonvulsant medications in the treatment of behavior disorders. Antipsychotic drugs have been used successfully for the treatment of several behavioral disturbances, especially in hospital settings, but they are prescribed with caution because significant side effects can occur. The antimanic medications have been successful with children having severe behavioral disturbances, but generally are not used because of their toxicity. The popularity of stimulant drugs dramatically decreased in the decade of the 1950s, but rebounded in the 1960s. Since that time stimulants have been used extensively for the treatment of attention deficit disorders. Today, stimulant medications are undoubtedly more widely used and researched in the pediatric age range than any other psychotropic drug. The antidepressant medications have been employed extensively for the successful symptomatic treatment of enuresis. Within the past 4 years, antidepressants have been integral in the treatment of childhood depression and continue to be used for the treatment of some anxiety states. A broad spectrum of so-called antianxiety medications have been used since the 1940s for the treatment of sleep disturbances in children, but interestingly not for childhood anxiety disorders. Antidepressant medications more commonly have been prescribed for the treatment of anxiety states in children.

The 1970s witnessed the emergence of an antidrug movement in this country, which stimulated the development of new federal regulations and safeguards for the clinical and research use of psychotropic medications. The decade of the 1970s also marked an increased interest in the search for alternatives to drug treatment of behavioral disturbances. The effects of environmental pollutants and diet on behavior began to receive a great deal of attention. Psychotropic medications continue to be used and studied, however, and in many cases provide the most reasonable treatment of choice.

DIETARY TREATMENT
HISTORICAL OVERVIEW

Long before Feingold (1968) postulated a relationship between diet and behavior, there were extensive speculations in this area by allergists and other physicians. Shannon (1922) is frequently quoted as one of the first physicians to note such a relationship. He asserted that allergic reactions, particularly to foods, could affect CNS functioning and give rise to a variety of physical and behavioral reactions. Behavioral reactions were of particular interest, as illustrated by the following case material from Shannon (1922, p. 91):

> A boy, 8 years old, was brought in because he was extremely irritable, did not eat well, was cruel to his playmates, and was unable to apply himself at school. As a result of the latter condition, he spent 2 years in the first grade. He had been perfectly normal, except that he had had head colds almost from birth until he was 4 years old. At that time he had had a series of convulsions without ascribable cause.

The patient was tested and found to have numerous food allergies. Shannon eliminated these foods from the boy's diet. Six weeks later he made the following observations (p. 91):

> Nothing was heard from him for 6 weeks, when the mother reported that the boy had been a different child from the time he had gone on the diet. His irritability was lessened; he was no longer cruel to his playmates; he was doing well in school; and his appetite was good. When heard from again 3 months after the diet was instituted, the improvement had continued and he had made his grade in school without difficulty.

This is a typical anecdotal case illustration. Clinical observations were made and conclusions drawn on the basis of the patient's behavior subsequent to the dietary eliminations. Shannon assumed that the behavioral disturbances were symptoms of a direct allergic reaction of central nervous system tissue and ruled out alternative interpretations. However, his arguments were not convincing: One obvious possibility is that the boy's allergic symptomatology gave rise to secondary behavioral and emotional reactivity, rather than a primary reactivity due to CNS hyperirritability mediated by an immunologic reaction. Shannon explicitly ruled out this possibility, because he felt marked behavioral and emotional reactivity occurred in cases with minimal physical discomfort due to allergic symptomatology. This latter point is particularly interesting, because subsequent anecdotal–clinical case reports have emphasized that allergic symptomatology may be quite minimal or even absent in children with behavior disorders who respond favorably to elimination diets or other allergy treatments (Rapp, 1978; Crook, 1980).

Kahn (1927) made observations similar to Shannon's, and to Rowe's (1931) and generally is credited with the description of what is currently called "allergic tension-fatigue syndrome." A paper by Speer (1958) frequently is referenced as providing an excellent description of the syndrome. Although variations exist in the reported symptomatology, Speer noted that two major behavioral categories emerge: hyperactivity and hypoactivity. Speer went on to state that the former is characterized by hyperkinetic behavior, poor gross and fine motor coordination, and school difficulties. He stated that teachers find these children to have short attention spans, to be distractible, and to be generally hyperirritable. Often peer relationships are poor. In hypoactivity there is general fatigue and withdrawal. These children show a lack of interest in academic as well as nonacademic activities and typically tire easily. As a result of their fatigue they often do poorly in school.

Speer (1958), like others before him (Shannon, 1922; Kahn, 1927; Rowe, 1931; Randolph, 1947; Clark, 1948), inferred a direct relationship between allergy, central nervous system functioning, and behavior. Based on anecdotal case histories of the past, Baldwin, Kittler, and Ramsay (1968) postulated the notion of minimal brain dysfunction occurring as a direct result of allergenic reactivity. Their study was one of the first to provide objective data, as opposed to purely clinical observation, regarding the possible relationship between allergies, CNS functioning, and behavior. The authors evaluated a series of children who had been referred to the Arkansas Child Development Center. The center served the entire state as a referral agency for children suspected of being mentally retarded. Each child received a complete physical, neurological, psychological, and speech evaluation. A detailed history was taken, and all patients received an EEG evaluation. From this referral population the authors obtained a group of subjects who had abnormal EEGs and a suspected history of allergy. This group was given a complete allergy work-up, and 20 subjects (15 boys and 5 girls) who tested positive for allergy were selected for further study. No information was provided to the center regarding the general characteristics of the referral population; the number of referred patients with an abnormal EEG in the absence of a history of allergy, with or without a history of cognitive or behavioral disturbance, was not indicated. Subjects were placed on individual elimination diets, excluding those substances to which they were allergic. Six weeks after initiation of the elimination diets, the subjects were reevaluated. The results revealed no change in intellectual test scores, but 11 of the 20 showed improved EEG tracings. The authors concluded that their results warranted a subsequent double-blind investigation with appropriate control groups.

Their study was typical of many in this area of research that are essentially no better than the clinical anecdotal studies, differing only in their inclusion of some objective test procedures and results. Nothing can be concluded from the Baldwin et al. study. There were no control groups, double-blind control of EEG readings, or monitoring of elimination diets. In a second publication Kittler and Baldwin (1970) essentially wrote a position paper, using their previous paper and clinical case studies to emphasize their firm belief in allergy as a cause of minimal brain dysfunction.

Campbell (1968, 1973) has taken a similar position, based on his own clinical experience and research.

Since the publication of these studies, five other studies have appeared that deal primarily with the issue of behavioral disturbance in children as a primary symptom of CNS-inferred allergy (Rapp, 1978; O'Banion, Armstrong, Cummings, & Strange, 1978; Tryphonas & Trites, 1979; Crook, 1980; O'Shea & Porter, 1981). Collectively, these studies are methodologically unsound, and therefore it is impossible to draw any conclusions from them regarding the primary role of allergy in behavior disturbances. As with the anecdotal case study literature, these authors would have us believe that (a) a significant number of behaviorally disturbed children (as high as 50–60%) are disturbed because of allergies; (b) the behavioral disturbance is mediated by CNS allergy, and not by a secondary response to the basic discomfort of allergic symptomatology; (c) most of the children improve dramatically with a diet that eliminates the substances to which they are allergic; (d) foods rather than other allergens are the primary culprits; and (e) behavioral disturbances in the absence of overt or classic allergic symptomatology does not rule out the possibility that the behavior is mediated by a CNS-allergic reaction.

Most allergists, or for that matter pediatricians, do not deny the extent to which allergies can make children feel miserable and place stress on their ability to cope with parents, peers, and schoolwork. This, however, is very different from inferring an allergy that interferes with CNS functioning, as reflected by impaired behavior or learning difficulties. Advocates of a primary CNS allergy argue that any body organ can be the target for an allergic reaction. However, this hypothesis lacks adequate scientific support. If CNS allergy is a valid entity, it is unlikely that it is as prevalent a cause of behavioral and learning disturbance as its advocates would suggest. In the November 1982 issue of the *Journal of the American Medical Association* that was devoted entirely to allergy and immunology, only scant reference was made to CNS allergy to food. In the article on food allergies, Buckley (1982) noted that there is no conclusive proof that food allergy causes behavioral disturbance.

We turn now to a related area of study that has focused on the adverse effects of common chemical substances found in foods and beverages, namely food additives—colors, flavors, and preservatives. Research in this area was pioneered by Feingold, an allergist, who believed additives are a primary cause of hyperactivity, behavior disturbance, and learning problems in children. In fact, he felt that additives are responsible for such problems in 50 to 60% of the children who present with such characteristics! Initially he hypothesized that additives produce an allergic reaction in much the same way that others postulated food allergies as a basis for CNS-mediated behavioral disturbance and learning problems. He quickly abandoned this notion in favor of the concept of a genetically mediated adverse reaction, as we shall see.

THE FEINGOLD HYPOTHESIS

In 1968 Feingold presented a paper to the Annual Congress of the American College of Allergists that was to mark the beginning of a great deal of public interest in the relationship between food additives and behavior and learning problems in children. The presentation focused on the adverse physical reactions that might occur from additives, particularly from color additives derived from coal tar dyes. Feingold noted that such additives are frequently used in medicinal tablets, capsules, and syrups, and asthmatic reactions had been reported in children that were thought to be induced by artificial color additives (Speer, 1958; Chafee & Settipane, 1967). Although all the coal tar dyes might give rise to adverse reactions, Feingold and others (Lockey, 1959; Chafee & Settipane, 1967) reported specific reactions to tartrazine (yellow dye no. 5), possibly because it is used so commonly. Feingold (1973) also noted that reactions produced by tartrazine were similar to aspirin (salicylate) intolerance, even though the two chemical compounds are structurally different. He further observed that in some patients with aspirin intolerance, symptoms were not relieved with the elimination of aspirin from the patient's system, but did clear with a diet free of additives and foods containing natural salicylates (e.g., almonds, apples, apricots, blackberries, cherries, nectarines, oranges, peaches, prunes, plums, tea, strawberries, and tomatoes, to mention a few). This discovery led to the formulation of the famous Feingold Kaiser-Permanente elimination diet while Feingold was chief of the Division of Allergy at the Kaiser-Permanente Medical Center in Santa Clara, California. Feingold's subsequent experience and the research of others (Conners, 1980) led to a deemphasis of the role of salicylates, and by the late 1970s foods that presumably contained natural salicylates no longer were eliminated from the Feingold diet.

Although not discussed in the 1968 presentation, Feingold's earlier clinical experience led him to suspect that adverse behavioral reactions could be triggered by additives. In 1965 he successfully treated a woman who had hives and swelling around the eyes with a diet that eliminated artificial food colors and flavors. Two weeks after she went on the diet, Feingold received a call from a psychiatrist who had been treating the woman for 2 years. The psychiatrist stated that over the past 2 weeks there had been a marked reduction in her hostile and aggressive behavior. This insight led Feingold to search for new cases, especially children. He was aware that hyperactivity, behavior problems, and learning difficulties had risen dramatically over the past 20 years, as had the use of food additives. As a result of this observation, along with the presumed effectiveness of the Feingold Kaiser-Permanente elimination diet, Feingold inferred a direct relationship between additive consumption and disturbances in behavior and learning. His position was formally presented at an annual meeting of the American Medical Association (Feingold, German, Brahm, & Simmers, 1973). His clinical findings were based on a study of 25 children placed on the Feingold Kaiser-Permanente diet (Feingold et al., 1973).

A dramatic change in behavior was observed within 1 to 4 weeks after instituting the diet. Children who were on medication with behavior-modifying drugs, e.g., amphetamines, methylphenidate, tranquilizers, and antidepressants, etc., could discontinue the medication within a few days after initiating dietary management. In addition, in school-age children a marked improvement in scholastic achievement was observed. . . . Any infraction of the diet, either deliberate or fortuitous, induced a recurrence of the clinical pattern within 2 to 4 hours, with persistence for 24 hours to 96 hours. In other words, we could turn the pattern on and off at will. (Feingold et al., 1973).

Their remarks were subsequently read into the Congressional Record by Senator Beall (1973). Newspaper articles and radio and television appearances, along with Feingold's 1975 book *Why Your Child is Hyperactive*, further popularized the notion that hyperkinesis could be controlled by a diet that eliminates food additives.

Unlike others (Shannon, 1922; Speer, 1958; Campbell, 1968; Rapp, 1978; O'Shea & Porter, 1981), Feingold did not accept allergy as a primary cause for behavioral and learning disturbances. Feingold favored the notion of a genetically mediated deficiency in the metabolism of food additives. He further speculated that this resulted from a sex-linked defect, because many more boys than girls presented with hyperkinesis and/or learning problems. He noted the well-known fact that the intermediate metabolism of many drugs or other chemical substances is controlled by genetic factors. Genetically mediated failure to metabolize a drug or chemical substance may give rise to an adverse reaction that might be expressed through behavioral or learning disturbances. He further noted that there are many genetically mediated metabolic deficiencies that have adverse effects on behavior or learning. One classic example is the genetically mediated defect in the metabolism of the amino acid phenylalanine. The systemic excess, or nonmetabolized, phenylalanine interferes with normal brain development, which results in mental retardation (Vaughan, McKay, & Behrman, 1979). This disorder, called phenylketonuria, can be diagnosed in the neonatal period, and the infant is placed on a phenylalanine-free diet to minimize adverse effects on brain development. Thus, as in phenylketonuria, children who manifested adverse reactions to food additives might have a genetically mediated defect that would interfere with their metabolism of food additives, as expressed through behavior and learning disturbances. Feingold's clinical observations and theoretical speculations generated tremendous public interest and led to the formulation of numerous parent groups that advocated his approach to the treatment of behavior and learning disturbances.

There continues to be strong public and professional support for Feingold's position (Adler, 1978, 1982; Wunderlich, 1981; Bobner, Marchionda, Benz, Newman, & Beaubien, 1982), despite limited support in the scientific literature.

Diet Elimination Studies

The first series of controlled studies on the Feingold hypothesis was conducted by Conners, Goyette, Southwick, Lees, and Andrulonis (1976). They selected 15 children, between the ages of 6 and 12 years, with a history of hyperactivity as defined by DSM-II criteria. This selection was accomplished by a medical and social history, parent and teacher symptom ratings, and use of a psychiatric rating scale. Parents and teachers of the children completed an abbreviated version of the Conners Parent–Teacher Rating Scale twice a week for 4 weeks to obtain baseline data on the children's behavior. Seven of the children had been on medication for control of their hyperactivity at the start of the baseline period, but medication was discontinued after the second week of observation. At the end of the 4-week baseline observation period, the children were randomly assigned to one of two diets. The experimental diet consisted of foods and beverages that did not contain artificial colors or flavors, or natural salicylates. The control diet contained the suspected problem ingredients, but was also designed as an exclusion diet. It was designed so that it would have the following characteristics: (a) that it was as difficult to follow as the experimental diet, (b) that it was believable as a potentially beneficial treatment, (c) that it required as much time in preparation, shopping, and implementation as the experimental diet, and (d) that it was nutritionally similar to the experimental diet.

Prior to the start of the experimental phase of the study, parents met with a nutritionist who explained the diets and procedures for implementing them, and for monitoring dietary violations. A double-blind crossover design then was used. The children were on each diet for 4 weeks, during which time parents and teachers continued to rate behaviors twice a week.

At the end of the first 4 weeks, the Clinical Global Impressions Scale (a subjective interview-rating instrument) was used to obtain parental impressions of behavior change. Analysis of the ratings indicated significant improvement in the behavior of children on the experimental diet when compared to the control-diet children. This result provided apparent support for the Feingold hypothesis (Conners, 1980), but closer analysis revealed that only 4 of the 15 children showed moderate improvement on the experimental diet, with either no improvement or slight improvement on the control diet.

Data from the somewhat more objective Abbreviated Conners Parent–Teacher Rating Scale revealed that both parents and teachers noted approximately a 15% reduction in symptoms when children were on the experimental diet, and roughly a 3% improvement on the control diet, when compared to ratings obtained during the baseline period. Conners noted, however, that improvement on the experimental diet was reported only for those children who were placed on it following the control diet. This phenomenon has been reliably noted in many studies and may be controlled by factors other than treatment effects (Conners et al., 1967). For example, the findings could be a function of chance assignment of the best treatment responders to the "control diet first" group. Another possibility is that the raters, with practice, developed a more accurate or clearly delineated framework on which to judge the behavioral improvement of the children.

When the diet-phase ratings were compared, it was found that the parent's behavioral ratings were essentially the same for both diets. Conversely, the teachers rated behavior as significantly worse on the control diet. When parent and teacher behavioral ratings were analyzed for congruence, the investigators noted a strong correspondence in ratings for only two children. Conners et al. (1976) suggested that the consistency of the ratings for these two children provided some assurance that the fluctuations in behavior reflect real behavior change in some instances. The lack of correspondence between parent and teacher ratings in most cases, however, make the data difficult to interpret. Conners concluded that there is some merit in the Feingold hypothesis, but he suggests that reactivity to additives and/or salicylates only occurs in a very small number of children who are described as hyperkinetic or behaviorally disturbed.

The most elaborate and highly controlled series of studies on the Feingold hypothesis was conducted by Harley, Ray, Tomasi et al. (1978). They decided to utilize the same diagnostic procedures and experimental design, with a similar double-blind crossover procedure, as outlined in the Conners et al. (1976) study. However, they provided greater experimental control of the diets by removing all foods and beverages from the homes of the subjects, and supplying foods and beverages specially packaged so that the experimental and control diets could not be differentiated. Other procedures were included to mislead the families—such as including items that looked like they might contain additives—to determine if parental ratings were influenced by parents' attitudes regarding the effects of additives. Additionally, they obtained laboratory measures of the cognitive and behavioral functions of the subjects. Finally, they studied a larger group of children than Conners et al. (1976), as well as a group of preschoolers.

Parental responses to the Conners Abbreviated Parent–Teacher Rating Scale revealed that most of the parents (12 of 13 mothers and 11 of 14 fathers) rated their child as improved on the Feingold diet. However, like Conners et al. (1976), this result occurred only for those children who were on the control diet first. In contrast to this finding, all of the mothers of the preschool children and 4 of 7 of the fathers reported improvement on the Feingold diet regardless of diet order. No differences were found in teacher ratings on the Conners Scale; on a variety of specific classroom behaviors that were monitored by trained observers; or in performance on the laboratory measures of cognition, attention, and motor functioning.

Harley, Ray, Tomasi et al. (1978, p. 826) concluded, "While there may well exist a subset of hyperactive children whose behavior is adversely affected by artificial food colors, the results of the present study of boys aged 6 to 12 suggest either that such a subset is very small or that the relationship of diet manipulation to behavioral change is much less dramatic and predictable than has been described in anecdotal clinical reports."

The dramatic effect noted for the preschool children was played down by the authors. They stated that parent ratings could not be relied on, and that the number of preschool children studied was too small to draw any firm conclusions regarding the effects of the diet. In view of the excellent control procedures used to disguise the diet phases, it seems unreasonable to dismiss the preschool findings. They at least suggest the need for replication with the inclusion of assessment measures thought to be less subjective, but to date no such replication with the dietary control of the Harley, Ray, Tomasi et al. (1978) study has been conducted.

Challenge Studies

The above studies attempted to evaluate the effectiveness of the Feingold diet by on–off diet comparisons within the same group of children. Another approach advocated by the National Advisory Committee on Hyperkinesis and Food Additives (1975) is to "challenge" individuals thought to be improved on the Feingold diet with substances presumed to be responsible for their behavioral or learning disturbances.

One of the most methodologically sound challenge studies was conducted by Harley, Matthews, and Eichman (1978). They selected for further study those children from their initial project (Harley, Ray, Tomasi et al., 1978) who appeared to be the most responsive to the Feingold diet. Nine children were selected on the basis of parent and teacher ratings, classroom observation data, and laboratory test performance. All nine children were in the 6- to 12-year age range, with an average age of 9 years. A control group of nonhyperactive children was selected on the basis of similar age, grade placement, and general academic ability.

As in the initial study, the subjects were assessed with the Conners Abbreviated Parent–Teacher Scale by the parents and classroom teacher; behavioral observations were made by trained classroom observers; and laboratory test data on cognition, memory, attention, and motor behaviors were obtained.

All children were assessed during a 2-week baseline period, during which time there were no dietary restrictions. A 4-week baseline assessment period followed in which the Feingold diet was implemented. As in the initial study, all foods were provided to the families of the nine experimental children. A 9-week experimental period followed in which the nine experimental children were challenged with cookies and candy bars containing precise amounts of food additives or were given placebo cookies and candy bars. Each challenge cookie or candy bar contained 13.5 mg of additives, and either two cookies or two candy bars were given each day of a challenge period. The 27 mg total per day was selected because it represented an estimated average daily consumption of additives. Five of the nine children began with the challenge, and four with the placebo. The challenge periods lasted 2 weeks and alternated with 2-week placebo periods, except for the last phase for each group, which lasted 3 weeks.

The initial analysis did not reveal any evidence of a challenge effect in parent or teacher ratings, classroom observations, or laboratory assessment of behavior. As expected, the nine experimental children, with their history of hyperkinesis, functioned significantly less well than the control children. Analysis of individual subjects revealed that only one child showed substantial evidence of being adversely affected by the challenge. Their findings led the authors to conclude, as they had in their initial study, that there is little support for Feingold's claim that 50% of children diagnosed as hyperkinetic can be helped significantly by his diet.

Conners (1980) also conducted a series of challenge studies. The children studied were selected on the basis of their initially favorable response to the Feingold diet. As in previous studies, many measures were used to assess the children. Conners was particularly interested in the dose-time relationship between ingestion of additives and any behavioral deterioration that occurred. Overall, the results indicated that very few children responded adversely to the food challenges. Of those few that did, the reaction usually occurred within 1 hour and was not detectable after 3 hours. Also of interest was the finding that when adverse reactions did occur, they were worse with subsequent challenges, even though the reactions were restricted to the 3-hour period following the challenge. This finding led Conners (1980, p. 68) to speculate:

These results raise the possibility that after the child has been on a diet which eliminates artificial colors, the first time he eats foods with such dyes in them he may not respond immediately, but have a delayed effect which depends upon a priming or loading effect from the previous day. This means that the dosage or amounts ingested, as well as the speed with which the substances are eliminated from the body, might be crucial in determining whether the child experiences an adverse reaction.

Another interesting point is that Conners found severe worsening of behavior to the food challenges in one child who did not show any marked improvement on the Feingold diet, and no behavioral deterioration in another child who showed marked improvement in behavior when placed on the diet. Such findings raise the possibility that factors other than food additives may give rise to adverse behavioral reactions.

Six other double-blind crossover challenge studies have been reported in the literature (Levy et al., 1978; Mattes & Gittelman-Klein, 1978; Rose, 1978; Swanson & Kinsbourne, 1980; Weiss et al., 1980; Adams, 1981). Rose (1978), in a well controlled behavioral study of two children maintained on the Feingold diet, found that both were adversely affected by a tartrazine cookie challenge of 1.2 mg. Swanson and Kinsbourne (1980) used 100 and 1,350 mg challenges of combined food additives to assess their effects on a paired-associates learning task in hyperactive and nonhyperactive children. The results revealed that both groups were affected significantly by the challenge and furthermore reacted adversely to the placebo, which was sugar. Frankly, it is difficult to conclude anything from the Swanson and Kinsbourne study! Weiss et al. (1980) challenged 22 children and found only 2 who responded adversely. The remaining studies did not reveal any children with adverse reactions to additive challenges.

One other interesting study by Williams, Cram, Tausig, and Webster (1978) assessed the relative effects of drugs and diet on hyperactive behaviors. The results revealed that medications (Ritalin® or dextroamphetamine) were superior to the Feingold diet in controlling hyperkinetic behavior. When the subjects were on medication, additive challenges did not affect behavior as assessed by the Conners Parent–Teacher Rating Scale, but their behavior was affected adversely by additive challenges when they were off medication (placebo condition). The effects of additive challenges were small, but no information was provided regarding the exact number of children who reacted negatively.

Summary

As with the elimination diet studies, the challenge studies suggest that a very small number of children respond adversely to additives. This effect has been demonstrated with tiny amounts of additives (Rose, 1978), as well as with massive doses (Swanson & Kinsbourne, 1980). Most studies, however, have been conducted with levels that attempt to approximate the average daily consumption of additives (20–30 mg). Adverse effects have been reported in children diagnosed as hyperkinetic, as well as in those who are not (Swanson & Kinsbourne, 1980). Negative behavioral reactions to additive challenges also have been found in children who do not show positive reaction to the Feingold diet (Conners, 1980). Finally, adverse reactions to additive challenges appear to occur 1 to 2 hours after ingestion and to dissipate 3 to 4 hours after ingestion (Rose, 1978; Conners, 1980; Swanson & Kinsbourne, 1980).

Thus, despite continued public interest in the Feingold diet, it does not appear to be a primary treatment for the DSM-III attention deficit or conduct disorders.

OTHER DIETARY TREATMENTS

Sucrose

There has been much speculation regarding the role of poor nutrition in behavioral and learning problems in school-age children (Mayer, 1972; Paige, 1975; Cheraskin, 1976; Knapczyk, 1979; Charlton-Seifert, Stratton, & Williams, 1980). Particular emphasis has been placed on the potentially adverse effect of excessive sugar (sucrose) intake (Charlton-Seifert et al., 1980). Some nutritionists have suggested that many behaviorally disturbed or learning-impaired children have hypoglycemia, a condition in which the pancreas produces excess insulin in response to the intake of carbohydrates such as sugar. The excess insulin rapidly lowers blood sugar levels and deprives the body, especially the brain, of needed nutrients. Sieben (1977) noted that reactive hypoglycemia is a rather rare condition and highly unlikely to play a primary role in most cases of behavioral disturbance or learning impairment. Despite the lack of sound scientific evidence, parents and school personnel continue to view sugar as a potential cause of hyperactivity, behavior disturbance, and, to a somewhat lesser extent, learning disabilities (Knapczyk, 1979; Charlton-Siefert et al., 1980). We know of only two experimental studies in which the potentially negative effects of sugar may be inferred (Swanson & Kinsbourne, 1980; Prinz, Roberts, & Hantman, 1980). In assessing the effects of dye challenges on the performance of hyperactive and nonhyperactive children Swanson and Kinsbourne (1980) used sugar for their placebo substance. Examination of their data revealed that sugar adversely affected the performance of both groups, a finding not discussed by the investigators but subsequently pointed out in a critique by Ferguson, Rapoport, and Weingartner (1981). In a controlled study by Prinz et al. (1980), sucrose challenges were correlated with increased aggressive and destructive play behaviors in a laboratory setting for a group of hyperactive children and with increased activity level in the nonhyperactive control group. The investigators point out alternative explanations that might account for their findings, but suggest that the role of sucrose on behavior deserves further study. A less well-controlled study by Gross (1984) did not reveal any significant negative effect on behavior following the ingestion of sucrose by 150 children. Rapoport and Kruesi (1983) suggested that the effect of sucrose on behavior is not clear-cut, and that it would be premature to advance any conclusions regarding the possible relationship between sucrose and behavior.

Vitamins

It is well known that vitamin deficiencies can significantly impair health and behavioral functioning. Unfortunately, this fact has lead to the erroneous conclusion that massive quantities of vitamins cure or greatly improve behavioral functioning and learning. Sieben (1977) noted that megavitamin therapy is the mainstay of orthomolecular psychiatry. Megavitamin therapy initially was applied to the treatment of schizophrenia and infantile autism (Rimland, 1973), but it has been extended to the treatment of less severe psychopathological conditions (Thiessen & Mills, 1975). There is virtually no sound scientific evidence in support of the efficacy of megavitamin therapy (Klein & Gittelman-Klein, 1976; Campbell, 1975). After an exhaustive review of the area, a task force of the American Psychiatric Association (1974) concluded that claims of the usefulness of megavitamin therapy were unfounded. A similar conclusion was reached by the committee on nutrition of the American Academy of Pediatrics (1976). Nor have more recent studies supported claims of the efficacy of megavitamin therapy (Bennett, McClelland, Kriegsmann, Andrus, & Sells, 1983; Haslam, Dalby, & Rademaker, 1984). Finally, recent articles in the *New England Journal of Medicine* point out the potential toxic effects of excessive vitamin ingestion (Schaumburg et al., 1983; Rudman & Williams, 1983).

SUMMARY

Shannon (1922) was one of the first allergists to report on the effects of diet on the behavior of children. The initial focus was on allergenic mediation of behavior and learning problems, especially to food allergens. Specifically, allergens were thought to directly affect the central nervous system. This notion persisted, and in the 1960s some investigators believed allergens that affect the CNS might give rise to minimal brain dysfunction. Although the notion of allergenically mediated behavior and learning problems persists to the present, there was a shift in emphasis in the 1970s to the investigation of the adverse affects of chemical dyes and preservatives (Feingold, 1975). Feingold's speculations were met with a great deal of interest and public support. However, subsequent well controlled scientific studies did not support his excessive claims. Despite the lack of scientific support for Feingold's ideas, they continue to receive public acceptance.

Although a number of excellent studies have been conducted on Feingold's speculations, virtually no well-controlled studies have appeared in the literature on the effect of megavitamin therapy on behavior and learning. Sugar, a substance long thought to adversely affect behavior, is just beginning to be studied scientifically. Like dyes and preservatives, it is doubtful that sugar will turn out to be a highly villainous substance adversely affecting the behavior of children.

FINAL COMMENTS

Two major biological treatment approaches to the treatment of childhood behavior problems have been discussed: psychopharmacological and dietary. The use of psychopharmacological agents began in the late 1930s and focused on the use of stimulants and anticonvulsants. By the 1970s five classes of psychopharmacological drugs were used to treat behavior problems: stimulants, antipsychotic drugs, antidepressants, antianxiety drugs, and antimanic agents. Stimulant medications appear to be the most widely used and researched in the pediatric age range and have been used primarily for the treatment of attention deficit disorders. Antipsychotics have been used for the control of severely disturbed children and adolescents, especially in residential treatment centers. Antidepressants, imipramine in particular, have been used extensively in the symptomatic treatment of enuresis and more recently for the treatment of preadolescent depression. Antianxiety and antimanic agents have been used sparingly. Anticonvulsants were used in the late 1930s and 1940s for the treatment of behavior problems thought to be neurologically based, but now are rarely used.

Although the dietary treatment of childhood behavior problems began earlier than psychopharmacological treatment, there was not great interest in this area until the work of Feingold appeared in the 1970s. The interest in dietary treatment undoubtedly was stimulated by a growing antidrug attitude in this country and by our desire as a nation to deal with life problems as naturally as possible. To date, there has been no compelling evidence that diet significantly affects the behavior of a large number of children. Although research is needed in this area, it is fair to state that psychopharmacological treatment has been more effective than dietary treatment of childhood behavior problems. Although psychopharmacological agents can be highly effective, they should not be considered the primary mode of therapy for most childhood behavior problems.

REFERENCES

Achenbach, T. (1978). Psychopathology of childhood: Research problems and issues. *Journal of Consulting and Clinical Psychology, 46* , 759–776.

Adams, W. (1981). Lack of behavioral effects from Feingold diet violations. *Perceptual and Motor Skills, 52,* 307–313.

Adler, S. (1978). Behavior management: A nutritional approach to the behaviorally disordered and learning disabled child. *Journal of Learning Disabilities, 11,* 651–656.

Adler, S. (1982). Nutrition and language-learning development in preschool programs for children with learning disabilities. *Journal of Learning Disabilities, 15,* 323–325.

Alderton, H. R., & Hoddinott, B. A. (1964). A controlled study of the use of thioridazine in the treatment of hyperactive and aggressive children in a children's psychiatric hospital. *Canadian Psychiatry Journal, 9,* 239–247.

Alexandris, A., & Lundell, F. W. (1968). Effect of thioridazine, amphetamine, and placebo on the hyperkinetic syndrome and cognitive area in mentally deficient children. *Canadian Medical Association Journal, 98,* 92–96.

Allen, R. P., & Safer, D. J. (1973). Factors influencing the suppressant effects of two stimulant drugs on the growth of hyperactive children. *Pediatrics, 51,* 660–667.

American Academy of Pediatrics, Committee on Nutrition (1976). Megavitamin therapy for childhood psychoses and learning disabilities. *Pediatrics, 58,* 910.

American Psychiatric Association. (1974). Megavitamins and orthomolecular therapy in psychiatry: Excerpts from the report of the Task Force on Vitamin Therapy in Psychiatry. *Nutrition Review, 32,* 44–74.

American Psychiatric Association. (1980). *Diagnostic and Statistical Manual of Mental Disorders* (3rd ed.). Washington, DC: Author.

Anderson, L. T., Campbell, M., Grega, D. M., Perry, R., Small, A. M., & Green, W. H. (1984). Haloperidol in infantile autism: Effects on learning and behavioral symptoms. *American Journal of Psychiatry, 141,* 1195–1202.

Angle, C. R., & McIntire, M. S. (1968). Persistent dystonia in a brain-damaged child after ingestion of phenothiazine. *Journal of Pediatrics, 73,* 124–126.

Annell, A. L. (Ed.) (1972). *Depressive states in childhood and adolescence.* Stockholm: Almquist & Wiksell.

Bair, H. V., & Herold, W. (1955). Efficacy of chlorpromazine in hyperactive mentally retarded children. *Archives of Neurology and Psychiatry, 74,* 363.

Bakwin, H. (1948). Benzedrine in behavior disorders of children. *Journal of Pediatrics, 32,* 215–216.

Baldwin, D. G., Kittler, F. J., & Ramsay, R. C. (1968). The relationship of allergy to cerebral dysfunction. *Southern Medical Journal, 61,* 1039–1041.

Baldwin, R., & Kenny, T. (1966). Medical treatment of behavior disorders. In J. Hellmuth (Ed.), *Learning disorders* (Vol. II). Seattle: Special Child Publications.

Barkley, R. (1976). Predicting the response of hyperkinetic children to stimulant drugs: A review. *Journal of Abnormal Child Psychology, 4,* 327–348.

Barkley, R. (1977). A review of stimulant drug research with hyperactive children. *Journal of Child Psychology and Psychiatry, 18,* 137–165.

Barkley, R., & Cunningham, C. (1980). Do stimulant drugs improve the academic performance of hyperkinetic children? A review of outcome research. *Clinical Pediatrics, 17,* 85–92.

Beall, G. (1973). *Congressional Record.* Senate, October 3rd. Section 19736–19742.

Beck, L., Langford, W. S., MacKay, M., & Sum, G. (1975). Childhood chemotherapy and later drug abuse and growth curve: A follow-up study of 30 adolescents. *American Journal of Psychiatry, 132,* 436–438.

Bender, L., & Cottington, F. (1942). The use of amphetamine sulfate (benzedrine) in child psychiatry. *American Journal of Psychiatry, 99,* 116–121.

Bender, L., & Nichtern, S. (1956). Chemotherapy in child psychiatry. *New York State Journal of Medicine, 56,* 2791–2796.

Bennett, F. C., McClelland, S., Kriegsmann, E. A., Andrus, L. B., & Sells, C. J. (1983). Vitamin and mineral supplementation in Down's Syndrome. *Pediatrics, 72,* 707–713.

Bindelglass, P. M., Dec, G. H., & Enos, F. A. (1968). Medical and psychosocial factors in enuretic children treated with imipramine hydrochloride. *American Journal of Psychiatry, 124,* 1107–1112.

Blackwell, B., & Currah, H. (1973). The psychopharmacology of nocturnal enuresis. In I. Kolvin, R. McKeith, & S. Meadow (Eds.), *Bladder control and enuresis. Clinics in developmental medicine* (Nos. 48/49). London: Heinemann.

Bobner, R. F., Marchionda, L. M., Benz, C. R., Newman, I., & Beaubein, M. J. (1982). Behavioral disorders: A nutritional checklist. *Academic Therapy, 17,* 457–484.

Bradley, C. (1937). The behavior of children receiving benzedrine. *American Journal of Psychiatry, 94,* 577–585.

Bradley, C. (1950). Benzedrine and dexedrine in the treatment of children's behavior disorders. *Pediatrics, 5,* 24–37.

Bradley, C., & Bowen, M. (1940). School performance of children receiving amphetamine (benzedrine) sulfate. *American Journal of Orthopsychiatry, 10,* 782–788.

Bradley, C., & Bowen, M. (1941). Amphetamine (benzedrine) therapy of children's behavior disorders. *American Journal of Orthopsychiatry, 11,* 92–103.

Bradley, C., & Green, E. (1940). Psychometric performance of children receiving amphetamine (benzedrine) sulfate. *American Journal of Psychiatry, 97,* 388–394.

Brown, P., Winsberg, B. G., Bialer, I., & Press, M. (1973). Imipramine therapy and seizures: Three children treated for hyperactive behavior disorders. *American Journal of Psychiatry, 130,* 210–212.

Brown, W. T., & Solomon, C. I. (1942). Delinquency and the electroencephalogram. *American Journal of Psychiatry, 98,* 499–503.

Buckley, R. H. (1982). Food allergy. *Journal of the American Medical Association, 248,* 2627–2631.

Byck, R. (1975). Drugs in the treatment of psychiatric disorders. In L. Goodman & A. Gilman (Eds.), *The pharmacological basis of therapeutics* (5th ed.). New York: Macmillan.

Campbell, M. B. (1968). Neurological allergy. *Review of Allergy, 22,* 80–89.

Campbell, M. B. (1973). Neurologic manifestations of allergic disease. *Annals of Allergy, 31,* 485–498.

Campbell, M. (1975). Psychopharmacology in childhood psychosis. *International Journal of Mental Health, 4,* 238–254.

Campbell, M. (1985). Schizophrenic disorders and pervasive developmental disorders/infantile autism. In J. M. Wiener (Ed.), *Diagnosis and psychopharmacology of childhood and adolescent disorders.* New York: Wiley.

Campbell, M., Anderson, L. T., Small, A. M., Perry, R., Green, W. H., & Caplan, R. (1982). The effects of haloperidol on learning and behavior in autistic children. *Journal of Autism and Developmental Disorders, 12,* 167–175.

Campbell, M., Cohen, I. L., & Perry, R. (1983). Psychopharmacological treatment.

In T. H. Ollendick & M. Hersen (Eds.), *Handbook of child psychopathology*. New York: Plenum.

Campbell, M., Fish, B., Shapiro, T., & Floyd, A. (1972). Acute responses of schizophrenic children to a sedative and stimulating neuroleptic: A pharmacologic yardstick. *Current Therapeutic Research, 14,* 759–766.

Campbell, M., Schulman, D., & Rapoport, J. L. (1978). The current status of lithium therapy in child and adolescent psychiatry. *Journal of the American Academy of Child Psychiatry, 17,* 717–720.

Cantwell, D. (1977). Psychopharmacologic treatment of the minimal brain dysfunction syndrome. In J. M. Wiener (Ed.), *Psychopharmacology in childhood and adolescence*. New York: Basic Books.

Cantwell, D., & Carlson, G. A. (1978). Stimulants. In J. S. Werry (Ed.), *Pediatric psychopharmacology*. New York: Brunner/Mazel.

Carlisle, C. L. (1937). Use of benzedrine sulfate in catatonic stupors. *Medical Bulletin of the Veterans' Administration, 13,* 224.

Chafee, F., & Settipane, C. A. (1967). Asthma caused by F. D. & C. approved dyes. *Journal of Allergy, 40,* 65–72.

Chao, D., Sexton, J., & Davis, S. D. (1964). Convulsive equivalent syndrome of childhood. *Journal of Pediatrics, 64,* 499–508.

Charlton-Seifert, J., Stratton, B. D., & Williams, M. G. (1980). Sweet and slow: Diet can affect learning. *Academic Therapy, 16,* 211–217.

Cheraskin, E. (1976). *Psychodietetics*. New York: Stein & Day.

Christenson, D. E., & Sprague, R. L. (1975). Effects of combining methylphenidate and a classroom token system in modifying hyperactive behavior. *American Journal of Mental Deficiency, 80,* 266–276.

Clark, T. W. (1948). The part of allergy in childhood neuroses. *Journal of Child Psychiatry, 1,* 177–180.

Conners, C. K. (1975). A placebo-crossover study of caffeine treatment of hyperkinetic children. *International Journal of Mental Health, 4,* 132–143.

Conners, C. K. (1976). Classification and treatment of childhood depression. In D. Gallant and G. Simpson (Eds.), *Depression: Behavioral, biochemical, diagnostic and treatment concepts*. New York: Spectrum.

Conners, C. K. (1980). *Food additives and hyperactive children*. New York: Plenum.

Conners, C. K., & Eisenberg, L. (1963). The effect of methylphenidate on symptomatology and learning in disturbed children. *American Journal of Psychiatry, 120,* 458–463.

Conners, C. K., Eisenberg, L., & Barcai, A. (1967). Effect of dextroamphetamine on children. *Archives of General Psychiatry, 17,* 478–485.

Conners, C. K., Goyette, C. H., Southwick, D. A., Lees, J. M., & Andrulonis, P. A. (1976). Food additives and hyperkinesis: A controlled double-blind experiment. *Pediatrics, 58,* 154–166.

Conners, C. K., Kramer, R., Rothschild, G., Schwartz, L., & Stone, A. (1971). Treatment of young delinquent boys with diphenylhydantoin sodium and methylphenidate. *Archives of General Psychiatry, 24,* 156–160.

Conners, C. K., & Taylor, E. (1980). Pemoline, methylphenidate and placebo in children with minimal brain dysfunction. *Archives of General Psychiatry, 37,* 922–930.

Conners, C. K., & Werry, J. S. (1979). Pharmacotherapy. In H. C. Quay & J. S. Werry (Eds.), *Psychopathological disorders of childhood* (2nd ed.). New York: Wiley.

Crook, W. G. (1980). Can what a child eats make him dull, stupid, or hyperactive? *Journal of Learning Disabilities, 13,* 281–286.

Cutts, K. K., & Jasper, J. H. (1939). Effect of benzedrine sulfate and phenobarbital on behavior problem children with abnormal electroencephalograms. *Archives of Neurology and Psychiatry, 41,* 1138–1145.

Cytryn, L., Gilbert, A., & Eisenberg, L. (1960). The effectiveness of tranquilizing drugs plus supportive psychotherapy in treating behavior disorders of children. *American Journal of Orthopsychiatry, 30,* 113–129.

Dabbous, A., & Bergman, A. B. (1966). Neurologic damage associated with phenothiazine. *American Journal of Diseases of Children, 111,* 291–296.

Davidoff, E. M. (1936). A clinical study of the effect of benzedrine therapy on self-absorbed patients. *Psychiatric Quarterly, 10,* 652.

Denhoff, E. (1973). The natural life history of children with minimal brain dysfunction. *Annals of the New York Academy of Science, 205,* 188–205.

Denhoff, E., & Holden, R. H. (1955). The effectiveness of chlorpromazine (thorazine) with cerebral palsied children. *Journal of Pediatrics, 47,* 328–332.

DiMascio, A. (1970). Classification and overview of psychotropic drugs. In A. DiMascio & R. I. Shader (Eds.), *Clinical handbook of psychopharmacology.* New York: Jason Aronson.

DiMascio, A. (1971). Psychopharmacology in children. In S. Chess & A. Thomas (Eds.), *Annual progress in child psychiatry and child development.* New York: Brunner/Mazel.

DiMascio, A., Solty, J., & Shader, R. (1970). Psychotropic drug side effects in children. In R. Shader & A. DiMascio (Eds.), *Psychotropic drug side effects.* Baltimore: Williams & Wilkins.

Dundee, J. W. (1954). A review of chlorpromazine hydrochloride. *British Journal of Anesthesia, 26,* 357–379.

Dyson, L., & Barcai, A. (1970). Treatment of children of lithium-responding parents. *Current Therapeutic Research, 12,* 286–290.

Eisenberg, L., Gilbert, A., Cytryn, L., & Molling, P. A. (1961). The effectiveness of psychotherapy alone and in conjunction with perphenazine or placebo in the treatment of neurotic and hyperkinetic children. *American Journal of Psychiatry, 117,* 1088–1093.

Eisenberg, L., Lachman, R., Molling, P. A., Lockner, A., Mizelle, J. D., & Conners, C. K. (1963). A psychopharmacologic experiment in a training school for delinquent boys: Methods, problems, findings. *Journal of Orthopsychiatry, 33,* 431–447.

Feingold, B. F. (1968). Recognition of food additives as a cause of symptoms of allergy. *Annals of Allergy, 26,* 309–313.

Feingold, B. F. (1973). *Introduction to clinical allergy.* Springfield, IL: Thomas.

Feingold, B. F. (1975). *Why your child is hyperactive.* New York: Random House.

Feingold, B. F., German, D. F., Brahm, R. M., & Simmers, E. (1973). *Adverse reaction to food additives.* Paper presented at the annual meeting of the American Medical Association, New York.

Feinstein, S., & Wolpert, E. (1973). Juvenile manic-depressive illness. *Journal of the American Academy of Child Psychiatry, 12,* 123–136.

Ferguson, H. B., Rapoport, J., & Weingartner, H. (1981). Food dyes and impairment of performance in hyperactive children. *Science, 211,* 410–411.

Fish, B. (1960a). Drug therapy in child psychiatry: Pharmacological aspects. *Comprehensive Psychiatry, 1,* 212–227.

Fish, B. (1960b). Drug therapy in child psychiatry: Psychological aspects. *Comprehensive Psychiatry, 1,* 55–61.

Flaherty, J. A. (1955). Effect of chlorpromazine medication on children with severe emotional disturbance. *Delaware State Medical Journal, 27,* 180–184.

Freed, H., & Peifer, C. A. (1956). Treatment of hyperkinetic emotionally disturbed children with prolonged administration of chlorpromazine. *American Journal of Psychiatry, 113,* 22–26.

Freedman, A. M. (1958). Drug therapy in behavior disorders. *Pediatric Clinics of North America, 5,* 573–594.

Freedman, A. M., Effron, A. S., & Bender, L. (1955). Pharmacotherapy in children with psychiatric illness. *Journal of Nervous and Mental Diseases, 122,* 479–486.

Freedman, R. (1971). Report of the conference on the use of stimulant drugs in the treatment of behaviorally disturbed young school children. *Psychopharmacology Bulletin, 7,* 23–29.

Frommer, E. A. (1967). Treatment of childhood depression with antidepressant drugs. *British Medical Journal, 1,* 729–732.

Garfield, S. L., Helper, M. M., Wilcott, R. C., & Murrly, R. (1962). Effects of chlorpromazine on behavior in emotionally disturbed children. *Journal of Nervous and Mental Diseases, 135,* 147–154.

Garfinkel, B., Webster, C., & Sloman, L. (1975). Methylphenidate and caffeine in the treatment of children with minimal brain dysfunction. *American Journal of Psychiatry, 132,* 723–728.

Gatski, R. L. (1955). Chlorpromazine in the treatment of emotionally maladjusted children. *Journal of the American Medical Association, 157,* 1298–1300.

Gibbs, E. L., & Gibbs, F. A. (1951). Electroencephalographic evidence of thalamic and hypothalamic epilepsy. *Neurology, 1,* 136–144.

Gittelman-Klein, R. (1975). Pharmacotherapy and management of pathological separation anxiety. *International Journal of Mental Health, 4,* 255–271.

Gittelman-Klein, R. (1978). Psychopharmacological treatment of anxiety disorders, mood disorders and Tourette's disorder in children. In M. Lipton, A. DiMascio, & K. Killam (Eds.), *A review of psychopharmacology.* New York: Raven.

Gittelman-Klein, R., & Klein, D. F. (1971). Controlled imipramine treatment of school phobia. *Archives of General Psychiatry, 25,* 204–207.

Gittelman-Klein, R., Spitzer, R., & Cantwell, D. (1978). Diagnostic classifications and psychopharmacological indications. In J. S. Werry (Ed.), *Pediatric psychopharmacology.* New York: Brunner/Mazel.

Gram, L., & Rafaelsen, J. (1972). Lithium treatment of psychotic children and adolescents. *Acta Psychiatrica Scandinavica, 48,* 253–260.

Grant, R. (1974). Sulthiame and behaviour. *Developmental Medicine and Child Neurology, 16,* 821–824.

Greenberg, L., Yellin, A., Spring, C., & Metcalf, M. L. (1975). Clinical effects of imipramine and methylphenidate in hyperactive children. *Journal of Mental Health, 4,* 144–156.

Greenhill, L. L., Hirsch, M. L., Halpern, F., & Spalten, D. (1980). *Molindone hydrochloride in the treatment of aggressive, hospitalized children.* Paper presented at the Annual NCDEU-NIMH Meeting, Key Biscayne.

Greenhill, L., Rieder, R., Wender, P., Bucksbaum, M., & Zahn, T. (1973). Lithium carbonate in the treatment of hyperactive children. *Archives of General Psychiatry, 28,* 636–640.

Gross, M. D. (1976). Growth of hyperkinetic children taking methylphenidate, dextroamphetamine, or imipramine/desipramine. *Pediatrics, 58,* 423–431.

Gross, M. D. (1984). Effect of sucrose on hyperkinetic children. *Pediatrics, 74,* 876–878.

Gross, M. D., & Wilson, W. C. (1964). Behavior disorders of children with cerebral dysrhythmias. *Archives of General Psychiatry, 11,* 610–619.

Gualtieri, C. T. (1981). Tardive dyskinesia. *Developmental Medicine and Child Neurology, 23,* 255–259.

Guilleminault, C., & Anders, T. F. (1976). The pathophysiology of sleep disorders in pediatrics. Part II. *Advances in Pediatrics, 22,* 151–174.

Harley, J. P., Matthews, C. G., & Eichman, P. (1978). Synthetic food colors and hyperactivity in children: A double-blind challenge experiment. *Pediatrics, 62,* 975–983.

Harley, J. P., Ray, R. S., Tomasi, L., Eichman, P. L., Matthews, C. G., Chun, R., Cleeland, C. S., & Traisman, E. (1978). Hyperkinesis and food additives: Testing the Feingold hypothesis. *Pediatrics, 61,* 818–828.

Haslam, R. H., Dalby, J. T., & Rademaker, A. W. (1984). Effects of megavitamin therapy on children with attention deficit disorders. *Pediatrics, 74,* 103–111.

Hayes, T., Panitch, M., & Barker, E. (1975). Imipramine dosage in children: A comment on imipramine and electrocardiographic abnormalities in hyperactive children. *American Journal of Psychiatry, 132,* 546–547.

Hechtman, L., Weiss, G., & Perlman, T. (1978). Growth and cardiovascular measures in hyperactive individuals as young adults and in matched controls. *Canadian Medical Association Journal, 118,* 1247–1250.

Huestis, R., Arnold, E., & Smeltzer, D. (1975). Caffeine versus methylphenidate and d-amphetamine in minimal brain dysfunction: A double-blind comparison. *American Journal of Psychiatry, 132,* 868–871.

Hunt, B. R., Frank, T., & Krush, T. P. (1956). Chlorpromazine in the treatment of severe emotional disorders of childhood. *Journal of Diseases of Children, 9,* 268–277.

Jasper, H. H., Solomon, P., & Bradley, C. (1938). Electroencephalographic analyses of behavior problem children. *American Journal of Psychiatry, 95,* 641–658.

Kahn, I. S. (1927). Pollen toxemia in children. *Journal of the American Medical Association, 88,* 241.

Kelly, J., Koch, M., & Buegel, D. (1976). Lithium carbonate in juvenile manic-depressive illness. *Diseases of the Nervous System, 37,* 90–92.

Kittler, F. J., & Baldwin, D. G. (1970). The role of allergic factors in the child with minimal brain dysfunction. *Annals of Allergy, 28,* 203–206.

Klein, D., & Gittelman-Klein, R. (1976). *Progress in psychiatric drug treatment* (Vol. 2). New York: Brunner/Mazel.

Klein, D., Gittelman, R., Quitkin, F., & Rifkin, A. (1980). *Diagnosis and drug treatment of psychiatric disorders: Adults and children* (2nd ed.). Baltimore: Williams & Wilkins.

Knapczyk, D. R. (1979). Diet control in the management of behavior disorders. *Behavioral Disorders, 5,* 2–9.

Krakowski, A. J. (1965). Amitriptyline in treatment of hyperkinetic children: A double-blind study. *Psychosomatics, 6,* 355–360.

Kupietz, S., & Balka, E. B. (1976). Alterations in the vigilance performance of children receiving amitriptyline and methylphenidate pharmacotherapy. *Psychopharmacology, 50,* 29–33.

Kurtis, L. B. (1966). Clinical study of the response to nortriptyline on autistic children. *International Journal of Neuropsychiatry, 2,* 298–301.

La Veck, G. D., De La Crug, F., & Simundson, E. (1960). Fluphenazine in the treatment of mentally retarded children with behavior disorders. *Diseases of the Nervous System, 21,* 82–85.

Lefkowitz, M. (1969). Effects of diphenylhydantoin on disruptive behavior: Study of male delinquents. *Archives of General Psychiatry, 20,* 643–651.

Lehmann, H. E., & Hanrahan, G. E. (1954). Chlorpromazine, new inhibiting agent for psychomotor excitement and manic states. *Archives of Neurology and Psychiatry, 71,* 227–237.

LeVann, L. J. (1961). Thioridazine, a psychosedative virtually free of side effects. *Alberta Medical Bulletin, 26,* 144–147.

Levitt, E. (1968). *The psychology of anxiety.* Indianapolis, IN: Bobbs-Merrill.

Levy, F., Dumbrell, S., Hobbes, G., Ryan, M., Wilton, N., & Woodhill, J. M. (1978). Hyperkinesis and diet: A double-blind crossover trial with a tartrazine challenge. *The Medical Journal of Australia, 1*(65th year), 61–64.

Lindsley, D. B., & Henry, C. E. (1942). The effects of drugs on behavior and the electroencephalograms of children with behavior disorders. *Psychosomatic Medicine, 4,* 140–149.

Lockey, S. D. (1959). Allergic reactions due to F. D. & C. yellow #5 (tartrazine). *Annals of Allergy, 17,* 718.

Looker, A., & Conners, C. K. (1970). Diphenylhydantoin in children with severe temper tantrums. *Archives of General Psychiatry, 23,* 80–89.

Lucas, A. P., Lockett, H. J., & Grimm, F. (1965). Amitriptyline in childhood depression. *Diseases of the Nervous System, 28,* 105–113.

MacLean, R. E. (1960). Imipramine hydrochloride (Tofranil) and enuresis. *American Journal of Psychiatry, 117,* 551.

Mahony, D., Laferte, R., & Mahony, J. (1973). Enuresis. Part IV. Observations on the sphincter-augmenting effect of imipramine in children with urinary incontinence. *Urology, 1,* 317–323.

Mattes, J., & Gittelman-Klein, R. (1978). A crossover study of artificial food colorings in a hyperkinetic child. *American Journal of Psychiatry, 135,* 987–988.

Mayer, J. (1972). *Human nutrition: Its psychological, medical, and social aspects.* Springfield, IL: Thomas.

McAndrew, J. B., Case, Q., & Treffert, D. A. (1972). Effects of prolonged phenothiazine intake on psychotic and other hospitalized children. *Journal of Autism and Childhood Schizophrenia, 2,* 75–91.

McNutt, B. A., Boileau, R. A., & Cohen, M. N. (1977). The effects of long-term stimulant medication on the growth and body composition of hyperactive children. *Psychopharmacology Bulletin, 13,* 36–38.

Miksztal, M. W. (1956). Chlorpromazine (Thorazine) and reserpine in residential treatment of neuropsychiatric disorders in children. *Journal of Nervous and Mental Diseases, 123,* 477–479.

Millichap, J. G., Aymat, F., Sturgis, L. H., Larsen, K. W., & Egan, R. A. (1968). Hyperkinetic behavior and learning disorders. Part III. *American Journal of Diseases of Children, 116,* 235–244.

Molitch, M., & Eccles, A. K. (1937). The effect of benzedrine sulfate on the intelligence scores of children. *American Journal of Psychiatry, 94,* 587–590.

Molitch, M., & Poliakoff, S. (1937). The effect of benzedrine sulfate on enuresis. *Archives of Pediatrics, 54,* 499–501.

Molitch, M., & Sullivan, J. P. (1937). The effect of benzedrine sulfate on children taking the new Stanford Achievement Test. *American Journal of Orthopsychiatry, 7,* 519–522.

Myerson, A. (1936). Effect of benzedrine sulfate on mood and fatigue in normal and neurotic persons. *Archives of Neurology and Psychiatry, 36,* 816–822.

Nathanson, M. H. (1937). The central action of beta-aminopropylbenzene: Clinical observations. *Journal of the American Medical Association, 108,* 528–531.

National Advisory Committee on Hyperkinesis and Food Additives (1975). *Report to the nutrition foundation.* New York: The Nutrition Foundation.

O'Banion, D., Armstrong, B., Cummings, R. A., & Stange, J. (1978). Disruptive behavior: A dietary approach. *Journal of Autism and Childhood Schizophrenia, 8,* 325–337.

O'Donnell, D. J. (1985). Conduct disorders. In J. M. Wiener (Ed.), *Diagnosis and psychopharmacology of childhood and adolescent disorders.* New York: Wiley.

Oettinger, L. (1962). Chlorprothixene in the management of problem children. *Diseases of the Nervous System, 23,* 568–571.

O'Shea, J. A., & Porter, S. F. (1981). Double-blind study of children with hyperkinetic syndrome treated with multi-allergen extract sublingually. *Journal of Learning Disabilities, 14,* 189–237.

Paige, D. (1975). Nutritional deficiency and school performance. In R. Halsam & P. Vallectutti (Eds.), *Medical problems in the classroom.* Baltimore: University Park Press.

Pasamanick, B. (1951). Anticonvulsant drug therapy of behavior problem children with abnormal electroencephalograms. *Archives of Neurology and Psychiatry, 65,* 752–766.

Paulson, G. W., Rizvi, C. A., & Crane, G. E. (1975). Tardive dyskinesia as a possible sequel of long-term therapy with phenothiazines. *Clinical Pediatrics, 14,* 953–955.

Pelham, W. (1983). The effects of psychostimulants on academic achievement in hyperactive and learning-disabled children. *Thalmus, 3,* 1–48.

Peoples, S. A., & Guttman, E. (1936). Hypertension produced with benzedrine. *Lancet, 1,* 1107.

Petersen, K. E., Anderson, O. O., & Hansen, T. (1974). Mode of action and relative value of imipramine and similar drugs in the treatment of nocturnal enuresis. *European Journal of Clinical Pharmacology, 7,* 187–194.

Physicians' Desk Reference. (1986). (40th ed.). Oradell, NJ: Medical Economics Co.

Poussaint, A. F., & Ditman, K. S. (1965). A controlled study of imipramine (Tofranil) in the treatment of childhood enuresis. *Journal of Pediatrics, 67,* 283–290.

Prinz, R. J., Roberts, W. A., & Hantman, E. (1980). Dietary correlates of hyperactive behavior in children. *Journal of Consulting and Clinical Psychology, 48,* 760–769.

Puig-Antich, J. (1982). Major depression and conduct disorder in prepuberty. *Journal of the American Academy of Child Psychiatry, 21,* 118–128.

Puig-Antich, J., Blau, S., Marx, N., Greenhill, L. L., & Chambers, W. (1978). Prepubertal major depressive disorder: A pilot study. *Journal of the American Academy of Child Psychiatry, 17,* 695–707.

Puig-Antich, J., Perel, J., Lupatkin, W., Chambers, W. J., Tabrizi, M. A., & Stiller, R. (1979). Plasma levels of imipramine and desmethyl imipramine and clinical response in prepubertal major depressive disorder: A preliminary report. *Journal of the American Academy of Child Psychiatry, 18,* 616–627.

Putnam, T. J., & Hood, O. E. (1964). Project Illinois: A study of therapy in juvenile behavior problems. *Western Medicine, 5,* 231–233.

Quinn, P., & Rapoport, J. (1975). A one-year follow-up of hyperactive boys treated with imipramine or methylphenidate. *American Journal of Psychiatry, 132,* 241–245.

Randolph, T. G. (1947). Allergy as a causative factor of fatigue, irritability, and behavior problems of children. *Journal of Pediatrics, 31,* 560–572.

Rapoport, J. (1965). Childhood behavior and learning problems treated with imipramine. *International Journal of Neuropsychiatry, 1*, 635–642.

Rapoport, J. (1976). Pediatric psychopharmacology in childhood depression. In D. Klein & R. Gittelman-Klein (Eds.), *Progress in psychiatric drug treatment* (Vol. 2). New York: Brunner/Mazel.

Rapoport, J., & Kruesi, M. J. (1983). Behavior and nutrition: A mini-review. *Contemporary Nutrition, 8*(10), 2–23.

Rapoport, J., & Mikkelsen, E. J. (1978). Antidepressants. In J. S. Werry (Ed.), *Pediatric psychopharmacology*. New York: Brunner/Mazel.

Rapoport, J., Quinn, P., Bradbard, G., Riddle, D., & Brookes, E. (1974). Imipramine and methylphenidate treatments of hyperactive boys: A double-blind comparison. *Archives of General Psychiatry, 30*, 789–793.

Rapoport, J., Quinn, P., & Lamprecht, F. (1974). Minor physical anomalies and plasma dopamine-beta-hydroxylase activity in hyperactive boys. *American Journal of Psychiatry, 131*, 386–390.

Rapp, D. (1978). Does diet affect hyperactivity? *Journal of Learning Disabilities, 11*, 383–389.

Rapp, D. (1980). *Allergies and the hyperactive child* (2nd ed.). New York: Cornerstone.

Remschmidt, H. (1976). The psychotropic effect of carbamazepine in non-epileptic patients with particular reference to problems posed by clinical studies in children with behavior disorders. In W. Birkmayer (Ed.), *Epileptic seizures–behavior–pain*. Baltimore: University Park Press.

Rettig, J. H. (1955). Chlorpromazine for the control of psychomotor excitement in the mentally deficient. *Journal of Nervous and Mental Diseases, 122*, 190–194.

Rimland, B. (1973). High-dosage levels of certain vitamins in the treatment of children with severe mental disorders. In D. Hawkins & L. Pauling (Eds.), *Orthomolecular psychiatry: Treatment of schizophrenia*. San Francisco: Freeman.

Rogers, W. J. (1965). Use of haloperidol in children's psychiatric disorders. *Clinical Trials Journal, 2*, 162–164.

Rose, T. L. (1978). The functional relationship between artificial food colors and hyperactivity. *Journal of Applied Behavior Analysis, 11*, 439–446.

Rosenblum, S., Buoniconto, P., & Graham, B. D. (1960). Compazine vs. placebo: A controlled study with educable emotionally disturbed children. *American Journal of Mental Deficiency, 64*, 713–717.

Ross, D. M., & Ross, S. A. (1982). *Hyperactivity: Research, theory and action*. New York: Wiley.

Rowe, A. H. (1931). *Food allergy: Its manifestations, diagnosis and treatment*. Philadelphia: Lea & Febiger.

Rudman, D., & Williams, P. (1983). Megadose vitamins: Use and misuse. *New England Journal of Medicine, 309*, 488–490.

Saraf, K., Klein, D., Gittelman-Klein, R., & Groff, S. (1974). Imipramine and side effects in children. *Psychopharmacologia, 37*, 265–274.

Sargant, W., & Blackburn, J. M. (1936). The effect of benzedrine on intelligence scores. *Lancet, 2*, 1385–1387.

Schaumburg, H., Haplan, J., Windebank, A., Vick, N., Rasmus, S., Pleasure, D., & Brown, M. (1983). Sensory neuropathy from pyridoxine abuse: A new megavitamin syndrome. *New England Journal of Medicine, 309*, 445–448.

Schmitt, B. D. (1982). Nocturnal enuresis: An update on treatment. *Pediatric Clinics of North America, 29*, 21–36.

Schrag, P., & Divoky, D. (1975). *The myth of the hyperactive child*. New York: Pantheon.

Schulterbrandt, J. G., & Raskin, A. (Eds.) (1977). *Depression in childhood: Diagnosis, treatment, and conceptual models.* New York: Raven.

Seignot, J. J. (1961). A case of tics of Gilles de la Tourette cured by R1625. *Annals of Medical Psychology, 119,* 578–579.

Shaffer, D., & Ambrosini, P. J. (1985). Enuresis and sleep disorders. In J. M. Wiener (Ed.), *Diagnosis and psychopharmacology of childhood and adolescent disorders.* New York: Wiley.

Shaffer, D., Costello, A.J., & Hill, I. D. (1968). Control of enuresis with imipramine. *Archives of Diseases of Children, 43,* 665–671.

Shaffer, D., Hedge, B., & Stephenson, J. D. (1978). Trial of an alpha-adrenolytic drug (Indoramin) for nocturnal enuresis. *Developmental Medicine and Child Neurology, 20,* 183–188.

Shannon, W. R. (1922). Neuropathic manifestations in infants and children as a result of anaphylactic reactions to food contained in their diet. *American Journal of Diseases of Children, 24,* 89–94.

Shapiro, A. K., Shapiro, E., Brunn, R. D., & Sweet, R. C. (1978). *Gilles de la Tourette syndrome.* New York: Raven.

Shapiro, A. K., Shapiro, E., & Wayne, H. (1973). Treatment of Tourette's syndrome. *Archives of General Psychiatry, 28,* 92–97.

Shaw, C. R., Lockett, H. J., Lucas, A. R., Lamontagne, C. H., & Crimm, F. (1963). Tranquilizer drugs in the treatment of emotionally disturbed children: Part I. *Journal of the American Academy of Child Psychiatry, 2,* 725–742.

Shields, W. D., & Bray, P. F. (1976). A danger of haloperidol therapy in children. *Journal of Pediatrics, 88,* 301–303.

Sieben, R. L. (1977). Controversial medical treatments of learning disabilities. *Academic Therapy, 13,* 133–147.

Silver, A. A. (1955). Management of children with schizophrenia. *American Journal of Psychotherapy, 9,* 196–215.

Solanto, M. V. (1984). Neuropharmacological basis of stimulant drug action in attention deficit disorder with hyperactivity: A review and synthesis. *Psychological Bulletin, 95,* 387–409.

Speer, F. (1958). Allergic tension-fatigue syndrome in children. *International Archives of Allergy, 12,* 207–214.

Sprague, R. L. (1978). Principles of clinical trials and social, ethical and legal issues of drug use in children. In J. S. Werry (Ed.), *Pediatric psychopharmacology.* New York: Brunner/Mazel.

Sprague, R. L., & Sleator, D. K. (1977). Methylphenidate in hyperkinetic children: Differences in dose effects on learning and social behavior. *Science, 198,* 1274–1276.

Swanson, J. M., & Kinsbourne, M. (1980). Food dyes impair performance of hyperactive children on a laboratory learning test. *Science, 207,* 1485–1486.

Thiessen, I., & Mills, L. (1975). The use of megavitamin treatment in children with learning disabilities. *Journal of Orthomolecular Psychiatry, 4,* 288–296.

Tryphonas, H., & Trites, R. (1979). Food allergy in children with hyperactivity, learning disabilities and/or minimal brain dysfunction. *Annals of Allergy, 42,* 22–27.

Ucer, E., & Kreger, K. C. (1969). A double-blind study comparing haloperidol and thioridazine in emotionally disturbed mentally retarded children. *Current Therapeutic Research, 11,* 278–283.

Valins, S., & Nisbett, R. E. (1971). *Attribution processes in the development and treatment of emotional disorders.* New York: General Learning Press.

van Krevelen, D., & van Voorst, J. (1959). Lithium in der behandlung einer psychose unklarer genese bei einem jugendlichen. *Acta Paedopsychiatrica, 26,* 148–152.

Vaughan, V. C., McKay, R. J., & Behrman, R. E. (Eds.) (1979). *Textbook of pediatrics* (11th ed.). Philadelphia: Saunders.

Waizer, J., Hoffman, S., Polizos, P., & Engelhardt, D. (1974). Outpatient treatment of hyperactive school children with imipramine. *American Journal of Psychiatry, 131,* 587–591.

Walker, C. F., & Kirkpatrick, B. B. (1947). Dilantin treatment for behavior problem children with abnormal electroencephalograms. *American Journal of Psychiatry, 103,* 484–492.

Wallace, I. R., & Forsythe, W. I. (1969). The treatment of enuresis: A controlled clinical trial of propoantheline, propoantheline and phenobarbitone, and placebo. *British Journal of Clinical Practice, 23,* 207–210.

Weiss, G. (1975). The natural history of hyperactivity in childhood and treatment with stimulant medication at different ages: A summary of research findings. *International Journal of Mental Health, 4,* 213–226.

Weiss, B., Williams, J. H., Margen, S., Abrams, B., Caan, B., Citron, L. J., Cox, C., McKibben, J., Ogar, D., & Schultz, S. (1980). Behavioral responses to artificial food colors. *Science, 207,* 1487–1488.

Wender, P. (1971). *Minimal brain dysfunction in children.* New York: Wiley.

Werry, J. S. (Ed.) (1978). *Pediatric psychopharmacology.* New York: Brunner/Mazel.

Werry, J. S. (1982). An overview of pediatric psychopharmacology. *Journal of the American Academy of Child Psychiatry, 21,* 3–9.

Whalen, C. K., & Henker, B. (1976). Psychostimulants and children: A review and analysis. *Psychological Bulletin, 83,* 1113–1130.

Whalen, C. K., Henker, B., & Dotemoto, S. (1980). Methylphenidate and hyperactivity: Effects on teacher behaviors. *Science, 208,* 1280–1282.

Whitehead, P., & Clark, L. (1970). Effect of lithium carbonate, placebo, and thioridazine on hyperactive children. *American Journal of Psychiatry, 127,* 824–825.

Wiener, J. M. (Ed.) (1985). *Diagnosis and psychopharmacology of childhood and adolescent disorders.* New York: Wiley.

Wiener, J. M., & Jaffe, S. (1977). History of drug therapy in childhood and adolescent psychiatric disorders. In J. M. Wiener (Ed.), *Psychopharmacology in childhood and adolescence.* New York: Basic Books.

Wilbur, D., MacLean, A. R., & Allen, E. V. (1937). Clinical observations on the effect of benzedrine sulfate. *Proceedings, Staff Meetings of the Mayo Clinic, 12,* 97–104.

Williams, J. I., Cram, D. M., Tausig, F. T., & Webster, E. (1978). Relative effects of drugs and diet on hyperactive behaviors: An experimental study. *Pediatrics, 61,* 811–817.

Winsberg, B., Bialer, I., Kupietz, S., & Tobias, J. (1972). Effects of imipramine and dextroamphetamine on behavior of neuropsychiatrically impaired children. *American Journal of Psychiatry, 128,* 1425–1431.

Winsberg, B. G., Goldstein, S., Yepes, L. E., & Perel, J. M. (1975). Imipramine and electrocardiographic abnormalities in hyperactive children. *American Journal of Psychiatry, 132,* 542–545.

Winsberg, B. G., & Yepes, L. E. (1978). Antipsychotics. In J. S. Werry (Ed.), *Pediatric psychopharmacology.* New York: Brunner/Mazel.

Wolpert, A., Hagamen, M. B., & Merlis, S. (1966). A pilot study of thiothixene in childhood schizophrenia. *Current Therapeutic Research, 8,* 617–620.

Wolpert, A., Hagamen, M. B., & Merlis, S. (1967). A comparative study of thiothixene and trifluoperazine in childhood schizophrenia. *Current Therapeutic Research, 9,* 482–485.

Wolpert, A., Quintos, A., White, L., & Merlis, S. (1968). Thiothixene and chlorprothixene in behavior disorders. *Current Therapeutic Research, 10,* 566–569.

Wunderlich, R. C. (1981). Nutrition and learning. *Academic Therapy, 16,* 303–307.

Yepes, L., Balka, B., Winsberg, B. G., & Bialer, I. (1977). Amitriptyline and methylphenidate treatment of behaviorally disordered children. *Journal of Child Psychology and Psychiatry, 18,* 39–52.

Zimmerman, F. T., & Burgemeister, B. (1955). Preliminary report upon the effect of reserpine upon epilepsy and behavior problems in children. *Annals of the New York Academy of Sciences, 61,* 215–221.

7

GROUP THERAPY

Like many new approaches, group therapy with children arose out of the perceived limitations of existing therapies. Clinicians realized that individual psychotherapy neither provided their child patients with social experiences nor optimally prepared them to function adaptively in groups. Initially, efforts were made to develop adjuncts to individual psychotherapy to provide children with social experiences by involving them in traditional groups such as activity clubs, scouting, or summer camps. Although such experiences were profitable for well-adjusted children, they were not therapeutic for the maladjusted child (Slavson, 1943). Thus, a more therapeutic group experience for disturbed children was needed. The present chapter deals with several approaches to treatment that grew out of this perceived need. The focus of this chapter is more technical than theoretical, since we found that many approaches to group treatment were similar despite their theoretical differences.

HISTORICAL DEVELOPMENT OF GROUP PSYCHOTHERAPY WITH CHILDREN

The inception of group psychotherapy with children began in the early 1930s with the work of S. R. Slavson, a psychiatrist at the Madelyn Borg Child Guidance Institute in New York. In 1943 Slavson published *An Introduction to Group Therapy*, which outlined the theory and clinical technique for Activity Group Therapy. The book was based on 8 years of group work, consisting of the systematic observation of over 750 clinical cases which formed the nucleus for 55 separate group treatment programs. Initially, group therapy was considered an adjunct to individual psychotherapy. Its primary goal was to provide socialization experiences that were not possible in individual therapy and usually did not occur in traditional socialization programs, such as scouting or summer camps. Slavson (1943) felt that traditional socialization groups did not provide the therapeutic milieu necessary to help the pathological child function more adaptively. In fact, he felt such programs could actually exacerbate the problems of such children.

Slavson appears to have been motivated pragmatically by the failure of traditional socialization programs to help youngsters with significant adjustment problems, but he was theoretically reinforced by neoanalytic ideas (Munroe, 1955) regarding determinants of psychopathology and personality development. As noted in chapter 4, the 1930s marked a period of increased emphasis on the role of family and social dynamics in the formulation of personality development and psychopathology, and on the intrinsic ability of individuals to work through their specific adjustment problems. Slavson (1943) felt that family and social dynamics play a major role in character formation by facilitating the reduction of egocentricity and increasing an awareness in the child of the rights and needs of others. Conversely, negative family and social experiences have an adverse affect on development as noted in the following quote from Slavson (1943, pp. 2–3):

> In group therapy, we work with children who are directly rejected by parents, family, school, street gangs, and community center, or whose powers and personalities are indirectly rejected by pampering and coddling, as a result of which they are unable to get on with their contemporaries and with adults. These children are actively hostile and destructive or reject the world by withdrawing from it. They are either excessively aggressive or excessively withdrawn; obsessed with great fears or guilt, they overcompensate for them by nonsocial or antisocial behavior. Having developed these deviant manners and methods for the sake of psychological (and often physical) survival, the child is further victimized by all the organized agencies of the community. Thus, he finds himself impeded at every turn by outer stresses and inner strains. What a child needs in such circumstances is a haven of relief, a sanctuary where these distressing, threatening, and hostile pressures can be removed and relief supplied.

This quote highlights Slavson's emphasis on family and social determinants. His fundamental orientation is psychoanalytic, and conceptually his thinking is like that of Anna Freud (1946, 1966, 1968). The final sentence of the quote emphasizes the type of environment necessary to ameliorate the destructive effects produced by negative and/or overly indulgent environments. Slavson felt that such children need an environment that affords them an opportunity to express their feelings and thoughts through play and action. The environment needs to be permissive and noncontrolling to promote a ''benign regression akin to a corrective emotional experience'' (Scheidlinger, 1977). The therapist's behavior in Slavson's Activity Group Therapy is very nondirective, or client-centered in nature, yet the underlying theory is psychoanalytic, as evidenced by Slavson and Schiffer's (1975) commentary on group transcripts. The nondirective and noninterpretative format of Activity Group Therapy is designed for a patient with reasonably adequate "ego development"; that is, one with a capacity for self-regulation and emotional control. Similar Activity Group Therapy formats were developed by Redl (1944), Axline (1947), and Ginott (1961). The treatment methods of Redl and Ginott are based on psychoanalytic theory, while Axline stressed Rogerian client-centered theory. All four treatment approaches emphasize ego development, but different aspects (Schamess, 1976). Slavson and Redl stressed individualization, autonomy, and sublimation through play, as well as constructive activities and a sense of personal accomplishment. Axline and Ginott, although also nondirective, stressed verbalization and reflection of feelings in the context of play. Schiffer (1969) modified the basic Activity Group Therapy format in the early 1950s for use with pre- and early latency-age school children.

Slavson (1943) also noted that many children were too disturbed to function in the nondirective Activity Group Therapy paradigm, but might profit from a more structured and interpretation-oriented group. This led to the development of Activity-Interview Group Psychotherapy. It is characterized by individual patient–therapist interpretative interactions, as well as by group discussion and interpretation designed to facilitate the resolution of each child's adjustment problems. Slavson's psychoanalytic orientation, much like that of Anna Freud, is reflected in the nature and depth of interpretation in Activity-Interview Group Psychotherapy. The activity-interview model was initially used with latency-age children, then extended to prelatency- and early latency-age children in the 1950s by Slavson and Schiffer (1975). A recent text by Schiffer (1984) provides an excellent clinical presentation of the Activity Group Therapy and Activity-Interview Group approaches.

Behavioral models of group psychotherapy emerged in the 1960s as an alternative to psychodynamic and client-centered therapy (Rose, 1967). Proponents of behavioral models stressed the need to define and operationalize specific, measurable therapeutic goals (Berger & McGaugh, 1965). Individual studies throughout the 1960s were followed by two major textbooks on behavioral group treatment models (Graziano, 1972; Rose, 1972).

A review of the research literature over the past 20 years reveals that group therapy studies have dealt with cognitive-developmental age differences (Schiffer, 1969; Barcai & Robinson, 1969; Slavson & Schiffer, 1975; Haizlip, McRee, & Corder, 1975; Azima, 1976; Schamess, 1976; Weisselberger, 1977), the relationship between specific approaches and type of psychopathology (Scheidlinger, 1960, 1965; Speers & Lansing, 1965; Frey & Kolodny, 1966; Rose, 1967; Brandt, 1973; Soo, 1974; Schamess, 1976; Frank, 1976; Anderson & Marrone, 1977; Maclennan, 1977; Plenk, 1978), the role of parents (Pasnau, Meyer, Davis et al., 1976; Gaines, 1981), the shift from activity-play models to verbal-oriented group models (Dannefer,

Brown, & Epstein, 1975; Kaczkowski, 1979; Blotcky, Sheinbein, Wiggins et al., 1980–1981), the use of psychodrama (Lockwood & Harr, 1973; Barsky & Mozenter, 1976), and length of treatment (Rhodes, 1973).

THREE GROUP MODELS

Individual and group psychotherapy cannot be differentiated on the basis of goals, because each seeks to help the child resolve basic adjustment problems. Nor can they be distinguished on the basis of general theoretical orientation, because both have been conceptualized within the context of psychoanalytic, client-centered, and social learning theory models. There is even considerable overlap in patient populations treated with group and individual psychotherapy. The role of the therapist can be very similar in terms of the initial formulation of a therapeutic alliance, delineation of goals, progression through the middle phase of treatment, and the final stage of therapy characterized by termination issues.

What then differentiates individual from group psychotherapy? The most obvious difference is the number of patients simultaneously treated; one versus a group composed of four to eight children. The group provides the basis for the formulation of patient–therapist, patient–patient, and therapist–group relationships, in contrast to the singular patient–therapist relationship of individual psychotherapy. Advocates of group psychotherapy assume that the additional relationships have therapeutic value. In addition, optimal personality development involves successful integration into group structures outside the immediate family, and group therapy provides the individual with a therapeutic social environment that functions as a bridge to more conventional social experiences.

Regardless of theoretical orientation, advocates of group psychotherapy assume that the roots of maladaptive behavior can be traced to experiences within the family. Dysfunctional behavior that emerges within the family is often extended to peer groups, the school, and the community. Conflict between the individual and the group serves to produce further adjustment difficulties and, as Slavson and Schiffer (1975) suggested, deprives the individual of experiences that contribute to optimal personality and social-emotional growth and development. Advocates of individual psychotherapy assume that the child's maladaptive behavior must be dealt with in a singular patient–therapist relationship before adequate progress can be made toward group functioning, or that the process of individual treatment occurs simultaneously with changes in a broader social milieu. In contrast, group psychotherapy advocates assume that group experiences have a profound effect on each individual's specific problems, and that as these problems begin to resolve within the context of the group, the group as a whole begins to function more adaptively. A sense of social responsibility develops through cooperation and mutual respect for one another.

Numerous group psychotherapy models have developed over the years to deal with a wide range of psychopathology (Slavson & Schiffer, 1975; Schamess, 1976; Scheidlinger, 1977). Some approaches have very different theoretical rationales, but are similar in actual practice (e.g., Slavson's [1943] Activity Group Therapy and Axline's [1947] Nondirective Play Group Therapy). Others are similar in clinical practice and theoretical rationale, but differ in name (e.g., Slavson's [1943] Activity Group Therapy, Redl's [1944] Diagnostic Groups, and Ginott's [1961] Group Therapy with Children). In some cases different names have been given to models based on the same theoretical rationale, but applied to children of different developmental ages (e.g., Slavson and Schiffer's [1975] Activity-Interview Group Psychotherapy for latency-age children and their Play Group Therapy for prelatency-age children).

Needless to say, it is not easy to categorize group psychotherapy models. While there are numerous ways to categorize group psychotherapy, none are completely satisfactory. We have chosen to present them by level of structure rather than by theory. Three structural categories have been conceptualized: group approaches in which the therapist provides limited structure and little or no interpretation; group approaches in which the therapist provides moderate structure and guidance, as well as interpretation of group and individual patient behavior; and highly structured behavioral groups that utilize social learning theory and behavioral principles.

NONINTERPRETATIVE LIMITED-STRUCTURE GROUPS

These groups are characterized by a therapist who is nondirective. Interpretation of the child's behavior is either reflective in nature or simply not given. Theoretically, both psychoanalytic and client-centered models can be found in this category. For example, the work of Slavson and Schiffer (1975) and Schiffer (1969) is based on psychoanalytic theory, while that of Axline (1947) is client-centered. Some variation occurs in the physical settings and materials, and in the children's developmental ages. The children best suited for groups within this category present with general behavioral problems and/or emotional immaturity. Children with severe psychopathology, such as autism, pervasive developmental disorders, or mental retardation are not appropriate candidates.

Slavson and Schiffer's (1975) Activity Group Therapy model will be presented descriptively as an example of a noninterpretative limited-structure approach to group treatment, followed by excerpts from a therapy session to highlight the process.

Activity Group Therapy (AGT)

Rationale. Children appropriate for AGT have the capacity to form adaptive and meaningful social relationships if given the opportunity. The goal of AGT is to provide an accepting and noncontrolling environment conducive to mild behavioral regression and a subsequent working through of individual emotional adjustment problems.

Physical Setting. AGT is designed to facilitate freedom and the spontaneous physical responsiveness of the group members. Both overly aggressive and withdrawn patterns of behavior are fostered by restrictive, harsh, or response-inhibiting environments and individuals. The AGT setting and therapist must be antithetical to the child's everyday maladaptive experiences for a corrective emotional response to occur. The setting is spacious (450–500 square feet) and conducive to group interactions as well as independent activity. The equipment consists of tools and related materials to be used with wood, metal, leather, and plastic construction projects. Art supplies and model boat and plane kits also are provided. There is an easily accessible bathroom and kitchen area for snack time.

The Therapist. The therapist must be noncontrolling, empathic, accepting, and supportive rather than directive and judgmental. This posture frees the child from the negative effects of his or her general environment so that an innate capacity for adaptive emotional growth and development can emerge. The therapist must be able to tolerate acting-out behavior, for it is expected and reflects the first stage of the corrective emotional process of group treatment. There is a limit, however; the therapist cannot allow the children to engage in serious aggressive behavior toward other group members, themselves, or the physical setting. Occasionally the therapist will set limits on an acting-out member if the behavior cannot be altered by the group. The therapist does not interpret behavior of the group or of individuals. He or she does help any child who requests aid, however, by conveying an emotionally supportive attitude. This nondirectiveness helps the child develop a sense of self-confidence in his or her ability to complete tasks and resolve confrontations with other group members. Finally, the therapist conveys a sense of responsibility through proper use and care of tools and supplies and the physical setting. This is done by example, and not by lecture or rule setting, as it usually occurs in the home, school, or recreational setting.

Group Composition and Balance. A group is composed of four to eight children. The success of AGT depends on group composition and balance. Slavson and Schiffer (1975) noted that two general conditions must be present for a child to be included in AGT. First, each child in the group must exhibit at least a moderate adaptation to life experiences and stresses.

Children with few emotional resources and little or no sense of social responsibility are unsuitable because they have great difficulty controlling their impulses and forming interpersonal relationships. They are inevitably destructive to the group and themselves because of the limited structure and noncontrolling nature of AGT.

The group must be balanced in terms of the interaction of its members. If the group is composed of too many aggressive children, it might be impossible to progress beyond the acting-out phase. Conversely, if there are too many timid, withdrawn, and overly dependent children, little progress will be made toward appropriate assertiveness and independence. Slavson and Schiffer (1975) have identified three behavioral types: instigators, neutralizers, and neuters. Instigators are subdivided into positive and negative types. Positive instigators tend to mobilize and reinforce strengths in individual children and contribute to adaptive intra- and interpersonal interactions. Negative instigators generate disruption, nonproductive activity, and hostility. According to Slavson, negative instigators are "true centers of infection," and if unchecked, they destroy the group. Neutralizers behave in ways that mitigate negative instigators without adding to group tension and conflict. Neuters are members without strong positive or negative positions in the group. The goal is for their behavior to shift over time in the direction of a neutralizer or positive instigator. The neuters, as expected, tend to be the more withdrawn, timid, or dependent members of the group.

Sex and Age. The group members and the therapist are of the same sex, primarily to facilitate general commonality of interest in activities. AGT is designed primarily for mid- to late latency-age children (8–12 years old). However, specific groups should not vary in age range by more than 1 to 2 years.

Group Process. As a result of the nondirective orientation of the therapist, minimal structure, and appropriate selection and balance of group members, the group interacts in a way that eventually leads to significant improvement in adaptive functioning. The group initially engages in much acting-out behavior. This occurs because there are few limits to inhibit pent-up frustrations and anger. The members "abreact" or act out in response to the tension and conflict that occurs within the group. There is also evidence of "reenactment," which reflects behavior toward the group that usually is directed toward the family, peers, or others in the child's general environment, a sort of group-based transference reaction.

The physical setting, tools, and materials provide one outlet for acting out. These initial behavioral reactions slowly give way to somewhat more adaptive functioning. Optimally, a great deal of group mobility occurs, characterized by members working and interacting with each other, but not restricting themselves over sessions to fixed relationships. This more fluid social phenomenon is viewed as a reflection of group members' capacity to form meaningful social relationships.

The reduction of conflicts, aggression, hyperactivity, and social withdrawal and the emergence of greater individual productivity and more adaptive social relationships occur slowly. It is not a smooth process, but one characterized by vacillating periods of adaptive and maladaptive behavior that give way to a more relaxed environment of productivity and adaptivity.

An activity group meets weekly for 2-hour sessions for approximately 2 years. As the group approaches termination, social outings are planned and consideration is given to placing some members in transitional groups. These groups are actually traditional recreational programs that provide a further testing ground for the newly acquired skills of the child. In some cases the therapist works with the transition group leader to help him or her understand the dynamics of the child.

Case Illustration of AGT

The following excerpt of AGT (Slavson & Schiffer, 1975, pp. 10–23) was taken from a single therapy session in the early stages of treatment, and it is characterized by a great deal of acting-out behavior. The session excerpt is preceded by character sketches of each boy and a brief summary of the preceding sessions.

> The group under consideration, composed of seven boys (six are present at this session), has been meeting for about 3 months, once weekly for the regular 2 hours. Four of the boys have been treated in exclusive group therapy. Two were in cooperative (individual and group) treatment for a time; but since both were resistive to individual therapy with their respective caseworkers, they were terminated by their caseworkers and continued in exclusive AGT.

The following statements were made about individual children in the group.

> Morris was 9 years old when originally referred to the child guidance clinic. He had had 2 years of individual treatment with caseworkers. The chief problems were that he resisted going to school, demanding that his mother dress him; had severe temper tantrums, including breaking windows; exhibited marked sibling conflict with a 16-year-old sister, who dominated him and ordered him around, and whom he once threatened to kill. Morris's mother had great difficulty controlling him. While he was stubborn and aggressive at home, he was quite fearful of children and polite with teachers and strange adults. The father, to whom the boy had been very close, died when Morris was 5 years old. The boy "reacted badly" to this death. The mother, a harassed woman, displayed little warmth for her only son. . . .

Paul was referred to the clinic by his school principal because of under-achievement, aggressive behavior, and association with "troublemakers." At home he was said to be "nervous and fearful." Also reported were occasional nocturnal enuresis, thumbsucking since birth, nightmares, and extreme sibling rivalry. His mother said Paul was dependent and close to her, and he often asked her to dress him. The family was intact, with one sibling, a brother several years older than Paul. The mother was an overanxious and rigid woman who overstressed physical care of both children. The father, on the other hand, was remote from the children, partially because he worked long hours. He tended to be overly lenient and passive. . . .

Arthur was referred by the school because he was inattentive, worked below capacity, and would not do assignments in written work. His parents described him as stubborn, with a severe temper, clumsy, and absent-minded. He had "nervous" habits: lip biting and eye rolling. Among other things reported were food fads, occasional nocturnal enuresis, rivalry with a younger sister, and some fear of going to sleep. Arthur's relations with peers were poor; he always wanted to "boss" them, which usually ended up in fights, so that he eventually had to play entirely by himself. When his father worked nights, he sometimes slept with his mother. Arthur frequently teased and provoked her to a point where she would beat him. . . .

Sol was referred because of poor schoolwork, although he had the capacity to do better. He had infantile mannerisms and fears of the dark and of being alone, and he played only with younger children, arguing with them constantly. The family situation was pathological. The father was separated from the family when Sol was 3 years of age, and the boy saw him only rarely. The mother was an extremely dominating and "castrating" woman, who was disturbed that she could not be involved in treatment. She focused her attention on an older son, 16 years of age, who acted the role of the father toward Sol. . . .

Ronald was first referred to the clinic by a school nurse because of "nervousness." He had difficulty in getting along with peers and had few friends. He was fearful, insecure, and anxious, was persistently enuretic nocturnally, had poor eating habits and fears of the dark, of being alone, and of "tough boys." There were also sleep disturbances. Ronald bit his nails, worried about being ill, and used to vomit a good deal. The family was intact. No problem was reported with respect to a younger daughter of 2. Both parents were extremely disturbed and frequently argued. The father was very strict with Ronald, expected instant obedience from him, and often beat the boy. . . . His mother, still dominated by her own mother who lived nearby, seemed overwhelmed. She was easily upset by Ronald, and she too hit him occasionally. More often, she yelled at him. . . .

Robert was referred by his mother, at the school's urging. He was disobedient, moody, and unhappy. He interrupted his teachers and was unable to get along with classmates because he tried to dominate them. Robert was markedly negativistic toward his mother, who complained that he did not respond when she spoke to him. She also complained that he had "terrible personal habits and ate like a pig." . . . His mother was 19 years old when she gave birth to him, and she resented him vigorously because he "interfered with her career as an artist." She was a tense, narcissistic person and did not hesitate to vent her anger on Robert at the slightest provocation. The father seemed to be more balanced, but did not see much of Robert because he worked nights and slept during the day. . . .

For the first 6 or 7 sessions the boys went through a phase of slow acclimatization. Several were frankly suspicious of the therapist. Conversation was limited and had to do mainly with the crafts work. The boys made only fleeting contact with each other; no real affiliations developed between any of them. The therapist pointedly stayed away from activities, allowing the boys to assess the permissive environment and react to it in accordance with their specific personalities. The more dependent ones began to seek him out, mainly for help; some attempted to work in close physical proximity to him. . . .

By the 8th and 9th sessions increasing signs of spontaneity in behavior began to appear, and as the growing assurance that the therapist was really permissive was demonstrated in various ways, some of the games became increasingly aggressive. Several boys made swords of wood and engaged in "duels," which made Morris manifestly very anxious. Increasing arguments for possession of tools and over sharing of supplies and distribution of food at refreshment time appeared. . . .

The noise level mounted rapidly; it had been quite moderate up to this time. By the 9th session distinct subgroup affiliations and supportive ego relations made their appearance. These were evidenced in the now aggressive "war games." Play grew rougher; pieces of plasticine and other small objects became the "ammunition" for the games. As these interactions mounted, work projects lagged, except for a few boys, who apparently used them for security against involvement in aggression, which still frightened them.

During the 12th group session much more open anger and deliberate provocations were displayed among some of the boys; they began to throw and hide each other's coats and locked some of the group members out of the treatment room. Vigorous wrestling on the floor and near fist-fights also occurred. This behavior continued to frighten two boys. Transference to the therapist was now fairly well established, and a good deal of unconscious acting out in the transference was observable in the behavior of some of them. It was acted out mostly indirectly; in messing up the room, painting chairs, careless and wasteful use of supplies, and other more subtle forms of defiance. Throughout, the therapist continued his neutral and accepting role and responded to any demands for help made upon him.

The following comments were extracted from session 14 to give the reader some feeling for the specific interactions that occurred between the children and the therapist and among individual children.

When the therapist arrived a few minutes early, Arthur and Paul were wrestling playfully in front of the door. On seeing him, both boys stopped and ran up to greet him. Arthur at once asked what refreshments they were having. The therapist replied, "cake, soda, and milk." He then added that since Arthur had asked at the preceding session for soda and Paul for milk, he had brought both beverages. . . .

[After this brief interaction the therapist and the two boys went up to the AGT room.]

The therapist first unlocked the tools and materials cabinet and then took off his jacket and hung it on the hook. The boys, however, threw their coats on chairs, a procedure they had followed at all previous sessions. Arthur commented on the fact that several more chairs had been covered with paint (by another group) and read the inscriptions on several of them. He immediately took two jars of paint and a brush out of the closet and, commenting that there was no red paint and that the red paint bottle was mostly water, began to paint one of the stools. He was quite sloppy in his work, so that drops of paint splashed to the floor.

Paul took some wood and began to saw on what looked like the outline of a gun. Sol, bundled up with his coat buttoned to the neck, came in a moment or two later. He looked at everybody but did not greet anyone. He stood in front of the supply cabinet for a few moments, stating that he did not know what to do. He wandered over to where Arthur was painting and became critical of him, calling attention to the fact that the paint was dropping to the floor and asking why he had to paint chairs. . . .

In the meantime the therapist had seated himself at the far worktable, away from where the boys had congregated, and worked on his linoleum block. For some time all three boys continued to work quietly. . . .

Ronald arrived, looking neat and clean. He lisped slightly as he approached the therapist and began to tell him some of the latest sports news. . . .

Morris arrived, entering in his characteristic energetic fashion, with his face beaming. He immediately came over to the therapist to ask what he was doing. The therapist told him, and Morris wondered if it was difficult. The therapist said it wasn't too difficult. Thereupon Morris asked if the therapist could show him how to cut his initials in a block. The therapist helped him get started, and Morris gradually took over working with the linoleum cutter. The therapist unobtrusively moved to another table. Several times in the ensuing hour, particularly when the play of the other boys got rather rough, Morris approached the therapist with his linoleum work. . . .

Arthur continued to use the paints sloppily and spilled part of a jar of red paint on the floor. Paul said it was a "stupid thing to do" and he should "clean it up." Arthur continued painting in his usual nonchalant and somewhat detached manner—he had a way of seeming unconcerned about activities going on around him while he worked. . . .

After a while the therapist fetched a rag and began to wipe some of the paint off the floor. Arthur ignored this, continuing his work. Since a good deal of paint was spilled, the therapist had to make several trips for water. While he was on one such trip, he heard Paul again criticizing Arthur, stating that he should not let the therapist do that. Arthur paid no attention, except to move the chairs away so there would be room for the therapist to do the cleaning. About five minutes after the therapist had finished cleaning and had replaced the cleaning implements, Arthur packed up the paintbrushes and put them back in the closet (this was contrary to his usual practice of leaving things around carelessly). . . .

[Later in the session the play of several of the boys got quite aggressive, but not enough to warrant intervention by the therapist, who simply continued to work on his own project.]

The mood grew increasingly playful as Ronald and Paul chased Robert around the room, pelting him with plasticine pellets. Robert picked some of these up from the floor and flung them back at them. Sol now ran to the door, held it wide open, and suggested to Paul and Ronald that they force Robert outside. This now became the emphasis of the play. Robert refused to be moved in the direction of the open door, and kept retreating before them. Sol then suggested that they just grab him and "throw him out," but the others did not follow this suggestion.

The plasticine battle was now becoming more violent as Robert was losing his good humor. Apparently afraid of his own anger, or growing fearful, he announced that he was "giving up" and that the others should stop. But Sol kept urging Paul and Ronald to throw Robert out of the room, and Paul insisted that the "fight" could not stop unless Robert was outside in the hallway. Robert, equally insistent, said he would not go, and the chase continued. Robert, finally losing his temper, shouted for them to stop and said again he did not want to fight anymore. The others still paid no heed. . . .

Robert picked up some of these [wood] squares and threatened Paul with them, demanding that he stop throwing "clay" at him, but Paul ignored him. After several threats, Robert threw a wooden block directly at Paul, striking him in the temple. Paul placed his hand to his temple and bent his head down as tears began to fill his eyes. The therapist walked over to him, noted there was no real injury, and left without comment, paying no attention to the others gathered around Paul. The boys were startled by the developments of their game and looked on silently at Paul for a moment or two. Robert exclaimed that he had told them to stop. Ronald said: "Now we'll show you!" Sol added: "Let's really throw him out." (Several times earlier, when Sol had left the door open, the therapist had gone over and closed it, but Sol kept returning to it, holding it open so that the boys could get Robert.) But, instead of trying to shove Robert out, the boys began to throw pellets at each other indiscriminately. . . .

[The boys' play became increasingly less aggressive and less directed toward Robert after the block-throwing incident. As refreshment time approached, the boys called a truce.]

Robert, in very good humor and in a playful mood, hurled back the pellets thrown at him. Paul had fashioned a piece of wood in the shape of a rifle, with which he directed "his men." He now seemed to notice the accumulation of trash from the broken "barricade" in the corner and proclaimed that it was "enough fighting." Obviously relieved, the others at once stopped throwing pellets. Paul, while acting "the general" and proclaiming that "things had to be cleaned up," now appeared in the role of a neutralizer. He directed Arthur to do something about the broken boards as the other boys were gathering up bits of plasticine strewn on the floor. Paul continued to give orders. Robert now also agreed, "That's enough," but Arthur countered, "We have to have a peace treaty." Saying this, he picked up a piece of drawing paper and ran to the refreshment table. The boys dropped what they were doing and sat around him as he began to frame the document.

The preceding excerpt is an example of noninterpretative limited-structure AGT. Although the session was marked by acting-out behavior, elements of self-control were evident when the boys' play reached a potentially dangerous level. As noted previously, children selected for groups in this category must exhibit a capacity for self-control because the therapist is so nondirective. The therapist, through his behavior, communicated his faith in the boys' capacity to resolve their differences. He was also supportive, accepting, and willing to help without being judgmental. All of these children came from environments that were rejecting, harsh, overly critical, and generally controlling. Group therapy provided them with an antithetical experience. Whereas elements of self-control, social responsibility, and concern for others could be seen in session 14, Slavson and Schiffer (1975) stated that truly significant changes did not begin to emerge until session 17. As therapy progressed over the 2-year period, the behavior of the boys slowly but progressively improved with fewer periods of conflict.

INTERPRETATIVE MODERATE-STRUCTURE GROUPS

These group approaches are characterized by a therapist who interprets individual and group dynamics and provides a generalized organizational structure for group activities and discussion. The nature of interpretation depends on the theoretical orientation of the therapist. Slavson and Schiffer's (1975) Activity-Interview Group Psychotherapy for 8- to 12-year-olds and Play Group Therapy for 4- to 7-year-olds are based on pyschoanalytic theory. Their approach to interpretation, as well as the physical setting and materials, are designed to facilitate expression of conflicts, emotions, and feelings as delineated in psychoanalytic theory. Gaines (1981) has developed a model that incorporates psychoanalytic and behavioral theory. Interpretation is social learning theory-oriented, but psychodynamics are considered relevant. For Gaines, the selection of a physical setting, activities, and materials is more a function of developmental age than personality theory. Ginott's (1961) model of group therapy is based on psychoanalytic theory and appears to be somewhat less structured than that of Slavson and Schiffer (1975), but clearly more highly structured and interpretative than AGT.

In general, a somewhat more disturbed group of children can be treated with models in the interpretative moderate-structure category because there are more external controls and guidance provided by the therapist. With the exception of Slavson and Schiffer (1975), who advocate the noninterpretative limited-structure type of group (i.e., AGT) for mildly disturbed children, interpretative moderate-structure groups are used with children of mild to moderate emotional disturbance.

There are many articles that describe specific formats for interpretative moderate-structure groups, or the transition from noninterpretative limited-structure groups to more highly structured groups involving interpretation (Dannefer, Brown, & Epstein, 1975; Schiffer, 1977; Kaczkowski, 1979). Again, we have chosen to present the Slavson (1943), Slavson and Schiffer (1975), and Schiffer (1984) model to illustrate an interpretative moderate-structure group approach. We have chosen their work because they provide an extensively detailed presentation of all phases of treatment. Their work represents the prototypical model in this category from which many subsequent variations have developed (Schamess, 1976; Abramowitz, 1976).

Activity-Interview Group Psychotherapy (A-IGP)

Rationale. A-IGP is designed for children who have the capacity to form adaptive relationships, but whose adjustment problems are severe enough to warrant the need for a structured situation characterized by limit setting and guidance through therapist's interpretation of significant individual and group conflicts. As Schiffer (1977, p. 378) stated, "A-IGP addresses itself to the internal sources of children's psychic conflicts within the limits of their emotional and intellectual capacities and their tolerance for analytic inquiry and interpretation." Without guidance and structure through limit setting and interpretation, no therapeutic progress is made toward the resolution of individual conflicts that interfere with emotional adjustment and personality growth and development through the social experiences of the group. In general, A-IGP is an extension of AGT designed to meet the needs of children who are not likely to benefit from the nondirective, ego-level structure of AGT.

Physical Setting. A-IGP usually is conducted in the same setting as AGT, although there is a major difference in the equipment and materials provided for the group. In AGT the equipment and materials are chosen to facilitate construction of projects. In contrast, the equipment and materials for A-IGP are like those found in typical playrooms used for psychotherapy and are designed to help the children act out their conflicts (see Slavson and Schiffer, 1975, chapter 15 for a detailed list of play materials).

The Therapist. In AGT the therapist is peripheral to the group and avoids initiating activities and discussions. The therapist in A-IGP, while remaining in a consistent, accepting, but fairly neutral role, does initiate contact with individuals in the group and with the group as a whole. The therapist's role is to provide structure and guidance through appropriate interpretation to facilitate the development of age-appropriate insight and the subsequent development of adaptive sublimation of emotional impulses. This process is facilitated by the equipment and materials through which internalized conflicts can be expressed. The therapist's interactions with the group occur during the general activities of the session and during a structured round-table discussion toward the end of each session. At the first session the therapist initiates the discussion. He might begin as Schiffer (1977, p. 378) suggests, by saying "I think you probably know that you came to the group because you had some problems in getting along, some at home, some at school and some in both, and that you are not happy about it. We want to talk about it and see if we can make things better for ourselves. Who would like to start?'' If no one volunteers, the therapist might choose a youngster he feels would be least threatened to speak. Through appropriate inquiry the therapist can help the child elaborate and bring other members into the discussion. Discussion among members is encouraged. The therapist can even bring up for discussion events he observed during the session.

This format of individual and group discussion is characteristic of all mid- to late latency-age interpretative moderate-structure groups. They differ principally in the theoretical orientation of the therapist, and hence with the nature of interpretations and the significance placed on individual and group behaviors.

Group Composition and Balance. A-IGP groups are usually composed of four to six children. Slavson and Schiffer's (1975) concept of group composition and balance as outlined for AGT holds for A-IGP. A somewhat more disturbed group of youngsters may be handled in A-IGP than in AGT, but A-IGP is still contraindicated for children who are psychotic, mentally retarded, or have severe behavior disorders.

Group balance is important in A-IGP, but not as crucial as in AGT or other noninterpretative limited-structure groups where the therapist is nondirective. In A-IGP the therapist provides guidance and structure to help children who are out of control or destructive to themselves or the group. Structure and guidance can be in the form of limit setting or interpretation of behavior.

Sex and Age. Groups can be homogeneous or mixed with respect to sex. If the group is mixed, the sex of the therapist is not important according to Schiffer (1977). However, he feels that a homogeneous group should have the same-sexed therapist. Homogeneous groups are advocated in AGT because there is a primary emphasis on constructive activities that are often homogeneous with respect to sex. In A-IGP, the materials are selected to facilitate expression of emotional conflicts and are less sex-specific.

A-IGP focuses on the mid- to late latency-age child (8–12 years old). Specific groups should not vary in age more than 1 to 2 years. Slavson and Schiffer (1975) developed Play Group Therapy, a modified version of A-IGP, for pre- to early latency-age children (4–7 years old).

Group Dynamics. The dynamics of A-IGP are similar to those of AGT, the primary difference being that the members receive the direct help of the therapist. There also may be some difference in the nature of conflicts presented by the children. Acting out occurs as in AGT, and both the physical setting and materials function as outlets for the children's emotional conflicts.

A group meets once a week for a 2-hour session, with 30 to 40 minutes devoted to group discussion. The general course of therapy is approximately 2 years.

Case Illustration of A-IGP

The following excerpt of A-IGP was taken from Slavson and Schiffer (1975), but was originally published by Gabriel (1939). This case illustration, considerably briefer than the previous one, focuses on a few selected interactions among the children and between the therapist and the children. The excerpt covers interactions from a number of sessions over the first few months of therapy. The group initially began with several children and increased to six children over a period of several months. Although this case study is several decades old, it illustrates a fundamental approach to treatment that has not changed (see A-IGP case study by Milstein in Schiffer, 1984).

We begin with brief statements about the children in the group that suggest that this group of children was no more or less disturbed than those involved in the foregoing AGT illustration. However, this group of children appears to have exhibited more problems with anxiety, oversensitivity, and emotionality in general than those noted in the children in the AGT group.

Linda was referred because of "nervous hysteria." She had many fears and somatic problems such as frequent vomiting spells when she was younger. She exhibited separation anxiety problems, generally would not allow her mother out of her sight, and refused to play with children.

Emma was the 11-year-old sister of Linda. Emma was not a particularly intelligent child and exhibited marked feelings of inadequacy. There was a great deal of conflict between her and Linda, which reflected Emma's feelings of hostility and anger toward her younger sister, who she felt was favored in the family.

Annette was a 10-year-old youngster who was referred by the school. She was an irritable and negativistic child who was greatly disliked by her classmates. She had marked feelings of inadequacy and felt unloved by her family.

Jean was a 10-year-old child who was referred by Linda's mother. Jean was an only child who presented with a history of bed-wetting. Her bed-wetting was considered to be symptomatic of a long history of parental rejection and general lack of emotional support and love. Additionally, she exhibited temper tantrums and negativistic behavior toward her family and peers.

Mike was a 10-year-old youngster who was referred by the school. He had few friends, was hypersensitive, and cried when called on to recite in the classroom. He was not a behavior problem at home, but mentioned briefly that he stuttered a little. He also indicated that his classmates thought he was insane because he cried for no reason. Hilton, aged 10, was referred by the school. He was a significant behavior problem in the classroom. He was described as disorderly and disobedient, and as having a stealing problem. He had spent many years in foster care and was frequently moved from one home to another because he was so uncontrollable.

The following comments reflect the therapist's perceptions of the group over a period of several months, with comments from individual sessions. The focus is on the interactions between the therapist and the group rather than on the overall process of treatment (Gabriel, 1939, pp. 150–151).

In December Linda and Jean played together, and although Emma was present she took an entirely negative role and merely chatted with others on a superficial basis. She felt that she was bringing her sister because "she presented with a particular problem." Annette joined later in December, and Mike and Hilton joined the group in February. At first the play was more individualistic, each child interesting himself in whatever drew his or her attention, but gradually they began playing together. It was then that the various problems, relationships, and attitudes were treated.

In the beginning Jean did not seem inclined to talk when other children approached her. However, the therapist felt that she enjoyed the opportunity of playing in a conditioned environment because the therapist was able at times to relieve her by turning the attention of the children to other things. Jean played quietly. Later, as she began to feel more secure, she frequently went into an adjoining room which was cut off by a movable wall. On these occasions the child looked uncomfortable when she returned, and the matter was discussed with her in private interviews. She generally acquiesced to suggestions made by the other children, resenting, however, Linda's constant domination of their activities and play. After several weeks she asserted herself and then blurted out to the therapist that she was "sick and tired" of having Linda always telling her what to play. This conversation brought forth information about their activity together in the neighborhood. Jean recognized that Linda was jealous of her, and that she sulked because Jean had friends. When Jean was asked what she did about it, she said that she refused to play with Linda. As the interviews with these children progressed, Jean spontaneously said that she and Linda were getting along much better.

When Hilton joined the group, he burst into the room in his accustomed manner, talking loudly and dominating the scene. The therapist introduced the children. Jean was very shy, looked askance at him, and during the rest of the time drew away from him whenever he came near. She was building a house and refused Hilton's help, telling him that she wanted to build her own house and play in her own way. At this point it seemed evident that the child's shyness reacted to some extent on Hilton's exuberant spirits, because he unconsciously lowered his voice whenever he spoke to her. . . .

During this session the children played at a table; some were drawing and others were building. Jean drew a picture of a man and brought it over to the therapist. Jean pointed to the belly button and giggled. Beside the picture she had written, "A man going to the bathroom in a nice clean pot on a summer day." On another occasion she drew a girl holding her skirt and urinating. Beside this picture she wrote, "The children are saying shame and one is wetting her pants." The children were all laughing good-naturedly as Jean came over to the therapist, and Jean laughed too. In a low voice the therapist said, "Are you ashamed when you wet?" She nodded. The therapist asked whether it bothered her, and she said she was trying to stop. She tried to stop masturbating too; she did it every night. She was afraid of being punished, and her mother knew, and she didn't want to do it any more. It was interesting to note at this point that Jean confided that whenever she played with Linda, Linda acted like a baby: "She always wants to play house." Jean wished she had a sister. Linda, overhearing her, said, "Maybe your mother could adopt a little girl." Jean replied, "Do you think I'd want that kind of a sister?" The therapist asked her what she meant. She said she would want her mother to have a baby, and giggled.

Jean continued to hold her own with the group, and the therapist never permitted them to take advantage of her. About 2 months after the group started, Jean brought her little friend Alice. Linda's jealousy took on an aspect of fury. She complained to the therapist that the children refused to play with her. When this was investigated, it was found that Linda made the complaint because the children refused to do her bidding. Finally, Jean and Alice went into the adjoining room while the therapist talked with Linda. Linda could not concentrate but kept calling out loudly, using names such as "dirty rat." Jean and Alice disregarded Linda. The therapist talked this through with Linda, and later, when the children came together, they played as though nothing had occurred.

Linda and Alice had retired to the other room while the therapist talked with Jean. Linda called out every few minutes, "Jean is talking about me." Jean looked at the therapist in surprise but said nothing. This conversation revealed that Jean had a good deal of insight in her play with children and in her own home situation. As she discussed the relationship between her mother and the grandparents, she ended by saying, "My grandmother always wants her own way and my mother always gives in to her. If I were my mother I wouldn't do it. My mother knows more than I do, but I won't give in to her all the time."

The foregoing excerpt illustrates the manner in which the therapist interacts with the children to provide interpretation of behavior as well as support and protection of an individual child when such assistance is necessary.

BEHAVIORAL GROUPS

Behavioral models of group psychotherapy are characterized by systematic observation of overt individual and group behaviors. Behavior is conceptualized in terms of basic learning theory, and social behavior is facilitated by the use of reinforcement principles, extinction, modeling, behavioral contracting, rehearsal, systematic desensitization, and stimulus generalization and discrimination, as well as other learning principles. Behavioral groups will vary in emphasis of techniques and the number of target behaviors to be dealt with in treatment. For example, a behavioral group might be formed specifically to treat highly anxious children through the use of systematic desensitization. In another behavioral group the therapist might use role modeling, rehearsal, and various reinforcement procedures to reduce aggressive behavior and facilitate socialization skills. Although the existence of psychodynamic processes is not denied, the behavioral approach emphasizes the delineation of observable maladaptive behaviors and the objective procedures needed to modify them. Interpretation of behavior does not play a role in behavioral models, but the therapist provides individuals and the group with a great deal of information regarding their behavior and specific ways in which they can work to alter it.

Behavioral Group Psychotherapy Models

Rationale. Behavior rather than personality is the target of change. Observable behavior is accessible and hence lends itself to description, evaluation, and prescriptions for change. The focus is on behaviors that are usually, but not exclusively, observed in groups. These include such skills as making friends, learning new ways to respond to others, and learning the impact of one's behavior on others. As Rose (1972, p. 9) stated,

> In group treatment a client is presented with a wider range of relationships than in dyadic treatment. There are many sources of feedback as to which of his behaviors or attitudes annoy others; he can explore different friendships until he finds his own style; he can try out new forms of communication with others in situations which closely simulate the real world. The group presents a wide range of problems and the client can observe these as well as the procedures, effective and ineffective, which have been utilized to cope with them. As a result of this exposure, he acquires the skills for dealing with new problems—skills that will serve him long after the group has terminated.

Physical Setting. The physical setting can vary greatly, depending on the specific goals for the group. Wodarski, Feldman and Flax (1974) suggested holding group meetings in a variety of places to facilitate generalization of behaviors that initially are learned in the context of a clinic setting. Such variations could increase over the course of treatment to afford the group opportunities to utilize newly acquired social and interpersonal skills while still under the structure and guidance of the group treatment process. The rationale behind this notion is reminiscent of Slavson and Schiffer's (1975) transition groups.

The Therapist. Consistent with other group models, the behavioral therapist must be understanding, concerned, and a model for adaptive behavior. In contrast to the other group models presented, the behavior therapist conceptualizes the group's behavior in terms of learning theory principles and directly attempts to convey the behavioral dynamics and contingencies to the group. This process is considered informative or descriptive rather than interpretative.

Sex and Age. Group members tend to be of the same sex, but heterogeneous groups are acceptable. There does not appear to be any major concern about the therapist's sex with respect to the group. Like all other models, behavioral groups are relatively homogeneous for age, which helps to maximize commonality of developmental interests and communication among group members.

Group Composition and Balance. Like other group models, a range of four to eight children is recommended. The size varies as a function of the degree of psychopathology treated. Because the group format is highly structured and organized, a broader range of psychopathology can be treated than in the noninterpretative limited-structure model.

Group balance is less important than in the first two models presented because of the highly structured nature and organization of behavioral groups. However, Rose (1972) points out that group progress can be hindered if individuals do not complement one another; hence groups can be too homogeneous or heterogeneous.

Group Dynamics. Therapy proceeds by a series of objectives that represent successive approximations to the desired treatment outcomes. The initial phase of treatment usually is characterized by high levels of reinforcement and control of the program by the therapist. As therapy progresses the therapist begins to shift responsibility for the program to the group members. In the final stages of treatment, the therapist begins to focus on alternatives to the specific group experience in order to generalize social skills learned in the group to daily living situations.

Case Illustration of Behavioral Group Therapy
The following case illustration was taken from Rose (1972, pp. 150–152) and represents an early session in the treatment process. A variety of learning principles are used to facilitate adaptive functioning of individuals and the group.

Ron, Paul, and Marv, 10, had been referred to the agency by the school. All had difficulty attending to the teacher, listening to peers, staying in their seats, and following instructions. When the therapist got to the room, he asked the boys to sit at the table while he set up the store. The boys sat down but soon came over to the store and expressed delight with what they saw. They discussed the price tags on each item and began to imagine how they would spend their chips. When the store was completed, the therapist again asked the boys to be seated. He took out the envelopes of chips and again explained how they could be used to buy models. There was a new envelope with Marv's name on it; giving it to Marv, he said, "You weren't here last week when we started. Last week each boy got three chips for coming. This week each of you will get one chip for coming and you, Marv, will get three more so you can start with the other boys. The boys also got a candy bar for coming last week, so you get one too."

The therapist then explained, "The first game we are going to play is Concentration. There are two rules you have to follow to earn the chips: you must stay in your seat—that means you have to have all your weight on the chair—and you must wait until the person before you turns his two cards back. If you follow the rules for 10 minutes you will earn one chip. If all three of you follow the rules, each of you will get one bonus chip." Ron and Marv each earned a chip but Paul didn't because he didn't wait until Marv had turned his two cards over. The therapist noticed that Ron went out of turn quite often.

The second game was Red Light, Green Light. Before the therapist started the game he said, "You guys have been calling each other names like "dirty rat" and "Frankenstein." If each of you can go for 3 minutes without calling anyone a name, including those two names, each of you will get a chip. If one of you calls someone a name, you won't get a chip, but the others will. There is no bonus this time." Marv asked "How about 'rat fink'?" The therapist replied, "Yes, that counts as a name." The boys played for 2 minutes, after which Paul stopped playing and just waited for the time to run out. No name-calling occurred, and all the boys got one chip. The boys again played the game fairly, and Ron offered Marv his turn in front: "Take my turn, you haven't been up front yet."

The longest activity was the writing exercise. The therapist showed the boys a picture (boat, men, ocean) and put it on the table in front of them. "This is going to be a writing exercise. I want each of you to write a two-part essay. In the first part, write down what you see in this picture. In the second part, write a story about what you see. Make up anything you want to. There is only one rule this time. You must stay in your seat the whole 20 minutes. Each person who stays in his seat the whole time gets four chips." The boys asked several questions about the writing, but all stayed in their seats and all got four chips. After this was completed, the therapist said that each would have a chance to earn one more chip if they would listen quietly while each person read his story. While this was intended to reward listening behaviors, it also rewarded standing up and reading in front of others. Marv said he wouldn't read his, but when it was his turn he did so, even though his grammer and presentation were poor. After all the stories were read and each had earned a chip, the therapist said that each boy should take a small piece of paper and write down which story was best. The one with the most votes would get one more chip. Paul won the chip.

Clay was put on the table, and the boys were told that if they stayed in their seats and did not throw any clay they would each receive three chips. The behaviors were interdependent, since one had to make a house, one a car, and one a fence around both. Toward the end of the 10 minutes Ron and Marv jumped out of their seats to get pencils to work in more detail, and Paul was the only one who got three chips.

The next activity was the arithmetic exercises the therapist had prepared. This apparently created an unpleasant situation for Marv, who was extremely weak in arithmetic. Whereas Paul completed most of the problems and Ron about half, Marv finished only two. There had been two rules—remaining in seat and raising one's hand before talking (whispering to self was allowed). This was a 15-minute exercise during which the boys were to do their best, without losing chips if the answers were wrong. Before they started, Ron said, "Yeah, you don't lose chips for getting them wrong, but you have to work on them real hard." During the period Marv quit doing the problems and stared at the models on the table across the room. He then looked at his pile of chips and with obvious effort picked up his pencil and began working again. At the end of the period Paul spoke without raising his hand, but the other two boys got four chips. The therapist did not grade the papers or make any comparisons.

Toward the end of the meeting the boys were at the store discussing how many chips were needed for each item. They were reminded that the store wouldn't be open until the meeting was over and asked which of the previous activities they would like to do again in the last 10 minutes. Concentration was their choice but they all asked to receive as many chips as possible this time. The game was played for 10 minutes with the same rules, but if they were followed each boy was awarded five chips and one bonus. Although Paul went out of turn, the other two received chips. At the close of the meeting Ron and Paul had 20 chips and Marv had 24. Ron traded his for a plane but both of the others asked that their chips be saved for the large models.

This example highlights the marked difference between behavioral models of group therapy and those previously discussed in this chapter. The behavioral group therapy session was highly structured, with specific tasks and goals outlined for the members. In addition to tasks having specific contingencies, other behavioral principles were used, such as rehearsal, modeling, and desensitization. As therapy progresses, the therapist gradually fades out the extensive "material reward contingencies" as group members experience a sense of personal reward from more adaptive functioning. Additionally, as their behavior improves they are more likely to experience natural social rewards from peers and adults that typically come with more adaptive functioning.

OUTCOME RESEARCH: GROUP THERAPY

A review of the literature over the past 20 years yields numerous studies on group treatment with children. They range from comparisons of a single approach to single or multiple control groups (e.g., Hugo, 1970; Hinds & Roehlke, 1970; House, 1971; Kelly & Matthews, 1971), to comparisons of multiple approaches versus controls (e.g., Irwin, Levy, & Shapiro, 1972; McBrien & Nelson, 1972; Randolph & Hardage, 1973;

Berry, Turone, & Hardt, 1980), and pre- and post-treatment comparisons without controls (e.g., Graziano, 1970; Johnson & Gold, 1971; Shere & Teichman, 1971; Berry, Turone, & Hardt, 1980). A wide variety of approaches have been assessed, including psychoanalytic (e.g., Coffey & Weiner, 1967; Clement, Fazzone, & Goldstein, 1970), client-centered (e.g., Moulin, 1970; Randolph & Hardage, 1973), and behavioral models (e.g., Hinds & Roehlke, 1970; Kelly & Matthews, 1971; Berry, Turone, & Hardt, 1980). Many have used eclectic approaches, but conceptualized their approaches as activity (play) or verbally oriented group models (e.g., Thombs & Muro, 1973; Taylor & Hoedt, 1974). Dependent measures include cognitive and academic achievement; personality variables such as anxiety, depression, and self-esteem; and specific ratings of individual and group behaviors. Patient populations have varied in age from 6 to 12 years, and degree of psychopathology has ranged from psychotic youngsters to ones with mild adjustment problems. Most studies, however, have dealt with mildly disturbed children, with an emphasis on measurement of social and academic adjustment within the school setting (e.g., Clement & Milne, 1967; Barcai & Robinson, 1969; Hinds & Roehlke, 1970; Kelly & Matthews, 1971; Berry, Turone, & Hardt, 1980).

There is a trend toward more favorable outcomes with behavioral group treatment models. Abramowitz (1976) found a similar trend. The somewhat more favorable results of behavioral studies might be a function of better design and utilization of sensitive and objectively delineated dependent measures. This does not necessarily imply that other group models are not effective, especially since many of the nonbehavioral group studies were less methodologically sound and often utilized dependent measures of questionable sensitivity, and poor reliability and validity. In terms of general methodological problems, most treatment periods were brief, and groups were not run by experienced therapists. Slavson and Schiffer (1975) maintain that both AGT and A-IGP groups must run 1 to 2 years to produce meaningful change. No other study in the literature approaches this criterion. Very little attention has been given to diagnostic evaluation, which is a very important consideration when studying models that place a major emphasis on group composition. Control groups have been used, but in many cases inappropriate control procedures were employed. As noted above, the sensitivity of dependent variables is a major problem, especially in studies that emphasize intrapsychic changes. Measures that purport to measure such changes (e.g., projective techniques) have notoriously poor reliability and validity.

Although there are far more outcome studies on group than individual child therapy approaches, our observations reveal a similar finding; namely, that the research is methodologically unsound and limited in scope and, as a result, no meaningful conclusions can be drawn regarding the efficacy of group treatment with children. This finding is in contrast to numerous case studies and textbook testimonials of the efficacy of group approaches. What is needed, then, is more effective research.

SUMMARY

Group treatment of children began in the 1940s. Slavson (1943) is most frequently cited as the innovator of group treatment with children, but other systematic programs and models of group treatment evolved in the same era (Redl, 1944; Axline, 1947). Although there are specific theoretical and technical differences across group treatment models, there is commonality with respect to the rationale for group treatment. Groups provide socialization experiences that cannot occur in individual psychotherapy; specifically, the child is exposed to a wider range of relationships. Group treatment is often more appealing to the child than individual treatment because there are many varied activities and experiences, and for some children it is often less emotionally threatening than individual treatment.

Group approaches were presented within the context of three structural categories: (a) noninterpretative limited-structure groups, (b) interpretative moderate-structure groups, and (c) behavioral groups. Regardless of level of structure or theoretical rationale, all advocates of group treatment specify guidelines for the type of child appropriate for treatment, in terms of the nature of psychopathology and requisites for group composition and balance. Noninterpretative limited-structure groups are appropriate for children with mild emotional adjustment problems, whereas more severe psychopathology can be treated with group models in the second and third categories.

A review of outcome studies over the past 20 years did not reveal much support for the efficacy of group treatment approaches, but research has been methodologically weak and too limited to draw definitive conclusions. From a technical standpoint the literature does provide many excellent examples of a wide range of group approaches.

REFERENCES

Abramowitz, C. V. (1976). The effectiveness of group psychotherapy with children. *Archives of General Psychiatry, 33*, 320–326.

Anderson, N., & Marrone, R. T. (1977). Group therapy for emotionally disturbed children: A key to affective education. *American Journal of Orthopsychiatry, 47*, 97–103.

Axline, V. (1947). *Play therapy.* Boston: Houghton Mifflin.

Azima, F. J. (1976). Group psychotherapy for latency-age children. *Canadian Psychiatric Association Journal, 21*, 210–211.

Barcai, A., & Robinson, E. H. (1969). Conventional group therapy with preadolescent children. *International Journal of Group Psychotherapy, 19*, 344–345.

Barsky, M., & Mozenter, G. (1976). The use of creative drama in a children's group. *International Journal of Group Psychotherapy, 26*, 105–114.

Berger, L., & McGaugh, J. L. (1965). Critique and reformulation of learning theory approaches to psychotherapy and neurosis. *Psychological Bulletin, 63*, 338–358.

Berry, K. K., Turone, R. J., & Hardt, P. (1980). Comparison of group therapy and behavioral modification with children. *Psychological Reports, 46*, 975–978.

Blotcky, M. J., Sheinbein, M., Wiggins, K. M., & Forgotson, J. H. (1980–1981). A verbal group technique for ego-disturbed children: Action to words. *International Journal of Psychoanalytic Psychotherapy, 8*, 203–232.

Brandt, D. E. (1973). A descriptive analysis of selected aspects of group therapy with severely delinquent boys. *Journal of the American Academy of Child Psychiatry, 12*, 473–481.

Clement, P. W., Fazzone, R. A., & Goldstein, B. (1970). Tangible reinforcers and child group therapy. *American Academy of Child Psychiatry, 9*, 409–427.

Clement, P. W., & Milne, D. O. (1967). Group play therapy and tangible reinforcers used to modify the behavior of 8-year-old boys. *Behavior Research and Therapy, 5*, 301–312.

Coffey, H. S., & Weiner, L. L. (1967). *Group treatment of autistic children.* Englewood Cliffs, NJ: Prentice-Hall.

Dannefer, E., Brown, R., & Epstein, N. (1975). Experience in developing a combined activity and verbal group therapy program with latency-age boys. *International Journal of Group Psychotherapy, 25*, 331–337.

Frank, M. G. (1976). Modifications of activity group therapy: Responses to ego-impoverished children. *Clinical Social Work Journal, 4*, 102–109.

Freud, A. (1946). *The psychoanalytical treatment of children.* London: Imago.

Freud, A. (1966). A short history of child analysis. *Psychoanalytic Study of the Child, 21*, 7–14.

Freud, A. (1968). Indications and contraindications for child analysis. *Psychoanalytic Study of the Child, 23*, 37–46.

Frey, L. A., & Kolodny, R. L. (1966). Group treatment for the alienated child in the school. *International Journal of Group Psychotherapy, 16*, 321–337.

Gabriel, B. (1939). An experiment in group treatment. *American Journal of Orthopsychiatry, 9*, 146–169.

Gaines, T. (1981). Structured activity discussion group psychotherapy for latency-age children. *Psychotherapy: Theory, Research and Practice, 18*, 537–541.

Ginott, H. G. (1961). *Group psychotherapies with children.* New York: McGraw-Hill.

Graziano, A. M. (1970). A group treatment approach to multiple problem behaviors of autistic children. *Exceptional Child, 35*, 765–770.

Graziano, A. M. (1972). *Group behavior modification for children.* New York: Pergamon.

Haizlip, T., McRee, C., & Corder, B. F. (1975). Issues in developing psychotherapy groups for preschool children in outpatient clinics. *American Journal of Psychiatry, 132*, 1061–1063.

Hinds, W. C., & Roehlke, H. J. (1970). A learning theory approach to group counseling with elementary school children. *Journal of Counseling Psychology, 17*, 49–55.

House, R. M. (1971). The effects of nondirective group play therapy upon the sociometric status and self-concept of selected second-grade children. *Dissertation Abstracts International, 31*, 2684A.

Hugo, M. J. (1970). The effects of group counseling on self-concept and behavior of elementary school children. *Dissertation Abstracts International, 30,* 3728A.

Irwin, E., Levy, P., & Shapiro, M. (1972). Assessment of drama therapy in a child guidance setting. *Group Psychotherapy and Psychodrama, 25,* 105–116.

Johnson, D. L., & Gold, S. R. (1971). An empirical approach to issues of selection and evaluation in group therapy. *International Journal of Group Psychotherapy, 21,* 456–469.

Kaczkowski, H. (1979). Group work with children. *Elementary School Guidance and Counseling, 14,* 44–51.

Kelly, E. W., & Matthews, D. B. (1971). Group counseling with discipline problem children at the elementary school level. *School Counseling, 18,* 273–278.

Lockwood, J., & Harr, B. J. (1973). Psychodrama: A therapeutic tool with children in group play therapy. *Group Psychotherapy and Psychodrama, 26,* 53–67.

Maclennan, B. W. (1977). Modifications of activity group therapy for children. *International Journal of Group Psychotherapy, 27,* 85–96.

McBrien, R. J., & Nelson, R. J. (1972). Experimental group strategies with primary-grade children. *Elementary School Guidance Counseling, 6,* 170–174.

Moulin, E. K. (1970). The effects of client-centered group counseling using play media on the intelligence, achievement, and psycholinguistic abilities of underachieving primary school children. *Elementary School Guidance Counseling, 5,* 85–98.

Munroe, R. L. (1955). *Schools of psychoanalytic thought: An exposition, critique, and attempt at integration.* New York: Holt, Rinehart.

Pasnau, R. O., Meyer, M., Davis, L. J., Lloyd, R., & Kline, G. (1976). Coordinated group psychotherapy of children and parents. *International Journal of Group Psychotherapy, 26,* 89–103.

Plenk, A. M. (1978). Activity group therapy for emotionally disturbed preschool children. *Behavioral Disorders, 3,* 210–218.

Randolph, D. L., & Hardage, N. C. (1973). Behavioral consultation and group counseling with potential dropouts. *Elementary School Guidance Counseling, 7,* 204–209.

Redl, F. (1944). Diagnostic group work. *American Journal of Orthopsychiatry, 14,* 53–67.

Rhodes, S. L. (1973). Short-term groups of latency-age children in a school setting. *International Journal of Group Psychotherapy, 23,* 204–216.

Rose, S. D. (1967). A behavioral approach to group treatment of children. In E. J. Thomas (Ed.), *The socio-behavioral approach and applications to social work.* New York: Council on Social Work Education.

Rose, S. D. (1972). *Treating children in groups: A behavioral approach.* San Francisco: Jossey-Bass.

Schamess, G. (1976). Group treatment modalities for latency-age children. *International Journal of Group Psychotherapy, 26,* 455–473.

Scheidlinger, S. (1960). Experimental group treatment of severely deprived latency-age children. *American Journal of Orthopsychiatry, 30,* 356–368.

Scheidlinger, S. (1965). Three group approaches with socially deprived latency-age children. *International Journal of Group Psychotherapy, 15,* 434–445.

Scheidlinger, S. (1977). Group therapy for latency-age children: A bird's-eye view. *Journal of Clinical Child Psychology, 6,* 40–43.

Schiffer, M. (1969). *The therapeutic play group.* New York: Grune & Stratton.

Schiffer, M. (1977). Activity-interview group psychotherapy: Theory, principles, and practice. *International Journal of Group Psychotherapy, 27,* 377–388.

Schiffer, M. (1984). *Children's group therapy: Methods and case histories*. New York: Free Press.

Shere, E. S., & Teichman, Y. (1971). Evaluation of group therapy with preadolescent girls: Assessment of therapeutic effects based on Rorschach records. *International Journal of Group Psychotherapy, 21*, 99–104.

Slavson, S. R. (1943). *An introduction to group therapy*. New York: The Commonwealth Fund.

Slavson, S. R., & Schiffer, M. (1975). *Group psychotherapies for children*. New York: International Universities Press.

Soo, E. (1974). The impact of activity group therapy upon a highly constricted child. *International Journal of Group Psychotherapy, 24*, 207–216.

Speers, R. W., & Lansing, C. (1965). *Group therapy in childhood psychoses*. Chapel Hill, NC: University of North Carolina.

Taylor, W. F., & Hoedt, K. (1974). Classroom-related behavior problems: Counsel parents, teachers, or children? *Journal of Counseling Psychology, 21*, 3–8.

Thombs, M. R., & Muro, J. J. (1973). Group counseling and the sociometric status of second-grade children. *Elementary School Guidance Counseling, 7*, 194–197.

Weisselberger, D. (1977). Developmental phases in activity-interview group psychotherapy with children. *A Journal of Group Dynamics and Psychotherapy, 8*, 20–26.

Wodarski, J. S., Feldman, R. A., & Flax, N. (1974). Group therapy and antisocial children. *Small Group Behavior, 5*, 182–210.

8

FAMILY THERAPY

At the suggestion of the school counselor, Mrs. Williams contacted Dr. Hastings, a clinical psychologist, by telephone regarding concerns she had about her 15-year-old daughter, Julie. Mrs. Williams indicated that Julie's behavior over the past several months had become quite troublesome and was very disruptive to the other family members. Julie's school performance was considerably below her intellectual capabilities, and she was often truant. Mrs. Williams reported that Julie refused to participate in family activities at home and defied most of the family rules. In addition, Julie had run away from home on several occasions following arguments with her mother about staying out late with her friends on school nights.

After his telephone conversation with Mrs. Williams, Dr. Hastings requested that the entire family come to the first session so that he could speak with everyone about their concerns. The family included Mr. and Mrs. Williams, Julie, and her 12-year-old brother, Paul. Mr. Williams indicated at the start of the session that he could not understand why they all needed to be there, because Julie was the one who needed "to be fixed."

Although Julie was presented as the reason that the family was seeking professional help, it soon became evident to Dr. Hastings that the other family members also were experiencing difficulties. It was revealed that Mrs. Williams was frequently depressed and often spent entire days in bed. Paul complained that no one in the family paid any attention to him, and he had to do too many things for himself because his parents were often not available when he needed them. In their interactions with each other during the sessions, Dr. Hastings observed that the family members were unable to focus on any single issue in order to resolve conflicts. It was impossible for any two members to talk to each other without being interrupted or having an argument ensue. Furthermore, Dr. Hastings noted that there was considerable disagreement between Mr. and Mrs. Williams regarding discipline and their expectations for the children.

Following several assessment interviews with the Williams family, Dr. Hastings suggested a contract of six family therapy sessions in which the entire family would be seen together. He indicated that his observations of the family's communication and interactional patterns had led him to the conclusion that the problem was within the family system, and not just within Julie. Thus, Julie's problem behaviors were viewed by Dr. Hastings as a symptom of problems in the larger family system.

During the past several decades, there has been an increasing realization that many behavior problems in children have their basis within maladaptive patterns of family interaction. As a result, there has been a greater trend toward the treatment of children within the context of the family.

Family therapy is a term applied to a complex collection of theories, therapies, and techniques that share a common orientation to human psychological dysfunction. The key element of family therapy is the identification of the family system as a whole, rather than the individual member, as the target of intervention. Deviant behaviors displayed by a child who is labeled as the ''identified patient'' are seen as symptomatic of a dysfunctional family system, and the goal of treatment is, therefore, the improvement of overall family functioning. Through family therapy, problematic family relationships and patterns of communication and interaction can be modified in a nonpathological direction, thereby effecting positive changes in behavior problems exhibited by individual family members.

The major types of family therapy presented in this chapter include psychodynamic, communicative, structural, and behavioral approaches to treatment. Following a brief discussion of the historical development of the family therapy movement, the theoretical foundations of the major approaches to family therapy are reviewed. An overview of a number of techniques of family assessment and treatment and several variations in family treatment approaches are presented. The final section of this chapter summarizes the research on the effectiveness of various approaches to family therapy.

THE ORIGINS OF FAMILY THERAPY

The family therapy approach began in the early 1950s when several groups of researchers and therapists independently broke away from established ideas about individual psychotherapy and began to investigate the role of family dynamics in the manifestation of symptoms by one family member. A number of important differences between individual therapy and family therapy are presented in Table 8.1. The four major groups in the 1950s in the United States centered on Gregory Bateson at the Men-

Table 8.1. Individual Therapy Contrasted with Family Therapy

INDIVIDUAL THERAPY	FAMILY THERAPY
Focus: illness of the individual patient. The primary interest is in intrapsychic disturbances of the individual.	*Focus:* illness of the family. The primary interest is in the processes that occur within the family as a group.
Responsibility: The therapist is responsible to the individual; the cure of the individual is the treatment goal.	*Responsibility:* The family is the patient. The therapist is responsible for the total family's welfare, rather than that of any one individual.
Process: The therapist studies the individual in depth, often apart from the individual's social environment and family relations.	*Process:* The therapist studies the individuals as members of the family group, relating behavior to interactions with other family members.
Content • The therapist relates present material to past experiences of the patient. • Fantasy, dream materials, and their meanings are used, more or less, as the content of treatment. • Fantasy and dream materials may be interpreted and related by the therapist to feelings, attitudes, and behavior. • Patient's identity often is clarified by examining the integrations the patient makes between conflicts of the superego and id. • Transference may be highly individualized, with distortion of the image of the therapist based on infantile emotional experiences. • Materials revealed by the patient are highly confidential.	*Content* • Emphasis is on the "here and now" and on ways the family can achieve healthy functioning. • Interactions between family members and their meanings form the focus of treatment. • Family interactions and processes are pointed out by the therapist; their meanings are explored as they occur. • Patient's identity evolves from a clarification of the role the patient plays in the family, the patient's self-image in this role, and the patient's role expectations. • Transference is diluted; the therapist is a reality figure. • Materials are openly shared by the family with the therapist.
Goals • Diagnosis, analysis, and cure of the individual's illness or disorder. • Understanding oneself as a unique individual. • Exploring, developing insights, and gaining relief from inhibiting conflicts.	*Goals* • Attaining effective family functioning, regardless of individual pathology. • Understanding oneself and other family members in relation to each other. • Establishing healthy interactions between family members.

Note. From "Family Therapy—Some Observations and Comparisons" by J. Carroll, 1964, *Family Process*, *1*, pp. 180–183. Copyright 1964 by Familly Processes, Inc. Reprinted by permission.

tal Research Institute in Palo Alto, California; Theodore Lidz at Johns Hopkins University and later at Yale University; Murray Bowen at the Menninger Clinic in Topeka, Kansas and later at the National Institute of Mental Health in Washington, D.C.; and Lyman Wynne, who succeeded Bowen at the National Institute of Mental Health (Goldenberg & Goldenberg, 1985). The research of all four groups focused on schizophrenics and their families and was largely the result of increasing frustration with the failure of individual psychiatric treatment with this population. Although each group studied different aspects of communication, they all concluded that schizophrenia was at least in part a response of the "identified patient" to his or her family, and that change in the entire family must occur if the schizophrenic symptoms (i.e., bizarre behaviors, confused thinking) were to be eliminated.

Because the early research focused almost entirely on families of schizophrenics, it was thought that the findings were limited to this patient population. In the late 1950s and throughout the 1960s, however, research and practice with families expanded to include families of delinquent youth, and later a wide range of normal and symptomatic families. As a result, it became clear that the same dysfunctional relationships observed in schizophrenic families were present, to some degree, in all families.

Nathan Ackerman, a psychoanalyst and child psychiatrist, is often credited as being one of the first to bridge the gap between theory, research, and practice in family therapy (Beels & Ferber, 1969). As an early pioneer in the treatment of families, Ackerman developed a psychodynamic model for family therapy in which he adapted psychoanalytic formulations of psychopathology to a family systems approach to treatment (Ackerman, 1958, 1966). In 1965, Ackerman founded the Family Institute in New York City to provide family therapy to primarily nonschizophrenic families and to train family therapists. Since the work of Ackerman and other seminal clinicians and theorists in this area, family therapy has gained considerable acceptance as a therapeutic modality for intervention with children exhibiting a wide range of behavior problems.

ASSESSMENT OF FAMILIES

There are many ways to obtain information about a family's functioning, as there are theoretical models of family pathology. Thus there is no single approach to assessment within family therapy. At the present time, assessment methods in family therapy tend to be practiced in a fairly unsystematic and subjective manner (Cromwell, Olson, & Fournier, 1976). The techniques of family assessment that a particular therapist uses generally depend to a large extent on his or her theoretical orientation regarding the causes of a person's symptomatic behaviors within the context of the family system.

Despite the diverse approaches to family assessment, a common element in the evaluation of families for treatment is a focus on what family therapists refer to as family process (McPeak, 1979). Process represents the ways in which a family operates and the patterns of interaction between and among family members. There are several methods that family therapists use to evaluate process, including an interview and behavioral observations of the family engaging in various tasks.

Haley (1979), for example, provides an outline for a family interview that follows several stages. In the first or "social" stage, the interviewer begins to establish rapport with the family and attempts to make them feel comfortable. The interviewer notes the family's seating arrangement and general mood and begins to evaluate the nature of the parent–child and marital relationships, as well as the manner in which the family members relate to the interviewer.

In the second stage, the interviewer investigates the reason the family has come for help. Each family member is asked to state his or her perception of the problems and changes that they would like to see in the family.

Following the "problem identification" stage, the interviewer begins to elicit greater interaction between family members. Family interaction is encouraged by having the members discuss their points of disagreement regarding the problem, and by directing the family members to speak to each other rather than to the interviewer. During this "interaction" stage, the interviewer notes, among other things, the way in which the generations within the family (i.e., children, parents, grandparents) relate to each other. For example, the interviewer watches to see if one parent sides with a child against the other parent. Various coalitions and roles within the family also are observed.

The final stage of Haley's assessment interview consists of clarifying the family's goals for therapy. In addition, a contract with the family is established for additional sessions, and arrangements are made for significant persons who were not present at the first interview to attend the next session.

Watzlawick (1966) proposes a more direct approach to eliciting family patterns of interaction in order to reveal the family's process. He has developed a "structured family interview" in which the family engages in a number of different tasks as the interviewer observes the process of their interaction.

In the first task, the interviewer asks each family member individually to state the "main problem" in the family. Later, the family is brought together and informed that their individual responses revealed discrepancies in their view of the problem. The family is then asked to discuss this issue and to come to some consensus on the family's main problems, during which time the interviewer leaves the room and with the family's knowledge observes the family from behind a one-way mirror.

Next, the interviewer asks the family members to "plan something together" and again leaves the room to observe them from behind a one-way mirror. In each of these tasks, the interviewer is not so much concerned with the actual decisions reached by the family as he is in the manner in which the decisions are reached, including who agrees and dis-agrees with whom, who leads the discussion, and so on.

For the next two tasks the children are asked to leave the room, and the parents discuss two questions. First they are instructed to discuss how they met. Then they are asked to discuss the proverb "a rolling stone gathers no moss" and to teach its meaning to their children.

In the final task the family is seated so that the father sits to the left of the interviewer, followed by the mother, and then the children in order from oldest to youngest. The family is asked to write down the "main fault" of the person to their left. In addition, the interviewer informs them that he or she is introducing statements of his own about two family members. All the statements are then shuffled and read aloud, and each family member is asked to indicate to whom each of the statements applies. This task enables the interviewer to evaluate patterns of incorrectly attributing blame to oneself or others, or of deflecting blame away from particular family members.

Many family therapists include as part of their assessment what Satir (1967) refers to as a "family life chronology," in which the interviewer takes a detailed history of the family's development over three or more generations. This longitudinal history of the family typically begins with questions regarding the mother and father's own parents and continues through an examination of the current family's characteristics and development. A family history often focuses on such areas as the development of the parents from childhood to adulthood; the parents' courtship and reasons for marriage; the nature and extent of past and current relationships of the parents to their own parents and siblings, as well as to their in-laws; the birth and development of their children; and significant family events such as separations, divorces, deaths, moves, and major illnesses.

To facilitate the history-taking with the family, some family therapists construct a family map representing multiple generations. This diagram of the family, referred to as a geneogram, helps both the interviewer and family members to visualize the various relationships and to highlight important events and experiences (Guerin & Pendagast, 1976). An example of a geneogram of a family and the symbols used in a geneogram are presented in Figure 8.1.

Another framework for assessment used by some therapists is to evaluate a family within the context of a family life cycle. The family life cycle is similar to the use of a geneogram in that it views the family within a developmental perspective. Each family goes through more or less the same set of developmental stages during its life cycle (Duvall, 1977; Hill & Rodgers, 1964). During each stage within the life cycle all families are confronted with potential challenges or stresses resulting from essential changes within that stage of development. These stresses are experienced

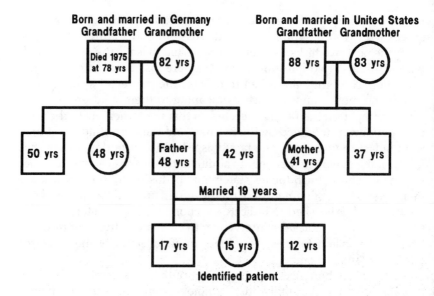

Figure 8.1. Sample geneogram of a family.

because of new roles and tasks that family members must assume at each stage (Boss, 1980). Most families are able to accommodate to these changes without significant difficulties; however, some families are unable to cope successfully with the new roles and tasks necessitated by one or more stages and subsequently develop problems in the functioning of the family system. Figure 8.2 illustrates an 8-stage model of the family life cycle of an average middle-class American family, as proposed by Duvall (1977). Each developmental stage is significant to the family in terms of budget, housing requirements, medical care, recreation, education, and home management. A similar developmental conceptualization of the typical life cycle of the family and the various tasks that must be mastered at each phase of the cycle are presented in Table 8.2. This approach to assessment enables the family therapist to ascertain a family's current stage of development and to determine whether the family is experiencing problems in accomplishing the various tasks at its current stage in the life cycle.

More recently, family researchers have attempted to develop standardized instruments for use in family assessment. Olson, Bell, and Portner (1978) have developed the Family Adaptability and Cohesion Evaluation Scale (FACES) to measure two dimensions that were found to subsume a variety of theoretical concepts within family therapy (Olson, Sprenkle, and Russell, 1979): cohesion and adaptability. Cohesion is defined as the degree to which family members are emotionally separated from or connected to their family. The adaptability dimension assesses the extent to which a family system can change its structure and rules in response to situational and developmental stresses. The FACES evaluates the adaptability and cohesion dimensions along four levels, ranging from extremely low to extremely high. By combining each of the four levels of cohesion and adaptability, 16 types of family systems can be identified.

Another self-report scale of family functioning is the Family Environment Scale (Moos, 1974), which assesses the impact of the family environment on individual and family functioning. The Family Environment Scale is comprised of 10 subscales. Three of the scales pertain to relationships and reflect the interpersonal transactions that are perceived by family

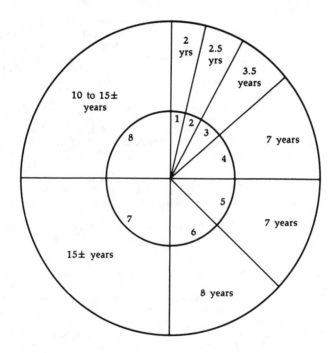

1. Married couples
   (without children)
2. Childbearing families
   (oldest child, birth−30 months)
3. Families with preschool children
   (oldest child 30 months−6 years)
4. Families with schoolchildren
   (oldest child 6−13 years)

5. Families with teenagers
   (oldest child 13−20 years)
6. Families as launching centers (first
   child gone to last child leaving home)
7. Middle-aged parents
   (empty nest to retirement)
8. Aging family members
   (retirement to death of both spouses)

Figure 8.2. The traditional family life cycle by length of time in each of the eight stages of life. From *Marriage and Family Development* (5th ed.) by E. M. Duvall (1977). New York: Lippincott. Copyright 1977 by J. B. Lippincott Co. Reprinted by permission.

Table 8.2. Developmental Phases in the Family's Life Cycle, with Typical Tasks to be Mastered at Each Phase

PHASE	DEVELOPMENTAL TASKS
Courtship	Contending with partner-selection pressures from parents; giving over autonomy while retaining some independence, preparing for marriage, including mutually satisfying sex life; becoming free of parents.
Early marriage	Sexual compatibility; sporadic contact with a partner becomes permanent; dealing with relatives; preparation for children; increased living standard with both partners working; interdependence.
Expansion	Children—new roles as parents; reduced income if wife loses earning power; agreements between spouses regarding birth control, pregnancy, child care; greater interdependence; dealing with rivalries between children; dealing with one or the other parent's overinvolvement with the children.
Consolidation	Family has no new additions but must contend with problems of school, adolescence. Sexuality in children must be dealt with; high earning power required of one or both parents; greater independence in children; generation clashes between parents and children.
Contraction	As children leave, the major activity of the couple—being parents—is gone; need for new interests; loss of involvement with children; increased economic prosperity.
Final partnership	Wife returns to work if she has not done so previously; new roles as spouses alone with each other; height of husband's career; high economic status.
Disappearance of family	Retirement with lower economic status and reduced prestige; increased dependency on others; maximum contact time between partners; problems of death—loss of partner, bereavement, loneliness.

Note. Adapted from *Principles of Family Psychiatry* by J. G. Howells, (1975). New York: Brunner/Mazel. Copyright 1975 by Brunner/Mazel, Inc. Adapted by permission.

members as taking place within the family. Five of the scales assess personal growth and various developmental processes supported by the family. The final 2 subscales represent systems maintenance and assess the family's general structure and internal role relationships. A score is obtained for each subscale, for each family member, and average scores for the entire family are used to develop a family profile.

MODELS OF FAMILY THERAPY

All family therapists share the view that the goal of treatment is the more effective functioning of the family system, but there are widely discrepant opinions as to how this goal is best accomplished. In addition to the approaches developed by the pioneers of the 1950s and early 1960s, there has been an ever increasing proliferation of new theories and techniques for intervention in family systems, to the point where it is difficult to estimate the number of different approaches. This section presents a summary of the theory and techniques of four major modes of family therapy: the psychodynamic approach, the communications approach, the structural approach, and the behavioral approach.

It should be noted that the classification of different approaches to family therapy as distinct "schools" or forms of treatment is somewhat artificial, since there are various degrees of overlap among the family therapy models in terms of their theoretical concepts and clinical techniques. Levant (1984, p. 73) has aptly noted:

> Because of the openness and flexibility with which the field has evolved, a great deal of cross-fertilization and exchanging of concepts and techniques has taken place among theoretically distinct groups. As a result, a lot of eclecticism has emerged, and it is somewhat difficult to discern the "pure strains" within the array of family-therapy approaches.

A slightly more complex scheme for organizing the various approaches to family therapy has been offered by Goldenberg and Goldenberg (1985). Table 8.3 presents their classification system and compares the different family therapy theories across eight dimensions.

THE PSYCHODYNAMIC APPROACH

Family therapists who subscribe to a psychoanalytic orientation view the family as a close relationship system in which family members are influenced by each other's psychological or intrapsychic characteristics. Psychoanalytically oriented family therapists are concerned with the way in which intrapsychic conflicts of individual family members interact within the family system to produce disturbed behavior in particular members of the family.

Nathan Ackerman, who was initially trained as a psychoanalyst and child psychiatrist, is credited as one of the earliest family therapists who adapted psychoanalytic theory to work with the entire family system. According to Ackerman, unconscious conflicts within individual family members interact to produce disturbed patterns of relating between the members, resulting in symptomatic behavior in one or more individuals.

Table 8.3. Comparison of Six Theoretical Viewpoints in Family Therapy

DIMENSION	PSYCHODYNAMIC	EXPERIENTIAL/ HUMANISTIC
Major time frame	History of early experiences needs to be uncovered.	Here-and-now data from immediate experience observed.
Role of unconscious processes	Unresolved conflicts from the past, largely outside of the person's awareness, continue to attach themselves to current objects and situations.	Free choice and conscious self-determination more important than unconscious motivation.
Insight vs. action	Insight leads to understanding, conflict reduction, and ultimately intrapsychic and interpersonal change.	Self-awareness of one's immediate existence leads to choice, responsibility, and change.
Role of therapist	Neutral; makes interpretations of individual and family behavior patterns.	Active facilitator of potential for growth; provides family with new experiences.
Unit of study	Focus on individual; emphasis on how family members feel about and deal with each other.	Dyads; problems arise from interaction between two members (eg., husband and wife).
Major theoretical underpinnings	Psychoanalysis.	Existentialism; humanistic psychology; phenomenology.
Major theorists and/or practitioners	Ackerman, Framo, Boszormenyi-Nagy, Stierlin, Skynner, Bell	Whitaker, Kempler, Satir
Goals of treatment	Insight, psychosexual maturity, strengthening of ego functioning; reduction in interlocking pathologies; more satisfying object relations.	Growth, more fulfilling interaction patterns; clearer communication; expanded awareness; authenticity.

Note. From *Family Therapy: An Overview* (2nd ed.) by I. Goldenberg and H. Goldenberg (1985). Monterey, CA: Brooks/Cole. Copyright 1985 by Brooks/Cole, Inc. Reprinted by permission.

BOWENIAN	STRUCTURAL	COMMUNICATIVE	BEHAVIORAL
Primarily the present, although attention also paid to one's family of origin.	Present and past; family's current structure carried over from earlier transactional patterns.	Current problems or symptoms maintained by ongoing, repetitive sequences between persons.	Focus on interpersonal environments that maintain and perpetuate current behavior patterns.
Earlier concepts suggested unconscious conflicts, although now recast in interactive terms.	Unconscious motivation less important than repetition of learned habits and role assignments by which the family carries out its tasks.	Family rules, homeostatic balance, and feedback loops determine behavior, not unconscious processes.	Problematic behavior is learned and maintained by its consequences; unconscious processes rejected as too inferential and unquantifiable.
Rational processes used to gain self-awareness into current relationships as well as intergenerational experiences.	Action precedes understanding; change in transactional patterns more important than insight in producing new behaviors.	Action-oriented; behavior change and symptom reduction brought about through directives rather than interpretations.	Activities prescribed to modify specific behavior patterns.
Direct but nonconfrontational; detriangulated from family fusion.	Stage director; manipulates family structure in order to change dysfunctional sets.	Active; manipulative; problem-focused; prescriptive, paradoxical.	Directive; teacher, trainer, or model of desired behavior; contract negotiator.
Entire family over several generations; may work with one dyad (or one partner) for a period of time.	Triads; coalitions, subsystems, boundaries, power.	Dyads and triads; problems and symptoms viewed as interpersonal communications between 2 or more family members.	Dyads; effect of one person's behavior on another; linear view of causality.
Family systems theory.	Structural family theory; systems.	Communication theory; systems, behaviorism.	Behaviorism; social learning theory.
Bowen	Minuchin	Jackson, Erickson, Haley, Madanes, Selvini-Palazzoli	Patterson, Stuart, Liberman, Jacobson, Margolin
Maximization of self-differentiation for each family member.	Change in relationship context in order to restructure family organization and change dysfunctional transactional patterns.	Change dysfunctional, redundant behavioral sequences ("games") between family members in order to eliminate presenting problem or symptom.	Change in behavioral consequences between persons leads to elimination of maladaptive or problematic behavior.

Ackerman proposes that a healthy family system is one in which there is a capacity to adapt to change and in which role relationships in the family are flexible and unambiguous. In order to change symptomatic behaviors in the family, intrapsychic conflicts must be brought into the open and addressed at the level of interpersonal conflicts and dysfunctional patterns of interaction. Ackerman (1966, pp. 90–91) states that the goal of therapy is to help the family "to accommodate to new experiences, to cultivate new levels of complementarity in family role relationships, to find avenues for the solutions of conflict, to build a favorable self-image, to buttress critical forms of defense against anxiety, and to provide support for creative development."

Murray Bowen's clinical and theoretical work in family therapy was also heavily influenced by his training as a psychoanalyst. His focus on affective issues within the family reflects his ties to the psychoanalytic school. He regards the family as an emotional relationship system and has introduced the concept of undifferentiated ego mass, derived from psychoanalysis, to explain the emotional closeness of families (Bowen, 1966). Bowen suggests that families can become so emotionally close or "stuck together" that the family's needs cannot be differentiated from the individual needs of its members. Symptoms may develop in one or more family members under stress when the emotional needs of each person are so fused that there is little sense of personal identity apart from the family. Within this framework the goal of therapy is to help the members to develop greater differentiation from the family emotional system. Family members must learn to relate to the family system in a meaningful way, without being emotionally fused.

In order to account for the family's response to stress and anxiety, Bowen (1976) developed the concept of the emotional triangle. According to Bowen, intimate dyadic relationships are inherently unstable. When stress and tension are low, most dyadic relationships in the family function without difficulty; however, when two people in the family become uncomfortable in their relationship, a third person in the family is likely to be "triangled" or pulled into the situation in an effort to reduce the tension. The person most likely to be triangled is the individual within the family who is most vulnerable; that is, the person who is least differentiated. Therefore, the most common triangle is mother–father–child, in which stress in the marital relationship inhibits the child's normal process of self-differentiation from the family. Repeated triangulation involving the child prevents the parents from resolving their own conflicts and makes the child vulnerable to developing symptomatic behavior.

Bowen's primary goal of therapy is to help each family member increase his or her level of differentiation from the family ego mass. His approach to therapy is designed to modify the family's typical patterns of triangulation by helping members to resolve conflicts with each other directly, so that they do not have to triangle others into their relationships. Bowen proposes two ways to modify dysfunctional triangles within the family. One method is to work with two persons in the triangle in order to release the third person from the triangle. This is accomplished by introducing another person (usually the therapist) into the triangle in such a way that the third person is outside the emotional maneuvers of the two family members.

Another method for changing relationships is to modify the behavior of one member of the triangle. By teaching a family member to identify triangles and ways to avoid becoming emotionally triangled, Bowen proposes that the therapist can effect change in the entire family system.

Bowen's usual method of family therapy is to work only with the parents of the symptomatic child. In his earlier work with families, Bowen saw all persons involved in the emotional triangle, including the problem child. He observed, however, that the parents often would focus their attention on the child's problem and avoid dealing with problems in their own relationship. He assumes that by helping the two adult family members to increase their level of differentiation, other family members will change in relation to the parents.

Bowen regards the therapist as a model and teacher for the family. The therapist demonstrates a high level differentiation of self by stating his or her own beliefs and values in a calm, emotionally neutral manner. In addition, the therapist instructs the family in the function of emotional systems and in ways to solve problems with each other directly, instead of bringing others into a triangular relationship.

The primary therapeutic technique used by Bowen is to direct the spouses to speak directly to him. He actively discourages them from discussing issues with each other during the therapy sessions or at home. Instead, he encourages them to talk to him about their feelings in a calm, factual manner, thus teaching them to respond to each other in more effective ways. Talking ''through'' the therapist enables the spouses to respond on a more intellectual level rather than on an emotional one.

An example of the therapeutic strategy used by Bowen is described by him as follows (1976, pp. 394–395):

> I open by asking the husband what kind of progress he has made since the last session, and ask him to give me his most objective report. If his report has reasonable content, I then turn to the wife and ask her thoughts while he was talking. Early in the course of therapy, my questions are designed to elicit the intellectual process by asking for thoughts, opinions, or ideas. In other situations I ask for her response or reaction, which is a little less intellectual. Only much later in therapy, and in special situations, do I ask for a reading from her subjective, inner feelings. After the wife has spoken, a question may be directed to the husband such as ''What was going on in your thoughts while she was talking?''

COMMUNICATIONS APPROACH

The communications approach to family therapy was an outgrowth of the work of a number of individuals associated with the Mental Research Institute in Palo Alto, California in the 1950s. The three major proponents of this approach—Don Jackson, Jay Haley, and Virginia Satir—share the basic assumption that the family system is best understood by studying the communication patterns between family members. They believe that all behavior, both verbal and nonverbal (i.e., tone of voice, facial expression, gestures), represents communication (Watzlawick, Beavin, & Jackson, 1967). Furthermore, communication theorists assume that it is impossible not to communicate, because even silence or a refusal to respond verbally has some message value, and therefore represents communication.

Communication has two levels: the content, or what is actually said; and metacommunication, which qualifies or modifies the content level (Watzlawick et al., 1967). Problems arise in a relationship when the metacommunication either is unclear or contradicts the content level of the message. In this instance the receiver of the message is placed in a conflict situation, since he or she is unclear as to which level of the message he or she should respond.

Therapists who subscribe to a communicative approach believe that modifying communication patterns can change relationships within the family system. Therefore, they focus on the ways in which family members send and receive messages and attempt to improve the ways in which a family communicates. Patterns of communication within a family are governed by family rules that are both implicit and explicit. According to communication theorists, problems arise within a family system when the rules become rigid or ambiguous. The goal of therapy is to clarify the family's rules, which results in improved communication and desirable behavioral changes in family members.

Jackson was one of the original members of the research group at the Mental Research Institute. In his research with schizophrenic patients and their families, he observed that disturbed families were particularly resistant to change. When the identified patient began to improve in therapy, other family members often began to develop symptomatic behavior. Thus, behavior changes in one member appeared to affect other members of the family system. In addition, Jackson found that improvements in the patient's problems often resulted in efforts on the part of other family members to sabotage the patient's treatment. As a result, the patient's symptoms frequently would reoccur.

Based on these observations, Jackson (1957) introduced the concept of family homeostasis; that is, the process that maintains the internal balance or status quo of family functioning. In addition, homeostasis describes changes in one family member as they relate to changes in other family members. Thus, behavioral change on the part of one family member can produce an imbalance in the system and affect the behavior of other members of the system. As a result, there is a pressure exerted from within the system to return to its former homeostatic state, either by interfering with behavior change on the part of the identified patient or by the development of symptomatic behaviors in other family members.

Jackson describes all communication as either symmetrical, a relationship of equality in which either person can take the lead; or complementary, a relationship in which one person leads and the other follows. He defines the family as an interacting communications network whose interaction patterns are maintained in the family system by the process of homeostasis.

There are two major goals in Jackson's family therapy: changing the homeostatic mechanisms that maintain the dysfunctional interaction patterns in the family, and clarifying the rules that operate within the family system. He focuses assessment and intervention on the communication patterns of the family, and he is particularly concerned with the rules of the family system that dictate how and with whom family members interact. Specifically, Jackson's primary focus is on the relationship between the sender and receiver of messages and not on the messages themselves. Thus, the content of the message is not important to Jackson; rather, he is interested in the patterns of interaction, or the family's process. Because of Jackson's focus on current patterns of interaction and the family rules that perpetuate the system, he is not concerned with a family's history unless it provides information about current interactional processes.

Jackson (1968) describes two basic techniques for changing a family's dysfunctional communication patterns and helping the family to clarify and understand those rules by which relationships are established. These therapeutic techniques are (a) relabeling, and (b) prescribing the symptom. Relabeling is a method of redefining or reframing behaviors to change the interpersonal meaning of the behaviors for the family. The therapist attempts to emphasize the positive aspects of the behavior and thereby reduces any possible negative interpretation of the behavior. Relabeling helps the family look at their interactions in a different way. An example is relabeling a mother's overcontrolling behavior as "concern" for her children.

In prescribing the symptom, the therapist instructs the family to continue and exaggerate the problem areas. This technique alters the meaning of the problem or symptom within the family system, because the symptom is now being prescribed by the therapist rather than by the family. The procedure also shifts power or control to the therapist and helps to deemphasize the symptom as a source of interpersonal control within the family. An example of the technique of prescribing the symptom is a situation in which the therapist instructs a child with a stealing problem to continue stealing from his parents, with the intention of helping to mobilize strong parental control and limit setting in a family in which such control is lacking.

Like Jackson, Jay Haley focuses on communication within the family, although his concern is primarily with power struggles in the relationships of family members. For Haley, power and control are central to understanding communication in the family system. In addition to helping the family to communicate more effectively, his goal in therapy is to help them to realize they are engaged in a power struggle (Haley, 1976). Family members seek power through messages that attempt to define and redefine their relationships. Developing symptoms to change the power relationship is another method for achieving control in the family system.

Haley (1976) refers to his treatment approach as problem-solving therapy. Because symptoms are a strategy that family members use for dealing with relationships in the system, Haley sees family therapy as a place to teach family members other methods for defining relationships so that the symptomatic behaviors will be eliminated.

The issue of power and control is also central to the relationship between the family and the therapist. According to Haley, it is essential for the therapist to remain in control if family therapy is to be successful. Haley (1976) views all forms of psychological treatment, including individual psychotherapy and family therapy, as involving interpersonal influence and manipulation. All therapies are, therefore, a power struggle between the client and therapist. In the case of family treatment, families attempt to manipulate the therapist in order to maintain their homeostatic balance and resist change. As a result, the therapist must take an active role in the therapy sessions and use methods that will counter the family's controlling maneuvers.

Many of Haley's therapeutic interventions with families attempt to shift the power from one family member to another, as well as from the family to the therapist. He uses several strategies to accomplish changes in the family's pattern of relating, such as giving paradoxical or conflicting directives to the family, or specifically instructing family members to engage in problematic behaviors. These techniques use therapeutic control as a means of facilitating behavior change; the family's typical response of resisting the therapist's directives in order to maintain its own control in the situation results in change in the dysfunctional behaviors. In a sense, the family changes its patterns of relating by rebelling against the therapist's controlling maneuvers.

Haley (1976) discusses the use of two types of directives in which the therapist assigns specific tasks for the family to follow outside the therapy sessions. In one type, the therapist tells the family what to do when he or she wants them to follow the directive. Such a directive typically involves instructing the family to stop a particular behavior.

The second type of directive involves telling the family what to do when the therapist does not want them to follow the instruction. The assumption is that the family will resist or rebel against the directive and thereby change their typical maladaptive behavior patterns. In a family with a school-phobic child, for example, Haley might recommend against altering the child's refusal to attend school, suggesting that it would be better if the child remained home because the family had grown comfortable with the situation. Because of the family's strategy to remain in a controlling position with the therapist, Haley assumes that the child would soon return to school and the family would change its behavior in order to prove the therapist wrong.

Satir, while subscribing to many of the concepts proposed by Jackson and Haley, also emphasizes the feeling aspects of communication. She is concerned primarily with the emotional interchanges that occur in family systems (Satir, Stachowiak, & Taschman, 1975).

Satir believes that dysfunction occurs within the family when communication is incongruent. Incongruent communication results when the content of the message and the metacommunicational aspects of the message do not agree (Satir, 1972). Dysfunctional communication occurs when family members consistently do not differentiate verbal and nonverbal levels of communication. Family members must therefore learn to give and receive clear messages.

Satir sees the therapist as a teacher and model of effective communication. She teaches family members to speak for themselves and to say as clearly as they can what they think and feel, in order to bring disagreements out into the open. Another goal of therapy is to help the family to discover its rules of communication, such as to whom one can talk in the family, what feelings can be expressed, and how members can seek clarification from each other when they do not understand the message sent by another family member.

Satir (1967, p. 72) provides an example of the approach she uses to help family members learn to communicate more directly with each other:

M: They never help around the house.
Th: Now you mean the kids?
M: Yes.
Th: Have you told them what you want them to do?
M: Well, I think so. They're supposed to know.

Th: But have you *told* them?
M: Well, no.

In another example, Satir (1967, pp. 97–100) illustrates how the therapist clarifies the process of the family members' interactions with each other:

Th: (To husband) I notice your brow is wrinkled, Ralph. Does that mean you are angry at this moment?
H: I didn't know that my brow was wrinkled.
Th: Sometimes a person looks or sounds in a way of which he is not aware. As far as you can tell, what were you thinking and feeling just now?
H: I was thinking over what she (his wife) said.
Th: What thing that she said were you thinking about?
H: When she said that when she was talking so loud, she wished I would tell her.
Th: What were you thinking about that?
H: I never thought about telling her. I thought she would get mad.
Th: Ah, then maybe that wrinkle meant you were puzzled because your wife was hoping you would do something and you did not know she had this hope. Do you suppose that by your wrinkled brow you were signalling that you were puzzled?
H: Yeh, I guess so.
Th: As far as you know, have you ever been in that same spot before, that is, where you were puzzled by something Alice said or did?
H: Hell, yes, lots of times.
Th: Have you ever told Alice you were puzzled when you were?
W: He never says anything.
Th: (Smiling, to Alice) Just a minute, Alice, let me hear what Ralph's idea is of what he does. Ralph, how do you think you have let Alice know when you were puzzled?
H: I think she knows.
Th: Well, let's see. Suppose you ask Alice if she knows.
H: This is silly.
Th: (Smiling) I suppose it might seem so in this situation, because Alice is right here and certainly has heard what your question is. She knows what it is. I have the suspicion, though, that neither you nor Alice are very sure about what the other expects, and I think you have not developed ways to find out. Alice, let's go back to when I commented on Ralph's wrinkled brow. Did you happen to notice it, too?
W: (Complaining) Yes, he always looks like that.
Th: What kind of a message did you get from that wrinkled brow?
W: He don't want to be here. He don't care. He never talks. Just looks at television or he isn't home.
Th: I'm curious. Do you mean that when Ralph has a wrinkled brow that you take this as Ralph's way of saying, ''I don't love you, Alice. I don't care about you, Alice.''?
W: (Exasperated and tearful) I don't know.
Th: Well, maybe the two of you have not yet worked out crystal-clear ways of giving your love and value messages to each other. Everyone needs crystal-clear ways of giving their value messages. (To son) What do you know, Jim, about how you give your value messages to your parents?
S: I don't know what you mean.

Th: Well, how do you let your mother, for instance, know that you like her, when you are feeling that way. Everyone feels different ways at different times. When you are feeling glad your mother is around, how do you let her know?

S: I do what she tells me to do. Work and stuff.

Th: I see, so when you do your work at home, you mean this for a message to your mother that you're glad she is around.

S: Not exactly.

Th: You mean you are giving a different message then. Well, Alice, did you take this message from Jim to be a love message? (To Jim) What do you do to give your father a message that you like him?

S: (After a pause) I can't think of nothin'.

Th: Let me put it another way. What do you know crystal-clear that you could do that would bring a smile to your father's face?

S: I could get better grades in school.

Th: Let's check this out and see if you are perceiving clearly. Do you, Alice, get a love message from Jim when he works around the house?

W: I s'pose—he doesn't do very much.

Th: So from where you sit, Alice, you don't get many love messages from Jim. Tell me, Alice, does Jim have any other ways that he might not now be thinking about that he has that say to you that he is glad you are around?

W: (Softly) The other day he told me I looked nice.

Th: What about you, Ralph, does Jim perceive correctly that if he got better grades you would smile?

H: I don't imagine I will be smiling for some time.

Th: I hear that you don't think he is getting good grades, but would you smile if he did?

H: Sure, hell, I would be glad.

Th: As you think about it, how do you suppose you would show it?

W: You never know if you ever please him.

Th: We have already discovered that you and Ralph have not yet developed crystal-clear ways of showing value feelings toward one another. Maybe you, Alice, are now observing this between Jim and Ralph. What do you think, Ralph? Do you suppose it would be hard for Jim to find out when he has pleased you?

THE STRUCTURAL APPROACH

Salvador Minuchin is most closely identified with the structural approach to family therapy. He developed much of the theory and techniques of structural family treatment when he was working at a residential treatment center for low-income delinquent youth in New York City (Minuchin, 1967).

The structural approach emphasizes the active, organized wholeness of the family system. Minuchin (1974, p. 89) describes his viewpoint:

> In essence, the structural approach to families is based on the concept that a family is more than the individual biopsychodynamics of its members. Family members relate according to certain arrangements [which], though

usually not explicitly stated or even recognized, form a whole—the structure of the family.

Minuchin considers the family to be a system that is governed by an invisible set of demands called a structure. The structure of the family system provides the primary social context in which the individual functions. The individual both influences and is influenced by this context. Consequently, changes in the family structure contribute to changes in the behavior and intrapsychic processes of the members of the system.

The family system differentiates and carries out its functions through subsystems consisting of one or more individuals. These subsystems may consist of dyads, such as father–son or mother–father, or they may be formed around generation, sex, interest, or function. Different levels of power and types of transactional patterns are associated with each subsystem. Contact between the various subsystems must be maintained, but members of each subsystem also must be allowed to carry out their functions without interference from other subsystems. Minuchin (1974) elaborates:

> Every family subsystem has specific functions and makes specific demands on its members; and the development of interpersonal skills achieved in these subsystems is predicated on the subsystem's freedom from interference from other subsystems.

Clear boundaries between the subsystems are essential for effective family functioning. Boundaries are the rules that define the members and how they participate in a subsystem. If the boundaries become blurred (e.g., if a child is permitted to enter the parental subsystem), the family system becomes enmeshed and may lack the resources to function effectively. On the other hand, if boundaries are too rigid, communication across subsystems becomes difficult and the family becomes disengaged. Members of disengaged families lack feelings of belonging and loyalty, as well as a capacity for requesting support when needed. Successful family functioning requires that the family structure be continually adaptive in response to demands for change. When enmeshment or disengagement occurs, dysfunctional transactional patterns within the family prevent adaptive responses.

Minuchin's goal in therapy is to transform the systematic structure of the family in three major steps. First, the therapist joins the family by becoming a member of various subsystems and adjusting to the transactional patterns, styles, affect, and language. The second step, evaluation of the family structure, evolves from the therapist's experiences and observations upon joining the family. This diagnostic process continues throughout the course of treatment, with constant revisions as the family restructures or resists attempts at restructuring. The creation of circumstances that allow for transformation of the structure is the third step, and it is accomplished by a variety of techniques facilitated by the therapist's assumption of a position of leadership in the family system (Minuchin, 1974).

One of the therapeutic strategies that Minuchin uses to alter the structure of the family is what he refers to as actualizing family transactional patterns. In this technique the therapist encourages the family during therapy sessions to engage in interactions with each other that help to highlight problems in their relationships. For example, the therapist might instruct an adolescent who is complaining about his father's absences from home to talk directly to his father about his concerns, rather than speak to the therapist about this issue. In a family where the boundaries are blurred between parental and child subsystems, the therapist might rearrange the seating in the therapy session so that the parents sit together on one side of the room and the children are on the other side.

Assigning tasks is another technique used by Minuchin to modify family structure. The family may be asked to engage in certain tasks during the sessions or be given homework assignments. For example, a child with too many parental duties might be assigned the task of going to a movie with friends rather than staying home to watch his or her siblings, or a mother who is underinvolved with her adolescent daughter might be directed to teach her daughter to cook.

Minuchin describes a series of techniques that utilize the child's symptoms to promote therapeutic change in the family, which in turn helps the child with his or her symptoms. An example might be helping a firesetter to learn to use matches in a safe and competent manner. The symptom can also be used in such a way as to deemphasize its significance to the family, such as having a family eat lunch with an anorectic child.

The following excerpt from a family therapy session illustrates some of the techniques used by Minuchin and Fishman (1981, pp. 155–157) to alter a family's patterns of interaction:

Alan: Would you give me a hand, Peg?

Peg: Tell Daddy that you want to make decisions by yourself. If you really want to do it.

Alan: Yeah, I would like to be more independent, but I guess it's a habit of letting people do things for me, and I've gotten into it.

Peg: And I guess it's going to be very hard for Daddy to stop. It will be hard for all of us, but especially Daddy, because he and Mommy tend more to be protective. And it's going to take a long time, and it's going to take a lot on your part, too, to make decisions and say, "Well, look, I don't want Peg to help." You can't be afraid to say it.

Alan: Yeah.

Minuchin: Peg, do you find yourself frequently in the job of being the helper?

Peg: Yes.

Minuchin: Who else is asking you for help?

Peg: Uh—my mother. . . .

Minuchin: Pete, exchange seats with your mom, because I want your mother to talk with Peg. (Pete unhooks his microphone to change chairs, and Peg starts to help him.) No, let him do it. (To Pete) Very good. You did it on your own. Nobody helped you. Maybe you will still be safe, Pete, since nobody will help you. Mom, talk with Peg because I think Peg gets herself saddled with helping a lot in the family. . . .

Mother: She does. Peg wants—

Minuchin: Talk with her about how you saddle her.

Mother: About how I saddle her with the problems?

Minuchin: Yeah.

Peg: Right. Well, I never realized it. It just happened that grandmother—

Mother: My mother used to live with us, and she was around all the time when Peg was growing up, and then when she wasn't there, I just automatically used to ask Peg—I didn't realize that I was putting pressure on Peg. I thought it was more or less conversation. Right, Peg?

Peg: Maybe you didn't realize it, but I know that you wanted me to help you decide things.

Mother: I always considered it more like we would talk over things together and then I would make my own decision, but I think maybe you felt that it was left on your shoulders to make the decision.

Peg: A lot of times you did. You would say, "What do you think I should do?" Or, "What do you think about this?" And I made a lot of decisions.

Minuchin: You did ask Peg to make decisions? . . .

Mother: Not about important things, like about if you're going to buy a house or something like that, but about—

Peg: About family things.

Mother: Yeah.

Minuchin: Family things. She would ask you?

Mother: Yes—I would ask her to help.

Minuchin: Father, where were you? You that were so helpful. You that were helping Alan. Where were you? Why didn't your wife ask you?

Father: I wasn't around too much then.

Minuchin: Oh, that's why. Are you saying that you were alone and that you used Peg because Nels was not around?

Mother: Nels was working two jobs for a long time. He's always working two jobs, but now he has more of an interest in the house. I feel Nels has time if it's something he's interested in, and if it's something he doesn't want to think about, he's just not there to hear it.

Minuchin: Peg, come here and move out from that center. Mom, you sit near your husband. You know, Peg, I think that it's a pity for you to be sitting here between them. I bet that you are too available. I bet you like that job. . . .

Mother: How do you think we can go about correcting this mess?

Father: Well, I think I should start being home nights for one thing. I'll
              leave the other job—
Minuchin: Can you stop shaking your head Peg? It's not your function.

Minuchin and his colleagues (Liebman, Minuchin, & Baker, 1974; Minuchin, Rosman, & Baker, 1978) describe the successful treatment of a number of psychosomatic disorders in children, using structural family therapy. They have identified five basic characteristics in families with children exhibiting psychosomatic disorders: enmeshment of family members, overprotective parents, rigidity between subsystems, a low threshold for resolving conflicts, and a weak spouse–subsystem boundary that encourages the child's involvement in parental conflicts. According to Minuchin, the child's "illness" becomes a means of helping the family to avoid resolving conflicts.

THE BEHAVIORAL APPROACH

The behavioral approach to family therapy is based upon the empirical methodology and specific principles drawn from the field of social-learning theory (LeBow, 1972; Liberman, 1972). Many of the behavior therapy techniques presented in chapter 5 have been adapted for use with families.

Therapists who subscribe to a behavioral approach to family treatment believe that the behavior of individual family members is shaped and maintained by events in the natural environment, and therefore behavior can best be changed by the modification of environmental contingencies. The major focus of this type of treatment has been the modification of the child's behavior by training parents in the effective use of contingency management.

Parent-training programs differ widely in their content, from those emphasizing the general theory and major techniques of behavior modification to those that focus on teaching specific interventions for specific problem behaviors (Gordon & Davidson, 1981; Dangel & Polster, 1984). Selection of the specific behavioral techniques to be included in a parent-training program depend on the level of sophistication of the parents, the time available for training, age of the target child, and the types of behavior to be changed.

Most programs include techniques for both accelerating desirable behaviors and decelerating undesirable behaviors. These techniques are typically used together. Several basic components typically are included in training programs. Parents are taught to define the problem behavior objectively and to analyze the effects of antecedent events and consequences on this behavior. They learn to monitor and record the frequency and duration of the behavior so that they can continuously assess the effectiveness of their intervention. Training in behavioral intervention often begins with instructions on how to state and enforce rules, and with the importance of being consistent.

The major technique for accelerating desirable behavior is to increase contingent positive reinforcement, especially social reinforcement, such as praise. In addition to changing the consequences for the child's behavior, parents are taught to alter antecedent events to increase the likelihood of prosocial behavior. Some behavior therapists train parents to decrease the number of commands they give their children. This practice is based on research findings that parents of clinic-referred children issued significantly more commands than mothers of nonclinic children (Forehand & McMahon, 1981). While a reduction in the number of commands may not directly increase a child's compliance, it may increase parental attention to positive behavior and thus provide reinforcement for such behavior.

The most commonly taught behavioral deceleration technique is time out from positive reinforcement. Time out consists of removing the opportunity to gain reinforcement, usually by isolating the child in an area devoid of reinforcing persons and objects immediately after undesirable behavior occurs. The use of time out is recommended primarily in cases of highly disruptive behaviors after other interventions have failed. Less aversive consequences, such as verbal reprimands or withdrawal of attention (ignoring problem behaviors), are often effective when applied consistently.

Parent training in behavioral techniques is typically used with young children who exhibit behavior problems. Older children or adolescents, however, are more actively involved in the therapy process and usually attend therapy sessions with their parents. One technique that is often used by behavioral family therapists in their treatment of families with adolescents is contingency contracting. A contingency contract is a written document that clearly specifies who does what to whom, and under what circumstances the behaviors are to occur. In addition, it specifies the consequences that will result when the behaviors are performed and when they are not performed. Contingency contracts are useful because they help to make explicit the expectations that family members have of each other. Furthermore, such contracts provide a structured approach to teaching families negotiation and problem-solving skills.

Weathers and Liberman (1975) have developed a program for helping families to construct a contingency contract in a brief period of time. Figure 8.3 outlines the steps that Weathers and Liberman (1975) use in their family contracting exercise. Family members learn to identify their needs and desires (rewards) for themselves and each other, to set priorities for rewards for self, to empathize with each other, to set costs on providing rewards to others, and finally to bargain and compromise.

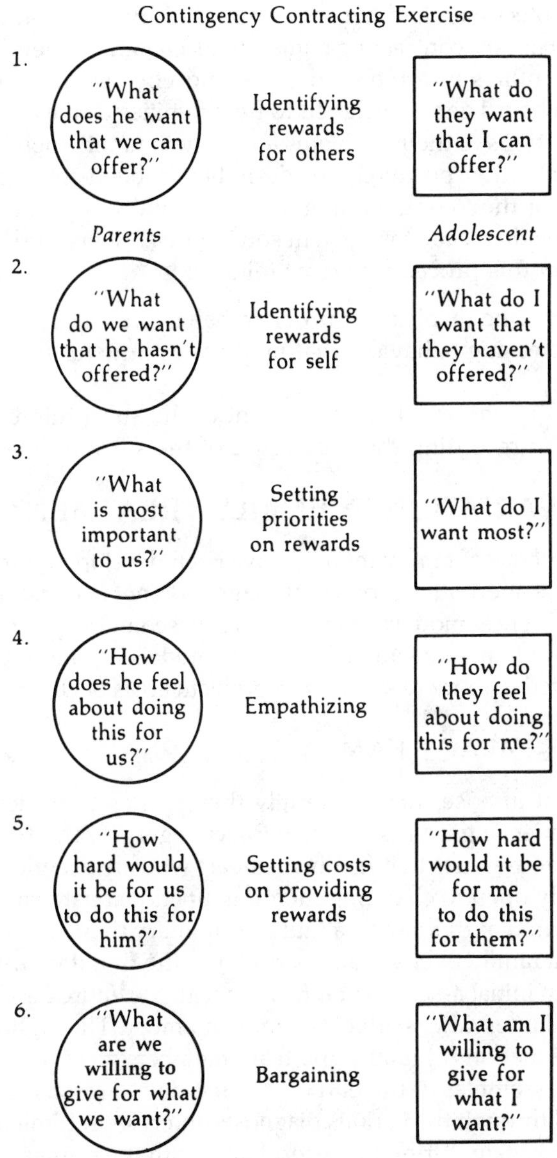

Contingency Contracting Exercise

Figure 8.3. Contingency contracting exercise between parents and an adolescent. This sequence is outlined for the parents in circles and for the adolescent in squares. From "The Family Contracting Exercise" by L. Weathers and R. P. Liberman, 1975, *Journal of Behavior Therapy and Experimental Psychiatry, 6*, pp. 208–214. Copyright 1975 by Pergamon Press, Ltd. Reprinted by permission.

Similarly, Blechman and her colleagues (Blechman, 1974; Blechman & Olson, 1976) use a "contracting game" to teach families negotiation skills to resolve conflicts in a more adaptive and effective manner. She has developed a board game designed to help families arrive at mutually acceptable solutions to their problems and to help family members learn to reinforce each other positively for desirable problem-solving behaviors. When playing the "contracting game" the family is guided through a series of steps that leads to problem solving in a brief period of time. The steps used in this procedure are as follows:

1. Discuss specific displeasing problem behaviors.
2. Propose pleasing behaviors that might substitute for the problem behaviors.
3. Arrange for contingent reinforcement of the substitute behaviors.
4. Arrange for recording the occurrence of the substitute behaviors.

VARIATION IN FAMILY TREATMENT

Several varieties of family therapy have been developed during the past decade. These alternative forms of treatment do not necessarily represent different theoretical models from those discussed in the previous section; rather, they are an extension of the basic models of family therapy and tend to be used with more specialized problem areas or client populations.

MULTIPLE-IMPACT FAMILY THERAPY

A brief, but intense, form of family therapy has been developed for families experiencing a crisis situation (MacGregor, 1971). Multiple-impact family therapy assumes that family members who are experiencing a crisis are maximally open to changing their dysfunctional patterns of relating.

In this method of treatment, a multidisciplinary therapy team typically works with a family over a 2-day period. On the first day, the treatment team holds an initial assessment interview with the entire family, followed by individual interviews with each family member. Throughout the day, various combinations of family and team members meet with each other. Everyone reassembles at the end of the first day to discuss the information revealed through the various diagnostic interviews. Similar interviews are conducted again during the second day, with the primary concern being the identification of dysfunctional patterns of communication and interaction in the family. A final meeting between the family and treatment team is held at the end of the second day. The therapists discuss their observations and make specific recommendations to the family for improving its ability to solve existing problems and those that may arise in the future. The treatment team also arranges to meet with the family after several months to assess whether the family has successfully implemented the recommendations.

MULTIPLE FAMILY THERAPY

A group treatment approach has been adapted to work with families in the form of multiple family therapy (Laquer, 1976). Four to six families typically are seen together for weekly sessions. A co-therapy team guides the discussion of their problems and facilitates a problem-solving orientation in the group. According to proponents of this approach, the group experience enables each family to learn new patterns of resolving conflicts by observing other families engaged in similar attempts at resolving their own problems. In addition, group support from other families may make the therapy experience less threatening, resulting in greater involvement in the therapy process.

SOCIAL NETWORK THERAPY

According to some family therapists, dysfunctional family relationships can result from problems in adapting to rapid social change and from loss of support from social resources. Social network family therapy was developed as a means of establishing an extensive supportive social network for families to enable them to cope more effectively with crises (Attneave, 1976; Speck & Attneave, 1973). Extended family members, friends, neighbors, and significant persons from school, work, and other social agencies are brought together to help the family learn to solve its own problems in a more adaptive manner. A team of therapists mobilizes the supportive and helping resources within the social network by strengthening social ties and creating new channels of communication within this large social unit. Over the course of several months, meetings are held in which the family presents its problems to the group. Various subgroups from the social network then discuss possible solutions to these problems. The therapy team assists the group members in implementing specific solutions to the family's problems and helps the social network to develop a plan for its continued supportive involvement with the family.

Speck and Attneave (1973) conceputalize social network therapy as progressing through six specific phases. These phases have been summarized by Rueveni (1979) and are presented in Table 8.4.

FAMILY THERAPY OUTCOME RESEARCH

Research on the effectiveness of family therapy has not kept pace with the growing interest in this field. Although much family therapy research has been published since the 1950s, it is only during the last decade that

Table 8.4. Family Network Intervention: Summary of Phases, Tasks, and Goals

PHASES	TASKS OF FAMILY AND NETWORK	TASKS OF INTERVENTION TEAM	GOALS
Retribalization	Family calls together network members and provides setting for meetings.	Explain rationale and significance of network meeting. Reduce tension through encounter-type exercises.	Make network visible. Begin re-building ties between network members.
Polarization	Family presents to network problems/issues creating crisis. Network members present different reactions to the issues.	Have subgroups of the network present, uninterrupted, their views and feelings about problems.	Draw out different attitudes and feelings of members. Promote confrontations that shake up old stereotypes and lead to new interpersonal perceptions.
Mobilization	The entire network or smaller groups work to generate possible solutions to specific problems.	Present specific problems to network. Facilitate group interactions, discourage unproductive communication.	Focus energy and resources of network on creating new solutions to problems.
Depression	Network members get discouraged or frustrated with difficulty of task.	Acknowledge difficulty and provide encouragement. Use psychodramatic techniques to help network break the impasse.	Regenerate positive feelings of solidarity and support to offset feelings of discouragement. Help network keep working on difficult tasks.
Breakthrough	"Activists" generate workable solutions.	Mobilize support structures for each family member. Promote effective small-group interaction.	Provide new solutions to problems.
Elation/exhaustion	Potential solutions are developed, new feelings of satisfaction and competence emerge. Future connections are planned.	Encourage support-group members to plan course of action.	Feelings of satisfaction and competence center in network, reinforcing value of network meeting.

Note. From *Networking Families in Crisis* by U. Rueveni (1979). New York: Human Sciences Press. Copyright 1979 by Human Sciences Press, Inc. Reprinted by permission.

investigations in this area have begun to address the methodological problems of earlier research. These methodological problems have made conclusions about the overall effectiveness of family therapy a difficult task. Many of the methodological problems that have hampered outcome research on psychotherapy also have contributed to problems in research into the effectiveness of family therapy (Wells, Dilkes, & Trivelli, 1972; Wells, Dilkes, & Burkhardt, 1976).

Outcome research in family therapy is complicated by several factors. First, unlike individual psychotherapy research, researchers in this field must simultaneously measure change in several people, and evaluate change in the interactions between and among them.

Another complexity in family therapy research is a lack of consensus as to what factors constitute evidence for the effectiveness of treatment. The diversity of criteria for evaluating the success of family therapy is reflected in a survey of family therapists that primarily included psychologists, psychiatrists, and social workers (Group for the Advancement of Psychiatry, 1970a). Among the questions that the respondents answered was one pertaining to their primary goals for therapy with a family. The results of this question are presented in Table 8.5 and illustrate the lack of agreement as to the most important factors that should be considered with evaluating the effectiveness of family therapy.

Other difficulties in conducting family therapy outcome research have been noted in the literature (Gurman & Kniskern, 1981; LeBow, 1981; Todd & Stanton, 1983). Some of these factors include problems in operationalizing the multitude of family therapy concepts, lack of clarity in delineating the exact components of family treatment, the reliability and validity of assessment procedures, the use of multiple assessment meth-

Table 8.5. Therapists' Stated Primary Goals with Families Currently in Treatment ($N = 290$)

PRIMARY GOALS	% OF ALL FAMILIES	% OF CERTAIN FAMILIES	TOTAL %
Improved communication.	85	5	90
Improved autonomy and individuation.	56	31	87
Improved empathy.	56	15	71
More flexible leadership.	34	32	66
Improved role agreement.	32	32	64
Reduced conflict.	23	37	60
Individual symptomatic improvement.	23	33	56
Improved individual task performance.	12	38	50

Note. From *The Field of Family Therapy* (GAP Report No. 78) by the Group for the Advancement of Psychiatry (1970a). New York: Group for the Advancement of Psychiatry. Copyright 1970 by the Group for the Advancement of Psychiatry, Inc. Reprinted by permission.

ods, experimental control in the research design, and the generalizability of the findings to various populations and settings.

Recent reviews of research in this area have concluded that the quality of outcome studies in family therapy have generally improved over time (Gurman & Kniskern, 1978, 1981; Todd & Stanton, 1983; Wells & Denzen, 1978; Wells, Dilkes, & Burkhardt, 1976). Gurman and Kniskern (1978), for example, note that there has been an 86% increase in the number of controlled studies of nonbehavioral approaches to family therapy since 1970.

In general, the reviews of family therapy outcome research have been cautiously optimistic regarding the effectiveness of family therapy as a treatment modality. Gurman and Kniskern (1978) have provided what is perhaps the most comprehensive review in this area. They evaluated over 200 studies of marital and family therapy, and approximately 5,000 persons were represented in these investigations. Included in their review were uncontrolled studies, single-group studies, investigations that compared family therapy to no treatment, and studies that compared family therapy to other forms of treatment such as individual therapy.

Table 8.6 summarizes the improvement rates for family therapy with different client populations and a wide range of presenting problems. Approximately half of the family therapy studies included children and adolescents as the "identified patient." Overall, the improvement rate for family therapy was 73%. It may be noted that where the child was the identified patient, the improvement rate was on the order of 68%, with somewhat higher improvement rates for adolescents (75%). While Gurman and Kniskern indicated that studies comparing family therapy with individual therapy often yielded results favoring family therapy, it is of interest to note that the 68% improvement rate for family therapy involving children is quite similar to the improvement rates for individual psychotherapy cited in chapter 3.

Table 8.6. Improvement Rates in Family Therapy

IDENTIFIED PATIENT	NO. OF STUDIES	PATIENTS IN STUDY	OUTCOME AT TERMINATION NO. OF PATIENTS (%)		
			IMPROVED	NO CHANGE	WORSE
Children	11	370	254 (68)	116 (32)	0 (0)
Adolescents	9	217	164 (75)	52 (25)	1 (0)
Adults	12	475	311 (65)	157 (33)	7 (2)
Mixed	8	467	380 (81)	78 (17)	9 (2)
Total	40	1529	1109 (73)	403 (26)	17 (1)

Note. Adapted from "Research on Marital and Family Therapy" by A. P. Gurman and D. P. Kniskern in *Handbook of Psychotherapy and Behavior Change* (2nd ed.) edited by S. Garfield and A. Bergin (1978). New York: Wiley. Copyright 1978 by John Wiley & Sons, Inc. Adapted by permission.

Finally, Gurman and Kniskern concluded that no one type of family therapy has been demonstrated as more effective than another when used with a broad range of presenting problems.

An additional review by Todd and Stanton (1983) also attempts to synthesize the research on marital and family therapy. Their findings can be summarized as follows:

1. Family therapy approaches are equal to or no more effective than individual or other forms of treatment.
2. Rates of deterioration in family therapy are approximately the same as those of other therapeutic modalities.
3. There is little comparative evidence that any particular type of family therapy is superior to all others across a diverse number of presenting problems.
4. Short-term and time-limited family therapy appear to be as effective as longer-term therapy.
5. The father's participation in family therapy substantially improves treatment outcome.
6. There is no empirical evidence to suggest that the use of a co-therapist is superior to family treatment conducted by a single therapist.

A number of research issues remain to be resolved, including operationalizing the numerous theoretical concepts in this area and developing objective measures of the process and outcome of family therapy.

SUMMARY

The family therapy approach to the treatment of childhood behavior problems was presented. It was noted that family therapy represents a diverse set of theories and techniques, with the common view that the family system as a whole, rather than an individual family member, should be the target of intervention. Behavior problems in children are seen as symptomatic of a dysfunctional family system, and the goal of treatment is therefore the improvement of overall family functioning.

Interest in family therapy developed during the early 1950s, when several research groups began to investigate the role of family dynamics in the manifestation of symptoms by a seriously disturbed family member. It was later observed that the same dysfunctional relationships seen in highly disturbed families are present to some degree in all families.

There is no systematic approach to the assessment of families. Instead, family therapists tend to use assessment procedures that reflect their theoretical orientation regarding the causes of symptomatic behaviors within the context of the family system. Despite the diverse approaches to family assessment, a common feature in the evaluation of families for treatment is a focus on family process. Structured interviews and tasks to facilitate interaction between family members often are used to evaluate family process. Some therapists include as part of their assessment a detailed history of the family's development over several generations. Another framework for assessment used by some family therapists is to evaluate a family within the context of the developmental stages in a family life cycle. This procedure enables the family therapist to determine whether the family is experiencing problems in accomplishing various tasks at its current stage in the life cycle. More recently, family researchers have developed standardized measures for use in family assessment.

Four major models of family therapy were reviewed in this chapter. The psychodynamic approach to family therapy focuses on the way in which intrapsychic conflicts of individual family members interact within the family system to produce disturbed behavior in particular members. This type of family treatment is represented by family therapists such as Nathan Ackerman and Murray Bowen.

In the communications approach to family therapy, the primary concern of the therapist is the manner in which family members send and receive messages. The three major proponents of this model are Don Jackson, Jay Haley, and Virginia Satir. Their goal of therapy is to help family members improve the manner in which they communicate with each other.

Salvador Minuchin is most closely associated with the structural approach to family therapy. Minuchin regards the family as a system in which family members relate according to certain rules, which he refers to as the structure of the family. Successful family functioning requires that the family structure continually adapt to demands for change. The goal of structural family therapy is the transformation of the systematic rule structure of the family.

The final model of family therapy presented was the behavioral approach. Behavioral family therapists believe that the behavior of individual family members is shaped and maintained by events in the natural environment, and therefore behavior can best be changed by modifying environmental contingencies. The major focus of behavioral family therapists has been the modification of a child's problem behavior by training parents in the effective use of contingency management. With older children and adolescents, a contingency contracting procedure often is used to help teach families negotiation and problem-solving skills to resolve conflicts in a more adaptive and effective manner.

Several variations of family therapy also were presented. Multiple-impact family therapy was developed for use with families experiencing a crisis situation. In this method of treatment, a multidisciplinary treatment team works with a family over a two-day period. Multiple family therapy is a group approach to family treatment in which several families are seen together in therapy sessions. Finally, social network therapy was developed as a method for creating an extensive supportive social network for families, to enable them to cope more effectively with crises. A team of therapists brings together a large network of significant others to help the family learn to solve its own problems in a more adaptive manner.

The final section of the chapter presented research on the effectiveness of family therapy. Many of the methodological problems that have hampered outcome research on psychotherapy also have contributed to problems in research into the effectiveness of family therapy. In general, the reviews of family therapy outcome research have been cautiously optimistic regarding the effectiveness of family therapy as a treatment modality for children.

REFERENCES

Ackerman, N. (1958). *The psychodynamics of family life.* New York: Basic Books.

Ackerman, N. W. (1966). *Treating the troubled family.* New York: Basic Books.

Attneave, C. L. (1976). Y'all come: Social networks as the unit of intervention. In P. Guerin (Ed.), *Family therapy: Theory and practice.* New York: Gardner.

Beels, C., & Ferber, A. (1969). Family therapy: A view. *Family Process, 8,* 280–332.

Blechman, E. A. (1974). The family contract game: A tool to teach interpersonal problem solving. *Family Coordinator, 23,* 269–281.

Blechman, E. A., & Olson, D. H. (1976). The family contract game: Description and effectiveness. In D. H. Olsen (Ed.), *Treating relationships.* Lake Mills, IA: Graphic.

Boss, P. G. (1980). Normative family stress: Family boundary changes across the life-span. *Family Relations, 29,* 445–450.

Bowen, M. (1966). The use of family theory in clinical practice. *Comprehensive Psychiatry, 7,* 345–374.

Bowen, M. (1976). Theory in the practice of psychotherapy. In P. J. Guerin (Ed.), *Family therapy: Theory and practice.* New York: Gardner.

Carroll, E. J. (1964). Family therapy—Some observations and comparisons. *Family Processes, 3,* 178–185.

Cromwell, R. E., Olson, D. H. L., & Fournier, D. G. (1976). Tools and techniques for diagnosis and evaluation in marital and family therapy. *Family Process, 15,* 1–49.

Dangel, R. F., & Polster, R. A. (1984). *Parent training.* New York: Guilford.

Duvall, E. M. (1977). *Marriage and family development* (5th ed.). New York: Lippincott.

Forehand, R., & McMahon, R. J. (1981). *Helping the noncompliant child.* New York: Guilford.

Goldenberg, I., & Goldenberg, H. (1985). *Family therapy: An overview* (2nd ed.). Monterey, CA: Brooks/Cole.

Gordon, S. D., & Davidson, N. P. (1981). Behavioral parent training. In A. S. Gurman & D. P. Kniskern (Eds.), *Handbook of family therapy.* New York: Brunner/Mazel.

Group for the Advancement of Psychiatry (GAP) (1970a). *The field of family therapy.* New York: Group for the Advancement of Psychiatry.

Group for the Advancement of Psychiatry (1970b). *Treatment of families in conflict.* New York: Science House.

Guerin, P. J., & Pendagast, E. G. (1976). Evaluation of family system and geneogram. In P. J. Guerin, Jr. (Ed.), *Family therapy: Theory and practice.* New York: Gardner.

Gurman, A. P., & Kniskern, D. P. (1978). Research on marital and family therapy: Progress, perspective and prospect. In S. Garfield & A. Bergin (Eds.), *Handbook of psychotherapy and behavior change* (2nd ed.). New York: Wiley.

Gurman, A. P., & Kniskern, D. P. (1981). Family therapy outcome research: Knowns and unknowns. In A. P. Gurman & D. P. Kniskern (Eds.), *Handbook of family therapy.* New York: Brunner/Mazel.

Haley, J. (1976). *Problem-solving therapy.* San Francisco: Jossey-Bass.

Haley, J. (1979). Family therapy. *International Journal of Psychiatry, 9,* 233–242.

Hill, R., & Rodgers, R. H. (1964). The developmental approach. In H. T. Christensen (Ed.), *Handbook of marriage and the family.* Chicago: Rand McNally.

Howells, J. G. (1975). *Principles of family psychiatry.* New York: Brunner/Mazel.

Jackson, D. D. (1957). The question of family homeostasis. *Psychiatric Quarterly Supplement, 31*(I), 79–90.

Jackson, D. D. (1968). The eternal triangle: An interview with Don D. Jackson. In J. Haley & L. Hoffman (Eds.), *Techniques of family therapy.* New York: Basic Books.

Laquer, H. P. (1976). Multiple family therapy. In P. J. Guerrin (Ed.), *Family therapy: Theory and practice.* New York: Gardner.

LeBow, J. (1981). Issues in the assessment of outcome in family therapy. *Family Process, 20,* 167–188.

LeBow, M. D. (1972). Behavior modification for the family. In G. D. Erickson & T. P. Hogan (Eds.), *Family therapy: An introduction to theory and technique.* Monterey, CA: Brooks/Cole.

Levant, R. F. (1984). *Family therapy: A comprehensive review.* Englewood Cliffs, NJ: Prentice-Hall.

Liberman, R. P. (1972). Behavioral methods in group and family therapy. *Seminars in Psychiatry, 4,* 145–156.

Liebman, R., Minuchin, S., & Baker, L. (1974). An integrated treatment program for anorexia nervosa. *American Journal of Psychiatry, 131,* 432–436.

MacGregor, R. (1971). Multiple impact psychotherapy with families. In J. G. Howells (Ed.), *Theory and practice of family psychiatry.* New York: Brunner/Mazel.

McPeak, W. R. (1979). Family therapies. In A. P. Goldstein & F. H. Kanfer (Eds.), *Maximizing treatment gains: Transfer enhancement in psychotherapy.* New York: Academic Press.

Minuchin, S. (1967). *Families of the slums: An exploration of their structure and treatment.* New York: Basic Books.

Minuchin, S. (1974). *Families and family therapy.* Cambridge, MA: Harvard University Press.

Minuchin, S., & Fishman, H. C. (1981). *Family therapy techniques.* Cambridge, MA: Harvard University Press.

Minuchin, S., Rosman, B. L., & Baker, L. (1978). *Psychosomatic families: Anorexia nervosa in context.* Cambridge, MA: Harvard University Press.

Moos, R. H. (1974). *Combined preliminary manual: Family, work and group environment scales.* Palo Alto, CA: Consulting Psychologists Press.

Olson, D. H., Bell, R., & Portner, J. (1978). *FACES-II*. St. Paul, MN: University of Minnesota.

Olson, D. H., Sprenkle, D. H., & Russell, C. (1979). Circumplex model of marital and family systems: I. Cohesion and adaptability dimensions, family types, and clinical applications. *Family Process, 18,* 3-28.

Rueveni, U. (1979). *Networking families in crisis.* New York: Human Sciences Press.

Satir, V. (1967). *Conjoint family therapy.* Palo Alto, CA: Science & Behavior Books.

Satir, V. (1972). *Peoplemaking.* Palo Alto, CA: Science & Behavior Books.

Satir, V., Stachowiak, J., & Taschman, H. A. (1975). *Helping families to change.* New York: Jason Aronson.

Speck, R. V., & Attneave, C. L. (1973). *Family networks.* New York: Pantheon Books.

Todd, T. C., & Stanton, M. D. (1983). Research on marital and family therapy: Answers, issues, and recommendations for the future. In B. B. Wolman & G. Stricker (Eds.), *Handbook of family and marital therapy.* New York: Plenum.

Watzlawick, P. A. (1966). A structured family interview. *Family Process, 5,* 256-271.

Watzlawick, P., Beavin, J. H., & Jackson, D. D. (1967). *Pragmatics of human communication: A study of interactional patterns, pathologies, and paradoxes.* New York: Norton.

Weathers, L., & Liberman, R. P. (1975). The family contracting exercise. *Journal of Behavior Therapy and Experimental Psychiatry, 6,* 208-214.

Wells, R. A., & Denzen, A. E. (1978). The results of family therapy revised: The nonbehavioral methods. *Family Process, 17,* 251-274.

Wells, R. A., Dilkes, T. C., & Burkhardt, N. T. (1976). In D. H. L. Olson (Ed.), *Treating relationships.* Lake Mills, IA: Graphic Publishing.

Wells, R. A., Dilkes, T., & Trivelli, N. (1972). The results of family therapy: A critical review of the literature. *Family Process, 7,* 189-207.

9

TREATMENT IN
RESIDENTIAL SETTINGS

Residential treatment may be the only alternative for children who display psychological difficulties of such a nature that community-based interventions are impossible to carry out or unlikely to be successful.

There are a range of situations where residential treatment is likely to be considered. Hersov and Bentovim (1977), for example, have suggested that inpatient care may be the treatment of choice where (a) the child's way of thinking and behaving is so irrational or bizarre that outpatient treatment is impossible, (b) the child may pose a danger to himself or herself or to others, (c) the child's behavior results from a severe form of psychopathology that is unresponsive to environmental change or outpatient treatment, (d) the child displays complex problems that require skilled observation, assessment, and intensive treatment over an extended period not possible on an outpatient basis, and (e) the family interactions are so pathological that living at home may seriously interfere with the child's developmental progress. Based on these considerations, children with pervasive developmental disorders and schizophrenia and children displaying serious antisocial and delinquent behavior are among those most often seen in residential treatment (Lewis, 1980), although children with other types of psychopathology are treated in residential settings as well.

The importance of inpatient/residential placement as a treatment alternative for severely disturbed children is emphasized by estimates suggesting that some 450 thousand children in the United States may require inpatient/residential psychiatric care of some type (Irwin, 1982).

THE CASE OF BILLY REVISITED:
ONE EXAMPLE OF RESIDENTIAL TREATMENT

One example of the type of problem that is appropriate for residential treatment was presented in chapter 1, in our discussion of Billy. It may be recalled that Billy was 12 years old, with a family history of mental illness and a medical history suggestive of possible neurological impairment. He displayed serious psychological problems, including inappropriate emotional responses, peculiarities of thought, and difficulties in relating to others. At times he was self-destructive (e.g., biting and hitting himself) as well as aggressive toward other children; sometimes hitting, biting, or scratching them to the point that he had to be restrained.

As indicated earlier, Billy's treatment took place on a child inpatient unit that was affiliated with the division of child psychiatry of a major medical center. This unit housed from 8 to 10 residents (ages 8 to 12) with diagnoses ranging from pervasive developmental disorders to severe behavior disorders. The physical facility consisted of rooms for residents (two children per room), a combined nurse's station and staff room, a kitchen and cafeteria, a recreation room equipped with ping-pong tables and television, and a time-out room. The unit also contained a teacher's office and two classrooms equipped with a variety of special educational materials. Adjoining the unit was a fenced-in play area with swings, slides, sandbox, and other recreational equipment.

The unit was directed by a child psychiatrist who also served as medical director. Additional staff included a nurse, a recreational therapist, two special education teachers, and a number of trained child-care workers who worked with and provided supervision of the residents on a 24-hour basis. Others from the division of child psychiatry who also were involved in working with the residents included child psychiatry residents, clinical psychology interns, and social work trainees, as well as faculty from each of these disciplines who supervised their activities on the unit.

Billy's treatment involved participating in a variety of educational and therapeutic activities. Each day he attended school from 8:30 until 2:30. His class, consisting of five children, was taught by a special education teacher who selected learning materials appropriate to Billy's level of achievement and worked closely with him to keep him on task and to reward successful academic performance. Billy was also seen in individual play therapy twice a week by a child psychiatry resident. Therapy was conducted within a psychodynamic framework and focused on working through conflicts contributing to Billy's problem behaviors. In addition to individual therapy, an individualized behavioral treatment program was developed to manage Billy's aggressivity on the unit. This approach involved using time-out procedures (see chapter 5) when Billy behaved aggressively toward other residents, and simultaneously rewarding his nonaggressive behavior. An attempt was made to teach Billy's parents how to use the same behavioral principles in dealing with his behavior at home. Finally, the entire family was seen for a number of sessions in order to deal with family-related issues contributing to Billy's problem behavior and, toward the end of his stay on the unit, with issues related to his return home.

Along with these programmed interventions, Billy also benefited from living on the unit, engaging in unit-related activities, and interacting with other children and staff. Teachers, child-care workers, and other unit staff were specifically trained to interact with residents in a therapeutic manner to help them deal with relationship problems that arose on the unit. For example, Billy's display of hostility on the playground might result in a child-care worker encouraging him to examine the effects of this behavior on other children and how his behavior might contribute to the negative reactions of others toward him. Likewise, disruptive behavior in the classroom would be responded to therapeutically by his teacher. Finally, through recreation therapy Billy was able to develop a degree of skill in working with handicraft projects and in play activities that resulted in increased self-confidence in his abilities.

After being on the unit for approximately 6 months, Billy's aggressive behavior was successfully brought under control. During this time the child-care workers reported that his interactions with other residents had improved considerably and he was beginning to develop at least one fairly close friendship. Billy's therapist reported that although he still displayed problems requiring outpatient treatment, significant gains had been made and inpatient care was no longer necessary. Billy's family also indicated that they felt more comfortable dealing with his problems at home than they had previously. As a result of this improvement Billy was discharged from the unit after 7½ months. Follow-up care involved individual therapy for Billy along with work with the parents in order to deal with issues arising subsequent to his leaving the unit. An additional aspect of the follow-up plan was for Billy's teacher on the unit to work with his teacher at home to find an appropriate academic placement and to discuss teaching methods that had been found useful with him.

THE NATURE OF RESIDENTIAL
TREATMENT PROGRAMS

Whereas this example illustrates the nature of residential treatment in one medical psychiatric setting, residential treatments, like approaches to individual therapy, vary markedly. As Hagemen (1978) has indicated, residential treatment can be described in the broadest sense as any 24-hour facility that devotes itself to the treatment of children with psychological disorders. In some instances treatment may be in a home-like setting in a group home located within the community and run by house parents, with the assistance of other staff, who are involved in the treatment of 10 to 12 children at a time. Some programs, like Billy's, take the form of a child inpatient unit in a medical school division of child psychiatry or within a state mental hospital. Others are residential treatment centers sponsored by community agencies, private foundations, or for-profit organizations. Although our focus here is on facilities for treating the "emotionally disturbed" child, state-run institutions for delinquents and the seriously retarded represent still other examples of residential treatment.

Some residential programs are designed to deal primarily with one type of child, whereas others provide services for children displaying a range of problems. Some provide only short-term care; others serve children requiring long-term placements. Programs also vary in terms of treatment philosophy and orientation and in the degree to which they provide a comprehensive treatment program. Finally, there are marked differences in the degree to which programs attempt to maintain ties with the child's home and community. For more detailed discussions of various inpatient and residential treatment programs see Davids (1972), Quay (1979), Schulman and Irwin (1982), and Whittaker (1979).

Despite this variability, an assumption basic to most residential programs is that the greatest treatment gains occur when the child is immersed in a continuous therapeutic environment. This environment, often referred to as the therapeutic milieu, includes aspects of ward structure and organization thought to help reduce problem behaviors, along with opportunities for children to interact in therapeutic ways with other children and staff members. The milieu may also provide a range of other therapeutic experiences, including educational, recreational, and behavior management programs and individual, group, or family therapy. As Whittaker (1979, p. 38) has suggested, "a therapeutic milieu seeks to activate every possible medium for learning—realizing that for some children the most effective "teachers" may be the cook or caretaker and the most fruitful lessons may be learned in a crafts shop or kitchen rather than a therapy room or classroom." Thus, the treatment milieu is a complex learning environment in which the child's difficulties are approached from many perspectives. The following listing, adapted from Whittaker (1979), illustrates a number of features that characterize a therapeutic milieu and which may contribute to constructive personality and behavior change.

Rules. The formal and informal guidelines of the unit that specify appropriate and inappropriate behaviors.

Routines. The regular patterns of getting up in the morning, eating meals, going to school, and going to bed that provide structure and add to the predictability of the treatment environment.

Program Activities. These frequently include arts and crafts, games, and sports, as well as a range of other informal group or individual activities. In addition to their recreational nature, these activities also encourage healthy competition among residents and opportunities to develop feelings of competence and enhanced self-esteem through successful participation (Group for the Advancement of Psychiatry, 1982).

Group Sessions. These may consist of unit meetings, formal involvement of residents in group therapy (e.g., as described in chapter 7), or participation in special interest groups, all of which are designed to foster better ways of relating.

Individual Psychotherapy. As Whittaker (1979) has noted, although individual child psychotherapy is often used in residential settings, it is usually thought of "not as the cornerstone of milieu treatment but as an important adjunctive therapy for those children who can develop and act on the basis of insight" (p. 38).

Life-Space Interviews. The life-space interview (see Redl & Wineman, 1957; Long, Morse, & Newman, 1971) is an approach to therapeutic interaction that was developed for use by child-care workers, but which can also be used by parents, to help them deal with children on the unit in a therapeutic manner when critical issues arise (e.g., when the child's parents fail to show up for an expected visit). The life-space interview is designed to help the child manage a particular upset and provide a sort of "emotional first-aid" (Whittaker, 1979). In other instances it may be used by unit staff to deal with chronic patterns of behavior that the child may display. It is a major vehicle through which staff on the unit can exert a therapeutic influence on the child at any opportune time during the day.

Incentive Systems. These are reward systems that may be used in the classroom or on the unit to increase positive social behavior. Such systems typically involve the use of operant procedures (e.g., those described in chapter 5) and often take the form of a token economy program, where children receive reinforcement for appropriate behaviors that later can be exchanged for reinforcers of their own choosing.

Special Education. Because children seen in residential treatment often show significant academic deficits, the inclusion of a special education program is usually essential. As Hersov and Bentovim (1977) have noted, these educational experiences not only provide remedial help, but also encourage feelings of competence in the learning situation.

Conjoint Family Treatment. Family therapy, like individual psychotherapy, is usually not a cornerstone of milieu treatment but rather an adjunctive approach in cases where some of the child's difficulties are related to patterns of family interaction. Family treatment may be undertaken from a variety of perspectives, such as those discussed in chapter 8. The general focus, however, is on treating the family as a total system.

Parent Education Groups. These groups involve work with the parents rather than with the entire family and have as their focus the development of effective parenting skills to assist the parents in dealing with the child's behavior after discharge.

Individual Behavior Modification Programs. Depending on the theoretical orientation of the unit, behavioral procedures like those described in chapter 5 may be used to modify any number of behavioral problems displayed by children in residential treatment. Examples are the use of modeling and reinforcement to teach speech to autistic children and the use of punishment to decrease self-injurious behaviors. An additional example was provided earlier in our discussion of the combined use of time-out and reinforcement procedures to deal with Billy's aggressive behavior.

The components listed here would not be useful with all children and are not found in all programs, but each is of value in dealing with specific problems displayed by children entering residential treatment. For example, the rules and routines built into the structure of the unit are useful in helping children with poor impulse control. Involvement in group activities helps some children overcome relationship deficits. Special education deals with self-concept problems, difficulties with impulse control, and learning problems. Likewise, individual psychotherapy has an impact on a variety of problem areas. Figure 9.1 presents in detail the relationship between the features of a therapeutic milieu and specific child problems.

From this discussion it should be clear that residential treatment involves a complex array of therapeutic components designed to deal with a range of problems. As Whittaker (1979, p. 40) has commented, "the milieu . . . must be conceived of as a 'multidimensional' context for teaching competence if it is to impact on the multiple life problems which children bring with them. No single teaching format—however powerful—can do the job alone."

Simply having a well-developed program that includes a range of treatment options is not enough to insure adequate treatment. It is necessary that such a program be staffed by personnel who have an understanding of developmental issues and the nature of childhood psychopathology, and who possess skills that enable them to interact with children in a therapeutic manner. Special attention must be given to the selection of staff and, when necessary, to providing in-service training. Although adequate training is often presumed in the case of professionals such as psychiatrists, psychologists, social workers, and teachers, this assumption cannot always be made in the case of other unit staff. It is especially important to insure that on-line personnel such as child-care workers be carefully selected and trained in the application of therapeutic techniques; the day-to-day contact between these workers and the residents may well have

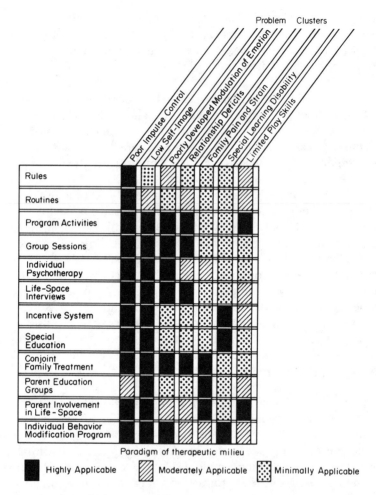

Figure 9.1. Paradigm of a therapeutic milieu. From *Caring for Troubled Children* by J. K. Whittaker, 1979, San Francisco: Jossey-Bass. Copyright 1979 by Jossey-Bass Inc., Publishers. Reprinted by permission.

a greater impact than the relatively shorter period of time children spend in individual or family therapy (Portnoy, 1973).

Along with a comprehensive program staffed by adequately trained personnel, an additional factor necessary for a long-term successful outcome is the maintenance of close ties with the child's community. Rather than attempting to treat the child in isolation, it is necessary to bring about changes in the child's home environment and community that generalize and maintain the behavior changes brought about in the residential setting. This may be accomplished, in part, by working with the child's parents when the child is in treatment. It may also involve work with the child's school and with community-based mental-health facilities that will serve the child after discharge. Indeed, it has been suggested that the nature of the post-treatment environment may be the most important determiner of the success of residential treatment (Allerhand, Weber, & Haug, 1966; Wilson & Lyman, 1983).

GUIDELINES FOR RESIDENTIAL TREATMENT

Wilson and Lyman (1983) have noted that residential treatment represents one end of a spectrum of treatment alternatives that should be considered in any given case. Citing the disruptive effects of removing a child from his or her home and the potential for stigmatization that may occur as a result of residential placement, these authors argue that it is essential to consider the full range of possible treatment alternatives when deciding on the most appropriate intervention with a given child. Treatment alternatives may include outpatient therapy using psychological and pharmacological approaches, such as those described in preceding chapters. They may include specialized educational placements or a therapeutic setting that is intermediate between an outpatient and a residential program. An example would be a day-hospitalization or day-treatment program where the child, rather than going to school, is involved in a specialized educational and treatment program during the day but spends evenings and weekends at home (see Hersov & Bentovim, 1977). And, as noted earlier, a range of residential programs have characteristics that make them appropriate for a given child *if* residential treatment is determined to be the treatment of choice.

In considering treatment alternatives, Wilson and Lyman (1983) suggest several basic principles that should be taken into account:

1. Care should be provided in the setting that is least disruptive of the child's natural environment. In the absence of extenuating circumstances (e.g., the child is in immediate danger or needs specific medical services), outpatient treatment should be attempted before day treatment, and day treatment should be considered before treatment in a group home or other more restrictive residential placement is chosen.

2. Treatment should be provided in a setting that allows for therapeutic effectiveness. The placement chosen must provide the programs and services necessary to adequately address the child's needs. Wilson and Lyman point out that problems in school-related behavior cannot be adequately dealt with on an inpatient unit that has no school program, and a program which is so far from the child's home that it allows little contact between the child and parent is clearly inappropriate where communication

problems between child and parent are a major issue. This principle also suggests, as noted earlier, that an optimal program would maintain strong ties with the child's community and home environment to increase the generalization of treatment effects.

3. The child's behavior and clinical condition should be matched to the structure and capabilities of the treatment environment (Wilson & Lyman, 1983, p. 1073).

> Some children require placement in programs with more resources, such as nighttime staff or locked facilities, while other children require only houseparent supervision. Placement of children in a program with inadequate resources to treat their condition effectively may lead to staff burnout, creation of a nontherapeutic environment, and dangerously uncontrolled circumstances. Placement of a child in a program with more resources than necessary may result in a loss of treatment effectiveness through decreased generalization as well as a squandering of limited resources.

4. Treatment should be implemented in a cost-effective way. Because treatment within residential programs is expensive, often costing as much as $15 to $40 thousand per year in public institutions (Romanczyk, Kistner, & Crimmins, 1980) and more in some private facilities, it is important to consider the issue of cost in assessing the most appropriate type of intervention. The obvious issue here is that one should not consider 24-hour residential placement if the treatment program offered within a day-treatment facility will suffice, and treatment within a day-treatment facility should not be pursued if the child can be treated just as well on an outpatient basis. In making this judgment, however, attention must be given not only to the initial cost of treatment, but also to treatment effectiveness. For example, it may be more cost effective to treat the child in a residential setting for several months than to pay for several years of outpatient therapy. Costs are not all measured in money; residential treatment may be the treatment of choice if the child's problems can be alleviated more rapidly than through extended outpatient therapy, where maladaptive behavior patterns and personal distress prevail over a longer period of time.

THE EFFECTIVENESS OF RESIDENTIAL TREATMENT

One faces a variety of problems in attempting to assess the effectiveness of residential treatment programs. Perhaps one of the greatest difficulties is in obtaining an adequate control group. To adequately assess the effectiveness of residential treatment, it is necessary to compare any changes observed in children receiving treatment with changes seen in children who show similar psychological difficulties but who do not receive treatment. This is to account for the possibility that changes observed in treated children may result from factors such as the passage of time, maturation, or other extraneous variables. Without such controls it is difficult to establish that the changes observed in treated children are indeed due to the treatment they have received. There are obvious ethical and practical problems associated with depriving children of needed treatment in order to serve as control subjects for a treatment effectiveness study. Thus, most outcome studies are of an uncontrolled nature (Whittaker, 1979).

A second problem in assessing effectiveness is that residential programs typically expose children to a range of therapeutic experiences, including individual therapy, special schooling, recreation, and the opportunity to interact with children and staff within a therapeutic milieu. An environment of multiple treatment experiences means that, even should it be demonstrated that the overall program is effective, it would be difficult to determine which of the various program components made the difference in child behavior.

Additional considerations are not unlike those faced in evaluating the effectiveness of individual treatment (see chapter 3). These include the selection of reliable and well validated outcome measures and the assessment of children not only after discharge, but at some follow-up period as well. As with individual psychotherapy, it is important to ask the right questions regarding effectiveness. Rather than simply asking whether residential treatment works, it is more appropriate to delineate the type of residential treatments that are effective with specific kinds of children under specific conditions (Wilson & Lyman, 1983). As noted in chapter 3, neither the literature on individual treatment nor that on residential treatment approaches this level of specificity (Wilson & Lyman, 1983).

There have been a number of studies designed to investigate the effectiveness of residential treatment programs, but relatively few are methodologically adequate in the sense of employing adequate controls and outcome measures (Hersov & Bentovim, 1977; Quay, 1979; Whittaker, 1979), and most provide equivocal findings regarding treatment efficacy. Although a detailed review of this outcome literature is beyond the scope of the present discussion, it is relevant to consider the general conclusions reached in two previously published reviews (Wilson & Lyman, 1983, p. 1084):

> What do studies of residential treatment find? Most report some improvement while the child is in the residential program, with this assessment typically based on a global judgment made at or after discharge. Few studies, however, demonstrate improvement compared to any control or comparison group. . . . Follow-up evaluations have been less positive.

These authors also note that research has found little relationship between behavior changes demonstrated within residential programs and behavior following discharge. Somewhat similar conclusions were reached by Hersov and Bentovim (1977, p. 897) in their review of the literature on inpatient and day-hospital treatment programs. Again lamenting the methodological problems inherent in much of the literature, these authors suggest:

> In general it appears that children with neurotic disorders do better than those with psychotic or organic disorders. . . . However, all studies tend to show that the goal of reuniting a child with his family without the need for further treatment is reached in only a small proportion of the cases, usually with neurotic children. The majority still require further special help in other hospital units or residential and day schools for maladjusted children (Capes, Gould, & Townsend, 1971). In Barker's (1974) words "inpatient care [is] a passport to further help rather than a complete treatment itself" (p. 307).

In considering these comments it is important to remember that children treated in residential settings are usually among the most severely disturbed, and perhaps it is not surprising that continued care after discharge is often needed. Further, as the reviewers of this literature have noted, good research on the effectiveness of residential treatment is the exception rather than the rule, thus making it difficult to draw more than tentative conclusions. Given that residential treatment often is required for children with severe psychopathology, more adequate research into the efficacy of this form of intervention is essential.

SUMMARY

We have briefly considered residential treatment as an alternative form of intervention for children displaying severe forms of psychopathology that are unresponsive to other therapies. It was noted that residential programs take a variety of forms (e.g., group homes, child psychiatry inpatient units, and public or private residential treatment centers in nonmedical settings) and usually include multiple treatment components, for example, individual, group, and family therapies; behavior management programs; special education programs; and recreational opportunities. Although various treatment components are part of residential treatment, it usually is assumed that the major factor in bringing about constructive personality and behavior changes is the child's participation in the total therapeutic milieu. Thus, the child is seen as benefiting from immersion in a 24-hour treatment environment consisting of opportunities for therapeutic interactions with children and staff on the unit as well as from more formal interventions. The rules and routines that contribute to the formal structure of the unit are also of therapeutic value.

While treatment within such a milieu is necessary in many instances, it was noted that residential treatment represents only one end of a continuum of treatment alternatives. Treatment in a residential setting should only be undertaken if this form of care is judged to be more appropriate than other less restrictive and less costly forms of treatment. The importance of determining that the specific residential treatment program selected meets the unique need of the individual child also was stressed.

Residential treatments are often seen as necessary for dealing with children displaying serious psychopathology, but we currently know less than we would like regarding the effectiveness of such programs. In this respect residential treatments are not unlike other forms of therapy we have discussed in earlier chapters. It is only through more adequate research in all of these areas that we can improve the quality of services that we as professionals offer to children and their families.

REFERENCES

Allerhand, M. E., Weber, R., & Haug, M. (1966). *Adaptation and adaptability: The Bellefaire follow-up study*. New York: Child Welfare League.

Barker, P. (1974). *The residential psychiatric treatment of children*. New York: Wiley.

Capes, M., Gould, E., & Townsend, M. (1971). *Stress in youth*. London: Oxford University Press.

Davids, A. (1972). *Abnormal children and youth: Therapy and research*. New York: Wiley.

Group for The Advancement of Psychiatry (1982). *The process of child therapy*. New York: Brunner/Mazel.

Hagemen, M. B. (1978). Childhood psychosis: Residential treatment and its alternatives. In B. Wolman, J. Egan, & A. Ross (Eds.), *Handbook of treatment of mental disorders in childhood and adolescence*. Englewood Cliffs, NJ: Prentice-Hall.

Hersov, L., & Bentovim, A. (1977). Inpatient units and day-hospitals. In M. Rutter & L. Hersov (Eds.), *Child psychiatry: Modern approaches*. London: Blackwell Scientific Publications.

Irwin, M. (1982). Literature review. In J. L. Schulman & M. Irwin (Eds.), *Psychiatric hospitalization of children*. Springfield, IL: Charles C Thomas.

Lewis, M. (1980). Residential treatment. In H. Kaplan, A. Freedman, & B. Sadock (Eds.), *Comprehensive textbook of psychiatry* (Vol. 3). Baltimore: Williams & Wilkins.

Long, N. J., Morse, W. C., & Newman, R. G. (1971). *Conflict in the classroom* (2nd ed.). Belmont, CA: Wadsworth.

Portnoy, S. M. (1973). Power of child care worker and therapist figures and their effectiveness as models for emotionally disturbed children in residential treatment. *Journal of Consulting and Clinical Psychology, 40*, 15–19.

Quay, H. C. (1979). Residential treatment. In H. C. Quay & J. Werry (Eds.), *Psychopathological disorders of childhood* (2nd ed.). New York: Wiley.

Redl, F., & Wineman, D. (1957). *The aggressive child*. New York: Free Press.

Romanczyk, R. G., Kistner, J. A., & Crimmins, D. B. (1980). Institutional treatment of severely disturbed children: Fact, possibility, or nonsequitur. In B. Lahey & A. Kazdin (Eds.), *Advances in clinical child psychology* (Vol. 3). New York: Plenum.

Schulman, J. L., & Irwin, M. (1982). *Psychiatric hospitalization of children.* Springfield, IL: Thomas.

Whittaker, J. K. (1979). *Caring for troubled children.* San Francisco: Jossey-Bass.

Wilson, D. R., & Lyman, R. D. (1983). Residential treatment of emotionally disturbed children. In E. Walker & M. Roberts (Eds.), *Handbook of clinical child psychology.* New York: Wiley.

EPILOGUE

The advantage of including a final section such as this is that it provides, at once, an opportunity to make summary comments, emphasize points that promote the authors' biases, and comment on issues that need to be addressed in the future while not being bound by the more formal structure of a book chapter. With these purposes in mind there are several points that seem worthy of comment.

Psychopathology in childhood can take many forms, and the treatment of childhood problems can be approached in a variety of ways. Among the treatments detailed in the preceding chapters are those that focus on the alteration of biological factors, the modification of intrapsychic determinants of behavior, the restructuring of family relationships, and the manipulation of environmental contingencies. Approaches range from those that focus on individuals to those that work with children in groups and those that treat children within an inpatient as opposed to an outpatient setting.

With such a diverse array of interventions, it is unfortunate that the selection of treatment methods is more often determined by the theoretical orientation of the clinician than by what is known regarding the effectiveness of specific treatments for specific problems. Thus, clinicians tending to emphasize the role of biological factors frequently utilize pharmacological treatments. Clinicians emphasizing intrapsychic determinants of behavior look for and find such factors to deal with in therapy. Those with a strong family orientation look for and find problems in family communication and interaction patterns and seek to change these in treatment. Likewise, external and environmental factors serve as a focal point for the intervention efforts of behaviorally-oriented clinicians. Although it would not be totally accurate to suggest that the causes of psychopathology are in the eyes of the beholder—as there are likely to be some instances where the factors emphasized by each theoretical orientation are of primary importance and all of these factors may well play some role in the majority

319

of clinical cases—approaches to child treatment are often unduly influenced by the clinician's theoretical predilections.

Given that no single model of psychopathology has been demonstrated as sufficient to account for the range of problems that are seen clinically, and that no one treatment approach is uniformly effective with all forms of child psychopathology, clinicians all too often approach childhood problems and their treatment from a limited theoretical perspective.

THE VALUE OF AN ECLECTIC APPROACH

As indicated in chapter 1, we would argue for an eclectic approach to clinical work. Instead of considering clinical problems from the perspective of a single theoretical model of psychopathology, an attempt is made to assess the range of possible contributors to the child's problem—including biological factors, family variables, relevant psychological conflicts, and environmental variables influencing the child's behavior. This approach involves a comprehensive approach to assessment of the child as he or she interacts with multiple social systems (e.g., family, school, and community). Such an approach may be contrasted with a focus on a select group of variables that sometimes occurs when assessment methods are dictated by a specific model of psychopathology; for example, ignoring relevant areas of psychological conflict by the avid behaviorist, or the denial of relevant environmental constraints by the psychodynamically-oriented clinician.

From this perspective, an optimal approach to treatment is determined by the nature of the assessment data collected and may or may not be consistent with a single theoretical orientation. As in the case of Terri discussed in chapter 1, for example, it may lead one to combine elements of behavioral, client-centered, and psychodynamic therapy. It was suggested in this case that a combination of approaches was valuable in dealing with the child's behavioral excesses (e.g., aggressivity, self-destructiveness), relationship difficulties, and possible conflicts associated with her prior sexual molestation. In other cases, the assessment data might lead to the use of different combinations of treatment methods. In any event, treatment should be the natural outgrowth of a comprehensive assessment of the child from the broadest possible perspective, designed to address the factors presumed to contribute to the child's current difficulties. As such, it may involve a single approach or the concurrent application of multiple modes of intervention associated with diverse models of psychopathology. Obviously, the components of the overall treatment program should have been empirically demonstrated as effective. If research data regarding effectiveness are unavailable, the approaches used should be consistent with accepted clinical practice. What we are advocating is a reasoned eclectic approach to child treatment.

This approach should not be confused with the sloppy eclecticism some-times seen in clinical practice where the clinician, acquainted with several approaches to treatment, haphazardly combines elements of each in some idiosyncratic manner that bears little relationship to the child's problems. Rather, "purposive eclecticism" involves a thorough consideration of the variables that contribute to the development and continuation of the child's difficulties and the selection of treatment methods based on their known or at least presumed effectiveness. In this regard the therapist might em-ploy any of a wide variety of the approaches discussed in the present text.

It must be acknowledged that this approach places a heavy burden on the clinician. He or she must be knowledgeable and skilled in diverse ap-proaches to child assessment and treatment. Likewise, he or she must be up-to-date on the research literature regarding the effectiveness of these treatment approaches (or at least those problems for which treatments are generally presumed to be effective, if research data are nonexistent). Final-ly, the clinician must be flexible enough to transcend the theoretical orien-tation in which he or she has been trained and consider clinical problems from a broader perspective. Despite the difficulties involved, such an ap-proach offers children an optimal opportunity to benefit from our interven-tion efforts.

THE NEED FOR CHILD TREATMENT RESEARCH

Whenever possible the clinician should rely on procedures that have been demonstrated as effective through empirical research. Unfortunately, although all of the approaches considered in the present text are of as-sumed value in dealing with certain childhood problems, empirical sup-port is often lacking. In many instances this lack of support is not so much evidence that an approach is ineffective, but that research related to the approach is so sparse or methodologically flawed that few conclusions regarding efficacy can be drawn. It is important that future research pro-vide a firmer knowledge base that can be used by eclectic therapists in-terested in providing the most effective treatments for troubled children.

PERMISSIONS

CHAPTER 2

Excerpts from *Psychopathology of Childhood: A Clinical and Experimental Approach* by S. Schwartz and J. H. Johnson. Copyright © 1985 by Pergamon Press.

CHAPTER 4

Excerpts from "Cognitive-Developmental Considerations in the Conduct of Play Therapy" by S. Harter in *Handbook of Play Therapy* edited by C. E. Schaefer and K. J. O'Connor (1983). New York: Wiley. Copyright © 1983 by John Wiley & Sons, Inc. Reprinted by permission.

Excerpts from *Therapies for Children* by C. E. Schaefer and H. L. Millman (1977). San Francisco: Jossey-Bass. Copyright © 1977 by Jossey-Bass, Inc., Publishers. Reprinted by permission.

Excerpts from "Play Therapy and Psychic Trauma: A Preliminary Report" by L. C. Terr in *Handbook of Play Therapy* edited by C. E. Schaefer and K. J. O'Connor (1983). New York: Wiley. Copyright © 1983 by John Wiley & Sons, Inc. Reprinted by permission.

Excerpts from "Play Therapy with the Aggressive, Acting-Out Child" by B. Willock in *Handbook of Play Therapy* edited by C. E. Schaefer and K. J. O'Connor (1983). New York: Wiley. Copyright © 1983 by John Wiley & Sons, Inc. Reprinted by permission.

Excerpts from "Psychoanalytic Play Therapy" by J. Finell in *Contemporary Psychotherapies* edited by G. S. Belkin (1980). Chicago: Rand McNally. Copyright © 1980 by Rand McNally & Co. Reprinted by permission.

Excerpts from *Theories of Personality* (2nd ed.) by C. S. Hall and G. Lindzey (1970). New York: Wiley. Copyright © 1970 by John Wiley & Sons, Inc. Reprinted by permission.

Excerpts from *Psychotherapy with Children* by C. Moustakas (1959). New York: Harper & Row. Copyright © 1959 by Harper & Row, Publishers, Inc. Reprinted by permission.

CHAPTER 7

Excerpts from *Group Psychotherapies for Children* by S. R. Slavson and M. Schiffer (1975). New York: International Universities Press. Copyright © 1975 by International Universities Press, Inc. Reprinted by permission.

CHAPTER 8

AUTHOR INDEX

Abelson, R. P., 37, 77
Abramovitz, A., 153, 190
Abramowitz, C. V., 153, 256, 265, 266
Abrams, B., 227, 241
Achenbach, T. M., 2, 5, 14, 22, 26, 74, 94, 107, 115, 135, 205, 231
Ackerman, N., 273, 279, 282, 302, 303
Adams, W., 227, 231
Adelman, H. S., 96, 97, 107
Adler, A., 126, 127, 135
Adler, S., 223, 231
Agras, W., 47, 74
Alderton, H. R., 200, 231
Alexandris, A., 200, 231
Alford, G. S., 160, 186
Allen, E. V., 197, 241
Allen, F. H., 127, 128, 135
Allen, K., 158, 186
Allen, L., 25, 26, 78
Allen, R. P., 40, 79, 212, 231
Allerhand, M. E., 313, 317
Ambrosini, P. J., 51, 66, 74, 79, 209, 211, 240
Anders, T. F., 214, 236
Andersen, A. E., 62, 64, 74
Anderson, L. T., 57, 75, 208, 231, 232
Anderson, N., 245, 266
Anderson, O. O., 209, 238
Ando, H., 55, 75
Andrulonis, P. A., 223, 233
Andrus, L. B., 229, 232
Angle, C. R., 208, 231
Annell, A. L., 210, 231
Anthony, E. J., 68, 75
Armstrong, B., 220, 238
Arnold, E., 202, 236
Ascione, F. R., 143, 187
Attneave, C. L., 297, 303, 305

Axline, V., 13, 109, 127, 128, 130, 135, 245, 247, 266
Ayllon, T., 182, 186
Aymat, F., 200, 237
Azima, F. J., 245, 266
Azrin, N. H., 67, 75, 161, 164, 165, 174, 186, 188, 191

Baer, D. M., 184, 186, 193
Bair, H. V., 199, 231
Baker, B. L., 194
Baker, L., 293, 304
Bakwin, H., 2, 22, 198
Bakwin, R. M., 2, 22, 231
Baldwin, D. G., 219, 231, 236
Baldwin, R., 203, 231
Balka, B., 209, 242
Balka, E. B., 211, 236
Bandura, A., 147, 148, 168, 169, 171, 173, 186, 187, 192
Barcai, A., 200, 202, 233, 234, 245, 265, 267
Barker, E., 211, 236
Barker, P., 316, 317
Barkley, R. A., 40, 77, 181, 187, 202, 212, 213, 231
Barlow, D. H., 181, 187
Barnes, R., 117, 136
Barrera, F., 163, 187
Barrett, C. L., 2, 22, 45, 78, 100, 102, 104, 107, 134, 135
Barry, E., 134, 137
Barry, V., 64, 78
Barsky, M., 246, 267
Barton, E. J., 143, 187
Baumeister, A. A., 181, 188
Beall, G., 222, 231
Beaubein, M. J., 223, 232

325

Beavin, J. H., 284, 305
Bechtel, D. R., 163, 188
Beck, L., 213, 231
Beels, C., 273, 303
Behrman, R. E., 222, 241
Beiser, H. R., 101
Bell, R., 15, 23, 276, 305
Bellack, A. S., 81, 104, 107, 181, 187
Bender, L., 198, 199, 232, 235
Bennett, F. C., 229, 232
Bennett, L. F., 157, 188
Bentovim, A., 306, 310, 313, 315, 317
Benz, C. R., 223, 232
Berger, L., 245, 267
Bergin, A. E., 103, 107
Bergman, A. B., 208, 234
Berkowitz, B. P., 184, 187
Berman, J. S., 102, 107
Bernal, M. E., 158, 187
Bernstein, D. A., 152, 192
Berry, K. K., 265, 267
Besserman, R. L., 157, 188
Bettelheim, B., 55, 75
Bialer, I., 209, 211, 232, 241, 242
Bijou, S. W., 183, 187
Bills, R. E., 134, 135
Bindelglass, P. M., 201, 232
Black, B. J., 100, 107
Blackburn, J. M., 197, 239
Blackwell, B., 209, 232
Blanchard, E. B., 147, 160, 186, 187
Blashfield, R., 5, 22
Blau, S., 202, 238
Blechman, E. A., 296, 303
Blotcky, M. J., 246, 267
Bobner, R. F., 223, 232
Boileau, R. A., 213, 237
Bond, L. A., 26, 76
Bonk, C., 167, 190
Bootzin, R. R., 165, 190
Borland, B. L., 40, 75
Bornstein, M. R., 181, 187
Bornstein, P. H., 2, 73, 77, 146, 187
Boss, P. G., 276, 303
Bowen, M., 198, 232, 282, 283, 302, 303
Bozarth, J. D., 103, 108
Bradbard, G., 209, 239
Bradford, D. C., 140, 141, 189
Bradley, C., 195, 197, 198, 200, 203, 212, 232, 236
Brahm, R. M., 222, 234
Brandt, D. E., 245, 267
Braswell, L., 10, 23, 41, 77, 149, 174, 190
Braukmann, C. J., 166, 190
Bray, P. F., 208, 240
Brierly, L. M., 55, 80
Brinbrauer, J. S., 160, 181, 187, 194

Brookes, E., 209, 239
Brown, P., 211, 232
Brown, R. I., 174, 188, 246, 255, 267
Brown, W. T., 203, 232
Bruch, H., 62, 75
Brunn, R. D., 201, 240
Buchsbaum, M. S., 61, 75
Buckley, R. H. 220, 232
Buckley, T. M., 160, 186
Bucksbaum, M., 202, 235
Buegel, D., 202, 236
Buell, S., 158, 186
Buonicaonto, P., 201, 239
Burchard, J. D., 163, 187
Burgemeister, B., 203, 242
Burkhardt, N. T., 299, 300, 305
Burton, N., 49, 78
Byck, R., 201, 210, 232

Caan, B., 227, 241
Cain, A. C., 116, 118, 120, 136
Cameron, N., 111, 112, 135
Campbell, M., 3, 23, 57, 75, 202, 203, 208, 209, 210, 213, 214, 215, 220, 229, 231, 232, 233
Campbell, M. B., 222, 232
Cantwell, D. P., 29, 40, 49, 51, 75, 78, 205, 212, 213, 233, 235
Capes, M., 316, 317
Caplan, R., 232
Carlisle, C. L., 197, 233
Carlson, G. A., 212, 233
Carlson, P. M., 173, 190
Carroll, E. J., 272, 303
Carson, G. A., 49, 75
Carson, R. C., 51, 60, 75
Carson, T. P., 51, 75
Case, Q., 208, 237
Casey, R. J., 102, 107
Casper, R. C., 63, 75
Cautela, J. R., 150, 187
Cayton, T. G., 155, 187
Cerny, J., 2, 23, 168, 183, 192
Chafee, F., 221, 233
Chamberlain, P., 72, 75
Chambers, W. J., 79, 202, 238
Chao, D., 203, 233
Chapin, H., 47, 74
Charlop, M. H., 181, 193
Charlton-Seifert, J., 228, 233
Cheraskin, E., 228, 232
Christensen, D. E., 182, 187, 213, 232
Christophersen, E. R., 65, 67, 75
Chun, R., 224, 225, 236
Ciminero, A. R., 142, 189
Citron, L. J., 227, 241
Clapp, R. K., 157, 188

Clarizio, H. F., 82, 83, 107
Clark, J., 40, 76
Clark, L., 202, 241
Clark, T. W., 219, 232
Cleeland, C. S., 236
Clement, P. W., 265, 267
Cobb, J. A., 15, 23, 142, 192
Coffey, H. S., 265, 267
Cohen, I. L., 203, 232
Cohen, M. N., 213, 237
Cohressen, J., 156, 182, 194
Combs, M. L., 181, 187
Conners, C. K., 3, 23, 39, 75, 196, 200,
   201, 202, 203, 205, 208, 209, 212, 213,
   214, 223, 224, 225, 226, 227, 228, 233,
   237
Coote, M. A., 156, 191
Corder, E. F., 245, 267
Corsini, R., 109, 135
Costello, A. J., 240
Cottington, F., 198, 232
Cox, C., 227, 241
Cox, P. N., 134, 135
Cram, D. M., 227, 241
Crane, G. E., 208, 238
Creer, T. L., 163, 187
Crimm, F., 200, 240
Crimmins, D. B., 314, 318
Crisp, A. H., 62, 63, 64, 75
Cristol, A. H., 182, 193
Cromwell, R. E., 273, 303
Crook, W. G., 218, 220
Crowther, J. H., 26, 76
Cummings, R. A., 220, 238
Cunningham, C., 202, 212, 213, 238
Currah, H., 209, 232
Cutts, K. K., 198, 234
Cytryn, L., 51, 78, 200, 204, 234

Dabbous, A., 208, 234
Dalby, J. T., 229, 236
Dalby, T., 181, 191, 236
Dally, P. J., 64, 76
Dangel, R. F., 184, 187, 293, 303
Dannefer, E., 245, 255, 267
Dare, C., 90, 107
David, O. J., 40, 76
Davidoff, E. M., 197, 234
Davids, A., 309, 317
Davidson, N. P., 184, 188, 293, 303
Davidson, W. S., 181, 192
Davies, R. V., 64, 76
Davis, J. M., 63, 75
Davis, L. J., 245, 268
Davis, M. T., 169, 194
Davis, S. D., 203, 233
Davison, G. C., 150, 187

Dawson, G., 60, 61, 76
De La Crug, F., 201, 236
Dec, G. H., 201, 232
Deffenbacher, J. L., 153, 188
DeGiovanni, I. S., 155, 189
DeLeon, G., 67, 76, 105, 107, 156, 182,
   188
Delprato, D. J., 48, 76
DeMyer, M. K., 55, 56, 76
Denhoff, E., 198, 213, 234
Denzen, A. E., 300, 305
Deutch, C. I., 3, 23
Devine, V. T., 183, 191
Diamond, S., 167, 188
Dilkes, T. C., 299, 300, 305
DiLorenzo, T. M., 161, 191
DiMascio, A., 201, 210, 234
Dinklage, D., 63, 78
Ditman, K. S., 201, 238
Divoky, D., 196, 239
Dixon, H., 29, 33, 80
Doleys, D. M., 66, 67, 68, 76, 156, 157,
   164, 188
Dorfman, E., 134, 136
Dotemoto, S., 212, 241
Douglas, V. I., 40, 80
Drabman, R. S., 165, 181, 190
Dubey, D. T., 40, 76
Dumbrell, S., 227, 237
Dundee, J. W., 199, 234
Duvall, E. M., 275, 276, 277, 303
Dyson, L., 202, 234

Eaton, P., 174, 188
Eccles, A. K., 198, 237
Eckert, E. D., 63, 75
Effron, A. S., 199, 235
Egan, R. A., 200, 237
Egel, A., 181, 193
Eggers, C., 60, 76
Ehrenreich, N. S., 90, 107
Ehrhardt, A. A., 38, 79
Eichman, P. L., 225, 236
Eisenberg, L., 200, 204, 233, 234
Ellinwood, C., 134, 137
Elliott, C., 153, 188
Emmelkamp, P. M., 48, 76
Engelhardt, D., 209, 241
Enos, F. A., 201, 232
Epstein, L. H., 147, 187
Epstein, N., 246, 255, 267
Evans, I. M., 142, 183, 188, 194
Evers, W. L., 173, 188
Eyberg, S. M., 15, 23

Farina, A., 15, 23
Farrington, D. P., 71, 80

Faschingbauer, T. F., 66, 76, 156, 188
Fazzone, R. A., 265, 267
Fehrenbach, P. A., 173, 194
Feingold, B. F., 196, 197, 217, 221, 222, 223, 224, 225, 226, 227, 228, 229, 234
Feinstein, S., 202, 234
Feldman, G. M., 167, 188
Feldman, R. S., 11, 23
Feldman, R. A., 261, 269
Fennell, E., 71, 72, 73, 77
Ferber, A., 273, 303
Ferguson, H. B., 228, 234
Ferguson, J. M., 172, 193
Feuerstein, M., 143, 190
Finch, S. M., 116, 118, 120, 136
Finell, J., 122, 129, 136
Finley, P. M., 157, 188
Finley, W. W., 157, 167, 188
Firestone, P., 40, 76, 142, 188
Fish, B., 200, 202, 233, 234
Fishman, H. C., 304
Fitzpatrick, J., 29, 33, 80
Fixsen, D. L., 166, 188, 190, 192
Flaherty, J. A., 199, 235
Flax, N., 261, 269
Floyd, A., 202, 233
Fonda, C. P., 29, 79
Forehand, R., 72, 76, 181, 184, 188, 294, 303
Forgotson, J. H., 246, 267
Forman, J. B., 33, 79
Forrester, R., 156, 182, 188
Forsythe, W. I., 209, 241
Fournier, D. G., 273, 303
Foxx, R. M., 67, 75, 163, 164, 165, 186, 188
Frame, C., 181, 190
Frank, M. G., 245, 267
Frank, T., 199, 236
Franklin, M., 167, 188
Frautschi, N., 173, 194
Freed, H., 199, 235
Freedheim, D. K., 85, 90, 107
Freedman, A. M., 199, 200, 235
Freedman, R., 235
Freeman, B. J., 57, 76, 79
French, J., 9, 23
Freud, A., 113, 114, 115, 116, 117, 119, 120, 121, 124, 136, 244, 267
Freud, S., 6, 23, 48, 76, 109, 110, 111, 124, 127, 128, 136
Frey, L. A., 245, 267
Fromm, E., 127, 136
Frommer, E. A., 201, 235
Fry, R. A., 173, 194
Furukawa, M. J., 168, 192

Gabriel, B., 258, 259, 267
Gadjos, E., 171, 187
Gaines, T., 245, 255, 267
Ganzer, V. J., 173, 193
Garcia, K. A., 155, 189
Gardner, R. A., 44, 76
Garfield, S. L., 201, 235
Garfinkel, B., 202, 235
Garfinkle, P. E., 64, 76
Garner, D. M., 64, 76
Gatski, R. L., 199, 235
Gelfand, D. M., 2, 23, 95, 96, 107, 142, 143, 173, 183, 189
Geller, E., 57, 76, 79
German, D. F., 222, 234
Gibbons, D. C., 72, 76
Gibbs, E. L., 203, 235
Gibbs, F. A., 203, 235
Gilbert, A., 200, 204, 234
Ginott, H. G., 245, 247, 255, 267
Girardeau, F. L., 165, 189
Gittelman, R., 43, 76
Gittelman-Klein, R., 204, 205, 206, 207, 209, 210, 227, 229, 235, 236, 237, 239
Glick, S. J., 100, 108
Goering, J. D., 40, 80
Goggins, E. B., 82, 107
Goggins, J. E., 82, 107
Gold, M. S., 64, 76
Gold, S. R., 265, 268
Goldberg, S. C., 63, 75
Goldenberg, H., 272, 279, 280, 303
Goldenberg, I., 272, 279, 280, 303
Goldfried, M., 11, 23, 140, 142, 150, 189
Goldstein, A. P., 184, 189
Goldstein, B., 265, 267
Goldstein, S., 210, 241
Gonso, J., 181, 188
Goodman, J., 174, 175
Gordon, S. B., 184, 189
Gordon, S. D., 293, 303
Gottman, J. M., 181, 189
Gould, E., 316, 317
Gould, J., 55, 80
Goyette, C. H., 223, 232
Graham, B. D., 201, 239
Gram, L., 202, 235
Grant, R., 204, 235
Graves, P. A., 9, 23
Graziano, A. M., 155, 173, 181, 184, 187, 189, 245, 265, 267
Green, E., 198, 232
Green, W. H., 3, 23, 57, 75, 231, 232
Greenberg, L., 209, 235
Greenhill, L. J., 39, 76
Greenhill, L. L., 38, 79, 202, 235, 238

Greenspan, N. I., 9, 23
Greenspan, S. I., 9, 23
Grega, D. M., 208, 231
Grimm, F., 200, 201, 237
Groden, J., 150, 187
Groff, S., 210, 239
Gross, A. M., 142, 189
Gross, M. D., 203, 213, 229, 235, 236
Grusec, J., 168, 187
Gualtieri, C. T., 208, 236
Guerin, P. J., 275, 304
Guerney, L. F., 109, 136
Guilleminault, C., 214, 236
Guirguis, E., 60, 77
Gurman, A. P., 299, 300, 301, 304
Guttman, E., 197, 238

Hagamen, M. B., 201, 241, 308, 317
Haier, R. J., 61, 75
Haizlip, T., 245, 267
Haley, J., 274, 284, 286, 287, 302, 304
Hall, C. S., 109, 110, 112, 126, 136
Hallahan, D. P., 181, 189
Halmi, K. A., 62, 63, 75, 77
Halpern, F., 202, 235
Hampe, E., 2, 22, 45, 78, 100, 107, 134, 135
Hanrahan, G. E., 199, 237
Hansen, T., 209, 238
Hantman, E., 228, 238
Haplan, J., 229, 239
Hardage, N. C., 264, 265, 268
Harding, V., 63, 75
Hardt, P., 265, 267
Harley, J. P., 224, 225, 236
Harper, R. A., 109, 136
Harr, B. J., 246, 268
Harris, R., 158, 164, 186
Harris, S. L., 164, 189
Hart, B., 158, 186
Harter, S., 116, 117, 118, 136
Hartmann, D. P., 96, 107, 140, 141, 142, 143, 173, 183, 189
Hasazi, J. E., 154, 194
Haslam, R. H., 229, 236
Hastings, J. E., 40, 77
Hatzenbuehler, L. C., 155, 181, 189
Haug, M., 313, 317
Hayes, T., 211, 236
Hechtman, L., 213, 236
Heckman, H. K., 40, 75
Hedge, B., 209, 240
Heinieke, C. M., 104, 107, 134, 136
Helper, M. M., 201, 235
Henker, B., 212, 216, 241
Henry, C. E., 203, 237

Herbert, M., 69, 70, 71, 72, 77
Herink, R., 109, 136
Herold, W., 199, 231
Hersen, M., 2, 12, 23, 81, 104, 107, 140, 143, 181, 187, 192
Hersov, L., 306, 310, 313, 315, 317
Hill, I. D., 201, 240
Hill, R., 275, 304
Hinds, W. C., 264, 265, 267
Hingtgen, J. N., 55, 76
Hirsch, M. L., 202, 235
Hobbes, G., 237
Hobbs, S. 174, 189
Hoddinott, B. A., 200, 231
Hodges, K. L., 51, 78
Hoedt, K., 265, 269
Hoefler, S. A., 73, 77
Hoffman, S., 209, 241
Hoffman, S. P., 40, 76
Holden, R. H., 199, 234
Holz, W., 161, 186
Honzik, M. P., 25, 26, 78
Hood, O. E., 203, 238
Horner, R. D., 174, 189
Horney, K., 127, 136
House, A. E., 15, 24, 142, 194
House, R. M., 264, 267
Howells, J. G., 60, 77, 278, 304
Hubert, N. C., 40, 80
Huestis, R., 202, 236
Hug-Hellmuth, H. V., 113, 114, 136
Hugo, M. J., 264, 268
Humphreys, L. E., 142, 189
Hunt, B. R., 199, 236

Irwin, E., 264, 268
Irwin, M., 306, 309, 317, 318

Jackson, D. D., 284, 285, 286, 287, 302, 304, 305
Jackson, R. K., 55, 76
Jacobson, E., 149, 150, 189
Jaffe, S., 200, 203, 241
Jasper, H. H., 203, 236
Jasper, J. H., 198, 234
Jeffrey, R., 171, 187
Jehu, D., 157, 189
Johnson, D. L., 265, 268
Johnson, J. H., 2, 24, 36, 38, 51, 58, 71, 72, 73, 77, 79, 94, 102, 107, 108
Johnson, S. B., 48, 77
Johnston, J. M., 162, 189
Jones, A. A., 157, 190
Jones, M. C., 149, 189
Jurgela, A. R., 154, 194

Kaczkowski, H., 246, 255, 268
Kahn, A. V., 167, 190
Kahn, I. S., 218, 219, 236
Kallman, W. M., 143, 190
Kalucy, R. S., 63, 75
Kandel, H. J., 182, 186
Kanfer, F. H., 11, 23, 140, 175, 176, 184, 189, 190
Kanner, L., 53, 54, 55, 77
Kaplan, S. J., 164, 186
Karoly, P., 175, 176, 190
Kaser-Boyd, N., 96, 107
Kashani, J., 49, 77
Kauffman, J. M., 181, 189
Kaufman, I., 118, 136
Kazdin, A. E., 2, 143, 157, 159, 161, 162, 165, 180, 181, 182, 190
Keilitz, I., 174, 189
Keller, J., 100, 101, 108
Keller, M. F., 173, 190
Kelly, E. W., 264, 265, 268
Kelly, J., 202, 236
Kemper, C. C., 153, 188
Kendall, P. C., 10, 23, 41, 42, 47, 77, 149, 174, 181, 190
Kennedy, H., 109, 137
Kennedy, W. A., 47, 77
Kenny, T., 203, 231
Kent, R. N., 140, 142, 188
Kerasotes, D., 39, 40, 41, 77
Kiesler, D. J., 102, 104, 107, 108
Kimmel, E., 66, 77
Kimmel, H. D., 66, 77
King, H. E., 184, 188
Kinsbourne, M., 227, 228, 241
Kirgin, K. A., 166, 190
Kirkpatrick, B. B., 203, 241
Kistner, J. A., 314, 318
Kittler, F. J., 219, 231, 236
Klawans, H. L., 64, 78
Klein, D., 207, 208, 209, 210, 212, 214, 229, 235, 236, 239
Klein, M., 113, 114, 115, 136
Kline, G., 245, 268
Klykylo, W. M., 64, 78
Knapczyk, D. R., 228, 236
Kniskern, D. P., 299, 300, 301, 304
Kniskern, J. R., 15, 23
Koch, M., 202, 236
Koegel, R. L., 181, 193
Koeppen, A. S., 150, 151, 190
Kolodny, R. L., 245, 267
Kolvin, I., 60, 77
Komper, C. C., 153, 187
Koocher, G. P., 21, 23, 98, 108
Kraepelin, E., 5, 23, 28, 77

Krahenbuhl, U., 50, 78
Krahn, G. L., 9, 23
Krakowski, A. J., 201, 236
Kramer, R., 203, 233
Krasner, L., 64, 79
Kratochwill, T. R., 48, 78, 153, 155, 181, 191
Krauft, C. C., 103, 108
Kreger, K. C., 201, 240
Kriegsmann, E. A., 229, 232
Kruesi, M. J., 229, 239
Krush, T. P., 199, 236
Kupietz, S., 209, 211, 236, 241
Kurtis, L. B., 201, 236

Lacey, J. H., 63, 75
Lachman, R., 234
Laferte, R., 209, 237
LaGreca, A., 88, 108
Lahey, B. B., 181, 174, 189, 190
Lamontagne, C. H., 200, 240
Lamprecht, F., 211, 239
Lang, P. J., 162, 190
Langer, E. J., 37, 77
Langford, W. S., 213, 231
Lansing, C., 245, 269
Lapouse, R., 25, 27, 45, 78
Laquer, H. P., 297, 304
Larsen, K. W., 200, 237
La Veck, G. D., 201, 236
Lawler, J. A., 160, 194
Layman, D., 182, 186
Lazarus, A. A., 153, 190
LeBow, J., 299
Lebow, M. D., 293, 304
Lees, J. M., 223, 232
Lefkowitz, M., 203, 237
Lefkowitz, M. M., 49, 78
Lehmann, H. E., 199, 237
Lehrman, L. J., 100, 107
Leon, G. R., 63, 64, 78
LeVann, L. J., 237
Levant, R. F., 2, 23, 279, 304
Levitt, E., 215, 237
Levitt, E. E., 9, 23, 100, 101, 102, 103, 108
Levy, F., 227, 237
Levy, P., 264, 268
Lewis, M., 306, 317
Lewis, S. A., 171, 190
Liberman, R. P., 293, 294, 295, 304, 305
Liebman, R., 293, 304
Lindsley, D. B., 203, 237
Lindzey, G., 110, 112, 126
Linehan, M. M., 142, 190
Lloyd, J. W., 181, 189
Lloyd, R., 245, 268

Lockett, H. J., 200, 201, 237, 240
Lockey, S. D., 221, 237
Lockner, A., 200, 234
Lockwood, J., 246, 268
Long, N. J., 310, 317
Looker, A., 203, 237
Loper, A. B., 181, 189
Lotter, V., 60, 78
Lovaas, O. I., 56, 78, 79, 181, 191
Lovibond, S. H., 155, 156, 191
Lucas, A. P., 200, 237
Lucas, A. R., 201, 240
Lundell, F. W., 201, 231
Lupatkin, W., 79, 238
Lupton, M., 64, 78
Lyman, R. D., 313, 314, 315, 318

MacFarlane, J. W., 25, 26, 78
MacGregor, R., 296, 304
MacKay, M., 213, 222
MacLean, A. R., 197, 241
MacLean, R. E., 201, 237
Maclennan, B. W., 245, 268
Mahoney, M. J., 190, 191, 209, 237
Mahony, D., 209, 237
Maloney, M., 64, 78
Mandell, W. A., 67, 76, 105, 107, 156, 182, 188
Marchionda, L. M., 223, 232
Margen, S., 227, 241
Marholin, D., 184, 191
Marrone, R. T., 245, 266
Martin, D. M., 64, 76
Marx, N., 202, 238
Mash, E. J., 142, 181, 189
Masters, J. C., 148, 192
Matson, J. L., 67, 78, 161, 163, 191, 192
Mattes, J., 227, 237
Matthews, C. G., 225, 236
Matthews, D. B., 264, 265, 268
Mattison, R., 29, 31, 78
Mayer, J., 228, 237
McAndrew, J. B., 208, 237
McBrien, R. J., 264, 268
McClelland, S., 229, 232
McCoy, G. F., 82, 83, 107
McCutcheon, S., 51, 77
McGaugh, J. L., 245, 267
McIntire, M. S., 208, 231
McKay, R. J., 13, 231
McKibben, J., 227, 241
McKnew, D. H., 51, 78
McMahon, R. J., 72, 76, 142, 191, 294, 303
McNutt, B. A., 213, 237
McPeak, W. R., 273, 304
McRee, C., 245, 267

Meichenbaum, D. H., 41, 78, 148, 174, 175, 191
Melamed, B. G., 162, 170, 173, 190, 191
Melton, G. B., 97, 107
Menlove, F., 168, 169, 187
Merlis, S., 201, 241, 242
Mesibov, G. B., 54, 60, 61, 76, 79
Metcalf, M. L., 209, 235
Methven, R. J., 29, 33, 80
Meyer, M., 245, 268
Michelson, L., 81, 104, 107
Mikkelsen, E. J., 211, 215, 239
Miksztal, M. W., 199, 237
Miller, L. C., 2, 22, 45, 47, 78, 100, 107, 134, 135
Miller, P., 189
Millichap, J. G., 200, 237
Millman, H. L., 118, 137
Mills, L., 229, 240
Milne, D. O., 265, 267
Minde, K., 40, 80
Minuchin, S., 289, 290, 291, 293, 302, 304
Mitchell, K. M., 84, 103, 108
Mitchell, S., 101, 108
Mizelle, J. D., 200, 234
Moguin, L., 174, 189
Molitch, M., 198, 237
Molk, L., 163, 187
Molling, P. A., 204, 234
Monk, M., 25, 27, 45, 78
Moos, R., 15, 23, 277, 304
Morgan, R. T. T., 157, 189, 194
Morison, P., 181, 190
Morris, R. J., 48, 78, 153, 155, 181, 191
Morse, W. C., 310, 317
Moulin, E. K., 265, 268
Moustakas, C., 89, 108, 109, 128, 130, 131, 132, 134, 136, 137
Mowrer, O. H., 66, 78, 155, 191
Mowrer, W. M., 66, 78, 155, 191
Mozenter, G., 246, 267
Mullins, L. L., 51, 78
Munroe, R. L., 116, 127, 137, 244, 268
Muro, J. J., 265, 269
Murrly, R., 201, 235
Myerson, A., 197, 237

Nathanson, M. H., 197, 238
Nee, J., 33, 79
Nelson, R. J., 264, 268
Nelson, R. O., 142, 188
Nemeth, E., 40, 80
Newman, A., 175, 176, 190
Newman, I., 223, 232
Newman, R. G., 310, 317
Newsom, C. D., 181, 191

Nichtern, S., 198, 232
Nisbett, R. E., 216, 240

O'Banion, D., 220, 238
O'Brian, P., 15, 23
O'Brien, F., 174, 191
O'Connor, K., 21, 24, 109, 137
O'Connor, R. D., 173, 191
O'Dell, S., 184, 191
O'Donnell, D. J., 216, 238
Oettinger, L., 201, 238
Ogar, D., 200, 241
O'Leary, K. D., 140, 165, 181, 183, 184, 191
O'Leary, S. G., 181, 184, 191
Oliveau, D., 47, 74
Ollendick, T. H., 2, 12, 23, 67, 78, 140, 142, 155, 163, 168, 173, 183, 192
Olson, D. H., 15, 23, 273, 276, 296, 303, 305
Oppenheim, B., 101, 108
O'Shea, J. A., 220, 238
Ozolins, M., 153, 188

Paige, D., 228, 238
Palmer, R. L., 63, 75
Panitch, M., 211, 236
Park, C., 159, 193
Parloff, M. B., 109, 137
Pasamanick, B., 203, 238
Pasnau, R. O., 245, 268
Patterson, G. R., 15, 23, 72, 75, 78, 142, 181, 184, 192
Paul, G. L., 152, 192
Paulson, G. W., 208, 238
Pavlov, I. P., 147, 192
Pearson, G. H., 118, 120, 137
Pedulla, B. M., 21, 23
Peed, S., 184, 188
Peifer, C. A., 199, 235
Pelham, W., 213, 238
Pendagast, E. G., 275, 304
Peoples, S. A., 197, 238
Perel, J., 79, 238
Perel, J. M., 210, 241
Perlman, T., 213, 236
Perry, M. A., 168, 192
Perry, R., 57, 75, 203, 231, 232
Petersen, K. E., 209, 238
Peterson, L., 2, 23, 95, 107, 176, 177, 193
Pettus, C., 29, 79
Phelan, P. W., 63, 64, 78
Phillips, D., 184, 190
Phillips, E. A., 166, 188, 192
Phillips, E. L., 165, 166, 188, 192
Phillips, J. S., 157, 192
Piaget, J., 117, 137

Pleasure, D., 229, 239
Plenk, A. M., 245, 268
Poliakoff, S., 198, 237
Polizos, P., 183, 209, 241
Polster, R. A., 184, 187, 293, 303
Porter, S. F., 220, 238
Portner, J., 15, 23, 276, 305
Portnoy, S. M., 312, 317
Pottash, A. L., 64, 76
Poulos, R. W., 183, 191
Poussaint, A. F., 201, 238
Poznanski, E. O., 50, 78
Prabhu, A. N., 40, 76
Pratt, J. M., 2, 20, 21, 24
Press, M., 211, 232
Prinz, R. J., 228, 238
Puig-Antich, J., 51, 74, 79, 202, 209, 210, 238
Putnam, T. J., 203, 238

Quade, D., 29, 79
Quay, H. C., 26, 34, 35, 36, 79, 80, 309, 315, 317
Quevillon, R. P., 146, 187
Quinn, P., 209, 211, 238, 239
Quintos, A., 201, 242
Quitkin, F., 207, 209, 236

Rademaker, A. W., 229, 236
Rafaelsen, J., 202, 235
Ramsay, R. C., 2, 19, 231
Randolph, D. L., 264, 265, 268
Randolph, T. G., 219, 238
Rank, O., 127, 128, 137
Rapoff, M. A., 65, 67, 75
Rapoport, J. L., 201, 202, 209, 211, 215, 228, 229, 233, 234, 238
Rapp, D., 3, 23, 197, 218, 220, 222, 239
Raskin, A., 209, 240
Rasmus, S., 237
Ray, R. S., 15, 23, 142, 157, 192, 224, 225, 236
Raynor, R., 47, 80, 147, 194
Redd, W. H., 183, 187
Redl, F., 245, 247, 266, 268, 310, 317
Redner, R., 181, 192
Reid, J. B., 181, 192
Reisman, J., 82, 87, 89, 91, 92, 93, 108
Remschmidt, H., 203, 239
Rettig, J. H., 199, 239
Rhodes, S. L., 246, 268
Richards, C. S., 155, 173, 192
Riddle, D., 209, 239
Ridley-Johnson, R., 181, 193
Rieder, R., 202, 235
Rifkin, A., 207, 209, 236
Rimland, B., 229, 239
Rimm, D. C., 148, 192

Risley, T. R., 184, 186
Ritvo, E. R., 57, 76, 79
Rizvi, C. A., 208, 238
Roberts, W. A., 228, 238
Robertson, R. E., 101, 108
Robins, L., 71, 79
Robinson, E. A., 15, 23
Robinson, E. H., 245, 265, 267
Rodgers, R. H., 275, 304
Roehlke, H. J., 264, 265, 267
Rogers, C., 13, 84, 108, 125, 126, 127, 128, 137
Rogers, W. J., 201, 239
Rolf, J. E., 26, 76
Romanczyk, R. G., 314, 318
Roper, B. L., 140, 141, 189
Rose, S. D., 245, 261, 262, 268
Rose, T. L., 227, 228, 239
Rosenblum, S., 201, 239
Rosenthal, T. L., 169, 171, 192
Rosman, B. L., 293, 304
Ross, A. O., 2, 24, 94, 95, 96, 98, 108, 183, 192
Ross, D., 40, 79
Ross, D. M., 40, 79, 213, 239
Ross, S. A., 213, 239
Rothschild, G., 203, 233
Rowe, A. H., 218, 219, 239
Rudman, D., 229, 239
Rueveni, U., 297, 298, 305
Russ, S. R., 85, 90, 107
Russel, M. L., 177, 178, 179, 192
Russell, A. T., 29, 78
Russell, C., 276, 305
Russo, D. C., 155, 181, 187, 193
Rutter, M., 2, 24, 55, 58, 79
Ryan, M., 227, 237

Safer, D. J., 40, 79, 212, 231
Sandifer, M. G., 29, 79
Sandler, J., 109, 118, 121, 137
Saraf, K., 210, 239
Sarason, I. G., 72, 79, 173, 193
Sargant, W., 197, 239
Saslow, G., 11, 23, 140, 190
Satir, V., 275, 284, 287, 302, 305
Schaefer, C. E., 21, 24, 66, 68, 79, 109, 118, 137, 156, 193
Schamess, G., 245, 247, 256, 268
Schaumburg, H., 229, 239
Scheidlinger, S., 244, 245, 247, 268
Schiffer, M., 244, 245, 246, 247, 248, 249, 250, 255, 256, 257, 258, 261, 265, 269
Schlalock, H. B., 134, 137
Schmidt, H. O., 29, 79
Schmitt, B. D., 211, 239
Schopler, E., 54, 79

Schrag, P., 196, 239
Schreibman, L., 181, 193
Schroeder, H. E., 155, 181, 189
Schuler, P., 181, 189
Schulman, D., 202, 215, 233
Schulman, J. L., 309, 318
Schulterbrandt, J. G., 209, 240
Schultz, S., 227, 241
Schwartz, L., 173, 188, 203, 233
Schwartz, S., 2, 24, 36, 38, 58, 79, 102, 108
Seeman, J., 134, 137
Seignot, J. J., 201, 240
Sells, C. J., 229, 232
Semenoff, B., 159, 193
Settipane, C. A., 221, 233
Sexton, J., 203, 233
Shader, R., 210, 234
Shaffer, D., 2, 24, 38, 66, 67, 79, 156, 193, 201, 209, 211, 239
Shannon, W. R., 196, 217, 218, 219, 222, 229, 240
Shapiro, A. K., 201, 202, 240
Shapiro, E., 201, 240
Shapiro, E. S., 149, 193
Shapiro, M., 264, 268
Shapiro, T., 202, 233
Shaw, D. A., 15, 23, 142, 192
Shaw, C. R., 200, 240
Sheinbein, M., 246, 267
Shepherd, M., 2, 24, 101, 108
Shere, E. S., 265, 269
Shields, W. D., 208, 240
Shure, M. B., 179, 180, 193
Sieben, R. L., 228, 229, 240
Siegel, L. J., 51, 78, 155, 166, 170, 173, 176, 177, 181, 184, 191, 192, 193
Silver, A. A., 199, 240
Simmers, E., 222, 234
Simon, L., 64, 78
Simonds, J. F., 49, 77
Sims, D., 2, 24
Simundson, E., 201, 236
Sirluck, H., 100, 108
Skinner, B. F., 147, 193
Slaby, D. A., 181, 187
Slavson, S. R. 243, 244, 245, 246, 247, 248, 249, 250, 255, 256, 257, 258, 261, 265, 266, 269
Sleator, D. K., 213, 240
Sloane, R. B., 182, 193
Sloman, L., 202, 235
Small, A. M., 57, 75, 231, 232
Smeltzer, D., 202, 236
Smith, E., 159, 193
Sneed, T. J., 67, 75, 164, 186
Snellman, L., 181, 192

Sobotka, K. R., 2, 24, 81, 84, 85, 86, 108
Solanto, M. V., 213, 240
Solomon, C. I., 203, 232
Solomon, P., 203, 236
Solty, J., 210, 234
Soo, E., 245, 269
Southwick, D. A., 223, 233
Spalten, D., 202, 235
Speck, R. V., 297, 305
Speer, F., 218, 219, 221, 222, 240
Speers, R. W., 245, 269
Spitzer, R. L., 33, 79, 205, 235
Spivack, G., 179, 180, 193
Spradlin, J. E., 165, 188
Sprafkin, J. N., 11, 23
Sprague, R. L., 182, 187, 196, 201, 213, 232, 240
Sprenkle, D. H., 276, 305
Spring, C., 209, 235
Stachowiak, J., 287, 305
Staerk, M., 167, 190
Stambaugh, E. E., 15, 24, 142, 194
Stange, J., 220, 238
Stanton, M. D., 299, 300, 301, 305
Staples, F. R., 182, 193
Stedman, J. M., 153, 154, 193
Stein, Z., 156, 188
Stephenson, J. D., 209, 240
Stevens-Long, J., 56, 79
Stiller, R., 79, 238
Stokes, T. F., 184, 193
Stone, A., 203, 233
Strassman, L. H., 104, 107, 134, 136
Stratton, B. D., 228, 232
Sturgis, L. H., 200, 237
Sullivan, H. S., 127, 137
Sullivan, J. P., 198, 237
Sum, G., 213, 231
Susser, M. A., 156, 188
Sverd, J., 40, 76
Swanson, J. M., 227, 228, 241
Sweeny, A. R., 64, 76
Sweet, R. C., 201, 240

Tabrizi, M., 79, 238
Taft, J., 127, 128, 137
Taschman, H. A., 287, 305
Tausig, F. T., 227, 241
Taylor, C. B., 172, 193
Taylor, E., 212, 233
Taylor, L., 96, 107
Taylor, W. F., 265, 269
Teichman, Y., 265, 269
Temerlin, M. K., 37, 79
Terdal, L. G., 142, 191
Terr, L. C., 119, 137
Tharp, R. G., 185, 194

Thelen, M., 173, 194
Thiessen, I., 229, 240
Thombs, R. R., 265, 269
Thoresen, C. E., 177, 178, 179, 192
Tobias, J., 209, 241
Todd, T. C., 299, 300, 301, 305
Tomasi, L., 224, 225, 236
Townsend, M., 316, 317
Traisman, E., 236
Treffert, D. A., 208, 237
Trites, R., 220, 240
Trivelli, N., 299, 305
Truax, C. B., 84, 108
Tryphonas, H., 220, 240
Tsuda, K., 55, 75
Tuma, J. M., 2, 20, 21, 24, 81, 84, 85, 86, 94, 107, 108
Turner, A., 157, 189
Turner, R., 156, 182, 194
Turone, R. J., 265, 267
Tyroller, M., 174, 189
Tyson, R. L., 109, 137

Ucer, E., 201, 240
Ullmann, L. P., 64, 79

Valins, S., 216, 240
Van Buskirk, S. S., 64, 65, 80
van Krevelen, D., 202, 240
van Voorst, J., 202, 240
Varni, J. W., 166, 181, 193, 194
Vaughan, V. C., 222, 241
Vick, N., 239

Wahler, R. G., 15, 24, 142, 194
Waizer, J., 209, 241
Waldrop, M. F., 40, 80
Walker, C. E., 39, 40, 77, 156, 194
Walker, C. F., 203, 241
Wallace, I. R., 209, 241
Wallander, J. L., 40, 80
Wansley, R. A., 157, 188
Ward, M. H., 194
Watson, J. B., 47, 80, 147, 194
Watzlawick, P. A., 274, 284, 305
Wayne, H., 201, 240
Weathers, L., 294, 295, 305
Weber, R., 313, 317
Webster, C., 202, 235
Webster, E., 227, 241
Weinberg, E., 163, 187
Weiner, I., 58, 61, 80
Weiner, L. L., 265, 267
Weingartner, H., 228, 234
Weiss, B., 227, 241
Weiss, G., 40, 80, 213, 236, 241
Weisselberger, D., 245, 269

Weithorn, L. A., 96, 108
Wells, R. A., 299, 300, 305
Wenar, C., 2, 24, 26, 28, 80
Wender, P., 202, 203, 235, 241
Wermuth, B. M., 172, 193
Werry, J. S., 3, 24, 26, 29, 33, 40, 80, 156,
  182, 194, 201, 203, 204, 205, 208, 212,
  213, 214, 215, 233, 241
West, D. J., 71, 80
Wetzel, R. J., 185, 194
Whalen, C. K., 38, 39, 80, 212, 216, 241
Whipple, K., 182, 193
White, L., 201, 242
White, W. C., 169, 194
Whitehead, P., 202, 241
Whittaker, J. K., 309, 310, 311, 312, 315,
  318
Wiener, J. M., 203, 213, 241
Wiggins, K. M., 246, 267
Wilbur, D., 197, 241
Wilcott, R. C., 201, 235
Will, L., 29, 78
Williams, C., 159, 194
Williams, J. H., 241
Williams, J. I., 227, 241
Williams, M. G., 228, 232
Williams, P., 229, 239
Williams, T., 160, 194
Willock, B., 120, 137
Wilson, D. R., 313, 314, 315, 318
Wilson, G. T., 150, 182, 183, 187, 190, 194

Wilson, W. C., 203, 236
Wilton, N., 227, 237
Windebank, A., 239
Wineman, D., 310, 317
Wing, L., 55, 80
Winsberg, B., 209, 242
Winsberg, B. G., 207, 209, 210, 211, 232, 241
Wish, P. A., 154, 194
Witmer, H. L., 100, 101, 108
Wodarski, J. S., 261, 269
Wolchik, S. A., 164, 189
Wolf, M. M., 158, 160, 166, 184, 186, 188,
  190, 192, 194
Wolpe, J., 149, 194
Wolpert, A., 201, 202, 241, 242
Wolpert, E., 202, 234
Woodhill, J. M., 237
Wright, C., 171, 187
Wright, L., 69, 80
Wunderlich, R. C., 223, 242

Yeates, S. R., 55, 80
Yellin, A., 209, 235
Yepes, L. E., 207, 209, 210, 211, 241, 242
Yorkston, N. H., 182, 193
Young, G. C., 156, 157, 182, 194
Yule, W., 71, 80
Yuwiler, A., 57, 76, 79

Zahn, T., 202, 235
Zimmerman, F. T., 2, 24, 203, 242
Zrull, J. P., 50, 78

SUBJECT INDEX

ABAB design, 143–144
Achievement Place, 73, 166
Activity group psychotherapy
  case example, 250–255
  composition of, 249
  defined, 248
  structure of, 248–250
Activity-interview group psychotherapy
  case example, 258–260
  composition of, 257
  defined, 256
  structure of, 256–257
Actualizing family transactional patterns, 291
Anorexia nervosa
  diagnosis of, 63
  etiology, 64
  prevalence, 62
  prognosis, 63
  relationship to bulimia, 63–64
  treatment of, 65–66
Anxiety disorders
  avoidant disorders of childhood and adolescence, 44
  overanxious disorder, 45
  separation anxiety disorder, 43
Assigning family tasks, 291
Asthma, treatment of, 163, 167
Attention deficit disorder
  etiology, 40
  prevalence, 39
  prognosis, 40
  treatment of, 6, 40–42, 174–176, 199–200, 202, 212–213
  with hyperactivity, 29, 38
  without hyperactivity, 38

Barbiturates, 204
Behavioral assessment

functional analysis in, 140–142
  methods of, 142–143
  and S-O-R-K-C model, 11, 40
  and traditional assessment, 140–141
Behavioral group psychotherapy
  case example, 262–264
  composition of, 262
  defined, 260–261
  structure of, 261–262
Behavioral parent training, 72, 184–185, 293–294
Behavior therapy
  defined, 139
  effectiveness of, 180–182
  misconceptions about, 182–183
  theoretical foundations of, 144–149
  therapeutic techniques, 149–180
  See also Behavioral assessment, Cognitive behavior therapy, Modeling, Operant conditioning, Respondent conditioning
Bell-and-pad procedure, 66, 105, 155–157
  See also Enuresis
Benedryl®, 200
Benzedrine, 197
Benzodiazepines, 204
Berkley growth study, 25–26
Biofeedback, 143, 166–167
Boundaries in family relationships
  disengaged, 290
  enmeshed, 290
Bulimia. See Anorexia nervosa

Caffeine, 212
Cascadia project, 72
CAT scan, 6
Childhood onset pervasive developmental disorder, 57–58, 306
Chlorpromazine (Thorazine®), 199
Chlorprothixene (Taractan®), 201

Client-centered therapy
  case example, 131–134
  developmental considerations in, 129
  effectiveness of, 134–135
  indications for use of, 129–130
  parental role in, 130
  personality, structure of, 126
  self-actualization, 125
  self-concept, 125–127
  theoretical foundations of, 124
  therapeutic relationship in, 128–129
Clinical child psychologists, theoretical
  orientations of, 20–21
Cognitive–behavioral therapy, 41, 148,
  174–180
Communication
  and behavior, 284
  congruence in, 287
  dysfunctional patterns of, 284–285
  emotional aspects of, 287
  levels of, 284
  and power, 286
Complementary relationships, 285
Conduct disorders
  case example, 69
  defined, 70
  diagnosis, 70
  etiology, 71–72
  prevalence, 71
  prognosis, 71
  treatment, 72–73
  types of, 69–70
Conners Parent–Teacher Rating Scale, 39,
  223–225, 227
Contingency contracting, 294–295
Contracting game, 296
Cylert®, 6, 41, 198, 202, 212

Day-treatment programs, 313
Defense mechanisms, 112
  See also Psychoanalytic psychotherapy
Deliquency, treatment of, 166, 173, 177–179
  See also Conduct disorders
Depression
  case example, 49
  etiology, 51
  prevalence, 49
  prognosis, 50
  treatment of, 51
Desipramine, 210
Developmental factors in
  psychopathology, 2, 26–28
Dextroamphetamine (Dexedrine®), 41,
  200, 202, 212, 227
Diagnosis
  labeling in, 37
  multivariate classification, 34–36

reliability of, 29–33
  validity of, 34–36
Diagnostic and Statistical Manual of Mental
  Disorders (DSM-III), 29–73
Diathesis stress model of schizophrenia,
  61
Diet
  effects of sucrose, 228–229
  food additives and behavior, 220–222
  food allergies, 218–220
  and phenylketonuria (PKU), 222
  See also Feingold Kaiser-Permanente diet
Differentiation of self, 282–283
Dilantin®, 203
Drug therapy
  antianxiety drugs, 203–204, 210, 214–215
  anticonvulsants, 203–204
  antidepressants, 6, 201, 209–210
  antimanic drugs, 202, 215–216
  antipsychotics, 6, 61, 199–201, 205–207
  for attention deficit disorder, 41, 200,
    202, 212–213, 227
  for conduct disorders, 215
  in EEG abnormalities, 203–204
  effects on learning and cognition, 208,
    211, 213, 215, 216
  effectiveness of, 208, 211, 213, 215, 216
  for enuresis, 66, 196, 201
  for Gilles de la Tourette's Syndrome,
    201–202, 208
  for schizophrenia, 56–57, 61, 199–200
  sedatives, 203–204
  side effects of, 207–208, 210–211,
    212–213, 215
  for sleep disorders, 204, 214
  stimulants, 6, 41, 197–198, 202, 212
  See also Specific drugs
Dry-bed training, 164
Dyadic Parent–Child Interaction Coding
  System, 15

Eating disorders, 158
  See also Anorexia nervosa
Eclectic approach to assessment and treat-
  ment, 17–20, 320–321
Ego, 6, 110–112
  See also Psychoanalytic psychotherapy
Elective mutism, treatment of, 159
Emotional triangle, 282
Emotive imagery, 153
Encopresis
  diagnosis of, 67–68
  etiology, 68
  treatment, 68–69
Enuresis
  defined, 65
  diagnosis of, 65

etiology, 65–66
treatment, 66–67, 105, 155–157, 164, 201, 209
Ethical issues in therapy
  children's rights, 95–98
  confidentiality, 97–98
  therapist competence, 94
  Ethical Standards for Psychologists, 94

Family Adaptability and Cohesion Scales, 15, 277–278
Family Environment Scale, 15, 276–277
Family life chronology, 275
Family life cycle, 275–276
Family rules, 284, 285, 287
Family system, 289–290
Family therapy
  assessment in, 273–278
  defined, 271
  effectiveness of, 297–301
  models of, 279–296
  origins of, 271–273
  and psychosomatic disorders, 293
Fears, 45
  See also Phobias
Feingold Kaiser-Permanente diet
  described, 221–223
  effectiveness of, 223–227
Free association, 113
Functional analysis of behavior. *See* Behavioral assessment

Generalization of treatment, 183–184
Genogram, 275
Group psychotherapy
  differences from individual psychotherapy, 246
  effectiveness of, 264
  models of, 246–264
  theoretical foundations of, 243–246
  See also Activity group psychotherapy, Activity-interview group psychotherapy, Behavioral group psychotherapy

Haloperidol (Haldol®), 56, 201–202, 208
Headaches, treatment of, 167
Homeostasis, 284–285
Hysterical conversion reactions, 118

Id, 6, 110–112
  See also Psychoanalytic psychotherapy
Imipramine (Tofranil®), 51, 66, 201, 210
Individual psychotherapy
  assessment for, 86–88
  characteristics of, 82–86
  effectiveness of, 98–105

research issues in, 103–104
setting for, 89–90
stages of, 90–94
structure of, 90
Infantile autism
  case example, 52
  description of, 53–54
  etiology, 55–56
  prevalence, 55
  prognosis, 55
  treatment of, 56–57, 164–165, 208
Inpatient treatment. *See* Residential treatment
Interviews, 4, 8, 11, 86–88, 142, 274–275

Labeling. *See* Diagnosis, labeling in
Life-space interview, 310
Lithium carbonate, 202–203, 215–216
Little Hans, 113

Megavitamin therapy, 6, 229
Mental retardation, treatment of, 174
Metacommunication, 284, 287
Methylphenidate (Ritalin®), 6, 41, 198–199, 200, 202, 212, 227
Modeling
  effectiveness of, 173
  live, 168
  participant, 171–173
  symbolic, 169–170
Models of psychopathology
  behavioral, 10–13
  client-centered, 13–14
  family, 15–16
  medical, 4–6
  psychodynamic, 6–10
Multiple baseline design, 144
Multiple family therapy, 297
Multiple-impact family therapy, 296–297

Neuroses, psychoanalytic explanation of, 117–118

Observational learning, 148
  See also Modeling
Oedipus complex, 112
  See also Psychoanalytic treatment
Operant conditioning, 147
  See also Behavior therapy
Operant methods
  biofeedback, 143, 166–167
  extinction, 159–160
  positive reinforcement, 157–159, 294
  punishment
    cautions in use of, 162
    overcorrection, 163–165
    presentation of aversive events, 161
    response–cost, 163
    time out, 161–163, 294

shaping, 158–159
token economies, 73, 165–166
Oppositional disorder, 70
See also Conduct disorders

Paradoxical directives, 286–287
Perphenazine (Trilafon®), 200
Phobias
case example, 46–47
defined, 45
etiology, 47–48
prevalence, 47
prognosis, 47
treatment of, 48, 149–155, 168–169, 171–173, 175–176
See also Fears
Physiological measures, 143
Play group therapy. See Activity-interview group psychotherapy
Play therapy, 14, 134
See also Client-centered therapy
Pleasure principle, 110
Preparation for hospitalization, 170–171
Prescribing the symptom, 285–286
Problem-solving therapy, 177–180, 286
Prochlorperazine (Compazine®), 200
Projective tests
Children's Apperception Test, 9
Draw-a-Person Test, 9
Rorschach Test, 9
Thematic Apperception Test, 9
Psychoanalytic psychotherapy
case example, 122–124
developmental issues in, 116–117
effectiveness of, 134–135
free association, 113
indications for use in, 117–121
interpretation in, 114–115, 121
parental role in, 121
personality, structure of, 6, 109–111
play, role in, 89, 114, 121
psychosexual stages, 6, 111
transference neurosis, 113, 115, 121–122
Psychosexual stages. See Psychoanalytic psychotherapy

Relabeling symptoms, 285
Relaxation training, 150–151

Residential treatment
case example, 306–308
effectiveness of, 314–316
guidelines for admission, 313–314
purpose of, 306
therapeutic milieu, description of, 308–311
Respondent conditioning, 144
See also Behavior therapy
Retention control training, 66–67
Revealed differences test, 15

Schizophrenia, childhood
case example, 59–60
diagnosis, 59
etiology, 60–61
prevalence, 60
prognosis, 60
treatment of, 61, 199, 205–207, 306
Self-actualization. See Client-centered psychotherapy
Self-control procedures, 175–176
Self-instructional training, 41–42, 174–176
Single subject designs, 143–144
Social learning theory, 147–148
See also Behavior therapy
Social network family therapy, 297
Social withdrawal, treatment of, 158, 173
Special education, 310
Structural family therapy, 289–293
Superego, 6, 110–112
See also Psychoanalytic psychotherapy
Symmetrical relationships, 285
Systematic desensitization, 12, 48, 149–155
See also Behavior therapy

Tantrums, treatment of, 159–160
Tardive dyskinesia, 208
Therapeutic milieu, 308–311
Thiordazine (Mellaril®), 200
Thiothixene (Navane®), 201
Time-Out procedure, 12–13, 161–163
Token economies. See Operant conditioning
Trifluoperazine (Stelazine®), 200
Trifluperidol (Triperidol®), 201

Undifferentiated ego mass, 282

Vomiting, treatment of, 160, 162–163

ABOUT THE AUTHORS

James H. Johnson received his PhD in clinical psychology from Northern Illinois University. He has previously served on the faculty of the University of Washington (Seattle) and is presently Associate Professor of Clinical Psychology at the University of Florida, where he is Director of Training in the clinical-child area. Dr. Johnson is currently President of the American Psychological Association's Section on Clinical Child Psychology and is Associate Editor of the *Journal of Clinical Child Psychology*. He has published over three dozen articles, chapters, and books dealing with areas such as assessment, child psychopathology, child treatment, the effects of stress on health and adjustment, and issues related to clinical child training. In addition to the present text, Dr. Johnson is co-author (with Steven Schwartz) of *Psychopathology of Childhood: A Clinical-Experimental Approach (Second Edition)* (Pergamon, 1985) and author of *Life Events as Stressors in Childhood and Adolescence* (Sage, 1986).

Wiley C. Rasbury received his doctorate in clinical psychology from Bowling Green State University. Dr. Rasbury has served on the faculty in the Department of Clinical Psychology at the University of Florida and is presently a diplomate (ABPP) in Clinical Psychology and Director of the Division of Pediatric Clinical Psychology at Henry Ford Hospital in Detroit. In addition to his involvement in the applied areas of child assessment, child treatment, and pediatric consultation, Dr. Rasbury has published widely in the areas of assessment, child neuropsychology, and correlates of chronic childhood illness.

Lawrence J. Siegel received his doctorate in clinical psychology from Case Western Reserve University. He has served on the faculty of the University of Missouri and the University of Florida and is currently Associate Professor and Director of the Division of Pediatric Psychology at the University of Texas Medical Branch at Galveston. Dr. Siegal has authored numerous research articles and book chapters dealing with such diverse areas as child stress management, surgery preparation, child behavior therapy, family therapy, and the correlates of childhood depression. Dr. Siegel serves as a reviewer for numerous professional journals, including the *Journal of Clinical Child Psychology* and *Health Psychology*. He is co-author (with B. Melamed) of *Behavioral Medicine: Practical Applications in Health Care* (Springer, 1980).

APPROACHES TO CHILD TREATMENT
INTRODUCTION TO THEORY, RESEARCH, AND PRACTICE

by James H. Johnson, Wiley C. Rasbury, and Lawrence J. Siegel

This comprehensive work provides a general introduction to a broad range of child treatment approaches that are commonly employed in mental health settings. Coverage of treatment methods is accomplished through discussions of the theoretical assumptions underlying specific approaches, the specific techniques involved in treatment, and the effectiveness of those methods as indicated by available research findings.

About the Authors

James H. Johnson (PhD, Northern Illinois University) is presently Associate Professor of Clinical Psychology at the University of Florida, where he is Director of Training in the clinical child area. He is currently President of the American Psychological Association's Section on Clinical Child Psychology and is Associate Editor of the *Journal of Clinical Child Psychology*. Dr. Johnson is co-author (with Steven Schwartz) of *Psychopathology of Childhood: A Clinical–Experimental Approach (Second Edition)* (Pergamon, 1985) and author of *Life Events as Stressors in Childhood and Adolescence* (Sage, 1986).

Wiley C. Rasbury (PhD, Bowling Green State University) is presently a diplomate (ABPP) in Clinical Psychology and Director of the Division of Pediatric Clinical Psychology at Henry Ford Hospital in Detroit. He has published widely in the areas of child assessment, child treatment, child neuropsychology, correlates of chronic childhood illness, and pediatric consultation.

Lawrence J. Siegel (PhD, Case Western Reserve University) is currently Associate Professor and Director of the Division of Pediatric Psychology at the University of Texas Medical Branch at Galveston. He has authored numerous research articles and book chapters and serves as a reviewer for several professional journals, including the *Journal of Clinical Child Psychology* and *Health Psychology*. He is co-author (with B. Melamed) of *Behavioral Medicine: Practical Applications in Health Care* (Springer, 1980).

ISBN 0-08-033629-9